INTERNATIONAL BUSINESS

Thomas Lindner & Jonas Puck

INTERNATIONAL BUSINESS

Mastering Strategic Challenges in the 21st Century

Sage

Sage

1 Oliver's Yard
55 City Road
London EC1Y 1SP

2455 Teller Road
Thousand Oaks
California 91320

10th Floor, Emaar Capital Tower 2
MG Road, Sikanderpur, Sector 26
Gurugram, Haryana – 122002
India

8 Marina View Suite 43-053
Asia Square Tower 1
Singapore 018960

Commissioning Editor: Amy Mitchell
Content Development Editor: Rhoda Ola-Said
Production Editor: Sarah Cooke
Marketing Manager: Elena Asplen
Cover design: Francis Kenney
Typeset by: C&M Digitals (P) Ltd, Chennai, India

Library of Congress Control Number: 2024941468

British Library Cataloguing in Publication data

A catalogue record for this book is available from the British Library.

ISBN 978-1-5296-8347-9
ISBN 978-1-5296-8346-2 (pbk)

CONTENTS

ABOUT THE AUTHORS

Thomas Lindner is a professor of management with affiliations at Copenhagen Business School, University of Innsbruck, and WU Vienna. Thomas is a co-owner and partner of intior GmbH, which consults SMEs on internationalization and digitalization topics. Thomas holds a BSc in economics and social sciences, a BSc in physics, an MSc and MIM in international management, a PhD in economics and social sciences, and a habilitation for business studies. His research investigates the role of institutions for corporate decision-making, data science and artificial intelligence, and international corporate finance. Thomas's research has appeared in some of the leading journals of business and management, including *Academy of Management Journal*, *The Journal of Finance*, *Journal of International Business Studies*, *Journal of Management Studies*, and *Management Science*.

Jonas Puck is a professor of international business at WU Vienna University of Economics and Business. In addition, he currently acts as WU Dean for International Affairs, as Academic Director of the MBA in Energy Management at the WU Executive Academy, and as Co-Director of WU's Research Initiative in Sports and Management. Jonas Puck is a Fellow of the European International Business Academy. Further, he is a co-founder and co-owner of intior GmbH, a consulting business focusing on internationalization strategies and international market analyses for SMEs. His current research interests lie in the overlaps of global strategy, finance, and political science. His research has been published in journals such as the *Journal of International Business Studies*, *Journal of International Business Policy*, *Journal of Management Studies*, *Journal of World Business*, and *Human Resource Management* (US), among others, and he serves on multiple editorial boards.

ACKNOWLEDGEMENTS

We are grateful for the outstanding support we received for creating this book. Overall, the book is the result of our teaching activities at Copenhagen Business School, FAU Nürnberg, LFU Innsbruck, and WU Vienna. Insights from colleagues and students at those universities, as well as other universities around the world where we were lucky enough to gain teaching experience, have helped us develop the materials that eventually led to the creation of this book. We are particularly grateful to our PhD students and student assistants in the years 2022–24, who have helped put together materials for this book and provided significant research assistance in the development of the chapters. We are particularly grateful for specific inputs to the contents in the book chapters from subject matter experts. We particularly thank Michael Wolfesberger (Chapter 2), Hubertus Reinprecht and Roman Gwosdilin (Chapter 3), Carmen Friedinger (Chapters 3-5), Mateo Mösli (Chapter 5), Leah Fischer (Chapter 6), Laurenz Tinhof (Chapter 7), Ana Andronovich (Chapter 8), Slavica Kurtovic (Chapter 9), Anna Lehmeier (Chapter 10), Julia Mittermayr (Chapter 11), Naomi Lutskes (Chapter 12), Andrea Vergeiner (Chapter 13), and Rodrigo Luna (Chapter 14). We also want to thank Evelyn Reithofer for her help with coordinating some of the work for the book, and we thank Frederic Ritter for his help with designing the figures. Nicole Bremstaller, Davide Finizia, Isabella Krasniqi, and David Miederhoff provided excellent assistance. At Sage, we received very good guidance from Rhoda Ola-Said and Amy Minshull.

LIST OF ABBREVIATIONS

AI	Artificial intelligence
AFTA	ASEAN Free Trade Area
APEC	Asia-Pacific Economic Cooperation
ASEAN	Association of South-East Asian Nations
B2B	Business-to-business
BCT	Blockchain technology
BMI	Business model innovation
BRI	Belt and Road Initiative
BRICS	Brazil, Russia, India, China and South Africa
CAGE	Cultural, administrative, geographic, economic
CARICOM	Caribbean Community
CCPA	California Consumer Privacy Act
CPTPP	Comprehensive and Progressive Agreement for Trans-Pacific Partnership
CEO	Chief executive officer
CFO	Chief financial officer
CIO	Chief information officer
CIVETS	Colombia, Indonesia, Vietnam, Egypt, Turkey, and South Africa
CME	Coordinated market economy
CPI	Consumer price index
CRA	Contingent Reserve Arrangement
CSA	Country-specific advantage
CSO	Civil society organization
CSR	Corporate social responsibility
DFT	Demand forecasting technique
DL	Deep learning
DMA	Direct market access
EMNC	Emerging-market multinational company
EMU	Economic and monetary union
EPRG	Ethnocentric, polycentric, regiocentric, and geocentric
ESG	Environmental, social, governance
EU	European Union
FASB	Financial Accounting Standards Board
FDI	Foreign direct investment
FOREX	Foreign exchange

FPI	Foreign portfolio investment
GAAP	Generally accepted accounting principles
GATT	General Agreement on Tariffs and Trade
GDP	Gross domestic product
GDPR	General Data Protection Regulation
GLOBE	Global Leadership and Organizational Behavior Effectiveness
GMM	Gaussian mixture model
GNP	Gross national product
GVC	Global value chain
HDI	Human development index
HQ	Headquarters
HFT	High-frequency automated trading
HRM	Human resource management
IASB	International Accounting Standards Board
IB	International Business
IBM	International Business Machines corporation
IBV	Institution-based view
ICE	Internal combustion engine
ICRG	International Country Risk Guide
IFRS	International Financial Reporting Standards
IGO	International governmental organization
IHRM	International human resource management
IJV	International joint venture
ILO	International Labor Organization
IMF	International Monetary Fund
IoT	Internet of Things
IP	Intellectual property
IPLC	International product life cycle
IPO	Initial public offering
IR	Integration-responsiveness
IRA	*Inflation Reduction Act*
IRP	Interest rate parity
IT	Information technology
JIT	Just-in-time
JV	Joint venture
KBV	Knowledge-based view
KPI	Key performance indicators
LBO	Leverage buyout
LME	Liberal market economy
LOFs	Liabilities of foreignness
LVMH	Luis Vuitton Moët Hennessy

Mercosur	Mercado Común del Sur
MFN	Most favoured nation
ML	Machine learning
MNC	Multinational company
MSCI	Morgan Stanley Capital International
NAFTA	North America Free Trade Agreement
NDB	New Development Bank
NGO	Nongovernmental organization
NLP	Natural language processing
NN	Neural network
NTM	Non-tariff measure
NTT	New trade theory
NYSE	New York Stock Exchange
OACPS	Organization of African, Caribbean and Pacific States
OECD	Organisation for Economic Co-operation and Development
OPEC	Organisation of the Petroleum Exporting Countries
OLI	Ownership, location, internalization
P&G	Procter & Gamble
PESTEL	Political, economic, social, technological, environmental, legal
POLCON	Political constraints
PPC	Pay-per-click
PPP	Purchasing power parity
PR	Public relations
PRI	Principles for Responsible Investment
PTA	Preferential trade agreement
RBV	Resource-based view
RCEP	Regional Comprehensive Economic Partnership
REE	Rare earth elements
RFID	Radio frequency identification
RMA	Return merchandise authorization
ROI	Return on investment
RTA	Regional trade agreement
R&D	Research and development
S&OP	Sales and operations planning
SCA	Sustainable competitive advantage
SCM	Supply chain management
SDGs	Sustainable development goals
SDR	Special drawing right
SEO	Search engine optimization
SMEs	Small and medium-sized enterprises
SMS	Short message service

SOE	State-owned enterprise
SPV	Special-purpose vehicle
SRI	Socially responsible investing
STV	Single transferable vote
SVM	Support vector machine
TCE	Transaction cost economics
TCT	Transaction cost theory
TPS	Toyota Production System
TTIP	Transatlantic Trade and Investment Partnership
TV	Television
UN	United Nations
UNCTAD	United Nations Conference on Trade and Development
UNDHR	United Nations Declaration of Human Rights
UNGA	United Nations General Assembly
UNGRI	United Nations Global Reporting Initiative
USD	United States Dollar
USMCA	United States-Mexico-Canada Agreement
VRIO	Valuable, rare, inimitable, organizationally embedded
VW	Volkswagen
WFOE	Wholly foreign-owned enterprise
WOS	Wholly owned subsidiary
WTO	World Trade Organization
WVS	World Value Survey
WWII	World War Two
WWF	World Wildlife Fund

ONLINE RESOURCES

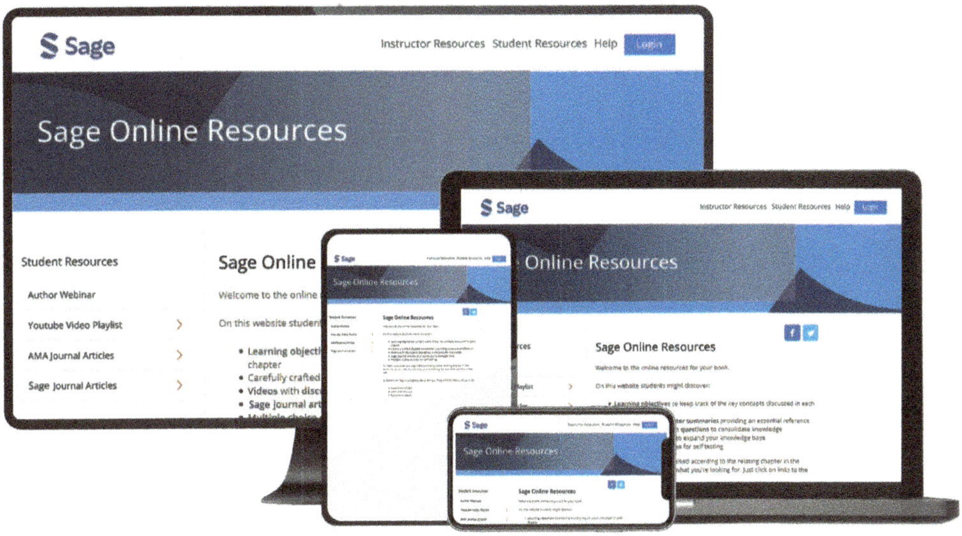

International Business is supported by online resources for lecturers to aid study and support teaching, which are available at **https://study.sagepub.com/lindner**

FOR LECTURERS

- **Image bank** featuring figures and tables from the book, which can be downloaded for use in your own presentations.
- **Testbank** containing questions related to the key concepts in each chapter can be downloaded and used in class, as homework or for exams.

1 INTRODUCTION

This book is designed to facilitate university-level courses on International Business. The book takes a global perspective and emphasizes the role of European companies in creating cross-border business. While other geographies of the world have seen a substantial increase in their relevance to the global economy, the European context is still home to most cross-border business activities in terms of their relevance to the open and relatively small national economies that make up much of the continent Having said that, this book is based on our experience of teaching International Business and global strategy in business schools around the world.

The book is structured to facilitate teaching on the fundamentals of global business, and building and managing multinational companies. It also provides the foundation for more specialized courses on functions (e.g. finance and marketing) and cross-functional aspects of International Business (e.g. sustainability and digitalization). We have provided extensive digital materials, which we will continue adding to. The book contains a number of case studies of companies that have faced challenges specific to issues we discuss in the chapters that follow. Sometimes, these companies managed to overcome the challenges in creative ways. In other cases, companies failed to address a challenge on time and had to work extra hard to recover from the resulting fallout. Our intention is not to illustrate particularly effective or ineffective management but to provide a glimpse into the complex reality of International Business as the basis for class discussion in which instructors and students can reflect on the circumstances in light of their own experience.

The opening chapters provide the basis for an introductory course on understanding the global business environment. An overview in Chapter 2 is followed by a discussion of formal institutions in Chapter 3, informal institutions in Chapter 4 and supranational institutions in Chapter 5.

Having gained an understanding of the global business environment, students with a more specialized interest in International Business typically take a course in international management or global strategy that introduces them to theories of trade and investment, explains how companies extend their operations around the world, and how management and strategizing in companies work once they have become multinational. We cover these foundational topics in the next three chapters. Chapter 6 outlines country-level theories of international economic exchange, which form the historical basis for an understanding of international management. Chapter 7 outlines the mechanisms that govern how firms grow their international activities and Chapter 8 introduces students to the topic of structure and strategy in the multinational company.

As well as courses on the International Business environment, international management, and global strategy, we have taught several function-specific courses that highlight the particular challenges of firms that operate globally. No one book can cover all functions and associated international complications, but we feel that it is important to discuss the most important concepts. More advanced students of International Business can then decide in an informed way which functional specialization they may want to pursue in more detail. Chapter 9 provides those basics for international finance, Chapter 10 for international marketing, Chapter 11 for international human resource management, and Chapter 12 for global supply chain management. Figure 1.1 shows the structure of the book.

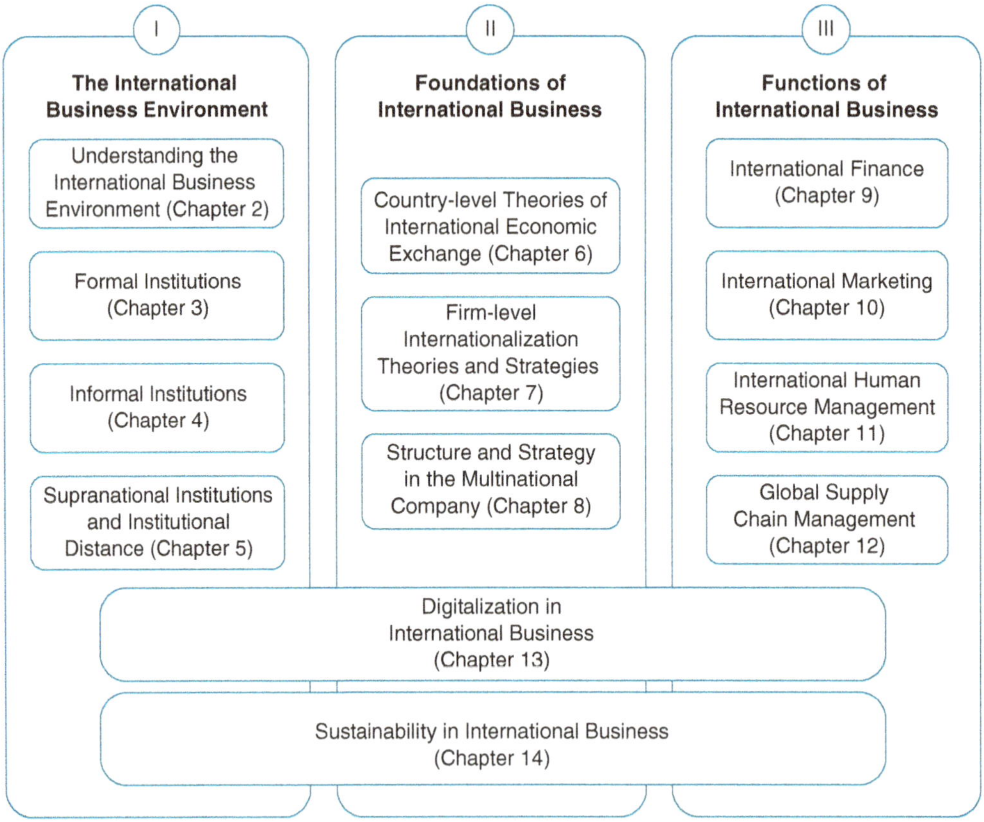

Figure 1.1 Structure of the book

Throughout the book, we emphasize the special roles that sustainability and digitalization play in today's business environment, providing special-insights boxes into these topics in all chapters. We draw together some of those insights and discuss the topics in two separate chapters. We introduce the specific international challenges and opportunities associated with digitalization in Chapter 13 and with sustainability in Chapter 14.

OVERVIEW OF CHAPTER 2

The International Business (IB) environment is highly complex, influenced by country-specific contexts such as language and institutions. Business studies has often overlooked these contextual factors, assuming a universal approach. However, increasing interconnectedness and globalization have made the importance of context undeniable. Since the 1980s, structured analysis of these contexts has become a significant field of study, essential for navigating the global business landscape. International Business involves cross-border activities, including trade and investment, with key players including individuals, companies, governments, international governmental organizations (IGOs), and non-governmental organizations (NGOs). Firms, particularly multinational companies (MNCs), are the most active in this arena, engaging in international trade (importing and exporting goods and services) and foreign direct investments (FDIs) which involve ownership and managerial control across borders. MNCs became prominent at the end of the nineteenth century, driven by technological innovation, trade liberalization, and the industrial revolution.

The history of globalization dates back to ancient times, with trade routes like the Silk Road facilitating early international commerce. After a decline in the early Middle Ages, cross-border trade revived during the Renaissance, leading to the rise of influential trading cities and families. Colonialism further expanded global trade, fostering the rise of international trading companies. The end of the nineteenth century saw the emergence of modern MNCs, spurred by liberal trade policies and technological advancements. Post-World War II, the ideological divide between the US and USSR had a significant influence on globalization. The US-led reconstruction of Western Europe, aided by the Marshall Plan and the establishment of institutions like the International Monetary Fund (IMF), the World Bank, and the General Agreement on Tariffs and Trade (GATT), fostered international trade. The triad of the US, Europe, and Japan dominated global trade until the 1990s. In recent decades, globalization has accelerated with the fall of socialist regimes, market-oriented policies in China, and the establishment of regional integration agreements driving further economic integration and global trade.

Technological advancements, economic liberalization, and political changes continue to drive globalization, presenting both challenges and opportunities for International Business. Understanding these historical and contextual factors is crucial for successfully navigating the International Business environment. Institutions, both formal and informal, shape the rules and norms guiding business practices, emphasizing the importance of contextual analysis in International Business. Formal institutions include political, economic, and legal systems, which interact and create a complex environment for businesses to operate in. Informal institutions, such as cultural norms and societal values, also play a crucial role in shaping business practices and strategies. Recognizing and adapting to these diverse institutional frameworks is essential for MNCs to thrive in the global marketplace. The continuous evolution of globalization demands that businesses remain agile and responsive to the changing international landscape, leveraging their understanding of institutional contexts to navigate challenges and capitalize on opportunities.

OVERVIEW OF CHAPTER 3

National institutions, distinct from supranational institutions, provide the rules for corporate decision-making, which is crucial for multinational companies operating across different nations. The formal national institutional environment is typically described by the political, economic, and legal systems of a country, which interact significantly with each other. For instance, political systems devise and vote on legislation, while legal systems define how these political actions can take place, often outlined in a country's constitution. The economic system's basic ideas are implemented within the legal environment, defining what is permissible in markets. These interdependencies between political, economic, and legal systems create a complex formal institutional system that significantly impacts how businesses operate in different national contexts.

This chapter explores political systems, differentiating between democratic and autocratic systems, and highlights how these systems impact MNCs through regulations, lobbying, and political risk. In democratic systems, political decision-makers are elected by the citizens, with features like regular and fair elections, rule of law, and separation of government powers. These systems vary in their electoral mechanisms, such as proportional representation and winner-takes-all systems, and forms of democracy, including direct and representative democracies, and federal vs national democracies. Conversely, autocratic systems concentrate power in the hands of a single leader or a small group, with limited citizen participation. These systems are characterized by centralized authority, uncontested elections, restricted individual freedoms, and state-controlled economic activities. Understanding the nuances of political systems is crucial for MNCs, as these systems determine regulatory frameworks, methods of influencing policies, and the stability of the business environment. Political risk, which can be macro (affecting all firms) or micro (affecting specific firms or industries), is a key consideration for MNCs operating in different political systems.

Legal and economic systems have a significant impact on International Business. The chapter distinguishes between civil law and common law systems. Civil law, prevalent in many countries, is based on codified statutes and comprehensive legal codes, with judges interpreting and applying these statutes. Common law, originating in England and adopted by countries like the United States, relies on judicial decisions and precedents. The adaptability of common law allows it to evolve with societal changes, making it a valuable framework for International Business transactions. Economic systems, ranging from pure market economies to pure planned economies, impact business operations through varying degrees of government intervention and market-driven dynamics. The chapter introduces the concept of varieties of capitalism, where liberal market economies (LMEs) like the United States and the United Kingdom rely on market mechanisms and hierarchies, while coordinated market economies (CMEs) such as Germany and Japan emphasize non-market interactions and relationships with other actors. Overall, understanding national institutions in IB is essential for analysing political, legal, and economic systems, providing students with the tools to navigate the complexities of international markets and make informed strategic decisions.

OVERVIEW OF CHAPTER 4

Informal national institutions are unwritten and uncodified, with implicit rules, norms, traditions, and social practices shaping human behaviour. Unlike formal institutions, which are enforced through written laws and regulations, informal institutions exert significant pressure on multinational companies to adapt their products, services, and practices to local standards. To understand these informal national institutions, this chapter introduces the iceberg model, originally developed to describe cultural dimensions but useful in structuring informal national environments. The Iceberg Model separates the informal national institutional system into three levels: artifacts and visible behaviours, values and social norms, and basic assumptions. Artifacts and visible behaviours are the most visible and easily understood elements of culture, including clothing, food, language, and rituals. Values and social norms lie just below the surface, guiding behaviour within a society through beliefs and ideals. At the deepest level are basic assumptions and beliefs, which are fundamental and often unconscious perceptions shaping individuals' worldviews and interactions.

Language is a critical artefact in the iceberg model, playing a vital role in shaping people's thinking and perceptions. It encompasses verbal, non-verbal, paraverbal, and extraverbal elements, each contributing to effective communication. Within MNCs, language can be both a barrier and a bridge. Language barriers can hinder intercultural communication and coordination, leading to misunderstandings and reduced communication among employees with limited foreign language skills. However, language diversity can also foster unique company-specific jargon and expressions that enhance cohesion and in-group feelings. Externally, language barriers pose challenges in legal communication, partnerships, and marketing. Effective communication within MNCs requires understanding these various elements and their impact on interactions. Moreover, communication difficulties often arise from varying language proficiencies, semantic differences, differing communication norms, linguistic mistrust, and anxiety. Addressing these challenges involves recognizing the multifaceted nature of language and its influence on business operations and relationships.

Culture, as defined by Hofstede, is the collective mental programming distinguishing members of one group from another. It encompasses shared values, rituals, heroes, and symbols, influencing behaviour, decision-making, and interpersonal interactions. Hofstede's model identifies six dimensions of culture: power distance, uncertainty avoidance, individualism vs collectivism, masculinity vs femininity, long-term vs short-term orientation, and indulgence vs restraint. These dimensions provide a framework for comparing cultures and understanding their impact on business practices. Despite criticism of Hofstede's model, it remains influential in cross-cultural management. The GLOBE study expands on Hofstede's work, introducing nine cultural dimensions and measuring both cultural values and practices. Hall's model, focusing on time, space, and context, highlights the role of communication in culture. Understanding these cultural models and their implications helps MNCs navigate the complexities of International Business environments. Finally, religion, as a fundamental aspect of culture, shapes beliefs, values, and behaviours. Recognizing the influence of religion on national cultures and organizational practices is crucial for MNCs operating in diverse cultural contexts.

OVERVIEW OF CHAPTER 5

Since the mid-twentieth century, supranational institutions have emerged to complement national and subnational institutions, playing a significant role in the global economy. The establishment of organizations like the United Nations, the European Union, and the World Trade Organization set the stage for the increasing influence of the supranational layer in the economy. Today, entities like the European Commission, USMCA, ASEAN, and the European Union have a substantial influence on global business practices. This chapter examines how supranational institutions co-create the institutional environment in which firms operate and characterizes the differences between countries by institutional distance. It also looks into the process of economic integration, highlighting the interaction between supranational and national institutions, and the role of MNCs in shaping these institutions.

Supranational institutions are characterized by six key properties: supraterritoriality, co-existence, contextuality, selectivity, consensuality, and co-evolution. Supraterritoriality refers to the power of these institutions to influence MNCs beyond national boundaries. Co-existence is about the need to understand both national and supranational components in a triadic institutional setting. Contextuality highlights the dependency of supranational institutions' effectiveness on national environments. Selectivity points out that these institutions selectively impact firms, creating advantages for some. Consensuality requires the consent of powerful agents for enforcement, and co-evolution indicates the mutual influence among MNCs, national, and supranational institutions. Formal components of supranational institutions include laws and treaties, while informal components encompass shared cultural and religious beliefs. Organizations such as civil society organizations (CSOs), the WTO, IMF, and World Bank play crucial roles in maintaining and developing these institutions, and influencing global business by providing information, setting standards, and modifying behaviour.

Economic integration, defined as agreements between countries to remove economic barriers, progresses through stages from free trade areas to economic unions, with each stage incorporating the provisions of the lower level. Free trade areas reduce tariffs on goods and services, customs unions establish common external tariffs, common markets allow the free movement of labour and capital, and economic unions harmonize economic policies. MNCs are key drivers of regional economic integration, benefiting from larger markets and economies of scale. However, the complexities of trade barriers, non-tariff measures, and rules of origin still pose challenges. The WTO's most favoured nation principle ensures non-discrimination in trade, but exceptions for regional trade agreements and preferential trade agreements complicate the landscape. Understanding these dynamics is crucial for MNCs to navigate the institutional triality of national and supranational institutions, and institutional distance, ultimately shaping successful international strategies.

OVERVIEW OF CHAPTER 6

This chapter explores the main theories of international economic exchange at the country level, connecting insights on the business environment from previous chapters to theories of international expansion at the firm level and the management of global firms. Understanding these theories is crucial for comprehending the complex dynamics of international trade and investment. Traditional economic theories in International Business (IB) offer valuable insights into why nations engage in trade, serving as a catalyst for growth and prosperity in the global economy. By facilitating the efficient use of local resources through specialization, trade helps maintain low product costs. Early economic thought, like eighteenth-century mercantilism, suggested that governments could enhance a country's economic well-being by promoting exports and restricting imports, resulting in a positive balance of trade. This chapter builds on foundational knowledge from previous discussions on strategic challenges, economic systems, and regional economic integration to provide a comprehensive understanding of international trade and investment theories.

The chapter investigates various traditional theories in the field of IB, covering international trade theories such as absolute and comparative advantage, factor endowment theory (Heckscher–Ohlin theory), the international product life cycle (IPLC) theory, the Leontief paradox, Linder's income-preference similarity theory, and the new trade theory (NTT). These theories explain factors influencing International Business activities, the role of countries' resources, and their ability to compete in international markets. For example, Adam Smith's absolute advantage theory posits that nations should specialize in producing goods they can produce more efficiently and trade for those they cannot. David Ricardo's comparative advantage theory refines this idea by emphasizing that even if one country is more efficient in all goods, trade can still be beneficial if countries specialize based on their relative efficiencies. Heckscher and Ohlin's factor endowment theory explains trade patterns based on countries' varying endowments of production factors. The chapter also covers the international product life cycle theory, which illustrates how a product's life-cycle stages influence trade patterns, and the Leontief paradox, which challenges the factor endowment theory by showing that countries often export goods that use less abundant resources.

In addition, the chapter examines recent developments in IB theories, highlighting insights that challenge traditional assumptions and provide new perspectives. For instance, it is crucial to understand the potential risks and complexities associated with international trade and capital mobility. Recent analyses suggest that trade and specialization are not always mutually beneficial and can sometimes lead to economic exclusion or imbalances. The chapter also emphasizes the importance of empirical research in validating and refining these theories, illustrating how real-world data can reveal nuances and shifts in international trade patterns. By integrating these theoretical frameworks with empirical findings, the chapter offers a comprehensive view of the factors driving international trade and investment, underscoring the dynamic and evolving nature of global economic interactions. This foundation is essential for exploring the complex interactions between countries and firms and informing effective decision-making in the global business environment.

OVERVIEW OF CHAPTER 7

This chapter builds on previous discussions about international economic exchange at the country level, looking into strategic questions related to the international expansion of firms. It explores why, when, where, and how firms internationalize, emphasizing that these decisions are interrelated and often considered jointly by internationalizing firms. By examining these dimensions one by one, the chapter provides a structured approach to understanding internationalization. The chapter outlines the main theories of International Business, such as the resource-based view (RBV), transaction cost theory (TCT), and the institution-based view (IBV), providing a comprehensive framework for understanding the strategic options available to firms. It also integrates real-life cases and contemporary topics like digitalization and sustainability, offering a broad and nuanced perspective on the internationalization process.

The chapter identifies four main motivations for internationalization: market seeking, resource seeking, efficiency seeking, and strategic asset seeking. Market seeking involves expanding operations to new markets to access new customer bases and extend product life cycles. Resource seeking aims to access natural resources or labour that is more affordable or of superior quality. Efficiency seeking involves optimizing costs through specialization and economies of scale by distributing production across various countries. Strategic asset seeking targets the acquisition of resources that enhance a firm's competitive edge or mitigate a competitor's advantage. These motivations are influenced by firms' competitive advantages and firm-specific assets (FSAs), which must be transferable to international contexts. The RBV posits that a firm's unique resources and capabilities, such as intellectual property, brand reputation, and proprietary technologies, are central to its success in foreign markets. These resources must be valuable, rare, difficult to imitate, and well organized (VRIO criteria) to provide a sustainable competitive advantage.

The chapter also discusses the importance of understanding the timing of internationalization, the speed of expansion, and the concept of born global firms, which rapidly internationalize from inception. First-mover advantages, the pace of internationalization, and the specific phenomena associated with rapid internationalization, such as born global firms, are explored to illustrate the diverse strategies firms employ. First movers can establish strong market positions, shape consumer preferences, and create barriers to entry for competitors, but they also face higher risks and uncertainties. In contrast, late movers can learn from early entrants and may benefit from lower uncertainties and refined market strategies.

Country market selection is another critical aspect of internationalization, driven by location advantages such as agglomeration economies, institutional factors, and macroeconomic conditions. Agglomeration economies refer to the benefits firms gain by being close to each other, such as better infrastructure, lower costs, and access to specialized labour pools. Institutional factors include the formal and informal rules that shape business environments, as highlighted by the institution-based view. The IBV emphasizes the importance of understanding the local institutional context, including laws, regulations, and cultural norms. Porter's diamond model provides a framework for assessing the competitiveness of industries in different countries by analysing factor conditions, demand conditions, related and supporting industries, and firm strategy, structure, and rivalry. The Uppsala internationalization model explains the incremental nature of internationalization, emphasizing the role of market knowledge and commitment. Firms often start with low-commitment entry modes and gradually increase their investment as they gain market knowledge and reduce perceived risks.

Market entry strategies, including ownership, establishment, and value chain decisions, are also covered in the chapter. Transaction cost theory provides a framework for evaluating ownership decisions, such as whether to enter a market through wholly owned subsidiaries, joint ventures, or non-equity modes like licensing and franchising. Establishment strategies involve deciding between greenfield investments (building new facilities) and brownfield investments (acquiring existing assets). Value chain decisions involve determining which parts of the value chain to locate in foreign markets, guided by Porter's value chain framework. The eclectic paradigm or OLI framework integrates various theories to explain the strategic decisions firms make in their internationalization journeys, highlighting the importance of ownership, location, and internalization advantages. This integrative model underscores that firms must possess a competitive advantage (ownership advantage), choose attractive locations (location advantage), and decide whether to internalize operations (internalization advantage) to succeed in international markets.

OVERVIEW OF CHAPTER 8

This chapter explores the strategic management of multinational companies like Apple, Microsoft, and Unilever, highlighting their substantial influence on the global economy. It draws parallels between business and military strategy, emphasizing the importance of competitive advantage, intelligence, and manoeuvring. Just as military leaders like Sun Tzu and Thucydides emphasized planning and adaptability, MNCs must navigate complex environments, anticipating competitors' moves, exploiting opportunities, and mitigating risks. These principles underpin modern business strategy, stressing the need for a clear strategic direction and effective organizational structures.

Porter's generic strategies – cost leadership, focus, and differentiation – provide a framework for achieving competitive advantage. Cost leadership parallels military force, focusing on efficiency and economies of scale. Differentiation, akin to military guile, involves unique offerings and innovation. Focus strategies target specific market niches with tailored cost or differentiation advantages. The chapter warns against the dangers of being 'stuck in the middle', lacking a clear strategic direction. Effective strategy development requires understanding internal strengths through the resource-based view (RBV) and analysing the external environment using Porter's five forces.

The chapter outlines essential components of corporate strategy: arenas, vehicles, differentiators, staging, and economic logic. Arenas define the markets where the firm would be competing, while vehicles are the means to enter these markets, such as mergers or joint ventures. Differentiators are the unique capabilities that set a firm apart, and staging refers to the timing and sequence of strategic moves. Economic logic explains how the strategy generates superior financial performance. Balancing global integration and local responsiveness is crucial for MNCs, requiring a careful trade-off between standardization and customization to meet diverse market needs.

Strategic orientations – ethnocentric, polycentric, regiocentric, and geocentric – shape global business operations. Ethnocentric focuses on home-country practices, polycentric adapts strategies to local markets, regiocentric balances regional control, and geocentric integrates a global perspective. Additionally, the chapter examines the organization of global value chains, highlighting strategic choices in outsourcing and offshoring. Effective global management requires aligning organizational structures, such as international divisions, global product structures, and matrix structures, with the overarching strategy.

OVERVIEW OF CHAPTER 9

This chapter on international finance focuses on incorporating risk into financial planning and understanding how risk influences company finances and investments. The chapter also provides insights into international accounting, particularly transfer pricing, and its significance in global business. Understanding risk is essential, especially when considering country risk, which encompasses economic, political, and social factors that might impact investment returns. Country risk is critical for MNCs as it can deter foreign investments and influence business decisions. Systematic risks, like economic crises, and unsystematic risks, such as company-specific issues, both play a role in international finance, requiring firms to conduct rigorous country risk analysis to make informed investment choices.

In international finance, understanding and managing country risk is paramount for multinational companies. Country risk encompasses various uncertainties, including economic instability, political turbulence, and social unrest, which can significantly impact investment returns. For instance, economic risks such as inflation, currency depreciation, fiscal deficits, and high unemployment rates can destabilize an economy, affecting MNC operations. Political risks, including policy instability, corruption, and lack of rule of law, can deter foreign investors and complicate business operations. Social risks like strikes, civil unrest, and cultural differences can disrupt business activities and pose physical and reputational threats. Recognizing and mitigating these risks through comprehensive country risk analysis allows MNCs to make informed decisions and strategize effectively.

International investment is explored through foreign direct investment (FDI) and foreign portfolio investment (FPI). FDI involves direct equity ownership and active management, while FPI includes investments in financial instruments like bonds and equities without active management. Brownfield and greenfield investments are two primary modes of FDI, each with its benefits and challenges. Brownfield investments involve acquiring existing entities, offering immediate market penetration but requiring significant capital. Greenfield investments, on the other hand, involve establishing new subsidiaries, allowing for location flexibility and potential tax benefits. FPI, comprising bonds and equities, provides opportunities for diversification but also involves market risks.

In the realm of international investment, FDI and FPI are two main avenues for channelling capital across borders. FDI allows investors to gain direct ownership and control over foreign assets, facilitating active involvement in management decisions. This form of investment can be categorized into brownfield and greenfield investments. Brownfield investments entail acquiring existing entities in the host country, providing immediate market access but necessitating substantial capital. Conversely, greenfield investments involve establishing new subsidiaries, offering advantages like location selection and potential tax incentives, though initial market share may be minimal. FPI involves investments in financial instruments, such as bonds and equities, without active management. This approach offers diversification opportunities but comes with market volatility risks.

Exchange rates and foreign exchange risk management are crucial aspects of international finance. Exchange rates can be fixed, floating, or pegged, and understanding these systems is vital for managing foreign exchange risk. For instance, fixed-rate systems maintain currency value through foreign exchange control or market intervention, while floating-rate systems allow currency values to adjust based on supply and demand. Pegged or crawling peg systems involve periodic adjustments to maintain stability. Managing foreign exchange risk involves hedging strategies, including using forward contracts, options, and other financial instruments to protect against adverse currency fluctuations.

OVERVIEW OF CHAPTER 10

Marketing involves promoting, selling, and distributing products or services by understanding customer needs and creating products that satisfy them. International marketing, however, requires a more complex approach due to varying institutional conditions such as legal, cultural, economic, geographical, and political dimensions across countries. Firms must develop multiple strategies to address these differences. The '7 Ps' of the marketing mix – product, price, place, promotion, people, process, and physical evidence – serve as a framework for coordinating marketing activities. For the product, companies must decide whether to standardize or adapt to local preferences. For instance, McDonald's modifies its menu to cater to local tastes, while luxury brands like Rolex maintain a standardized product globally.

Promotion involves stimulating demand through advertising, which can either be standardized or adapted based on market conditions. Identical products may have different advertising messages tailored to local preferences or regulations. For example, car companies might emphasize luxury in one market and fuel efficiency in another. The choice of advertising channels – such as classical advertising, digital marketing, and public relations – varies according to local consumer behaviour and market dynamics. Pricing strategies, including cost-based, market-based, skimming, and penetration pricing, must consider factors like production costs, market demand, competition, and purchasing power. Currency fluctuations, government regulations, and cultural differences also play a significant role in pricing decisions. For instance, German cars are priced higher in many markets due to their perceived quality, whereas other markets might require price adjustments to match local purchasing power.

Distribution, the place aspect of the 7 Ps, involves selecting appropriate channels to deliver products to consumers, whether directly or through intermediaries, considering local shopping habits and infrastructure. Evaluating potential partners' financial strength and market reach is crucial. People, or the employees who interact with customers, play a vital role in delivering customer satisfaction and reflecting company values. Effective recruiting, training, and cultural sensitivity are essential. Process focuses on creating efficient and customer-friendly systems, managing enquiries, orders, and service delivery. Physical evidence includes tangible aspects like store design, signage, and staff appearance, reinforcing the brand image and enhancing customer experiences. International marketing requires adapting the 7 Ps to local conditions, balancing standardization and customization to achieve global success. This involves evaluating market potential, legal, cultural, economic, and competitive factors, and employing strategic approaches based on research findings.

OVERVIEW OF CHAPTER 11

Human resource management (HRM) is a critical strategic element for multinational companies (MNCs) in today's globalized business landscape. Effective HRM practices, such as selecting, training, and compensating personnel, help MNCs cultivate a talent pool that provides a competitive edge. Key areas in international human resource management (IHRM) include personnel selection, training, managerial development, compensation, and labour relations, all tailored to the unique challenges of operating globally. IHRM facilitates managing a diverse and geographically dispersed workforce to achieve strategic objectives, addressing the complexities of international operations.

International staffing policies play a crucial role in IHRM. Organizations can adopt one of three staffing policies: employing parent-country nationals (ethnocentric approach), host-country nationals (polycentric approach), or third-country nationals (geocentric approach). Each approach has its advantages and disadvantages, depending on the context and industry of the MNC. Initially, many MNCs rely on home-country managers for overseas positions, but as they gain experience, they often transition to incorporating more host-country nationals. This strategy leverages local market knowledge and reduces operational costs while fostering better integration with local markets. Successful international hiring requires selecting candidates based on criteria such as technical proficiency, adaptability, and personal characteristics. These criteria help identify individuals most likely to succeed in cross-border roles.

International training is essential for expatriate success, addressing the high failure rates associated with overseas assignments. Expatriate adjustment involves adapting to the general environment, work situation, and interactions with host nationals. Effective international training programmes, both standardized and tailor-made, help expatriates navigate these challenges. Standardized programmes cover universal skills, while tailor-made programmes address specific cultural nuances. Additionally, compensation packages for expatriates must include elements such as base salary, incentives, tax considerations, and allowances (e.g. cost-of-living and hardship allowances) to ensure equity and fairness. By integrating international coaching with HR practices, MNCs can enhance expatriate performance and retention, providing personalized support for navigating cultural and professional challenges.

To successfully manage international operations and local employees, expatriates must adapt to new cultural perspectives and values, facing challenges such as cultural shock and acculturation. Organizations play a vital role in supporting expatriates by providing training, coaching, and carefully selecting candidates who demonstrate the potential to navigate these challenges. Addressing personal, cultural, and organizational factors is crucial to mitigating expatriate failure and ensuring the success of international assignments. By refining selection criteria, offering comprehensive training, and providing ongoing support, MNCs can enhance cross-cultural adjustment and increase the likelihood of successful international assignments.

OVERVIEW OF CHAPTER 12

Navigating the global business environment presents substantial challenges for MNCs, particularly in supply chain management (SCM). SCM has become crucial in orchestrating the movement of goods, services, and information across international borders. Intense globalization has created international networks of firms, and SCM has emerged as a vital function in this context. Rapid globalization during the twentieth century brought SCM to the core of business strategies. Free trade agreements and technological innovations enabled firms to internationalize their supply chains, creating global networks. The strategic considerations driving SCM's importance include market expansion, cost benefits, customer satisfaction, collaboration benefits, and risk management. Effective SCM allows firms to access diverse customer bases, optimize costs, meet customer expectations, and manage risks associated with geopolitical, economic, and natural disruptions.

Key theories in international SCM include the resource-based view (RBV), transaction cost economics (TCE), and institutional theory. The RBV emphasizes the strategic importance of efficient resource allocation and leveraging core competencies. TCE focuses on the make-or-buy decision, helping managers assess the risks, coordination costs, and benefits of global sourcing. Institutional theory explores how organizations adapt their supply chain strategies to comply with diverse regulations, cultural norms, and ethical considerations in various countries. Understanding these theories helps firms design and manage their supply chains effectively in a dynamic global context. The activities in international SCM include procurement, manufacturing, inventory management, logistics management, return management, and planning. Effective procurement involves sourcing materials from different countries, managing trade regulations, and building strong supplier relationships. Manufacturing activities are distributed globally to leverage cost advantages and specialized skills. Inventory management aims to balance stock levels to meet customer demands while minimizing costs. Logistics management involves selecting transportation modes and managing customs compliance. Return management handles returned goods, repairs, and recycling. Planning aligns sales forecasts, production plans, and inventory management to maintain an optimal balance between demand and supply.

To manage international supply chains successfully, firms must implement methods and strategies that ensure smooth operations and a competitive advantage. Building resilience into supply chains is crucial to mitigate disruptions and facilitate swift recovery. Preventive resilience strategies include designing flexible and robust supply chains, while recovery strategies involve managing inventory and demand forecasting techniques. Emerging trends in international SCM, such as digitalization, sustainability, and agility, are essential for firms to remain competitive and responsive in a global, interconnected world. Digital technologies, sustainable practices, and agile supply chains are key enablers for successful international SCM.

OVERVIEW OF CHAPTER 13

Digitalization is transforming the global business landscape by integrating digital technologies into various aspects of business and society. This shift has prompted a reevaluation of traditional theories in International Business, as digitalization impacts both developed and developing countries uniquely. In developed nations, digitalization drives business innovation, competitive strategies, and new business models, utilizing digital platforms, data analytics, and automation for operational efficiency. Research in these contexts often explores the interplay between digitalization and organizational structure, strategy, and performance, highlighting the transformative potential of digital technologies. Conversely, developing countries face distinct challenges and opportunities, leveraging mobile technology and localized digital solutions to address social and economic issues despite infrastructural limitations and digital divides.

Digitalization also brings significant methodological implications for International Business research. The surge of big data and data science methods enables researchers to adopt innovative techniques for data collection, analysis, and interpretation. Big data analytics allows for improved market forecasting, customer segmentation, operational efficiency, and innovation, contributing to an MNC's competitive advantage. Automation enhances process innovation within MNCs, improving operational efficiencies and enabling firms to scale operations. However, successfully leveraging digitalization requires more than just adopting advanced technologies; it involves aligning these tools with the company's strategic objectives to create unique value propositions. The resource-based view (RBV) framework provides a lens to examine how digital trends can foster a competitive edge by perceiving them as strategic resources.

Furthermore, the integration of AI and data science in International Business is reshaping decision-making processes. AI, machine learning, and deep learning enable predictive analytics and data-driven strategies, transforming various business functions, including marketing, supply chain management, customer service, and human resources. However, this integration raises concerns about job displacement, privacy, and security, necessitating a balanced approach. The interplay between AI and human decision-making creates augmented decision-making processes that can reduce biases and enhance strategic decisions. The optimal balance between automation and augmentation depends on the nature of tasks, available technology, and broader societal and regulatory contexts. Overall, digitalization, AI, and data science hold vast potential for increased efficiency, innovation, and strategic advancement in International Business, demanding a comprehensive understanding and strategic application of these technologies.

OVERVIEW OF CHAPTER 14

In this chapter, we look into the complex interplay between ethics, social responsibility, and sustainability in business, posing the central question: what is the role of businesses in our society? This discussion spans the concepts of corporate social responsibility (CSR) and sustainability, emphasizing their importance in International Business operations. Students will explore the roles diverse stakeholders play in promoting social responsibility and learn the distinctions between sustainability and CSR. Additionally, the chapter covers the United Nations Sustainable Development Goals (SDGs) and examines how multinational companies (MNCs) contribute to and can mitigate climate change. Ethical dilemmas faced by MNCs, such as corruption, workplace standards, and human rights, are scrutinized, highlighting the challenges managers face in maintaining ethical behaviour across different cultural and regulatory environments.

The discussion on ethics includes the challenges of navigating different ethical standards in various countries, illustrated by cases like IKEA's controversial catalogue modifications for Saudi Arabia. The chapter also examines corruption and bribery, with notable examples like the Odebrecht scandal, which underscores the global prevalence and impact of corrupt practices. Furthermore, the importance of workplace standards and human rights is addressed, with a focus on the International Labour Organization's guidelines and the persistent issues in industries like cocoa farming, where illegal child labour remains a significant concern. The role of stakeholders is analysed through the lens of stakeholder theory, which argues that businesses should exercise responsibility that goes beyond maximizing shareholder profit. This perspective emphasizes the interconnected relationships between businesses and their internal and external stakeholders, each with distinct interests and influences.

Corporate social responsibility is dissected into ethical, business, and agency perspectives. The ethical case for CSR asserts that businesses have a moral duty to contribute positively to society, while the business case argues that socially responsible practices can lead to long-term benefits, such as improved reputation and financial performance. However, there is also a critique that CSR can sometimes be used by managers to further personal agendas, potentially leading to greenwashing. This phenomenon, where companies falsely portray their environmental efforts, is exemplified by the Volkswagen emissions scandal. Lastly, the chapter explores the concept of sustainability, which encompasses economic, social, and environmental dimensions, and the role of the SDGs in guiding global efforts towards sustainable development. MNCs' impact on climate change and the strategic decisions they must make in response to shifting regulations and environmental pressures are also discussed, highlighting the complex and multifaceted nature of ethical business practices in the global context.

2

UNDERSTANDING THE INTERNATIONAL BUSINESS ENVIRONMENT

CHAPTER INTRODUCTION

The general assumption in International Business is that context is critical for business. This means that doing business in different countries, using different languages, and following different institutional backgrounds will result in substantial variation in how companies operate. While this general idea may seem obvious to the polyglot traveller of the world, business studies has often ignored the central role of context for business and assumed an approach to doing business that followed the logic that 'a deal is a deal, and a contract is a contract' logic. With increasing international connections and globalization, the challenges of operating in different contexts have become too obvious to ignore. As a result, the structured analysis of context has only really become a separate field of study since the 1980s, and it has picked up steam over the last 25 years. Today, understanding the context in which a company considers starting to operate has become the norm, and to successfully navigate the global business environment, students of International Business, both undergraduate and executive, have to understand how to analyse the global business environment. This chapter introduces students to the main ideas underlying the analysis of the International Business environment and draws on current institutional perspectives to provide applied tools and the theoretical background needed to succeed.

LEARNING OUTCOMES

After reading this chapter you should be able to:

1. Demonstrate understanding of how context influences business
2. Critically reflect on globalization today and how it has developed over time
3. Identify the drivers behind globalization and discuss how current trends influence globalization
4. Analyse global business from an institutional perspective.

Case Study: Walmart in Germany

Walmart aimed to replicate in Germany its low-cost, high-volume retail model, that had been so successful in the United States. In 1997, Walmart made its first attempt to enter the German market via an acquisition of the Interspar and Wertkauf operations, which together accounted for around 2-3% of the retail market in Germany. The company sought success in the German retail market by offering discounted prices, standardized products, and a large-scale, self-service shopping experience. Walmart intended to challenge established German retailers by leveraging its renowned operational efficiency and logistical expertise while becoming a prominent player in the country's retail landscape.

However, the company's success in the United States did not translate well into the German retail landscape, leading to its eventual retreat from the market in 2006. Walmart's failure to penetrate the German retail market in the late 1990s illustrates how difficult it can be to translate a business model to a foreign market and a different context. Several key factors contributed to Walmart's unsuccessful venture in Germany.

Cultural differences played a pivotal role in Walmart's inability to connect with German consumers. The company's business model relied heavily on low prices, bulk buying, and standardized products. However, German consumers prioritized quality over price and were accustomed to a diverse range of high-quality goods, personalized service, and a preference for fresh, locally sourced products. Walmart's large-scale, self-service approach conflicted with German retail culture, which emphasized smaller, specialized stores with a focus on customer service and quality.

Moreover, Walmart faced formidable competition from well-established German retailers like Aldi, Lidl, and Metro AG. These competitors had already established a strong foothold in the market, offering a unique mix of affordable products, superior quality, and a shopping experience that resonated with German consumers. Their deep understanding of local preferences and efficient supply chain management gave them a competitive edge that Walmart struggled to match.

Another significant challenge for Walmart was its failure to adapt its business model to suit German consumer preferences and regulatory requirements. The company's centralized decision-making approach clashed with the decentralized nature of the German retail market. Walmart's attempts to impose its standardized practices, including its employment policies and management style, did not align with German labour laws and employee expectations. This led to discontent among the German workforce and hindered the company's ability to integrate into the local business environment effectively.

Supply chain inefficiencies further compounded Walmart's struggles in Germany. The company's renowned logistical expertise in the United States did not translate seamlessly to the German market. Issues related to inventory management, distribution, and supplier relationships resulted in difficulties in maintaining adequate product availability and responding swiftly to shifting consumer demands. These challenges undermined Walmart's competitiveness and hindered its ability to offer the assortment and quality that German consumers expected.

Moreover, Walmart's lack of understanding of the cultural nuances and regulatory framework led to marketing missteps. The company's advertising campaigns failed to resonate with German consumers, and its communication strategies did not effectively convey the value proposition tailored to local preferences. This inability to connect with the target audience limited Walmart's ability to build brand loyalty and gain traction in the competitive German retail landscape.

In conclusion, Walmart's failure in Germany stemmed from a combination of factors, including cultural differences, intense competition, an inability to adapt its business model, supply chain inefficiencies, and marketing missteps. The company's departure from the German market serves as a cautionary tale for multinational companies entering new territories, highlighting the importance of comprehensive market research, cultural sensitivity, adaptation to local laws and regulations, and flexibility in business strategies.

Source: Alcácer et al. (2013)

Case Study Questions

1. What are the cross-national differences that made it difficult for Walmart to succeed in Germany?
2. How could Walmart have worked towards overcoming these cross-national differences?

2.1 WHAT IS INTERNATIONAL BUSINESS?

International Business refers to business activities and transactions across national borders. This involves the transfer of goods, resources, services, information, knowledge, skills, capital, and so forth. The main actors in International Business are individuals (e.g. tourists, consumers), companies, public bodies (e.g. governments, regulators), international governmental organizations (IGOs; e.g. the UN and the IMF), and non-governmental organizations (NGOs; e.g. the WWF). The primary and most active players among these actors are firms, which have gained in relevance since the end of the nineteenth century.

The two main International Business transactions are international trade and international investments. Historically, the most important form of International Business activity is international trade with its two components – importing and exporting. Importing refers to activities associated with firms buying and bringing into the country goods and services produced in another. Exporting refers to activities associated with firms selling and sending goods or services produced in one country to another. Inter-country trade therefore always represents both an exporting and an importing activity. International investments became more important in the late nineteenth century alongside the rise of multinational companies (MNC)s. While 'international (or foreign) investments' refers to any movement of capital across national borders, the term 'foreign direct investment (FDI)' denotes investments by companies which involve, beside ownership, strategic and managerial control. This differentiates FDI from 'portfolio' investments in shares, stocks, and other financial products abroad for the sole purpose of risk diversification and rent generation.

The key actors conducting international trade and investment are firms. Companies that are internationally active by directly controlling business activities and/or affiliates/subsidiaries in foreign locations are MNCs. There are many different definitions of MNCs. One sees MNCs as multi-plant firms that control operations in more than one country (Caves, 1996), while another emphasizes the characteristics that distinguish MNCs from firms that are simply active internationally (Dunning, 1988). We adopt a definition throughout the book that is unrelated to the size of the company; rather it is close to the first example. We define MNCs as firms that directly control and coordinate operations or affiliates in more than one country. Whereas the term MNC usually evokes images of big corporates (e.g. Siemens, Apple, Samsung, and Airbus), the applied definition also includes smaller firms (e.g. many family-owned firms and small- and medium-sized enterprises).

MNCs are the most important actors in International Business today. However, this has not always been the case. MNCs as we know them today emerged at the end of the nineteenth century and since then have continuously grown in importance, assuming a key role in driving and benefiting from globalization. Factors contributing to the rise of MNCs are, for example, technological innovation during the industrial revolution, increasing liberalization of trade, the introduction of the gold standard, and advanced financing opportunities, specifically the introduction of stock exchanges.

2.2 HISTORY OF GLOBALIZATION

While globalization has increased, particularly in the last century, the phenomenon is not new. Transactions across borders have existed since ancient times. For instance, trade flourished along the Silk Road between Asia and Europe, where traders transported silk, porcelain, and spices. While transactions across borders already existed, environmental conditions in ancient times were different and presented various obstacles to international trade. Despite these obstacles, trade depended on distance – that is, trade and economic exchange happened most often and were strongest amongst actors that were geographically close.

Following ancient times, cross-border trade experienced a decline in the early Middle Ages. It was not until the late Middle Ages and the beginning of the Renaissance that cross-border trade again picked up in Europe. Among the factors driving this development was an increase in the size of the population, accompanied by the rise of various trading cities (e.g. Florence, Genoa, Venice, Bruges, Antwerp, and Nuremberg) and the ascent of various influential trading families, such as the Tucher family in Nuremberg and the Medici family in Florence, which built a trading empire consisting of various international branches. These changes led to the development of a growing trading network within Europe and beyond. Another important example is the German Hanseatic League, considered to be one of the first free trade areas. Although it did not have a bureaucratic structure or its own finances, this association of trade cities was united by strong informal rules and norms that facilitated trade and exchange. These informal institutions helped overcome obstacles to international trade and the League remained influential until the late seventeenth century.

Another phenomenon connected to globalization was the growing colonization of parts of the world, especially India and Africa. European colonialism began as European nations expanded their influence beyond their borders, starting in the late fifteenth century. It was fuelled by factors including economic motives (such as the search for new trade routes and resources), religious zeal, and the desire for power and prestige. European countries including Portugal, Spain, England, France, Germany, and the Netherlands established colonies in regions across Africa, Asia, and the Americas.

Colonialism not only expanded the political influence of these countries but also led to the rise of private international trading companies (e.g. the British East India Company) that had extensive rights (e.g. to use weapons and exercise jurisdiction in colonies) and established trading posts, made conquests, and imposed political control over Indigenous populations. European nations exploited resources, imposed their cultures and systems of governance, created new borders, and often engaged in the subjugation or displacement of native populations. In consequence, colonialism reshaped societies, economies, and cultures worldwide, creating long-lasting effects that are still felt in many parts of the world today.

The end of the nineteenth century saw the rise of the first MNCs as we know them today. While international exchange was conducted by international traders importing and exporting products from local producers, environmental developments promoted the creation of modern MNCs. The first such companies originated in England, the Netherlands, and Belgium with the aim of securing natural resources abroad (e.g. oil and minerals). Liberalism and the introduction of the gold standard at the beginning of the nineteenth century enabled companies from Great Britain to establish an extensive business network of trade and overseas subsidiaries that strengthened Great Britain's position as an economic superpower of that time. While European companies (e.g. Siemens, Philips) also started to increase their international operations towards the end of the nineteenth century, US companies restricted their business activities to their large home market and only played a minor role until World War I. The interwar period then changed international trade relations considerably. While the growth of nationalism and protectionism together with the Great Depression resulted in a decline in international trade, FDI was not severely affected as companies tried to circumvent trade barriers by setting up overseas subsidiaries.

The economic and political aftermath of WWII changed the structure and characteristics of globalization markedly. The ideological divide between East and West, between the USSR and the US, was a significant feature of international economic developments until the 1990s. The US-led reconstruction of Western Europe via the Marshall Plan after WWII and the convergence towards democratic market economies reinforced international trade relations in the Western world. A key feature of this development was the introduction of US-centric economic policies. The Bretton-Woods agreement, established in 1944, created a system of fixed exchange rates with the US dollar as the leading currency. This agreement along with the foundation of other IGOs, such as the International Monetary Fund and the World Bank, established a standardized economic system for international trade and exchanges. The General Agreement on Tariffs and Trade (GATT), established in 1947, was a further multilateral agreement to reduce trade tariffs and barriers, and set up an international trade system. These institutional frameworks promoted international trade that was fuelled mainly by the European Union, the US and – since the 1970s – by countries from Asia, specifically Japan. This triad dominated the world economy largely in terms of trade and FDI until the 1990s.

Meanwhile, other regions (Africa, South America and Eastern Europe) were largely unintegrated into global trade and investment. Development in countries under the influence of the USSR followed a different path from those in the West. Socialist countries in Central and Eastern Europe operated a state monopoly of foreign trade and exchange. Instead of being a driver of economic growth as in the West, this system conceptualized foreign trade as merely a means to balance planning errors and supply unavailable goods to these countries. Similarly, the participation of many countries from Africa or Latin America in the international economy remained limited until the 1990s. Even China and India did not assume an important role in international trade and investments during that time.

Since the 1990s, we have seen a strong increase in globalization fuelled by various contemporaneous factors. The collapse of socialist regimes in Central and Eastern Europe in the late 1980s opened up these economies to foreign trade and investment. China started to implement market-oriented policies in 1979, slowly began to open up to foreign investments over the course of the next decades, and today is one of the biggest global investors itself. Further de-regulation and privatization laid the foundation for intensified economic cooperation in industrialized and developing countries. The EU increased the number of member countries and intensified their cooperation by moving towards a single European market. At the same time, other regional integration agreements (e.g. NAFTA, ASEAN and Mercosur) were established to promote economic exchange. Further liberalization in Africa, Asia, and Latin America provided additional economic opportunities. The Uruguay Round extended the GATT to include areas such as agriculture, capital, services, and intellectual property. While it eventually led to the foundation of the World Trade Organization (WTO), it was also the first multilateral trade agreement in which developing countries assumed a more important role. All these developments resulted in a much more multipolar world economy.

2.3 THE FACTORS DRIVING GLOBALIZATION

As is evident from this summary of the history of globalization, the factors that drive globalization are diverse and interdependent. Technological, economic, political, social, cultural and ecological factors have impacted and driven globalization.

2.3.1 Technological

Telecommunication innovations such as the telegraph, telephone, and internet have enabled instantaneous communication and exchange of information across distant locations in real time and at considerably reduced cost. Improvements in transportation and logistics (e.g. cargo containers, aeroplanes, and ships) have allowed companies to move goods and people across space in a short time at low cost. These and other technological improvements have driven globalization at an unprecedented speed over recent decades and continue to do so.

2.3.2 Economic

A second factor influencing globalization was the liberalization of world trade via agreements and institutions such as the GATT, the Uruguay Round, and the WTO. The economic opening of previously closed countries created further business opportunities for companies. The de-regulation of markets, which facilitated the movement of capital and goods, further promoted globalization. These developments enabled companies to locate their activities in an economically efficient way across the globe. This led to an increase in International Business and the interdependence of economies.

2.3.3 Political

The increasing mobility of companies and the International Business activities that have followed have increased competition among countries to provide environments that are more conducive to business. While companies can move their operations to the environment that best fits their needs, countries do not have this opportunity. They therefore try to develop attractive investment conditions to benefit from international business activity. As a result, the political environment not only provides the legal and regulatory environment for international business, but is also a driver of further globalization.

2.3.4 Social

The social dimension is a driver in terms of income and living standards. There is much discussion in the literature about whether globalization results in an increase in overall wealth or in a stronger divergence between industrialized and developing countries. Scholars provide differing perspectives on this issue. On the one hand, studies by the IMF show that in many countries the per-capita income of those who are more affluent has increased much more strongly than of those who are less affluent. This suggests a rather diverse and negative consequence of globalization. On the other hand, many studies provide evidence of poverty lessening and living standards increasing as a result of international business activity, which is why many countries see international investment as well as integration in international trade as important pathways for development and support the international activities of firms.

2.3.5 Cultural

A core part of globalization is convergence towards a global culture. The worldwide mobility of people, information, and products has resulted in increased cultural and social connections across borders. While previously national traditions played a key role in culture, with globalization age, job, income and lifestyle assume a much more important role. Although we can observe these cultural changes, national cultural differences still matter. Whether a unified global culture emerges or a stronger divide between cultural clusters remains to be seen.

2.3.6 Ecological

Many of the previously mentioned factors have contributed to an increase in ecological problems. Technological innovations have increased the pollution of air and water, enlarged the ozone hole, and supported the greenhouse effect. Extensive use of fossil fuels has had severe effects on nature, reducing forestation and the natural habitats of many species. The causes and effects of the ecological dimension can be observed and felt on a global level. Equally, ecological issues can only be solved via global initiatives and cooperation, such as the Earth Summit in Rio de Janeiro in 1992, the Kyoto Protocol, and the Paris Agreement of 2015, which established measures and goals to mitigate climate change. Despite these important efforts, we also see the difficulties in agreeing on global climate protection measures, among them the differing abilities of industrialized and developing countries to combat pollution and climate change.

Spotlight: Digitalization and Globalization

Since the 1960s, digitalization has profoundly facilitated globalization by transforming how information is exchanged, how businesses operate, and how people connect. The advent of computers and the internet revolutionized communication, making it instant and borderless. Email, social media, and video conferencing have allowed individuals and organizations to interact and collaborate globally in real time, breaking down geographical barriers.

In business, digital technologies have streamlined operations and opened new markets. E-commerce platforms enable companies to sell products and services worldwide, reaching a broader customer base than ever before. Supply chain management systems and digital logistics have optimized international trade, making it more efficient and cost effective. Cloud computing has further enabled businesses to operate globally by providing scalable and flexible IT resources accessible from anywhere.

The digitialization of information and data has also played a crucial role. Access to digital databases, online journals, and research materials has democratized knowledge, fostering international collaboration in science, education, and innovation. Moreover, digital banking and financial technologies have facilitated global transactions, investment, and the integration of financial markets. Similarly, cryptocurrency and blockchain technologies are starting to impact global finance, offering new avenues for secure and transparent transactions.

Recently, the emphasis on artificial intelligence (AI) has added a new dimension to digital globalization. AI technologies, such as machine learning and natural language processing, are enhancing decision-making processes, automating tasks, and providing insights from vast amounts of data. AI-driven analytics help businesses understand global market trends and consumer behaviours, allowing for more strategic international expansion. AI-powered tools are also improving communication across languages and cultures, further bridging gaps between different regions.

AI's impact extends to various sectors, including healthcare, where it aids in global research collaboration and the sharing of medical data, and in manufacturing, where it optimizes production processes and supply chains. Additionally, AI is playing a critical role in addressing global challenges such as climate change, by analysing environmental data and developing sustainable solutions.

Source: United Nations (www.un.org/en/un75/impact-digital-technologies)

2.4 EMERGING MARKETS AND CONTEMPORARY STRATEGIC CHALLENGES

The landscape of International Business is changing continuously. New operational locations, consumer markets, and competitors have emerged that alter the way of doing business internationally. Despite discussion about de-globalization among scholars, we can still observe an ongoing integration of the world economy. This development is particularly driven by the rise of emerging markets and their growing involvement in the world economy. The term emerging markets, although widely used, comes with some form of vagueness due to the variety of measures, classifications, and indices (MSCI, World Bank, OECD, UN) applied. For instance, countries can be advanced in terms of economic measures, but behind in terms of social measures. Emerging economies are commonly countries with a young population, an expanding middle class, and prospering economies growing since the 1980s (e.g. China, Russia, Brazil). These countries should be differentiated from developing economies, which are usually low-income economies with high birth rates, and little discretionary money to spend (e.g. Zambia, Cambodia, Bolivia). A few countries have established themselves as key players of global economic growth, such as the continuously expanding BRICS (Brazil, Russia, India, China, South Africa) or the CIVETS (Colombia, Indonesia, Vietnam, Egypt, Turkey, South Africa). Furthermore, the Covid-19 pandemic and geopolitical animosities pose further contemporary challenges for MNCs. The way these developments unfold will have a major impact on the future development of global business.

2.4.1 Emerging Operational Locations

Emerging economies provide opportunities for MNCs as operating locations for production and resource access. While industrialized nations still provide a considerable amount of the global economic output, many emerging economies have become attractive investment locations. Emerging economies commonly feature a low-cost manufacturing base, but these countries often have a developing commercial infrastructure, an evolving legal system, and a generally high-risk business environment. Further, these countries often feature strong involvement of government in national and international business transactions.

Emerging economies often start out as manufacturing locations for developed-market firms attracted by their natural resources. South America, Africa, and Central Asia has large resources of fossil fuels and minerals. The lower wages in these economies give them a competitive advantage over industrialized economies as manufacturing locations. Activities located in emerging economies were at first less advanced operations with industrialized economies retaining the high, value-added activities, but this development has started to shift. Emerging economies, particularly the BRICS countries, are increasingly attracting investment for high, value-added activities as they catch up in terms of skills, knowledge, and technology. Global value chain (GVC) analysis is about understanding the distribution and fine slicing of value chain activities in different economies.

The importance of emerging economies as production locations was hastened by liberalization policies across these countries that made it much easier for MNCs to operate there. This was particularly evident in post-communist countries transitioning from a centrally planned to a free-market economy. By the end of the twentieth century there was widespread acceptance that an open economy and trading with MNCs would be beneficial for economic growth, reflected in the accession of most countries to the WTO, which aims to reduce barriers to trade and cross-border business. The increasing number of bilateral investment treaties between countries to facilitate FDI exemplifies this development. However, economic liberalization and being open to the world economy do not take the same form across countries. For example, whereas India has measures in place to protect small local businesses from foreign MNCs, Russia has an abundance of so-called 'oligarchs' who control a big portion of the economy and are commonly connected to the domestic government. In addition, emerging economies are often still characterized by problematic institutional and political conditions. One such factor is the prevalence of corruption. Similarly, mismanagement of the domestic economy and the local currency can result in price instabilities, which can affect the asset values of foreign MNCs. At the same time, the administrative processes of repatriating profits from the currency of an emerging economy can be cumbersome and severely obstructive. Risks related to intellectual property can pose another challenge to foreign MNCs as local governments are interested in foreign MNCs transferring knowledge to them. For instance, for a long time China required investors to engage in joint ventures with local firms when entering the Chinese market.

Spotlight: Offshoring Carbon Emissions

The offshoring of carbon-intensive production has become a significant factor in making developed economies appear less carbon-intensive than they really are. This phenomenon involves transferring manufacturing and production processes from high-income, developed countries to lower-income, developing countries. Such transfers are often economically motivated by the lower labour costs and less stringent environmental regulations in the host countries. However, this shift also has substantial implications for global carbon emissions.

When developed countries offshore carbon-intensive industries, such as steel, cement, and chemical manufacturing, they effectively export the associated carbon emissions as well. This results in a decrease in domestic emissions within these developed economies, which can misleadingly suggest progress towards decarbonization and climate goals. However, globally, the total emissions do not necessarily decrease; instead, they are simply redistributed to other parts of the world.

This displacement of emissions complicates the measurement and comparison of national carbon footprints. The standard practice of calculating a country's emissions based on territorial output - emissions produced within a country's borders - does not account for emissions embedded in imported goods and services. Consequently, developed countries may report lower emissions and appear more environmentally sustainable, while the developing countries to which production has been offshored experience increased pollution and greenhouse gas emissions.

(Continued)

The concept of 'carbon leakage' is relevant here, where efforts to reduce emissions in one country lead to an increase in emissions in another, often because of the relocation of industries to regions with laxer environmental controls. This not only masks the true environmental impact of developed economies but also places an unfair environmental burden on poorer nations.

Moreover, addressing this issue requires a global perspective and cooperative international policies. Strategies such as carbon pricing, which includes taxes or cap-and-trade systems, and consumption-based emissions reporting, which accounts for the carbon costs of imported goods, are critical. These approaches can help ensure a more accurate representation of a country's environmental impact and promote a more equitable distribution of responsibility for climate change mitigation.

Sources: German Federal Ministry for Economic Affairs and Climate Action (www.bmwk-energiewende.de/EWD/Redaktion/Newsletter/2021/11/Meldung/direkt-erklaert.html) and European Commission (https://climate.ec.europa.eu/eu-action/eu-emissions-trading-system-eu-ets/free-allocation/carbon-leakage_en)

2.4.2 Emerging Consumer Markets

Emerging markets not only became attractive targets as production locations but subsequently often developed as new consumer markets. Economic growth in emerging markets leads to greater buying power for households in these countries and in turn to a change in consumption behaviour. Higher consumer income in emerging markets gives millions of consumers access to previously unaffordable consumer goods (e.g. electronic equipment and cars), which represents a huge opportunity for MNCs. The emerging economies' new middle class, defined as households with 50% to 150% of the national median income, has grown dramatically in many countries, particularly in some of the BRICS countries (e.g. China, Brazil, and India). Other BRICS and emerging market countries paint a similar picture with excellent growth opportunities.

Some sectors have already outgrown industrialized countries in terms of demand. The energy sector has become a key factor in driving the growth of emerging markets. Energy demand due to increasing manufacturing capacity, rapid population growth, and urbanization – construction and lifestyle – increases energy consumption in emerging markets, outpacing industrialized countries. The same reasons account for massive growth in the construction sector to build even bigger cities. The environmental footprint of such development will lead to a growth in investment in environmental protection and mitigation measures. Information technology (IT) is another sector that often has an advantage over industrialized economies as consumer markets. Due to the lack of legacy infrastructures, consumers in emerging economies purchase the newest technology as first-time buyers.

Products that are popular in industrialized economies are, however, not necessarily appropriate products in emerging markets. Many people in these markets lack the financial resources to purchase products from industrialized economies. In order to succeed, MNCs need to adapt their products or establish their own distribution channels to gain brand loyalty. This involves reducing packaging size and lowering retail prices (e.g. Unilever selling smaller detergent packages at lower prices or Procter & Gamble selling single-serve shampoo sachets). The challenges MNCs from industrialized countries face are that their business models are not adapted to operating profitably in these circumstances. This is an area where MNCs originating from emerging markets have a considerable advantage that they can also leverage in industrialized economies.

2.4.3 New Competitors

The rise of emerging economies also creates new competitors for established MNCs from developed countries. MNCs originating in emerging economies might enjoy significant advantages compared to their peers from developed economies. Emerging market MNCs (EMNCs) are more attuned to the difficult operating conditions in emerging countries, which they can then leverage to enter less developed countries (Cuervo-Cazurra & Genc, 2008, 2011). At the same time, many EMNCs have improved their ability to design and produce high-end technological products and start competing with MNCs from developed economies. For instance, Brazil's commercial aircraft company Embraer has assumed a globally leading role in the market for regional jets. Similarly, China features an abundance of companies that have established themselves as worldwide leading companies in their sectors. Huawei, for instance, has become a leading ICT software and hardware producer, and is the target of geopolitical animosity (Luo & van Assche, 2023). EMNCs have also led developments in some service-based industries, making clear that EMNCs are a force to be reckoned with today but especially tomorrow. Consequently, EMNCs have been shown to engage in different internationalization behaviour, which is due not only to cultural differences in management but also their latecomer status. A particular form of internationalization that EMNCs have exhibited has become known as 'the springboard' theory, whereby EMNCs aggressively acquire key assets and resources abroad to mitigate their latecomer status and reduce institutional and market constraints at home (Luo & Tung, 2007, 2018).

2.4.4 De-Globalization, De-Coupling, and the Role of the Covid-19 Pandemic

While the story of International Business has largely been associated with an ever tighter integration of world economies and thus increasing globalization, recent developments have led some scholars to believe that the world might be facing an era of de-globalization. De-globalization refers to 'the process of weakening interdependence among nations' (Witt, 2019: 1054). The level of analysis is the world and not nations (Witt, 2019; Chase-Dunn et al., 2000). At the same time, scholars have emphasized that we may also witness an era of de-coupling, which is 'the process of weakening interdependence between two nations or blocs of nations' (Witt et al., 2023: 1) with the level of analysis being dyadic ties between nations or economic blocs (Witt et al., 2023). The latter decline is particularly evident in the US–China context and the geopolitical issues that came with it. The Covid-19 pandemic intensified these (de-)globalization and (de-)coupling discussions. Whereas scholars disagree about whether the world is entering a phase of de-globalization or just a time of shifting economic exchange patterns via de-coupling between nations, the world economy confronts different factors that drive this development.

Scholars have suggested that current political, economic, and technological factors are major drivers in the on-going de-coupling of nations (Ahlstrom et al., 2020; Ghauri et al., 2021; Witt et al., 2023). Geopolitical rivalry between the US and China for global dominance and the war in Ukraine, resulting in further geopolitical animosity between large nations, are major political factors. Falling growth, labour costs, governance uncertainty, and the Covid-19 pandemic and its consequences are some of the economic factors. Digitalization, additive manufacturing, and platform business models are major technological factors in the de-globalization and de-coupling movement (Witt et al., 2023).

The Covid-19 pandemic brought globalization to an abrupt halt and highlighted a weak spot in the global economy – that is, finely attuned and cost-efficient global supply chains, which were severely disrupted, with long-term and ongoing effects. The pandemic intensified the globalization and de-globalization discussion (Delios et al., 2021), raising questions about whether the world would see globalization return to pre-pandemic levels (Ciravegna & Michailova, 2022; Contractor, 2022). Airlines and airports reduced their growth outlook and capacity, only to see travelling bounce back in 2022, resulting in chaos during the peak holiday season. The effects of the global pandemic have combined with geopolitical animosity between blocs of countries and led to a shift in focus from cost-efficient supply chains to alliances based on shared values and geopolitical interests (Cui et al., 2023).

2.5 THE INSTITUTIONAL PERSPECTIVE ON IB: INSTITUTIONAL TRIALITY

It is clear that International Business faces substantial contextual challenges as well as remarkable opportunities in the current dynamic environment. Some researchers (e.g. Beugelsdijk, 2022) even argue that understanding how context influences business is the central question in International Business. But how can we understand context, and what are its components? Here we introduce 'institutional theory' to understand context. This perspective has received a lot of attention, and the pre-eminent scholar on institutional theory, Douglass C. North, received what is commonly called the Economics Nobel Prize in 1993 for his pioneering work on institutions. The thirty-plus years since 1993 have seen quite a bit of work adding to North's foundational contributions, and we now have a good understanding of how we can characterize the context in which business takes place, using what has become known as the institution-based view. We will explore these challenges and opportunities from theoretical and practical perspectives in the following chapters. We differentiate three levels of institutions in IB: the national level, the supranational level, and institutional distances. Jointly, the three levels represent the institutional triality (Hartmann et al., 2022) that internationally active firms need to navigate.

Spotlight: The Economics Nobel Prize

The Sveriges Riksbank Prize in Economic Sciences in Memory of Alfred Nobel, commonly referred to as the Economics Nobel Prize, is awarded annually to individuals who have made outstanding contributions to the field of economics. Established in 1968, it was not part of the original Nobel Prizes established by Alfred Nobel's will but was created in his memory to acknowledge the significance of economic research. The prize recognizes achievements in economic theory, empirical research, and policy analysis, and it covers a wide range of economic topics, from macroeconomics and microeconomics to development economics and behavioural economics.

- In 2023, Claudia Goldin received the Prize for her groundbreaking research on women's historical and contemporary roles in the labour market. She has pioneered work on the gender pay gap and has developed and advanced data necessary to understand the role of gender in the workplace.
- In 2021, David Card and Joshua D. Angrist were awarded the Prize for their pioneering work in empirical labour economics. Card's research on minimum wage effects and Angrist's contributions to the field of causal inference have had a profound impact on understanding the labour market and public policy.
- Oliver E. Williamson was awarded the Prize in 2009 for his pioneering work in the field of economic governance. Williamson's research explored the complex relationships between firms, markets, and institutions, focusing on how transactions and contractual arrangements are structured in the business world.
- Douglass North, who received the Prize in 1993, was acknowledged for his work in institutional economics, shedding light on the role of institutions in shaping economic outcomes.

The Prize highlights some of the most important research in different areas of economics, and many of this book's chapters draw on applications of research on questions of International Business awarded Nobel Prizes. Even if some of the research awarded Nobel Prizes was published years or sometimes decades ago, the insights continue to be remarkably predictive of how firms operate today.

Sources: National Science Foundation (www.nsf.gov) and The Nobel Foundation (www.nobelprize.org/prizes/economic-sciences)

When discussing institutions at national level, we will look into formal as well as informal institutions. The formal institutions relate to the rules and laws that structure what companies can do in the International Business environment. The informal institutions relate to the norms and beliefs that frequently drive many business decisions, in terms of both conscious rational decision-making, and the underlying heuristics and biases. We will shed particular light on the supranational institutions that serve as coordination frameworks for International Business, bridging the differences in national institutions, both formal and informal. We will also investigate the roles of supranational organizations and civil society. These organizations and social movements have substantial influence over both institutions and multinational firms, particularly in the areas of sustainability and digitalization. Lastly, we also discuss the relevance of institutional distance.

Case Study: Context Matters for Starbucks

Starbucks, the American coffee giant, opened its first store in Italy in 2018 - entering the home of the espresso 47 years after the company was founded and after it had entered much of the rest of the world. Still, entering Italy was a bold move considering Italy's rich coffee culture and tradition. Starbucks chose to open its first store in Milan, which is the financial and economic hotspot in Italy, but not the core of Italy's coffee culture, which is in Rome and Naples. Despite much effort, Starbucks was faced with some concerns regarding its entry into Italy, notably because of differences in coffee culture between Italy and the USA. These are some of the contextual aspects that have created complications.

1 Coffee culture: Italy is known for its deep-rooted coffee culture, centred around traditional espresso served at the bar. Starbucks, with its focus on large-sized, customizable, and often sweetened coffee drinks, did not align with the Italian coffee culture. Starbucks' offerings were seen as foreign and at odds with the local preference for small, strong, and unadulterated espresso.
2 Competition: Italy has a highly competitive coffee market with a multitude of small, independent coffee shops and established, iconic brands. Starbucks faced competition not only from these traditional coffee shops but also from established international coffee chains that had adapted to the local market.
3 Pricing: Starbucks' pricing strategy differs from the traditional Italian market. The premium prices of Starbucks' coffee were significantly higher than Italians were used to paying for their espresso. This made Starbucks seem expensive and less attractive to local customers. Also, the price of espressos and some other coffee options is subject to heavy regulation in Italy, and Starbucks had to balance this with its international pricing strategy and positioning.
4 Location selection: Starbucks opened its first store in a historic, upscale area of Milan, which was seen as an attempt to make a statement. However, this choice

was not fully aligned with the Italian coffee tradition, which emphasizes simple and unpretentious coffee bars in local neighbourhoods.

While Starbucks struggled to enter the Italian market for decades, it has now gained a foothold in Italy. In 2023, Starbucks opened its first location in the centre of Rome, finally penetrating the very heart of Italian coffee culture. It remains to be seen what Starbucks' long-term performance in Italy will look like. It seems, though, that careful adjustment to the formal and informal institutions in Italy, particularly the regulation of coffee prices and the cultural preferences for coffee types, will eventually bear fruit.

Sources: Forbes (www.forbes.com/sites/jennawang/2018/09/13/why-it-took-starbucks-47-years-to-open-a-store-in-italy/?sh=60030180fc00), *The Washington Post* (www.washingtonpost.com/travel/2023/05/11/starbucks-rome-italy)

Case Study Questions

1 What are the differences in coffee culture between the USA and Italy which made it difficult for Starbucks to get a foothold in the Italian market?
2 How does Starbucks perform in Italy today? Find out about their store locations and recent growth in outlets in Italy.

SUMMARY

Institutions play a crucial role in shaping global business activities. According to the seminal work of Douglass North (1990), institutions set the 'rules of the game' that guide the choices and actions of organizations (for our purposes the relevant 'players'). From an institution-based view, organizations (or players) are defined as groups of individuals working towards a common goal or objective, including political bodies (e.g. political parties, regulators, government agencies), economic bodies (e.g. firms, trade unions), and social bodies (e.g. churches, schools, universities). The dynamic interaction between institutions and organizations enables and constrains the successes and failures of organizations because institutions provide the framework for economic activity and human interaction. Well-functioning, predictable, and stable institutions reduce uncertainty and consequently reduce the costs (of doing business) and limit the potential for opportunistic behaviour (of acting out of self-interest). In the business field, firms typically adapt their practices to conform to a prevailing institutional framework in their pursuit of acceptance in international markets. Hence, institutions have a bearing on the strategic choices firms make about dimensions such as location, governance, technology, and investment sequence.

There are different types and levels of institutions. For instance, we can differentiate between national and supranational institutions. National institutions encompass formal and informal rules, regulations, and social norms established within a country, while supranational institutions are entities that transcend national boundaries and govern interactions across multiple countries. Further, the two most prevalent distinctions between types of institutions are formal vs informal institutions (North, 1990, 1994) and regulative vs normative vs cultural–cognitive institutions (Scott, 1987, 1995), as outlined in Table 2.1.

From an economics perspective, Douglass North (1990) argues that institutions are either formal or informal. Formal institutions refer to the explicit and codified rules, laws, regulations, and organizational structures created and enforced by governments, authorities, and other governing bodies. These rules are often written down and have a legal or official character that help establish order, resolve disputes, protect property rights, ensure contracts are upheld, and provide a stable environment for social and economic activities. Informal institutions, on the other hand, are unwritten, uncodified, and involve implicit rules, norms, traditions, and social practices that shape human behaviour. They are often deeply rooted in culture and history and do not have a formal enforcement mechanism. Instead, they are typically enforced through social sanctions, peer pressure, reputation effects, and other forms of informal social control. In other words, organizations typically follow shared understandings of what is considered acceptable or unacceptable within a national or supranational informal institutional setting. While informal institutions can complement formal ones by providing additional stability and social support for compliance – especially when formal constraints are unclear or fail – they may also cause tensions when formal laws and regulations are implemented.

From a social science perspective, Richard Scott (1995) describes the three pillars of an institutional framework, which overlap with the dichotomy described above. As with formal institutions, the regulatory pillar of the institutional framework consists of formal rules, laws, and regulations that govern behaviour and interactions within a society, often based on legal mechanisms and sanctions (i.e., rewards or punishments). The other two pillars, normative and cultural–cognitive, share more similarities with informal institutions. The normative pillar refers to social norms, values, and moral beliefs that guide behaviour and interactions and is largely based on prescriptive, evaluative, and obligatory dimensions. Normative systems set goals (e.g. win the game, make profits) but also determine appropriate ways to pursue them (e.g. rules of the game, notions of fair business practices). The third pillar of the institutional framework encompasses the cultural–cognitive elements, which involve shared beliefs, assumptions, and mental models shaping individuals' perceptions of reality and their understanding of the world. This influences the way people and organizations think, interpret information, and make judgements based on shared understandings. While economists often stress the regulative, formal elements of the institutional logic, sociologists, rather, relate to informal, normative elements and more recently also cultural–cognitive elements.

Table 2.1 Institutional frameworks and examples

North (1990)	Scott (1995)	Examples
Formal institutions	Regulatory institutions	Laws
		Regulations
		Rulings
Informal institutions	Normative institutions	Norms
	Cultural–cognitive institutions	Cultures
		Global societal movements

It is vital to recognize that institutions are not static but actually undergo incremental and revolutionary changes over time. Endogenous processes (e.g. conflicts, contradictions between institutional elements) and exogeneous shocks (e.g. wars, financial crises) lead to changes in economic, political, and social conditions. This, in turn, may lead to the adaptation or replacement of existing institutions to better suit the prevailing environment. Given the broad applicability and continuous changes in institutional environments, scholarly interest in drawing upon institutional theory for a multitude of research questions has been evident across disciplines, including IB.

3
FORMAL INSTITUTIONS

CHAPTER INTRODUCTION

We touched upon the different levels of institutions in the previous chapter, focusing on the distinction between national and supranational institutions. This chapter focuses on national institutions in the context of International Business (IB). While supranational institutions, as well as several layers within countries, definitely matter, the defining level of analysis for IB (and hence this book) is the nation state. As a result, it is particularly important to have a good grasp of national institutions. This is because multinational companies (MNCs) operate in different nations and are thus faced with different institutional frameworks. Following the institution-based view we introduced in Chapter 2, companies need to be aware of the nature of these different factors as they provide the 'rules of the game' for corporate decision-making. Because they are easier to understand, we are starting with formal institutions, and move on to investigate informal institutions in Chapter 4.

The formal national institutional environment is typically described in terms of the political, economic, and legal systems of a country. These dimensions of the formal institutional system are not independent but significantly interact with each other. For example, members of the political system design, propose, and vote on legislation. Further, the legal system defines how the political system can propose, adapt, and remove rules; in most cases this is outlined in a country's constitution). The basic ideas of the economic system are, on the one hand, implemented in a nation's legal environment. On the other hand, laws and rules define what is allowed in markets and what is not. It becomes evident that the different formal institutional systems can rather be viewed as a system with strong interdependencies than as three independent elements.

LEARNING OUTCOMES

After reading this chapter you should be able to:

1. Identify the key formal components of national political, legal, and economic systems
2. Compare countries in terms of their systems of governance

3 Translate the characteristics of the formal institutional environment into country risk.
4 Critically reflect on the changing role of formal national institutions in relation to global trends and multinational influences.

Case Study: Barrick Gold in Tanzania

In the early 2000s, Barrick Gold entered a joint venture with a Tanzanian company to operate the Bulyanhulu gold mine in Tanzania. However, disputes arose between Barrick Gold and the Tanzanian government over tax claims, export regulations, and a significant fine was imposed on the company for alleged environmental breaches and unpaid taxes.

In 2017, the Tanzanian government imposed a ban on the export of gold and copper concentrates, affecting Barrick Gold's operations and profitability. The government also demanded a payment of US$190 billion in back taxes and penalties from Acacia Mining, a subsidiary of Barrick Gold, accusing the company of underreporting export revenues.

This situation led to a prolonged negotiation period between Barrick Gold and the Tanzanian government. In an attempt to resolve the dispute, Barrick Gold reached a settlement with Tanzania in 2019, agreeing to pay US$300 million to resolve outstanding tax claims and to share future economic benefits from the mines.

Despite the challenges and disputes with the Tanzanian government, Barrick Gold has tried to promote sustainable mining practices in Tanzania. The company has implemented various initiatives aimed at environmental conservation, community development, and responsible resource extraction. It has invested in sustainable development projects in Tanzania that focus on environmental stewardship, community engagement, and economic empowerment. These initiatives include programmes relating to reforestation, water conservation, and biodiversity around its mining sites. It has also established community development programmes to enhance education, healthcare, and local infrastructure. Moreover, it has emphasized responsible mining practices, striving to minimize the environmental impact of its operations. This includes implementing modern technologies and techniques to reduce water usage, control emissions, and manage waste generated from mining activities.

In the context of the disputes with the Tanzanian government, Barrick Gold's commitment to sustainability serves as a crucial aspect of its negotiation strategy. The company has leveraged its efforts in sustainable mining and community development to demonstrate its commitment to responsible practices and establish a positive relationship with the government and local communities.

By showcasing its investment in sustainability, Barrick Gold aims to mitigate tensions, showcase its contribution to Tanzania's development, and potentially find common ground with the government regarding tax issues and regulatory compliance. These efforts reflect the company's recognition of the importance of sustainable practices, not only for environmental and social reasons but also to foster positive relationships with host governments in the mining industry.

This case illustrates how disputes between multinational companies and governments over contractual obligations, taxes, and regulatory issues can strain relationships, having a significant financial impact and leading to prolonged negotiations. It also highlights the challenges faced by companies operating in countries where governments may change regulations or enforce unexpected measures, impacting contractual obligations and profitability. At the same time, the case highlights how MNCs can play a role in promoting sustainable business practices, and how these practices can be used as a vehicle for improving MNC-government relationships.

Sources: Barrick Gold (www.barrick.com/English/operations/north-mara/mining-with-integrity/tanzania/default.aspx); Institute of Developing Economies (www.ide.go.jp/English/Data/Africa_file/Company/tanzania03.html); CGTN Africa (https://africa.cgtn.com/tanzania-and-barrick-gold-reach-final-operating-agreement)

Case Study Questions

1. How have mining companies in this case traditionally engaged with local communities?
2. Why are such approaches unlikely to succeed today?
3. How can a humble approach help Barrick Gold and similar companies gain a foothold in local markets?

3.1 POLITICAL SYSTEMS

The national political system refers to the political organization of a country. As extremes, we can differentiate democratic and autocratic national political systems. Firms usually do not directly interact with the political system of a country. However, the rules and regulations established by political systems bear strong relevance for firms.

MNCs directly and indirectly interact with political systems by, for example, lobbying policymakers and being tied to regulations, respectively. For firms and especially MNCs given their cross-border operations, political systems may act as significant sources of political risk. Political systems typically come in layers, with two extremes: democracy and authoritarianism or totalitarianism.

3.1.1 Democracy

Democracy is a system of government in which the power to make decisions is vested in the people, either directly or through elected representatives. In general, democratic governments gain legitimacy from being elected by their country's citizens.

Democratic government systems are characterized by (1) regular and fair elections, (2) active engagement of citizens through the right to express their opinions, join political parties and participate in political debate, (3) a rule of law that protects individual rights and freedoms such as individual property, freedom of speech, religion, press, and assembly, (4) separation of legislative, executive, and judicial powers, and (5) a relatively apolitical bureaucracy and defence policy to safeguard the political system's continuity in case of regime changes.

These common features allow for some variation from one democracy to another – for example, differences in electoral system such as proportional representation (PR) and winner-takes-all systems. In PR systems, the distribution of seats in a legislative body reflects the proportion of votes received by the candidate or political party. These electoral systems are based on the idea that voters' preferences should be accurately represented in choosing the country's leaders and are adhered to in most European countries. In practice, we see different PR systems across countries. The most widely used PR system is party-list PR in which citizens vote for a political party and seats are allocated to parties based on vote shares. The order of candidates on political-party-provided lists, in turn, often determines who gets elected. Mixed-member PR (MMP) systems allow citizens to cast two votes: one for a party and one for a candidate. Seats are allocated to parties proportionally and additional seats are filled with candidates to ensure overall proportionality. Finally, in single transferable vote (STV) systems, citizens rank candidates in order of their preference with candidates elected if votes pass a predetermined minimum threshold. These candidates' surplus votes are then redistributed to other candidates according to the order of voters' preferences.

In contrast, in winner-takes-all systems, such as first past the post, the candidate or political party with the most votes wins the seat. These electoral systems tend to emphasize majority governance and simplicity, giving less influence to candidates with fewer votes and smaller parties.

In a democratic national political system, political decision-makers are elected by the citizens of a country. However, how votes are translated into representation in the parliament and the decision-making authority that comes with being elected vary significantly across different democratic systems. Usually, this is determined by the constitution of a country.

- *Direct vs indirect elections*: In direct elections voters directly elect their preferred candidate, while indirect elections involve an additional step where voters choose representatives or electors who, in turn, make the final decision. Germany is an example of a country with both direct and indirect elections. The national parliament is directly elected by voters and elected members of the parliament subsequently elect and control the government (chancellor and ministers). The presidential election in the United States is a good example of a direct election in which voters directly elect a president with executive powers.
- *Direct vs representative democracies*: Representative democracies rely on elected officials to represent the interests of voters and make decisions on their behalf.

It is the most common form of democracy in most countries today. Direct democracy involves citizens actively participating in the decision-making process through mechanisms such as referendums and initiatives. Referendums are votes on specific issues or laws, and initiatives allow citizens to propose new laws or changes to existing ones. Many countries combine both mechanisms in their systems and include elements of direct democracy in their generally representative democratic systems.

- National vs federal democracies. Countries vary based on the relevance of national vs federal democratic systems. While in purely national systems political power is centralized, federal systems – as in Germany, the US, and Austria – give considerable decision-making power to the subnational federal level.

3.1.2 Authoritarianism

An autocratic national political system, also known as an autocracy, is a form of government in which power and authority are concentrated in the hands of a single leader or a small group of individuals with no accountability to the public. This means that autocratic leaders are usually less constrained in decision-making than democratically elected governments.

Authoritarianism (or totalitarianism) represents a system of government characterized by exclusive control vested in an individual or a singular political party. This often involves refusing to acknowledge alternative political parties or even suppressing them.

Totalitarian regimes are characterized by (1) centralized authority with little to no political constraints, (2) uncontested elections with little to no political competition, (3) limited rights to express individual opinions and limited freedom of speech, religion, press, and assembly, (4) state-controlled economic activities through extensive state ownership and central planning, (5) propaganda and censorship, and glorification of the country's leader or leaders.

Spotlight: The Social Credit System in China

The digital social scoring mechanism proposed for some regions in China, often referred to as the Social Credit System (SCS), aims to monitor and assess the behaviour of individuals and businesses. This system uses a wide range of data sources, including financial records, social media activity, public behaviour, and even social connections, to generate a score that reflects the trustworthiness and social responsibility of a person or entity.

High scores can provide numerous benefits, such as easier access to loans, priority in job applications, and expedited public services. Conversely, low scores can result in

(Continued)

various penalties, including travel restrictions, reduced access to social services, and public shaming. The system is intended to promote trustworthy behaviour and adherence to laws and social norms by rewarding positive actions and punishing negative ones. This incentivizes compliance with societal standards and legal regulations, theoretically fostering a more harmonious society.

The Social Credit System is underpinned by advanced artificial intelligence (AI) technologies, which play a crucial role in its operation. AI algorithms analyse vast amounts of data from multiple sources, identifying patterns and behaviours that contribute to an individual's or business's social credit score. Machine learning techniques allow the system to continuously improve its predictive accuracy and responsiveness to new types of data and behaviours.

AI-driven facial recognition technology, for example, is used to monitor public spaces and identify individuals, ensuring compliance with public norms and rules. Natural language processing (NLP) algorithms scan social media and other online communications for content that may impact social credit scores. Additionally, AI-powered data analytics integrate information from different databases, ensuring a comprehensive evaluation of each entity's behaviour.

Critics argue that the SCS poses significant privacy concerns and risks of abuse, as it grants the government extensive surveillance capabilities. They also raise concerns about fairness, potential errors, and the impact on personal freedoms, warning that such a system could lead to social stratification and discrimination. Proponents, however, believe it can enhance public safety and trust, reduce fraud, and encourage responsible behaviour.

Sources: Universität Wien (https://rudolphina.univie.ac.at/das-social-credit-system-in-china) and Horizons (https://joinhorizons.com/china-social-credit-system-explained)

Over time, we have seen a range of totalitarian variants emerging, each exhibiting unique attributes, while we also observe totalitarian systems declining and becoming democracies. The most widely known variant of totalitarianism is communism. Communism, as an ideology, envisions a classless, stateless society with communal ownership of property. In practice, historical communist regimes have often centralized decision-making on production and distribution, frequently under authoritarian or totalitarian governance. Other variants include theocratic, secular, and right-wing totalitarianism. In theocratic totalitarianism, political power is vested in an individual or group that governs according to religious principles, often repressing non-conforming religions. In secular totalitarianism, political power is vested in the military. In right-wing totalitarianism, political power is vested in those that allow individual economic liberties while curtailing individual political freedom, stemming from the concern that individual political freedom may lead to communism.

In practice, most countries are hard to classify along the continuum from democratic to authoritarian. Take Russia and China as examples. Russia is nominally democratic, but in reality it is a highly centralized authoritarian state. China is a more decentralized authoritarian state with some democracy at the local level and even calls for democracy within the communist party. In fact, governments are made up of competing political and bureaucratic interests – this is true for all political systems.

In the realm of International Business, understanding the political system should be of utmost importance to managers of MNCs. First, political systems determine where decision-making power is vested, which regulations are established and whose interests these regulations may reflect. Second, political systems shape the methods by which businesses can exert influence on policymaking and regulations – whether through legitimate means (e.g. political connections, political contributions, lobbying) or illicit means (e.g. corruption, bribery). Last, political systems determine the frequency of potential regime changes that may lead to adverse firm-level effects, causing political risk and uncertainty. To protect against political risks, checks and balances as constraints come into effect, mostly in democratic systems of governments. Henisz (2000) developed a widely used framework for assessing political constraints (POLCON). This framework is based on the idea that institutions that have counterbalancing powers will lead to a reduction in risk. As foreign firms generally fear changes to the political environment, more checks and balances are assumed to be positive for international investments.

Political systems, arguably, provide the structural foundation (e.g. regarding the role of the government, or the degree of centralization or decentralization in decision-making) for the functioning of economic systems. Economic systems tend to follow political systems as the latter primarily influence the rules, regulations, and policies that guide economic activities within a country and determine resource allocation, wealth generation, and private–public regulation.

The national political system is relevant to MNCs as different systems are associated with different degrees of political risk for MNCs. Political risk refers to the potential negative effects of political factors, such as government stability, policy changes, and geopolitical tensions on business operations and foreign investments. Uncertainties posed by the political environment stem from actions by governmental and non-governmental actors and may lead to changes in the 'rules of the game' (i.e., formal and informal institutions). Political risk can be classified into two categories, namely macropolitical risks (e.g. war, change of government), which affect all firms in a country, and micropolitical risks (e.g. regulations, taxes), which affect only specific firms, industries, or venture types.

Case Study: MNC-Government Interaction in Venezuela

The Venezuelan oil sector offers a fascinating insight into the complex dynamics of multinational companies (MNCs) and governments in the context of a valuable natural resource - oil. The history of the Venezuelan oil sector consists of several critical episodes, each marked by shifts in the balance of power, changing government policies, and legal disputes. Müllner and Puck (2018) highlight the key political events and strategies employed by both MNCs and the Venezuelan government.

1 The golden age (1930s): In the 1930s, Venezuela became the world's largest oil exporter, a position that attracted substantial foreign investment, primarily from MNCs. The dependence of Allied forces on oil during World War II further strengthened the bargaining position of the Venezuelan government. This period saw the establishment of the Hydrocarbons Law in 1943, which introduced a concession scheme, splitting oil revenues evenly between foreign MNCs and the state. Oil revenues quickly became Venezuela's primary income source, but this growing dependence on foreign MNCs initiated a period of sustained power balance between the government and these enterprises.
2 Obsolescing bargaining I - *La Gran Venezuela* (1943-75): In the post-war years, the government's revenues from oil began to stagnate. The first democratic election in 1958 led to a unilateral increase in the government's share of oil revenues to 65%. This shift in bargaining power marked the start of extended negotiations, resulting in government revenues reaching 95% by 1975. Meanwhile, MNCs, facing decreasing profit margins, neglected well maintenance and explored alternative investments. Eventually, Venezuela lost its position as the world's largest oil exporter.
3 Sovereignty at bay I - *Apertura Petrolera* (1989-99): Over this decade, various governments attempted to establish a new institutional framework to attract foreign investors. This framework bypassed the Venezuelan government and made PDVSA, the state-owned oil and gas company, a private partner for incoming foreign direct investment (FDI). Based on this framework, foreign MNCs could recover their investments from PDVSA in case of government intervention (at least in theory). This created more flexibility for MNCs and shifted the power towards the MNC side. In auctions held during this period, many oil fields were sold to foreign MNCs, re-establishing a state of mutual dependence.
4 Obsolescing bargaining II - Bolivarian revolution: In late 1998, Hugo Chavez came to power, initiating the Bolivarian revolution. The government initially focused on consolidating power over PDVSA, which led to disputes and strikes. To address the controversy, Chavez replaced the board of PDVSA in 2002 and fired approximately 19,000 workers to finally secure the government's access to oil resources. He used increasing oil revenues for social development programmes to maintain support among the electorate. Tensions between foreign MNCs and the Venezuelan government escalated, with government threats of economic sanctions and creeping expropriation.

5 Epilogue - International arbitration: ExxonMobil and ConocoPhillips refused to accept government terms and pursued legal strategies to recover their investments. This resulted in substantial arbitration awards. As well as the legal consequences, Venezuela experienced a decline in incoming FDI, increased political isolation, and difficulty attracting future investment on favourable terms.

This historical overview of the Venezuelan oil sector illustrates the dynamic nature of political institutions, and how MNCs navigate the politics in their global operations. The Venezuela example showcases the profound impact of changing governments, legal disputes, and shifting economic dynamics on the global oil industry. The case offers valuable insights into the intricate interplay between economic and political forces in a resource-dependent nation.

Source: Müllner & Puck (2018)

Case Study Questions

1 What are the different degrees of government intervention that governments can use to absorb some of the profits from multinational companies?
2 Under what circumstances are government interventions in MNC operations justified? How can you draw a line?
3 How can MNCs engage with governments in order to avoid partial or full expropriation?

3.1.3 Political Ideologies

An ideology is 'a set of beliefs or principles, especially one on which a political system, party, or organization is based' (Cambridge University Press, n.d.) that often guides people's behaviours, decisions, and perspectives. Political ideologies often provide the philosophical and theoretical foundation upon which governance systems are built and operated. Michael Freeden, a leading theorist of ideology, defines political ideology as 'a set of ideas, beliefs, values, and opinions, exhibiting a recurring pattern, that competes deliberately as well as unintentionally over providing plans of action for public policy making, in an attempt to justify, explain, contest, or change the social and political arrangements and processes of a political community' (Freeden, 2001: 7174). Because of their central role in all activities in a society, political ideologies have implications not only for political systems, but also for the legal and economic systems we will discuss below. Over time and especially since the nineteenth century, we have seen many political ideologies emerging, some more enduring than others, some with more government intervention than others. In the following, we briefly outline some of the most common ideologies as well as distinct 'hybrid' ideologies from a political point of view: capitalist, laissez-faire, mercantilist, neoliberal, protectionist, social market, communalist, and socialist/communist ideology.

Capitalism, as a political ideology, advocates for private ownership of resources and means of production, emphasizing individual economic freedom and competitive markets. In capitalist ideology, government intervention is limited but may vary in degree. Governments might intervene to safeguard fair competition and mitigate the consequences of market failures over and above self-regulation by markets themselves. Proponents of capitalism argue that it promotes innovation and growth while critics argue it leads to inequality and exploitation.

Closely related to capitalism and also referred to as free market capitalism is laissez-faire ideology. In contrast to capitalism, however, laissez-faire advocates minimal government intervention, arguing that the less government intervenes, the better off businesses and, as a result, societies will be. Proponents emphasize the ideology's efficiency (e.g. no costly government regulation is needed) and individual economic freedom, while critics – most famously John Maynard Keynes – point to negative externalities that primarily affect the weakest in society or those who are in most need of government protection.

Mercantilism, as a political and economic ideology that dominated Western economic thought from the sixteenth to the eighteenth centuries, emphasizes the accumulation of wealth from a favourable balance of trade, often by promoting exports (e.g. through subsidies) and restricting imports (i.e., through protectionism). Of its time, it was often associated with colonial expansion to secure valuable resources (e.g. precious metals).

Neoliberalism advocates for limited government interaction and market-driven policies, free markets and deregulation, as well as individual economic freedom and privatization. Neoliberalism emerged as a political ideology in the mid-twentieth century.

Protectionism, in contrast, makes the protection of domestic production through government intervention a nation's top priority. Domestic production and jobs are to be preserved and protected from foreign competition by imposing trade barriers such as tariffs or quotas on imported goods and services. Critics argue that protectionism, while trying to safeguard local jobs, leads to reduced consumer choice given fewer and more expensive imported options.

Next, we outline two hybrid ideologies that combine key elements of distinct ideologies. One is social market ideology, which combines elements of both capitalism and social welfare and aims to balance economic freedom with social protection. Governments guided by social market ideology intervene to prevent excessive inequality and provide social safety nets, healthcare, and education for their nation's citizens.

The second is communalist ideology, which advocates for community ownership and management of resources and means of production. Thus, communalist ideology opposes both capitalist ideology (promoting private ownership) and socialist/communist ideology (promoting state ownership).

Finally, two closely related political ideologies – socialism and communism – advocate collective (state) ownership and control of resources, means of production, and the distribution of wealth. While they share common goals, they differ in the radicality of their approaches and degree of government involvement.

All these ideologies have important and far-reaching implications for what their respective proponents consider to be the best political and economic system. However, what we see in reality are not these archetypical ideologies; rather, we observe elements from different ideologies combine to form different forms of national governance systems.

3.2 LEGAL SYSTEMS

The national legal system has significant and direct effects on firms active in a market as home-country laws do not apply abroad. Across legal systems of the world, we can differentiate between two core types of legal system. Civil law systems are based on written law that has been approved by political authorities. Common law systems, in contrast, are developed through judicial decisions and precedents over centuries.

3.2.1 Civil Law

Civil law is a legal system primarily derived from Roman law and is prevalent in many countries across Europe, Latin America, Asia, and parts of Africa. Unlike common law, which relies on judicial decisions and precedents, civil law is based on codified statutes and comprehensive legal codes established by legislatures. It emphasizes detailed and extensive statutes that provide the framework for legal interpretation and application.

In civil law systems, judges have a more restricted role in creating law compared to common law jurisdictions. Their primary duty is to interpret and apply statutes rather than create legal precedents through judicial decisions. The principle of *stare decisis*, or 'to stand by things decided', is not central in civil law systems to the extent it is in common law.

One of the primary influences of civil law on International Business relates to its structured and comprehensive approach to legal codes. These legal codes often cover a broad range of matters, including contracts, property, torts, and more. For instance, when a multinational company from a civil law jurisdiction conducts business in a foreign country with a similar legal system, it might rely on the codified laws and statutes to govern its contractual agreements and operations. Consider a French multinational company entering into a business partnership in a country that follows a civil law system, such as Spain. When drafting contracts or agreements, the French company would likely focus on adhering to the specific provisions outlined in the civil code of Spain regarding contractual obligations, rights, and responsibilities.

Civil law principles governing contracts, such as rules concerning offer and acceptance, form, interpretation, and performance, will strongly influence how the French company structures its agreements with local partners or clients. Adherence to the explicit provisions outlined in the civil code helps ensure legal clarity, as civil law systems typically provide detailed regulations governing various aspects of contracts. Moreover, in the event of a contractual dispute arising in a foreign civil law jurisdiction, courts in that country would primarily rely on the codified statutes and legal codes to interpret and resolve the disagreement. Unlike common law systems, where judges often look to precedents, courts in civil law countries tend to focus on applying the specific statutes and regulations outlined in the legal codes to resolve disputes.

The structured nature of civil law can provide a level of predictability and clarity in International Business dealings. Companies operating in civil law jurisdictions can navigate legal requirements, draft contracts, and resolve disputes by following the explicit provisions outlined in the legal codes of those countries.

In summary, civil law's reliance on codified statutes and comprehensive legal codes significantly influences how multinational companies conduct business in foreign countries with similar legal systems. The emphasis on detailed legal provisions helps companies structure contracts and operations according to specific statutory requirements, ensuring legal compliance and predictability in International Business transactions.

3.2.2 Common Law

Common law is a legal system that originated in England and spread to various countries, particularly those in the British Commonwealth and the United States. It is characterized by the development of legal principles and precedents through judicial decisions and interpretations rather than codified statutes or legislative enactments.

At its core, common law relies on the doctrine of *stare decisis*, meaning 'binding precedent'. This principle emphasizes that courts are bound to follow the precedents established by previous judicial decisions when deciding similar cases. Judges have the authority to interpret laws and apply legal principles based on past rulings, ensuring consistency and predictability in the legal system.

One of the fundamental aspects of common law is its adaptability and flexibility. It evolves over time as judges interpret existing laws in light of societal changes, technological advancements, and shifting moral values. This evolutionary nature enables common law to remain relevant in addressing new legal challenges and scenarios that were not explicitly foreseen when the laws were initially written.

A prime example of common law's influence on doing business in a foreign country is its impact on contract law. Contracts are essential in business dealings, outlining the terms and agreements between parties. Common law principles surrounding contracts, such as offer, acceptance, consideration, and implied terms, have been influential worldwide due to their adaptability and comprehensive nature.

For instance, consider a multinational company based in the United States engaging in a business venture in a foreign country with a different legal system. When forming contracts, the company might rely on common law principles to ensure clarity and enforceability. Elements like an offer made by one party, acceptance by the other, and the presence of consideration (something of value exchanged between parties) form the foundational elements of a contract.

Common law principles regarding contractual obligations, such as implied terms (terms not expressly stated but understood to be part of the contract) or the doctrine of good faith and fair dealing, may also guide the multinational company in structuring agreements with foreign partners or clients. These principles help establish a framework for fair and equitable business dealings, even in jurisdictions where statutory laws might differ significantly. Moreover, in cases of contractual disputes arising in a foreign legal system, common law principles of contract interpretation and precedent may influence how courts in that country resolve the conflicts. Judges might look to precedents established in common law jurisdictions to interpret ambiguous clauses or resolve contractual ambiguities, especially if the local legal system lacks specific statutes addressing such issues.

The adaptability of common law allows businesses operating internationally to navigate diverse legal landscapes more effectively. Companies can utilize established legal principles and precedents to structure agreements, mitigate risks, and resolve disputes in a manner consistent with established legal norms, even when operating in countries with different legal traditions.

In conclusion, common law principles have a significant impact on doing business in foreign countries by providing a framework for contractual relationships, dispute resolution, and legal predictability. The flexibility and evolution of common law make it a valuable tool for multinational company seeking to conduct business in various jurisdictions while adhering to established legal norms and ensuring enforceable agreements.

3.3 ECONOMIC SYSTEMS

The national economic system relates to the organization of the economy in a market. There are multiple options to organize and govern a market that range from a pure market to a pure planned economy, with multiple varieties of capitalism in between the two extremes.

A pure planned economy, also known as a 'command economy' or a 'centralized economy', is an economic system in which the government or a central authority has significant control over the production, allocation, and distribution of goods and services. In a command economy, the government typically makes key decisions regarding what to produce, how much to produce, and for whom to produce.

In a pure planned economy, the government or a central authority creates comprehensive plans that outline production targets, resource allocation, and economic priorities. These plans can cover various sectors of the economy. In many planned economies, the government or state owns and controls the means of production, including factories, farms, and major industries. Private ownership is limited or non-existent in key sectors. Further, the government often sets prices for goods and services, wages, and rents, rather than allowing them to be determined by market forces.

Planned economies have often been associated with socialist and communist political systems and ideologies, with some countries, such as the former Soviet Union and China under Mao Zedong, fully or partially implementing planned economies at various points in their history. However, critics argue that a pure planned economy never really existed, as black or grey markets for certain goods existed almost everywhere.

The conceptual counterpoint to a pure planned economy would be a pure market economy. A pure market economy largely refers to a market that is totally unregulated by the government and follows the ideas that Adam Smith described in *The Wealth of Nations* (1937/1776). The core assumption of a pure free market economy is that the market is most efficient if governments take a hands-off approach, giving all power to the 'invisible hand of the market'. This limits the role of the government to being a provider of infrastructure and safety that cannot be provided by the market itself. Consequently, in a pure market economy the production, allocation, and distribution of goods and services are purely determined by market forces of supply and demand, rather than by government control or central planning. In a pure market economy, individuals and businesses have a very high degree of economic freedom and autonomy in making decisions about what to produce, how to produce, and for whom to produce.

In a pure market economy, economic decisions are decentralized, meaning that individual consumers and producers make choices that collectively shape the economy. The price system conveys information that guides these choices. Most of the means of production, such as land, resources, and businesses, are privately owned. This includes a wide range of economic entities, from small businesses to large corporations. Further, market economies rely on competition among businesses to drive innovation, efficiency, and consumer choice. For market participants, the pursuit of profit is a fundamental driving force in a market economy. Individuals and businesses aim to generate profits. Prices of goods and services are determined by the interaction of supply and demand in the marketplace. When demand for a product or service increases, its price tends to rise, and when demand decreases, prices tend to fall.

Political economists have been exploring a more actor-centric approach in explaining economic systems, dubbed 'varieties of capitalism' (Mariotti & Marzano, 2019). According to Hall and Soskice (2001), in this context, actors can be individuals, companies, or governments. However, they emphasize the role of firms, regarding them as the key actors in a capitalist economy, advancing their interests rationally and strategically interacting with other actors in the system through coordination. Hence, according to Hall and Soskice (2001: 6), firms 'are the key agents of adjustment in the face of technological change or international competition whose activities aggregate into overall levels of economic performance'.

In this relational view of the economy in general and firms in particular, economic success ultimately depends on the ability of firms to establish effective coordination with a broad range of actors. In order to resolve these coordination problems, firms must build relationships across five spheres: industrial relations, vocational training and education, corporate governance, inter-firm relations, as well as employees. In this framework, two main 'varieties of capitalism' emerge: liberal market economies (LMEs), mainly relying on market mechanisms and hierarchies, and coordinated market economies (CMEs), emphasizing the importance of non-market forms of interaction and relationships with other actors.

3.3.1 Liberal Market Economies

The free market, often associated with neoliberal and Anglo-Saxon capitalist economic systems, refers to an economic model wherein the state's intervention in the economy is minimal, with the market predominantly driven by supply and demand. This economic philosophy, which emphasizes individual entrepreneurship, private property, and competition.

The United States, United Kingdom, Canada, Australia, and Hong Kong are examples of countries that have adopted an economic model most closely related to liberal market economies. In these systems, the state typically plays a limited role in the marketplace. Instead, businesses and consumers are mostly free to determine prices, production, and distribution. This hands-off approach, however, has exceptions. Crucial sectors like defence, healthcare, and education are often subject to significant government intervention, be it through funding, regulation, or direct operation. The rationale behind this selective involvement is the belief that certain essential services are best maintained or regulated by the state to ensure universal accessibility or quality.

In Latin America, Chile stands out as the most free-market-oriented economy, having undergone significant market-oriented reforms since the 1970s, which have been referred to as the 'Miracle of Chile'. These reforms, ranging from the privatization of state-owned enterprises to deregulation and opening up to foreign investment, have made Chile a regional benchmark for free-market economics. Peru, though further behind in its adoption of these policies, has been making strides towards liberalizing its economy, reducing trade barriers, and encouraging foreign investment.

In a liberal market economy, the primary goal of the state is seen as maximizing economic efficiency, which usually translates to fostering an environment conducive to economic growth. Contrary to models where governments have an active role in directing economic activities or supporting specific industries, the free-market model resists the idea of the state 'picking winners and losers'. Rather, the economy is seen as a 'convoy system' in which many firms enter many industries with some firms succeeding and some failing. The rationale is that the market, if left largely alone, will lead to optimal outcomes by ensuring resources are allocated where they generate the most value. However, this does not leave the state completely passive. Instead, its role is to maintain the conditions for the market to function effectively, such as enforcing contracts, protecting property rights, and ensuring competition.

Several distinctive characteristics emerge in economies that lean heavily towards a free-market approach. First, labour unions tend to be weaker in these economies. The rationale is that powerful unions can distort labour markets, leading to inefficiencies. However, this has raised concerns about worker protection and rights in such settings.

Second, free-market economies often have comparatively lower taxes; advocates of the free market argue that high taxes can discourage entrepreneurship and economic activity. Consequently, many countries that lean towards a free-market economy have comparatively lower corporate and sometimes personal income taxes in order to incentivize business growth and investment.

Third, at the same, free-market economies are often characterized by higher inequality. While the free-market system can lead to significant generation of wealth, the distribution of this wealth usually is not equal across society. On the contrary, free-market wealth generation often results in higher levels of economic inequality. Without strong redistributive mechanisms, the wealth generated in such systems can become concentrated in the hands of a few.

In conclusion, the liberal-market model emphasizes a limited role for the state in economic affairs, trusting the invisible hand of the market to guide resource allocation. While this approach has yielded rapid economic growth in many instances, it also brings challenges, especially in addressing inequality and ensuring that the benefits of growth are broadly shared.

Spotlight: The Laffer Curve

The Laffer Curve, named after economist Arthur Laffer, illustrates the relationship between tax rates and tax revenues. It suggests that there is an optimal tax rate that maximizes government revenue, beyond which further increases in tax rates could lead to diminishing returns or even a decrease in revenue. The curve takes into account taxpayers' behaviour in relation to changes in tax rates.

Increasing taxes where rates are very low is likely to increase revenue proportionally because even though the government takes a small cut, people tend not to adjust their behaviour because they experience the tax as an insubstantial reduction to their income. However, as tax rates rise, individuals might change their behaviour to mitigate the tax burden. Higher taxes can disincentivize work, investment, and entrepreneurship as people may decide to work less, invest less, or find ways to avoid taxes (legally) or evade taxes (illegally). This reduced economic activity can lead to a decrease in overall taxable income despite higher rates, resulting in lower tax revenues.

Conversely, reducing tax rates from excessively high levels can stimulate economic growth. Lower taxes can incentivize individuals and businesses to work harder, invest more, and expand operations, ultimately leading to increased economic activity. This increased economic output could potentially offset the loss in revenue from lower tax rates.

The Laffer Curve implies that there is a point at which raising tax rates becomes counterproductive, as it can stifle economic activity and lead to diminishing tax revenue. Similarly, reducing tax rates beyond a certain point may lead to a temporary reduction in revenue but could stimulate economic growth, which might eventually increase overall tax revenue.

The curve does not pinpoint an exact tax rate but suggests that there is a level at which tax rates can be optimized to maximize government revenue without burdening taxpayers excessively. Policymakers need to consider this trade-off between tax rates and tax revenue to strike a balance that fosters economic growth while generating the necessary funds for government operations.

Sources: Gahvari (1989) and Heijman & Ophem (2005)

3.3.2 State-Led Or Directed Economic Systems

State-led or directed economic systems represent a unique blend of capitalist mechanisms with pronounced government intervention. In these systems, while market mechanisms do operate, the government has a significant say in directing economic activities, often to achieve broader development or strategic objectives. These models offer a stark contrast to both free-market models and mixed economic systems.

Countries such as Japan, France, Korea, Singapore, and many developing nations have historically witnessed governments steering economic resources and protection to certain favoured firms and industries. Such practices are not only about ensuring a level playing field but are intended to foster certain sectors deemed critical for national development or strategic interests. Contrasting 'convoy system' approach (see above) that is characteristic of free-market economies, the state-led model often features a 'bullet train' approach. This means that the government institutes policies to support industries that they believe are of strategic importance or will be particularly profitable, allowing very fast development of these industries. The resulting businesses are often (partially) state-owned enterprises (SOEs).

Case Study: Singapore's Industrial Strategy

Since gaining independence in 1965, Singapore has strategically developed its economy through a series of industrial strategies, propelling itself from a developing nation into a global economic powerhouse. The nation's industrial strategy has been multifaceted, adapting to changing global trends, leveraging its strategic location, investing in education, and fostering innovation. These efforts have transformed Singapore into a thriving advanced economy.

The industrial strategy of Singapore in the 1960s primarily focused on industrialization to reduce dependence on imports and create jobs for its burgeoning population. The government, under the leadership of Lee Kuan Yew, pursued policies that attracted foreign investment, particularly in labour-intensive industries such as textiles and electronics. This kick-started the nation's export-oriented industrialization, fostering economic growth and job creation.

In the 1970s, Singapore recognized the importance of diversification and embarked on a strategy of developing high-value industries. The government invested heavily in infrastructure, education, and technology to attract multinational companies (MNCs) in sectors such as petrochemicals, pharmaceuticals, and electronics. The creation of Jurong Industrial Estate and the development of the Port of Singapore bolstered its position as a regional hub for manufacturing and trade.

(Continued)

The 1980s saw Singapore adapting to global shifts by emphasizing productivity and innovation. The Economic Development Board (EDB) encouraged companies to adopt advanced technologies and improve efficiency. The government also invested in research and development (R&D) to foster innovation, leading to the establishment of institutions such as the Agency for Science, Technology, and Research (A*STAR).

By the 1990s, Singapore recognized the importance of transitioning into a knowledge-based economy. The government implemented initiatives to attract talent, enhance education, and promote entrepreneurship. The establishment of Biopolis and Fusionopolis, dedicated research hubs, showcased Singapore's commitment to becoming a global centre for research and development.

In the twenty-first century, Singapore continued to evolve its industrial strategy, focusing on emerging sectors like biotechnology, clean energy, and digital innovation. The government launched initiatives such as the Research, Innovation, and Enterprise (RIE) Plan to drive innovation across various industries and invested in developing a skilled workforce adaptable to the demands of the digital era.

Today, Singapore stands as a testament to the success of its industrial strategy. It has transitioned from labour-intensive industries to a diverse, knowledge-based economy, driven by innovation and technology. The nation's GDP per capita ranks among the highest globally, and it serves as a regional financial hub, attracting global talent and investment.

Singapore's industrial strategy has shaped its advanced economy by fostering a conducive environment for businesses, investing in human capital, nurturing innovation, and adapting to global economic shifts. Its success serves as a model for nations aspiring to achieve economic development through strategic industrial planning and continuous adaptation to changing global dynamics.

Sources: Bercuson (1995) and Yeo (2016)

Case Study Questions

1 What are the upsides and downsides of industrial policy?
2 How can multinational firms influence the creation of industrial policy?

China presents another one of the most emblematic examples of a state-led economic system. Its government exerts control over vast segments of its economy, dominating most of the financial system. Unlike models that allow market forces to determine winners and losers, the Chinese government explicitly selects industries and companies to support, reflecting its strategic and developmental priorities.

Further amplifying the state's role, a significant portion of China's economy is dominated by SOEs. These entities, while operating in a market environment, are owned (wholly or in majority) by the government. SOEs play a pivotal role in numerous sectors, from energy and telecommunication to transportation and banking.

These economies, though rooted in capitalism, diverge significantly from free-market systems. The state often prompts firms to venture into specific industries, grants preferential treatment to certain firms, or establishes SOEs to dominate sectors deemed vital. Large governmental bureaucracies are tasked with planning, monitoring, and sometimes controlling economic activities.

The model of export-led growth adopted by Korea provides an insightful illustration of state-directed economic policy. Drawing parallels with Japan and other Asian nations, Korea's strategy pivoted on promoting industries that catered to export markets. By focusing on external demand, these countries hoped to accelerate economic development and technological advancement.

Singapore, often hailed for its economic success, similarly embodies a system with a robust governmental role. While its economy is vibrant and globally integrated, the government plays a decisive role in strategic sectors, aiming to ensure long-term stability and growth.

The efficacy of state-led economic systems is a topic of enduring debate. Asian countries, notably the 'Asian Tigers' (Hong Kong, Singapore, South Korea, and Taiwan), registered unparalleled economic growth using such models. However, critics argue that these nations could possibly have achieved even more rapid growth without state intervention.

Conversely, in various parts of the world, especially where the focus was on import substitution, state-led systems led to the emergence of stifling bureaucracies, curbing innovation and entrepreneurial spirit. The intention behind import substitution – to reduce dependency on foreign goods by promoting local industries – often resulted in inefficient industries being shielded from global competition. In some cases, however, import substitution policies are not entirely voluntary but rather implemented due to economic sanctions following political conflict, such as in the aftermath of Russia's annexation of Ukrainian Crimea in 2014 (Council of the EU & European Council, 2023).

In conclusion, state-led or directed economic systems aim to leverage the potential of government intervention in shaping economic trajectories. While there is historical evidence of state-led systems achieving rapid economic growth in several countries, their efficacy remains a topic for contested discussions among economists. The success of such systems is highly dependent on the delicate balance between leveraging market efficiencies while guiding them towards national objectives. The challenge lies in ensuring that the state's role as a guiding hand does not hinder the entrepreneurial spirit and innovation that are hallmarks of thriving economies.

3.3.3 Characteristics of Economic Systems

The diverse tapestry of global economic systems is more than a backdrop for managers of MNCs. It is an ever-evolving environment, guiding strategic planning and influencing decision-making, including fine-tuning operations. Several aspects determined by the type of economic system companies operate in are therefore crucial to understand.

3.3.3.1 Market Dynamics

In free-market systems, the forces of demand and supply play a pivotal role. Competition is fostered due to minimal state intervention. Managers must be adept at understanding market-driven prices, rapidly changing consumer preferences, and evolving industry trends. It is crucial for MNCs to remain agile, continuously innovate, and frequently assess market position to sustain profitability. In state-led systems, certain sectors might be dominated or heavily influenced by state-owned enterprises. Market access, pricing, and even the volume of goods/services produced might be directed or capped by state policies. For MNC managers, aligning with these predetermined state objectives, while carving out a market niche, becomes a unique challenge.

3.3.3.2 Regulatory Environment

With fewer regulations, businesses enjoy operational flexibility in free-market systems. However, global standards, especially those relating to environmental, health, and safety concerns, require rigorous self-regulation to avoid reputational risks. The regulatory maze can be intricate in state-led systems. Managers might encounter policies on local sourcing, technology transfers, and mandatory partnerships with local entities, or obligations to contribute to national economic and socio-cultural goals. Navigating these often necessitates local strategies and partnerships.

3.3.3.3 Labour Dynamics

With market-determined wages, MNCs must be competitive to attract and retain talent in a free-market system. This often translates into comprehensive HR strategies encompassing competitive salaries, benefits, training, and growth opportunities. State-led systems might feature standard wage structures, mandatory benefits, and strong labour unions. Strikes and labour unrest can be more frequent, necessitating robust labour relations strategies and contingency planning. However, these factors are more characteristic of European-style mixed economies. Modern state-led economic systems – such as nominally communist China – often place only limited focus on worker rights and representation.

3.3.3.4 Financial and Investment Landscape

In free-market systems, the financial landscape is marked by competitive taxation and reduced trade restrictions, making these regions attractive for foreign direct investment. However, especially in the case of developing countries embracing a free-market economic system, currency volatility can be a challenge, demanding adept financial hedging strategies. Profits can be influenced by higher taxes, tariffs, or other state-imposed financial directives in state-led systems. Such systems might also control currency exchange rates to maintain economic stability, affecting pricing and investment decisions for MNCs.

3.3.3.5 Corporate Social Responsibility and Ethics

While corporate social responsibility (CSR) initiatives are primarily voluntary in free-market systems, market pressures and brand reputation often drive companies to adopt commendable initiatives. Ethical considerations extend beyond compliance, as global audiences hold companies accountable. In state-led systems MNCs might encounter state-mandated CSR activities or specific ethical standards. In certain regions, a percentage of profits might be legally directed towards social development projects.

3.3.3.6 Supply Chain Management

Supply chain optimization in free-market systems is primarily driven by efficiency, cost, speed, and global best practice. Managers aim for lean operation, rapid delivery, and minimal disruption. Supply chains in state-led systems might need to adhere to local sourcing mandates, quotas, or utilize specific domestic industry services. This can lead to challenges in quality control, synchronization, and efficiency.

3.3.3.7 Access to Resources

Access is predominantly determined by market availability, competition, and costs in free-market systems. Managers strategize based on the best sources, costs, and logistical considerations. In state-led systems, key resources, especially minerals or energy sources, might be state-controlled. This can lead to monopolistic scenarios, where managers need to negotiate directly with state entities or authorized distributors.

3.3.3.8 Technology and Innovation

A competitive environment spurs innovation. In free-market systems, investment in R&D becomes a necessity, and managers often scout for disruptive technologies or startups for potential partnerships or acquisitions. While innovation is essential in state-led markets too, technology transfers or sharing with local partners might be mandated for market access. MNCs need to balance technology sharing with intellectual property protection.

3.3.3.9 Trade Policies and Tariffs

Liberal trade policies and minimal tariffs facilitate smoother international trade in free-market economies, but global geopolitical tensions can still introduce uncertainties. In state-led systems, protective measures to support domestic industries can introduce tariffs, quotas, or licensing requirements. MNC managers must be well versed in these policies and anticipate potential trade barriers.

3.3.3.10 Intellectual Property Rights

In free-market systems, intellectual property (IP) rights are typically robust, protecting innovations and brand identities. MNCs can confidently invest in R&D, knowing that their intellectual assets are safeguarded. IP protection in state-led systems might vary, with some regions notorious for counterfeiting or weak enforcement. Managers need to strategize on how to protect and leverage intellectual assets effectively. While it might seem from this overview that in state-led systems the government controls all the factors of production and in free-market systems the state's share is marginal, this is not quite the case. In reality, if one looks at central government's expenditure with share of GDP as a proxy of state control, the global picture is more homogenous than the reader might expect. Figure 3.1 shows an overview of this indicator. Two things become clear: first, state-led economies such as Japan and Korea do not necessarily have higher government spending ratios than free-market economies such as the USA or Australia; rather, they are similar, mostly around the 30% mark. Second, the highest shares can be observed in Europe with its predominantly mixed economic systems and countries such as France or Norway quite close to the 50% mark.

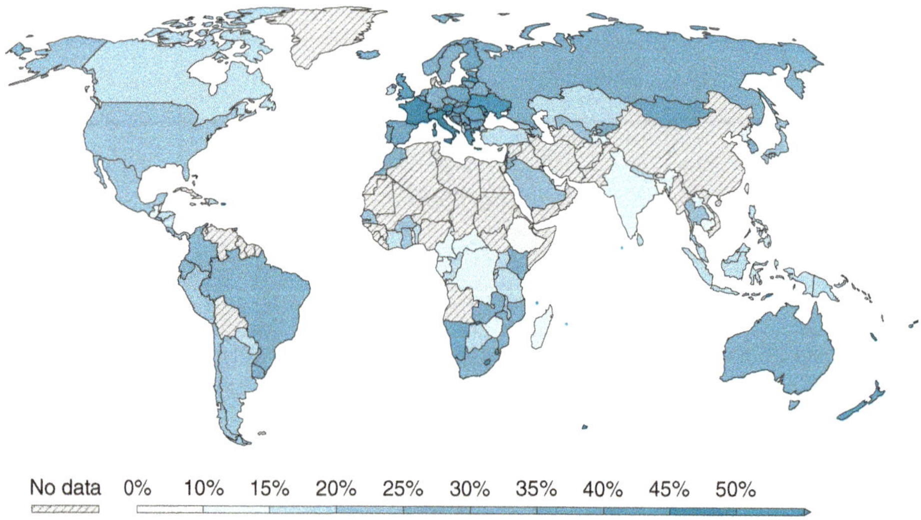

Figure 3.1 Total central government expenditure as share of GDP

Source: Graph compiled from World Bank data: OurWorldInData.org/government-spending

In sum, the intricacies of economic systems influence every facet of an MNC's operations. For an MNC to be successful, managers need a deep understanding of these systems, ensuring that strategies are tailored, adaptable, and resilient across diverse economic landscapes. This alignment ensures that MNCs not only navigate global challenges but also reap the ample opportunities that different economic systems present.

3.3.4 Mixed Economic Systems: European Social Democratic Models

The concept of mixed economies stems from a blend of market-driven capitalist dynamics and state-driven interventions, reflecting a balance between private enterprise and public welfare. In the European context, many nations, particularly those embracing social-democratic or socialistic policies, exhibit these mixed economic tendencies. Such systems aim to harness the efficiency of the market mechanism while ensuring that social objectives, such as reducing inequality and providing essential services, are achieved.

European states, exemplified by countries like Portugal, adopt a significantly more pronounced role in the economy than their free market counterparts. This interventionist approach seeks to guide and regulate market forces to achieve broader social goals. Portugal, for instance, has been characterized by especially restrictive labour rules, emphasizing worker protection and aiming to provide stability in employment. While such regulations can provide enhanced job security and worker benefits, they may at times be criticized for potentially hampering business flexibility and competitiveness.

A striking feature of European social-democratic and socialistic models, especially in Scandinavian nations, is the societal emphasis on equality and the eradication of poverty. There is a pervasive belief that while markets can be efficient in allocating resources, they are not always equitable. Hence, there is less faith in the absolute efficiency of markets, and a conviction that state intervention is necessary to correct market failures and ensure the welfare of all citizens, especially the most vulnerable. This results in policies that prioritize social well-being over unhindered economic growth.

In alignment with their social objectives, governments in these mixed economic systems typically allocate a substantial share of their GDP to social services. The state's expenditure in areas such as healthcare, pensions, education, and other social welfare programmes is markedly higher than in more free-market economies. For example, nations such as Sweden, Denmark, and Norway invest heavily in comprehensive healthcare systems, ensuring almost universal access. Education, from primary to tertiary levels, is highly subsidized or even free in many of these countries, emphasizing the societal value placed on knowledge and skills.

Labour unions hold a pivotal role in European mixed economies. Contrary to the weakened stature of unions in more market-driven economies, in countries like Germany, Sweden, and France, they remain formidable entities, in terms of both membership and influence. These unions actively engage in collective bargaining, ensuring that wages and working conditions are favourable for their members. Furthermore, they play a critical role in social dialogues, shaping labour market policies and broader economic strategies. The cooperative relationship between employers, unions, and the state, often referred to as the 'social partnership model' in countries such as Germany, underscores the collaborative approach adopted to achieve both economic and social objectives.

Spotlight: Wage Setting Via Collective Bargaining in Austria

Collective bargaining in Austria is a cornerstone of the country's labour relations system, playing a pivotal role in shaping employment conditions, wages, and overall workers' rights. It operates within a framework that emphasizes cooperation between employers and employees, fostering a balanced and harmonious working environment. This system is underpinned by a strong tradition of social partnership between trade unions, employers' associations, and the government.

At the heart of the Austrian collective bargaining system are sectoral collective agreements negotiated between trade unions, representing employees, and employers' associations, representing employers within specific industries or sectors. These agreements cover a wide range of issues, including wages, working hours, holidays, occupational safety, and social benefits. They set minimum standards that employers within a particular sector must adhere to, often providing better conditions than are stipulated in law.

One distinctive feature of the Austrian collective bargaining system is its comprehensive coverage. The vast majority of employees, in both the public and private sectors, are covered by these agreements. Even though union membership rates have declined over the years, the reach of collective agreements remains extensive due to the legal provision of extending agreements to non-unionized workers within a specific sector.

The negotiating process typically involves a coordinated approach between the Austrian Trade Union Federation (ÖGB) and various employers' associations. These negotiations occur at both national and regional levels, allowing for flexibility to address specific regional needs and economic conditions.

Austria also practises a system of 'social partnership', whereby the government actively engages with social partners (unions and employers' associations) to shape labour market policies, economic reforms, and social welfare measures. This tripartite cooperation fosters consensus-building and helps in crafting policies that consider the interests of all stakeholders.

The role of works councils, representing employees within individual workplaces, is another crucial aspect of Austria's collective bargaining system. Works councils facilitate communication between employers and employees, ensure compliance with collective agreements, and participate in decision-making processes concerning workplace matters.

In case of disputes or disagreements arising from the interpretation or application of collective agreements, Austria relies on a well-established system of labour courts and arbitration boards. These institutions provide a mechanism for resolving conflicts through mediation, conciliation, or arbitration, thereby reducing the likelihood of prolonged industrial conflicts.

The Austrian collective bargaining model has contributed significantly to the country's economic stability, low unemployment rates, and relatively low levels of income inequality. Providing a platform for negotiation and compromise has helped maintain a balance between the interests of employers and employees, fostering a conducive environment for economic growth while safeguarding workers' rights and social protections.

However, challenges such as globalization, technological advancements, and evolving labour market trends continue to impact the effectiveness of the collective bargaining system. Adapting to these changes while maintaining the relevance of the collective bargaining system and promoting inclusivity remains an ongoing task for Austrian social partners and policymakers. Overall, Austria's system of collective bargaining stands as a testament to the success of social dialogue and cooperation in shaping the country's labour relations.

Sources: Austrian Federal Ministry for Labour and the Economy: www.entsendeplattform.at/en/collective-agreements/principles; OECD & AIAS (2021)

In conclusion, European social-democratic and socialistic economic systems present a nuanced blend of market operations and state intervention. At their core, these mixed systems prioritize societal well-being and equality, endorsing the belief that while markets are powerful tools for resource allocation, their outcomes need guidance and occasionally correction to ensure broader societal objectives are met. Through substantial state expenditure on social services and the robust influence of unions, these economies strive to strike a balance between economic efficiency and social equity.

3.4 FOREIGN DIRECT INVESTMENT AND ECONOMIC DEVELOPMENT

Traditionally, economic development has been associated with economic growth, typically measured by gross domestic product (GDP) or gross national product (GNP) growth rates. Economic growth is indeed a foundational pillar of economic development, representing an increase in a country's output of goods and services over time, but while it is a vital component, economic development goes far beyond the singular focus on GDP expansion to encompass a broad spectrum of improvements. It is a multidimensional and dynamic process that affects economic, social, political, and institutional aspects of society, and is transformative in bringing about sustained improvements in the standard of living and well-being of individuals within a nation.

In terms of human development, it emphasizes the enhancement of human capabilities and quality of life, encompassing aspects of society such as education, healthcare, nutrition, access to clean water, housing, and overall well-being. Indices like the Human Development Index (HDI) are used to measure and compare these aspects across nations, providing insights into how well a country is progressing in terms of improving its citizens' lives.

With the recognition that resources are finite and the environment must be preserved for future generations, sustainable development has gained prominence within the framework of economic development. Sustainable development aims to meet present needs without compromising the ability of future generations to meet their own needs

(United Nations, 1987). It involves balancing economic growth with environmental sustainability and social inclusivity, taking into account factors such as resource management, climate change mitigation, and the promotion of environmentally friendly practices.

Economic development entails equitable distribution of wealth and opportunities among various segments of society. Addressing poverty and reducing income disparities are fundamental goals. Policies aimed at poverty alleviation, social safety nets, and programmes focusing on marginalized communities contribute significantly to a more inclusive and equitable society.

Strengthening institutional frameworks – including governance structures, legal systems, property rights, and regulatory environments – is integral to sustainable economic development. Well-functioning institutions ensure transparency, accountability, and respect for the rule of law, fostering an environment conducive to economic activities, investment, and growth.

Economic development is not a linear process; rather, it is characterized by progress, setbacks, and continuous adaptations. It involves a combination of factors and policies that interact and evolve over time in response to changing societal needs, technological advancements, and global dynamics. Furthermore, economic development is contextual and varies across different countries and regions. Developing countries often face unique challenges such as limited access to capital, inadequate infrastructure, lack of technological advancement, and institutional weaknesses. Strategies for economic development must be tailored to address these specific challenges while leveraging available resources and opportunities.

In essence, economic development is a comprehensive and evolving concept that encompasses economic growth, human development, sustainability, equitable distribution of resources, and the strengthening of institutions. Achieving sustainable economic development requires a holistic approach, sound policies, effective governance, and a focus on inclusivity to ensure that the benefits of development are shared by all parts of society.

Spotlight: Slovakia's Economic Development

Slovakia, located in Central Europe, has undergone significant economic transformation since gaining independence in 1993. Initially, it faced challenges following the split from what is now known as Czechia, but by the early 2000s, Slovakia emerged as one of the fastest-growing economies in the European Union.

The country's economic development has been marked by several key factors. One crucial element was its shift from a centrally planned economy to a market-oriented one. Slovakia implemented economic reforms, including privatization, liberalization, and adjusting taxation, which encouraged foreign investment and fostered a more competitive business environment.

The automotive industry became a cornerstone of Slovakia's economy, attracting major global car manufacturers like Volkswagen, Kia, and Peugeot. This sector made a significant contribution to economic growth, employment, and technological advancement. The country also focused on developing other industries such as electronics, manufacturing, and services, diversifying its economic base.

Slovakia's accession to the Organisation for Economic Co-operation and Development (OECD) in 2000 was a milestone, reflecting its economic progress. OECD membership provided the country with a platform for policy dialogue, sharing best practices, and aligning its policies with international standards. This integration into a network of developed nations facilitated further economic reforms and improvements in governance.

Moreover, joining the European Union in 2004 opened up opportunities for trade, investment, and access to EU structural funds. Slovakia utilized these resources for infrastructure development, education, and innovation, contributing to its overall economic advancement.

Despite these achievements, Slovakia faced challenges, including high unemployment rates, regional disparities, and the need for ongoing structural reforms. Efforts were made to address these issues through education and labour market reforms, investment in innovation and technology, and support for small and medium-sized enterprises (SMEs).

Additionally, Slovakia aimed to enhance its energy efficiency and diversify its energy resources, reducing dependency on imported energy. This involved investing in renewable energy sources and improving energy infrastructure to ensure sustainability and competitiveness in the long term.

In conclusion, Slovakia's economic development journey since independence has been remarkable. The country transformed from a centrally planned economy to a market-oriented one, with a focus on industries like automotive manufacturing that drove economic growth. Joining the OECD and the EU each played a pivotal role in shaping its economic policies and fostering international integration. Despite the challenges, Slovakia continues to strive for sustainable economic development, aiming for greater innovation, competitiveness, and inclusive growth.

Sources: OECD Snapshot on the Slovakian Economy: www.oecd.org/economy/slovak-republic-economic-snapshot; IMF Country Report of Slovakia: www.imf.org/external/pubs/ft/scr/2014/cr14254.pdf

Foreign direct investment (FDI) serves as a catalyst in driving economic development by channelling essential resources into a country. FDI brings in not just financial capital but also technological know-how, managerial expertise, and access to global markets. This infusion of resources helps to stimulate economic growth by creating jobs, improving infrastructure, and enhancing productivity. Moreover, FDI often acts as a conduit for the transfer of skills and knowledge, particularly in emerging economies. It plays a pivotal role in supporting the development of local industries, fostering innovation, and contributing to the overall competitiveness of a nation in the global market. However, the extent to which FDI translates into tangible benefits for economic development depends on the host country's policies, institutional frameworks, and the ability to absorb and utilize the incoming investments effectively.

The infusion of technology through FDI is a critical driver of industrial upgrading and economic progress. Technology transfer, often associated with FDI, aids in boosting productivity, improving efficiency, and adding value to local industries. This process facilitates the transition from traditional activities with low added value to more sophisticated production processes with high added value. As countries acquire technological advancements through FDI, they can diversify their economies, moving away from reliance on resource-based industries towards knowledge-intensive sectors. This shift enables economies to be more resilient, adaptable, and competitive in the global marketplace.

Beyond the economic sphere, FDI's influence extends to various socio-economic aspects in a host country. While it contributes significantly to economic growth and development, it also brings about changes in employment patterns, labour conditions, and societal structures. FDI can positively impact job creation, providing employment opportunities and fostering skills development. However, its effects on income distribution and wealth accumulation might not always be equitable, potentially exacerbating social inequalities. Moreover, the environmental impact of FDI activities can be substantial, necessitating stringent regulations and sustainability measures to mitigate adverse effects on the environment and local communities. Governments must balance economic gains with social well-being and environmental sustainability with care when formulating policies to attract and manage FDI.

Effective policy formulation and implementation are crucial in maximizing the positive impact of FDI on economic development. Governments play a pivotal role in creating a conducive business environment that attracts and retains FDI while safeguarding national interests and promoting sustainable growth. Policies aimed at improving infrastructure, education, and innovation ecosystems are instrumental in enhancing the absorptive capacity of the host economy, ensuring that incoming FDI translates into long-term developmental gains. Additionally, regulatory frameworks need to strike a balance between facilitating FDI inflows and safeguarding the autonomy and interests of the host country, preventing exploitative practices and promoting fair and mutually beneficial partnerships between investors and the local economy.

There are, however, also a number of challenges when using FDI to foster economic development, and it is important to bear in mind the challenges when critically assessing the role FDI plays in economic development.

First, over-reliance on FDI for economic growth can create dependency and vulnerability for host countries. Heavy dependence on foreign investment makes economies susceptible to external shocks, market fluctuations, and the whims of multinational companies. Sudden shifts in global market dynamics or policy changes in investor countries can significantly impact the host nation's economy, leading to instability and vulnerability.

Second, while FDI inflows can spur economic growth, the benefits might not be evenly distributed across society. Often, FDI-led growth exacerbates income inequality and marginalizes certain socio-economic groups. This disparity can stem from unequal access to employment opportunities, skill requirements that leave some parts of the population behind, or skewed wealth distribution.

Third, rapid industrialization fuelled by FDI can pose environmental challenges if sustainability measures are overlooked. The pursuit of economic growth may lead to environmental degradation, resource depletion, and pollution. Balancing economic development with environmental sustainability is crucial to ensure that growth is not achieved at the expense of long-term ecological health and resilience.

3.5 COUNTRY RISK

Case Study: A PESTEL Analysis for Brazil

A PESTEL analysis is a strategic framework used by organizations to assess and understand the external macro-environmental factors that can impact their operations and business environment. The acronym PESTEL stands for political, economic, social, technological, environmental, and legal factors. By analysing these elements, businesses can identify opportunities and threats, enabling them to make informed decisions and develop strategies to navigate their operating environment more effectively.

1. Political factors: These encompass government policies, stability, trade regulations, and taxation laws that can influence businesses. For example, changes in government leadership or policies such as tariffs on imports or exports can significantly impact industries like international trade or manufacturing.
2. Economic factors: Economic variables like inflation rates, exchange rates, economic growth, and interest rates directly affect businesses. For instance, a recession may lead to decreased consumer spending, impacting retail and luxury goods industries.
3. Social factors: These involve societal trends, demographics, cultural aspects, and lifestyle changes that can influence consumer behaviour and demand for products or services. An example could be the increasing trend towards healthier eating habits impacting the food and beverage industry.
4. Technological factors: Technological advancements, innovation rates, automation, and digitalization impact industries profoundly. For instance, the rise of e-commerce has transformed retail, changing how consumers shop and affecting traditional brick-and-mortar businesses.
5. Environmental factors: These factors focus on ecological and environmental aspects, including climate change, sustainability concerns, and regulations. Businesses, particularly in industries like energy and manufacturing, face pressure to adopt environmentally friendly practices due to increased awareness of climate change.
6. Legal factors: Legal factors involve laws, regulations, and compliance standards that businesses must adhere to in their operations. For example, changes in employment laws or data protection regulations can significantly impact HR policies or tech companies dealing with user data.

(Continued)

Let us consider the example of a PESTEL analysis applied to the country of Brazil:

1. Political: Brazil's political stability, government policies, and regulatory framework greatly impact businesses. Changes in leadership, trade agreements, and government stability can influence investment decisions and market dynamics.
2. Economic: Economic factors like inflation rates, GDP growth, and currency fluctuations affect business operations. Brazil's economic growth or recession directly impacts consumer spending, investment, and market expansion opportunities.
3. Social: Socio-cultural factors in Brazil encompass diverse demographics, cultural diversity, lifestyle changes, and consumer behaviour. Trends in population growth, education levels, and shifts in consumer preferences influence market demand for goods and services.
4. Technological: Brazil's level of technological advancement, innovation, and infrastructure development affect industries. The integration of technology into various sectors, digitalization, and internet penetration rates impact business operations and market competitiveness.
5. Environmental: Brazil faces environmental challenges such as deforestation in the Amazon rainforest, sustainability concerns, and regulations affecting industries like agriculture, energy, and mining.
6. Legal: Legal factors include regulatory frameworks, labour laws, and compliance standards. Changes in taxation policies, trade regulations, and business laws impact market entry, operations, and investment strategies in Brazil.

A PESTEL analysis of Brazil provides insights into the external factors influencing the country's business environment. Understanding these factors helps businesses, investors, and policymakers anticipate changes, mitigate risks, and capitalize on opportunities within the Brazilian market. At the same time, it is important to understand the shortcomings and limits of PESTEL analysis. For example, PESTEL has been criticized for being static and not being able to capture dynamic developments, for a lack of priority-setting (what matters most in an analysis?), and for limited strategic guidance. That is why a PESTEL analysis is often used as a starting point for an in-depth and structured analysis rather than a single sufficient tool to analyse environments.

Source: World Bank (www.worldbank.org/en/country/brazil/overview)

Building on the PESTEL idea which helps get a bird's-eye perspective on formal institutions, IB scholars often employ country-risk reports and indices, such as those provided by Witold (Henisz, 2000) and the PRS Group (n.d.). Henisz (2000) developed the POLCON index, which measures the level of political constraints on the executive branches of a country's government with veto power. It assesses the degree of institutionalization of political constraints and the potential for policy reversals and disruptions. The index helps businesses gauge the likelihood of government intervention and the stability of policy environments in different countries. However, a potential limitation of the POLCON index is its focus on executive constraints, which may not fully capture the complexities of the overall political risk landscape. Another widely used political risk index is the International Country Risk Guide (ICRG) index by the PRS Group, which evaluates various political risk factors, including government stability, corruption, socioeconomic conditions, and external threats. While aiding businesses in making informed decisions about international investments and operations, the ICRG index's complexity and the vast number of indicators it considers may pose challenges for users who seek a simplified and straightforward evaluation of political risk. Table 3.1 shows an overview of political risks and their potential impact on firms.

Table 3.1 Types of political risks and their likely impacts

Type	Impact on firms
Expropriation of companies by foreign governments	Loss of sales, assets, and future profits
Tariffs and campaigns against imported goods	Loss of sales, increased marketing cost
Stricter employee law	Increased operating costs
Increased taxation	Loss of profits, potential relocation
Inflation	Increased operating costs
Foreign exchange rate changes	Reduced value of repatriated earning (currency depreciation), reduced competitiveness overseas (currency appreciation)
Terrorist acts (e.g. violence, kidnapping)	Increased security and managerial costs, lower productivity
Civil wars	Loss of sales, lower productivity, destruction of property, increased security costs

Source: Based on Müllner & Dorobantu (2022)

3.6 CURRENT DEVELOPMENTS IN FORMAL INSTITUTIONAL ENVIRONMENTS

Recently, the global economic landscape has been shaped by tectonic shifts in policies, ideologies, and overarching priorities as well as country-level competition between states with differing economic systems. These developments significantly influence the modus operandi of MNCs navigating today's intricate global market.

3.6.1 Increasing Protectionism and Economic Nationalism

The shift towards protectionism and economic nationalism has become one of the most defining features of the contemporary economic era. As countries place more emphasis on safeguarding domestic industries and ensuring national interests, MNCs face a changing landscape.

Under the first Trump administration, the USA started to adopt a more confrontational stance towards China, leading to escalating trade tensions between the world's two largest economies. Tariffs, sanctions, and rigorous regulatory scrutiny became instrumental tools in this economic tug-of-war. These measures disrupted global supply chains, requiring MNCs to reassess their business strategies and sourcing logistics, a recent example being the restriction on exports of advance US-made AI semiconductors during the Biden administration (Chu et al., 2023). With the export controls introduced in 2022, the US banned the sale of the most advanced chips that China might use to train AI systems for military purposes (Leahy, 2023; Sevastopulo, 2023).

3.6.2 Chinese Belt and Road Initiative (BRI)

China's Belt and Road Initiative is an ambitious global infrastructure development and investment strategy, aiming to boost trade connectivity between Asia, Europe, and Africa. This vast network of railways, roads, ports, and pipelines seeks to recreate the ancient Silk Road (Huang, 2016).

The BRI exemplifies the state-led approach of the Chinese government, which strategically funnels investment to areas deemed geopolitically and economically crucial. This development is especially remarkable in the sense that state-led economic policy is reaching beyond China's borders, singling out global trade infrastructure as a strategic focus area.

3.6.3 Resurgence of State Capitalism and SOEs as Political Tools

While capitalism has predominantly been seen as a domain of private enterprises, there has been a resurgence in the concept of state capitalism, especially in nations such as Russia and China. Here, the state doesn't just play the role of a regulator but is an active market player, often holding significant stakes in key sectors through state-owned enterprises (SOEs) (Mariotti & Marzano, 2019).

Russia's energy giants like Gazprom and China's tech behemoths like Alibaba, while operating in a capitalist market framework, have close ties with their respective governments. This association affords them strategic advantages but also subjects them to geopolitical crosshairs. A textbook example of this dynamic is the weaponization of energy supplies by Russia in the context of its invasion of Ukraine in 2022 (Sheppard, 2022). While Russia used oil and gas supplies in previous geopolitical tensions as leverage, the virtually complete halt of gas deliveries to force Europe into limiting support for Ukraine was unprecedented, highlighting the blurred lines between business and politics. Another result of Russia's invasion of Ukraine and weaponization of Gazprom was the large number of sanctions imposed, affecting not only Russia's ability to maintain its aggression but also MNCs operating in the country. Consequently, many MNCs left the Russian market while some were even forcibly nationalized by the state, such as Carlsberg's local subsidiary in 2023 (Speed, 2023).

3.6.4 Shift Towards Green Economics

There's a palpable global movement towards building sustainable, green economies. As environmental concerns become central to global discourse, there's a noticeable policy and consumer preference shift towards green and sustainable products and practices.

While the title of the Biden Administration's Inflation Reduction Act (IRA) of 2022 emphasized inflation, its subtext revealed efforts to foster sustainable, eco-friendly growth, signalling a broader shift in US economic priorities at that time. The IRA could be seen as a historical shift in the US's traditionally free-market economic policy towards a more state-led approach. By creating a tremendous domestic market for decarbonization and green technologies as well as providing sustainability-related tax credits, the US was significantly shifting global market attractiveness and country-level competitiveness (Boston Consulting Group, 2022). With the second Trump administration, many of these developments were cancelled, and policy moved back to a more laissez-faire approach, particularly regarding climate change.

Overall, these exemplary trends in global economic dynamics reflect the world's attempts to reconcile economic growth aspirations with geopolitical considerations, environmental sustainability, and nationalistic imperatives. For managers of MNCs, staying abreast of these trends and understanding their nuanced implications becomes pivotal. Adapting to this dynamic landscape requires a blend of strategic foresight, operational flexibility, and an appreciation for the socio-political contexts of the markets they operate in. As the global economic fabric gets continually reshaped so too must the strategies of multinational companies navigating this intricate tapestry.

SUMMARY

This chapter introduced the formal institutional environment. The chapter provided structures and understanding of the key formal components of national political, legal, and economic systems, discussed the relationship between foreign direct investment and economic development, and highlighted recent trends. All elements of the formal national institutional environment strongly influence the risks associated with doing business in a specific market (country risk).

The national political system of a country, which ranges from democratic to autocratic, significantly influences firms and multinational companies (MNCs). The regulations and rules established by these systems are crucial for firms. Democracies are characterized by features like fair elections, the rule of law, and the separation of powers, whereas autocracies concentrate power in a single leader or party, limiting public participation and political competition. Political ideologies, such as capitalism, neoliberalism, and socialism, further underpin these systems, guiding the extent and nature of government intervention in economic activities. Understanding the formal political environment is essential for MNCs to manage political risks and influence policymaking, as these systems shape the regulatory environment and potential for regime changes that impact business operations.

Legal systems vary globally between civil law and common law. Civil law systems, prevalent in many regions, are based on codified statutes approved by political authorities, emphasizing detailed legal codes and limited judicial precedent. In contrast, common law systems, originating in England, rely on judicial decisions and precedents, allowing for greater flexibility and adaptability over time. Civil law offers predictability through explicit statutes, while common law provides adaptability through evolving precedents. For MNCs, understanding these legal systems is crucial for navigating contracts, ensuring legal compliance, and resolving disputes.

Economic systems range from pure market to pure planned economies, with various forms of capitalism in between. A pure planned economy, also known as a command economy, involves significant government control over production, allocation, and distribution of goods and services, often through comprehensive plans and state ownership of key sectors. Conversely, a pure market economy operates with minimal government intervention, relying on supply and demand to determine economic outcomes, characterized by high economic freedom and private ownership. Between these extremes, varieties of capitalism emerge, such as liberal market economies, which emphasize minimal state intervention and competition, and coordinated market economies, which focus on non-market interactions and relationships among firms. Finally, state-led or directed economic systems combine market mechanisms with substantial government intervention, aiming to direct economic activities for strategic and developmental purposes, as seen in countries such as China and Singapore. Foreign direct investment (FDI) plays a significant role in economic development by introducing financial capital, technological advancements, managerial expertise, and access to global markets. FDI stimulates economic growth, job creation, and productivity enhancement, while also facilitating industrial upgrading and diversification. However, the benefits of FDI depend on the host country's policies and ability to utilize the investments effectively. Despite its advantages, FDI can also create dependency, exacerbate income inequality, and pose environmental challenges if not managed sustainably.

4

INFORMAL INSTITUTIONS

CHAPTER INTRODUCTION

After formal institutions, informal institutions are the other half of the story when seeking to understand the institutional environment in a country. Informal national institutions are the unwritten, uncodified, and implicit rules, norms, traditions, and social practices that shape human behaviour. In contrast to formal institutions, they are not enforced through written laws or regulations, but they are still of critical importance to MNCs, as informal rules are often used to apply pressure on them to adapt products, services, and practices to local standards.

In this chapter, we introduce the iceberg model. Originally developed to describe and analyse different dimensions of culture, it can also be used to describe, understand and structure the different layers of informal national institutions. We then analyse phenomena on all three levels of the model to provide a picture of the informal institutional environment. First, we focus on language as an informal institution that is all around us. Second, we address national culture. And third, we discuss the role of religion.

LEARNING OUTCOMES

After reading this chapter you should be able to:

1. Outline the general structure of informal institutions based on the iceberg model
2. Describe the role of language as an element of informal institutions
3. Define national culture and explain different models of national culture
4. Discuss the role of religion in forming basic beliefs in an informal institutional environment.

Case Study: Japanese Culture and Efficiency at Toyota

Toyota's integration of Japanese cultural principles into its manufacturing processes has been instrumental in developing its renowned efficient manufacturing techniques, known as the Toyota Production System (TPS). This integration leverages key elements of Japanese culture such as continuous improvement (*kaizen*), respect for people, teamwork, and discipline. These cultural underpinnings enabled Toyota to achieve unparalleled efficiency, quality, and innovation in its manufacturing operations, setting a global standard for the automotive industry. TPS has become a model for manufacturing excellence worldwide.

Kaizen, meaning 'continuous improvement', is a core element of TPS. This cultural concept encourages all employees to continuously seek ways to improve processes and products. Toyota's founder, Kiichiro Toyoda, and later Taiichi Ohno, who developed TPS in the 1940s and 1950s, embedded this mindset deeply into the company's operations. Employees at Toyota are encouraged to voice their suggestions for improvements, fostering a culture of innovation and engagement that maintains high standards of efficiency and quality. This continuous feedback loop enhances operational processes but also contributes to the company's long-term adaptability and resilience.

Respect for people is another foundational principle in both Japanese culture and TPS. This principle is reflected in Toyota's treatment of its employees, customers, and suppliers. Toyota invests in employee training and development, ensuring workers have the skills to contribute effectively. This respect creates a motivated workforce committed to the company's success, evident since the company's early years in the city of Toyota, Japan. By fostering a respectful and inclusive work environment, Toyota enhances employee satisfaction and retention, which are crucial for sustained operational excellence.

Japanese culture emphasizes collectivism and teamwork, values integral to TPS. Teamwork is encouraged at all levels of the organization. Toyota employs team-based problem-solving techniques, such as quality circles and cross-functional teams, enabling the company to respond quickly to challenges and continuously improve its processes. This collaborative culture allows for the sharing of knowledge and best practices across different departments, driving continuous improvement and innovation. It also promotes a sense of unity and shared purpose among employees, which is essential for achieving the company's strategic goals.

Discipline and standardization are key aspects of Japanese culture influencing Toyota's manufacturing. Meticulousness and precision are reflected in Toyota's rigorous adherence to standardized work procedures, ensuring consistency and reducing errors. This disciplined approach has been part of Toyota's practices since the development of TPS in the mid-twentieth century. Standardization also facilitates training and scalability, allowing Toyota to replicate its high standards across global operations. It ensures that quality and efficiency are maintained regardless of location, contributing to Toyota's reputation for reliability and excellence.

Jidoka, or 'automation with a human touch', involves designing equipment and processes that automatically detect and respond to problems. Introduced by Sakichi Toyoda, this principle integrates human oversight into automated processes, ensuring quality and addressing defects promptly. It has been a fundamental aspect of Toyota's manufacturing philosophy since the early twentieth century. *Jidoka* not only improves product quality but also empowers employees to take an active role in maintaining and enhancing production standards, fostering a proactive and engaged workforce.

Lean manufacturing, emphasizing the elimination of waste (*muda*), is rooted in the Japanese cultural focus on efficiency. Developed by Taiichi Ohno in the post-WWII era, this principle encourages efficient use of resources and minimizing non-value-adding activities. By continuously identifying and eliminating waste, Toyota maximizes efficiency and reduces costs, contributing to its global competitive advantage. Lean manufacturing principles have been adopted widely across industries, highlighting Toyota's influence on modern production practices. This approach also supports environmental sustainability by reducing resource consumption and waste generation.

Taken together, Toyota's embedding of Japanese cultural principles into its manufacturing processes has been a key factor in its development of efficient manufacturing techniques. The integration of *kaizen*, respect for people, teamwork, discipline, *jidoka*, and lean manufacturing has enabled Toyota to achieve high standards of efficiency, quality, and innovation, fostering a motivated workforce committed to continuous improvement and success. These principles have not only driven Toyota's growth but also set benchmarks for manufacturing excellence globally, influencing practices across various industries. Toyota's commitment to these values continues to propel its leadership in the automotive sector.

Sources: Toyota (www.toyota-global.com/company/history_of_toyota/75years/data/conditions/philosophy/toyotaway2001.html) and Harvard Business Review (https://hbr.org/2008/06/the-contradictions-that-drive-toyotas-success)

Case Study Questions

1 To what extent does a focus on efficiency detract from innovative ability? What are the kinds of innovations that you would expect to see in a highly efficient organization?
2 What are some of the negative consequences of Japanese work culture?
3 To what extent is it possible to replicate Toyota's approach in companies in Europe?

4.1 ICEBERG MODEL

The iceberg model provides a good opportunity to structure the informal institutional environment. It has been applied for different purposes in the field with slight adaptions (e.g. Osgood, 1951; Hall, 1976; Schein, 2010). Some authors have used it to structure national culture, some to analyse organization culture, and we are using it to structure the holistic informal national environment.

Using the metaphor of an iceberg (Figure 4.1), the informal national institutional system can be separated into three levels: (1) artefacts and visible behaviours, (2) values and social norms, and (3) basic assumptions. The model emphasizes that while visible elements are readily noticeable and easily understood, they are just a small part of a larger context. The true essence of a society lies beneath the surface, in the implicit, often unconscious, and deeply ingrained aspects of culture. These hidden elements have a significant influence on how individuals within a culture perceive and interpret the world, interact with others, and behave in different situations.

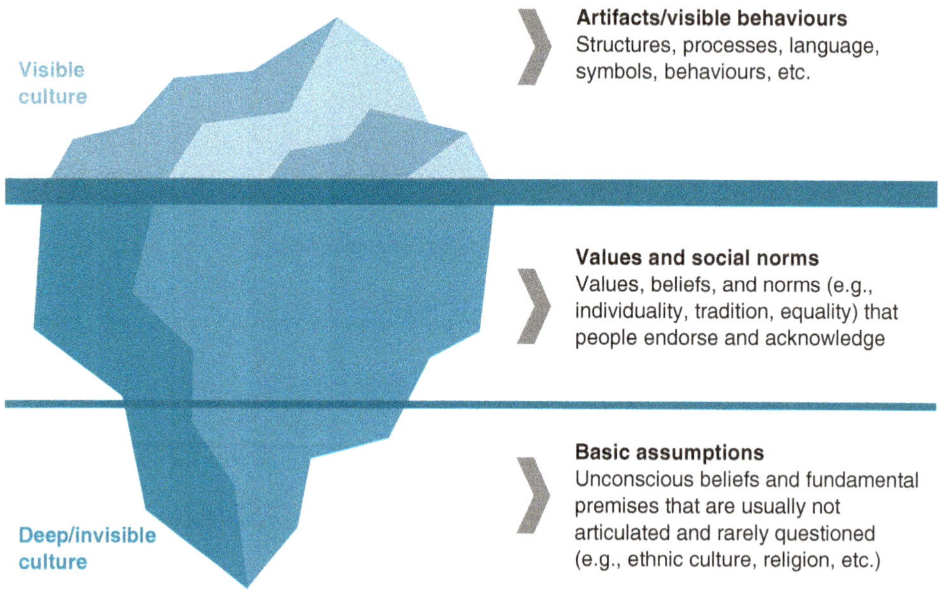

Figure 4.1 The iceberg model

Artefacts and visible behaviours are often referred to as the 'tip of the iceberg', suggesting that the majority of a national culture remains invisible. Artefacts and behaviours include clothing, food, architecture, music, art, language, greetings, gestures, rituals, ceremonies, and other customs, which are easily identifiable by outsiders and represent the surface expressions of a culture. They are often the first things people notice when encountering a new environment.

At the second level – 'just below the surface' – lie values that members of a national culture acknowledge and endorse. Such values can be differentiated into beliefs and norms and are harder to observe than artefacts. Norms refer to the rules and expectations that guide behaviour within a society or group. They can be social norms (accepted behaviours in a society), folkways (common customs or habits), or mores (strongly held norms with moral significance). Values represent the beliefs and ideals of a culture, influencing attitudes and behaviours. They are deeply ingrained and shape individuals' perceptions, judgements, and decision-making. Values can include concepts such as family, honour, honesty, individualism, and collectivism. These values guide how people interact and respond to various situations within their culture.

On the deepest and third level of the iceberg model lie basic assumptions and beliefs. Basic assumptions are the core beliefs and unconscious perceptions of individuals within a culture. They are so ingrained that they often go unquestioned and operate on an unconscious level, but they shape individuals' worldview, understanding of reality, and perceptions of truth. They influence how people interpret events, understand relationships, and make sense of the world around them. Beliefs are convictions and understandings that individuals hold about various aspects of life, and include religious beliefs, philosophical views, and perspectives on societal roles. These beliefs contribute to the formation of basic assumptions and influence behaviour.

4.2 LANGUAGE

Arguably, language is one of the most important artefacts, given its potential to shape people's thinking and the way they perceive and interpret the social world around them. Language is a complex system of communication used by humans to convey meaning, express thoughts, share ideas, and interact with one another. It is a fundamental aspect of human culture and society, allowing individuals to communicate, share knowledge, pass on traditions, and build relationships. Communication consists of verbal, non-verbal, paraverbal, and extraverbal elements.

- *Verbal elements of communication* involve the use of words, spoken or written, to convey messages. They include what is explicitly stated in speech or writing (e.g. conversations, dialogues, speeches, letters, texts, emails, books, and articles).
- *Non-verbal communication* consists of cues and signals that convey meaning without the use of words. These include gestures like facial expressions (e.g. smiling, raising eyebrows), body language (e.g. posture, body movements), and other physical actions that communicate emotions, intentions, and messages (e.g. the use of gaze or eye movements to express interest, attention, and emotions).
- *Paraverbal communication* refers to vocal aspects that accompany verbal communication. It includes tone of voice (e.g. modulation, pitch, volume, intonation, or rhythm) and the speed or rate of speech, as well as the strategic use of pauses, which can affect the message's meaning and impact.
- *Extraverbal communication* encompasses elements beyond verbal and linguistic components. It includes contextual factors (e.g. the broader context in which communication occurs, such as the physical environment, historical background, and situational factors influencing the message) and the use of symbols, images, signs, and visuals that complement or reinforce verbal communication and aid understanding.

These elements collectively contribute to effective communication. Verbal and non-verbal elements work in tandem to convey messages comprehensively, while paraverbal and extraverbal aspects add nuance, context, and depth to the communicated information, enhancing the overall understanding and interpretation of the message. Language skills, consequently, represent much more than the ability to participate in verbal or written communication. They also include the ability to understand the three other dimensions of communication.

Language matters for communication, both within the MNC and with its stakeholders. Within the MNC, the effect of language is twofold. On the one hand, language can be a prominent barrier to inter-cultural communication, cooperation, and coordination where employees speak a wide variety of different languages needing translation. In addition, some employees may reduce their communication because of limited language skills or anxiety. This has negative effects on firms given the ever-increasing need for global communication and exchange of data, information, and knowledge across borders. Further, communication about strategy becomes more challenging when management needs to function across multiple language contexts.

On the other hand, language diversity within the MNC can also have positive effects. For example, company-specific languages may develop ('company speak') that lead to stronger cohesion in the MNC. In an environment where almost everybody speaks 'bad English', communication can lead to the development of firm-specific words and sentences that subsequently increase in-group feelings within a company.

When considering interaction between the MNC and its external stakeholders, the language barrier creates challenges when communicating about legal matters, interacting with partner firms, and marketing, among others. There are many examples of language blunders in marketing communications, often having a significant impact on foreign activity.

Difficulties in communication, whether within a firm or between a firm and its stakeholders, typically stem one or more of the following:

1. Different levels of proficiency in a language can cause communicative challenges. Individuals with limited proficiency may struggle to express themselves accurately or understand others, resulting in miscommunications, misunderstandings, and misinterpretations, and potentially confusion or conflict.
2. Difficulties in finding semantic equivalents across languages can create challenges. Individuals typically make sense of a foreign message using their native language's frame of reference. Consequently, unskilled use of language may lead to misinterpretation, as illustrated in the 'language blunders' or 'marketing fails' in Table 4.1 – intended meanings may be interpreted very differently in other settings, particularly when translation is literal.
3. Even when the same language is used, communication norms may differ in significant ways. For instance, in spite of sharing a native tongue with local dialects, Swiss and Germans favour concise and brief performance reviews,

whereas Austrians prefer a more elaborate, colloquial style. Another example is the Japanese word *hai*, which translates to 'yes', does not necessarily mean 'Yes, I agree with what you are saying' but often 'Yes, I understand what you are saying.' Because there is no equivalent word for 'no' in Japanese, *hai* may still indicate disapproval. Furthermore, whereas head-nodding signals consensus in the US, it only indicates that the message has been received in Japan.

4 Linguistic differences can create mistrust and prejudice between native and non-native team members. In social and professional settings, differing levels of language proficiency can make it much more difficult to form strong relationships or connections. In extreme cases, weak language skills in foreign subsidiaries can result in shadow MNC structures.

5 Non-natives may experience high levels of discomfort or even anxiety when they have to speak in a foreign language. One reason may be the fear of losing face and status in a foreign language. People with lower levels of competence in another language may therefore be reluctant to participate in conversations, discussions, and group activities.

Table 4.1 Examples of language blunders

Company	Example
Pepsi	The ad-slogan 'Come alive with Pepsi' can be literally translated to 'Come out of the grave with Pepsi' in Germany or 'Pepsi brings back your ancestors from the dead' in Taiwan
Mercedes-Benz	Mercedes-Benz entered China with a car model called 'Bensi', which translates to 'rush to die'. They quickly rebranded it to 'Benchi', meaning 'run quickly as if flying'
IKEA	When IKEA introduced the 'Fartfull workbench', meaning 'full speed' in Swedish, it received some chuckles from English-speakers
American Airlines	When American Airlines wanted to advertise their leather seats, they used the slogan 'Fly in Leather'. For the Spanish-speaking market in Mexico, however, this translated to 'Fly naked'
Ford	Ford has experienced some difficulties with Spanish-speaking markets: both their low-cost truck that was initially marketed as the Feira, meaning 'ugly old woman' in Spanish, and their high-end car, Comet, that was sold as Caliente in Mexico, which is local slang for 'prostitute', did not do so well in these markets

4.3 CULTURE

Communication may seem fairly straightforward on the surface, but the potential for miscommunication and misinterpretation – at multiple levels – is high. Difficulties are likely to arise, particularly where there are differences in communication style and context (Hall, 1976). Linguistic preferences are mostly based on the deeper dimensions of the informal environment, which we will now discuss in more detail.

4.3.1 Definition and Relevance

Hofstede (2001) defines culture as the collective mental programming that distinguishes the members of one group from those of another. The term 'mental programming' initially appears strongly deterministic. However, this impression is softened by Hofstede's definition of culture. According to Hofstede (2001), culture encompasses the combination of shared values, rituals, heroes, and symbols. Symbols are words, gestures, images, etc., that carry specific meanings recognized only by those belonging to the same culture (hairstyles, status symbols, etc.). Symbols change rapidly and are often adopted or imitated by other cultural groups. Heroes are individuals, alive or deceased, real or fictional, possessing qualities highly esteemed in a culture and thus serving as role models (e.g. politicians, actors, etc.). Rituals are collective activities that are technically unnecessary but socially essential within a culture (handshakes, bowing, etc.). Values reflect the deepest level of culture. They are broad feelings, partially unconscious, determining what is good or bad, ugly or beautiful, abnormal or normal. The iceberg model describes this stage as the underlying assumptions; they are typically implicit, learned in childhood, and often remain unconscious, making them difficult or impossible to discuss. Further, they are often not invisible; one can only infer them from how people act under different circumstances. They constitute the distinct core of a culture, while other elements may vary. Specifically, these permitted variations, explicitly acknowledged by Hofstede, mitigate the concept of 'mental programming', suggesting that while fundamental assumptions may not change, other elements of a culture can be intentionally or unintentionally altered.

Culture, therefore, is an orientation system for members of a social group, comprising observable actions, languages, and artefacts, as well as imperceptible values, norms, and attitudes. In sum:

- Culture is a group-level phenomenon and can be situated between individual personality and the biological characteristics of all humans.
- Culture is learned in a social environment and is often handed down from generation to generation.
- Culture distinguishes members of one group from another.
- Members of a culture share similar behaviours, norms, and values.

In an interconnected world where businesses operate across borders, understanding the role of national culture is crucial for effective collaboration and understanding in multinational companies. However, it is important to understand that culture also exists at levels other than the national level. Organizational culture, regional culture, music cultures, shopping cultures (and many more) exist, too. Interestingly, significant parts of national culture are invisible to outsiders, at least at first sight. Complicating the situation even more, even members of a culture are often unaware of specific norms and values in their own cultures as they have internalized them to an extent that makes them unquestioned. And if they are aware of a specific norm, they are sometimes not able to explain why a certain norm is important for them.

Spotlight: Being On Time Is Important for Germans!

As an example, take a stereotypical German cultural trait, punctuality. Most people who have interacted with Germans have noticed how important punctuality is for the (stereotypical) German. Using the iceberg model, the importance of punctuality is a clearly observable artefact of German culture. Going beyond artefacts, Germans also share the feeling that being on time is 'the right thing to do'. In that sense, there is an underlying shared norm that punctuality is not only important but also the right way to behave. So where does this focus on punctuality in the German culture come from? Surprisingly, it is hard for Germans to explain why punctuality is so important to them. The underlying basic assumptions remain unclear, even to some strong advocates of punctuality. There are some historical pointers that punctuality has long been an important characteristic of German culture, but there is no clear reason why. As with many cultural traits, German punctuality remains a shared norm and emphasized trait, but the underlying basic assumptions remain invisible and far below the waterline.

Sources: DW Germans and Punctualilty (www.dw.com/en/germans-and-punctuality/a-16430264)

Discussion Questions

1. Outline the components of stereotypical punctuality in Germany that represent cultural artefacts, norms, and underlying values.
2. Where else in the world have you observed people to be exceptionally punctual?
3. While punctuality is a big issue in some cultures, it is less so in others. Nevertheless, things work similarly well in those cultures. Why is that?

4.3.2 Concepts of Culture

To capture the phenomenon of 'national culture', researchers have presented many concepts of culture that can be differentiated in emic and etic approaches. Etic approaches involve an external or outsider's viewpoint when studying cultures or behaviours. This approach emphasizes the objective analysis and comparison of cultures using universal or cross-cultural categories, theories, and frameworks. Researchers adopting an etic approach aim to observe, analyse, and interpret cultural phenomena through a lens that is detached from internal viewpoints and specificities of the culture being studied. They apply external standards or theoretical constructs to compare and understand cultural similarities, differences, and patterns across various societies.

Emic approaches focus on understanding behaviours, concepts, and phenomena from within the cultural context being studied. They involve examining things from the insider's viewpoint, emphasizing the internal meanings, values, and interpretations that members of a specific culture attribute to their experiences. Researchers employing an emic approach strive to grasp the unique perspectives, beliefs, symbols, and practices that hold significance within a particular cultural group. This method often involves intense engagement with individuals within the culture, employing their native language, and seeking to understand their worldview on their own terms.

Both perspectives have their strengths and limitations. While the emic approach offers cultural specificity and depth, it may lack generalizability. Conversely, the etic approach provides broader comparisons and generalizations but might oversimplify or overlook crucial cultural nuances.

By definition, 'models' of cultures will always be of etic nature. A key motif for the development of etic models of culture is the ability to compare different cultures. This is in contrast to emic approaches which seek to provide a deep understanding of a single culture. We will therefore present five etic approaches: Hofstede's model (1980), the GLOBE project (House et al., 2004), Hall's concept (1966, 1976, 1983), Trompenaars' model (2011), and Kluckhohn and Strodtbeck's model (1961). While Hofstede, GLOBE, Trompenaars and (partially) Kluckhohn and Strodtbeck represent etic approaches that are based on empirical approaches (i.e., they try to operationalize culture), Hall's concept is a purely theoretical one (i.e., there is no quantitative comparison of cultures).

4.3.2.1 Hofstede's Study and Model of Culture

Dutch researcher Geert Hofstede (1980) identified four (later six) dimensions of culture based on an empirical study of IBM, the large MNC, conducted in 1968. To arrive at the concept, Hofstede (who was working for IBM at that time) surveyed over 116,000 respondents from 70 different countries and 66 national subsidiaries and identified four dimensions: power distance, uncertainty avoidance, individualism vs collectivism, and masculinity vs femininity (see Figure 4.2).

The 'power distance' dimension relates to power distribution and the degree to which less powerful members of a society accept and expect power to be distributed unequally. Whereas low power distance is associated with an egalitarian society, minimum inequality, and flat hierarchies, high power distance entails strong authorities, inequalities, and the superiority of power holders. High power distance countries (e.g. many Asian and African cultures) thus exhibit a greater acceptance of hierarchical structures, where power is centralized, and superiors are respected and unquestioned. Low power distance countries (e.g. Nordic countries) have flatter organizational structures, value equality, and prefer power to be more evenly distributed. Employees might challenge authority and expect participative decision-making.

Spotlight: The Lowest Power Distance Score in the World: Austria

When investigating the cultural dimensions via the www.hofstede-insights.com website, European students stumbled upon an interesting artefact in the data: Austria seems to be one of the countries with the lowest power distance score (PDI = 11) in the world. This is surprising, because other than, for example, the Scandinavian countries such as Denmark (PDI = 18), which are known for their egalitarian societies, Austria is known to be a country of formality and status-rich titles and honorifics. At a conference in Vienna, the issue was discussed with leading figures in psychology. The explanation points towards some of the methodological constraints under which the studies underlying Hofstede's dimensions were conducted. First, the original study focused on managers in IBM, which is a rather specific sub-stratum of society. Second, the interpretation of power distance is a question of social norms and beliefs. The kind of cultural narrative that is represented in the IBM managers' responses, however, points in a different direction. The lower power distance score for Austria might be a consequence of a culture of 'I can do the job better than my manager', which translates to a lower power distance score in the culture study.

Source: Cultural Atlas (https://culturalatlas.sbs.com.au/austrian-culture/austrian-culture-core-concepts)

'Uncertainty avoidance' expresses the degree to which the members of a society feel uncomfortable with uncertainty and ambiguity. The fundamental issue here is how a society deals with the fact that the future can never be known: should we try to control the future or just let it happen? Under low uncertainty avoidance, individuals show a higher tolerance for ambiguity, uncertainty, and innovation and have a higher propensity for risk, whereas high uncertainty avoidance relates to the perception of uncertainty as a threat and resistance to change. High uncertainty avoidance cultures (e.g. Greece, Japan) tend to have more rigid structures, strict rules, and a low tolerance for ambiguity. They seek security through laws, technology, and religious beliefs. In contrast, low uncertainty avoidance cultures (e.g. Denmark, Singapore) are more open to change, tolerate ambiguity better, and have fewer rules and formalities.

'Individualism vs collectivism', the third dimension, reflects the degree to which individuals prioritize self-interest over group interests. Individualistic cultures share an 'I mentality', which is based on individual needs, personal achievement, and autonomy, whereas collectivist cultures share a 'we mentality' in which decisions are based on what is best for the group and higher levels of loyalty and interdependence prevail. More individualistic cultures (e.g. the United States) therefore prioritize personal achievement, independence, and individual rights over group interests. People take responsibility for themselves and their immediate families. More collectivist cultures (e.g. China, Japan) emphasize group harmony, loyalty to the larger community, and the well-being of the group over individual desires.

The dimension labelled 'masculinity vs femininity' distinguishes between cultures that are 'traditionally' more masculine and those that are more feminine. More masculine societies tend to emphasize assertiveness, competition, and material success, whereas more feminine societies focus on cooperation, quality of life, and empathy. Very masculine cultures (e.g. Japan) prioritize assertiveness, competition, and success, often valuing material achievement. Roles are clearly defined based on gender stereotypes. Feminine cultures (e.g. Sweden) emphasize nurturing and caring for others. Gender roles tend to be less distinct, and empathy is valued.

Over the years, Hofstede added two additional dimensions to the model. These dimensions do not relate to the original study but are – from his perspective – important additions to the original model.

The time dimension describes society's 'long-term vs short-term orientation'. Long-term orientation emphasizes perseverance, life-long personal networks, self-discipline, and future-oriented thinking, whereas short-term orientation stresses short-term profits and emphasizes a need for achievement, respect for tradition, and saving face. In cultures oriented to the long term, businesses might invest in relationships for future gains, while in cultures oriented to the short term, immediate profits and quick results might be prioritized.

The sixth and final dimension of 'indulgence vs restraint' refers to different perspectives on gratification. Indulgent societies allow relatively free personal gratification related to enjoying life and having fun, but also emphasizing freedom of speech. Restrained societies, however, defer and suppress gratification and promote self-control and strict social norms, often indicated by higher numbers of police officers. In indulgent cultures, workplaces might have a more relaxed atmosphere, and leisure time might be valued. In restrained cultures, work ethic and self-discipline might be emphasized, and leisure activities might be more restricted.

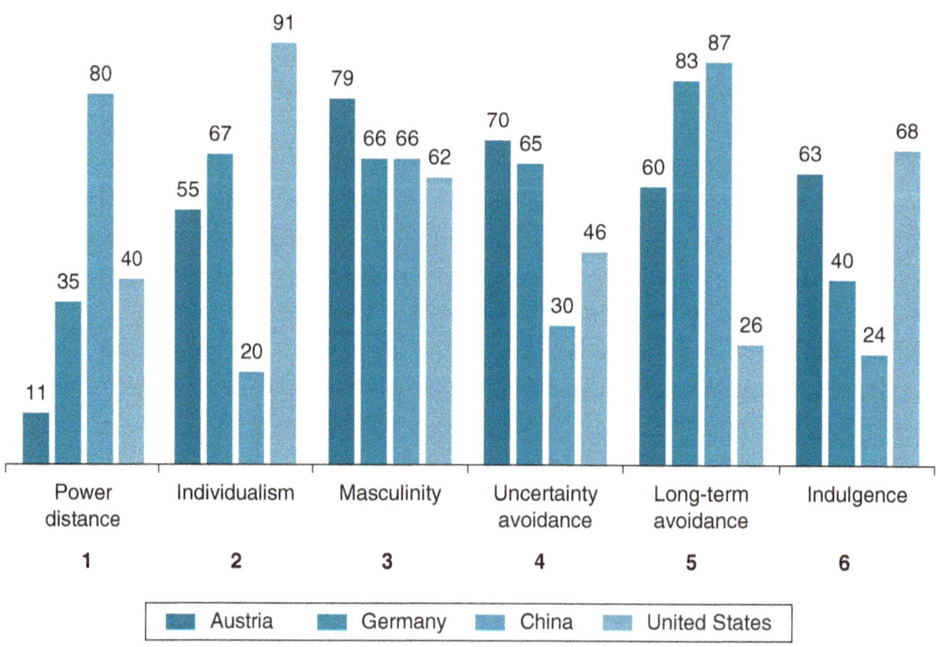

Figure 4.2 Examples of cultural dimensions according to Hofstede

Source: Based on data from www.hofstede-insights.com

Hofstede's study had a significant impact on IB research, and his statement that 'the business of International Business is culture' received strong support after publication of the study. However, the study has also been strongly criticized. Criticism includes the assumption that all cultures in the world can be described with the same four (or six) dimensions (a frequent and largely unavoidable point of criticism for etic approaches). The fact that all respondents came from the same firm, that within-country cultural diversity had been neglected, and that, from today's perspective, the study is rather old have been additional relevant points of criticism. While at least part of this criticism appears to be fair, the study still deserves recognition as a landmark study in the field of cross-cultural management that created substantial awareness of the topics and triggered a lot of follow up research.

4.3.2.2 GLOBE Study and Model of Culture

Partially triggered by the criticism of the Hofstede study, the GLOBE (Global Leadership and Organizational Behavior Effectiveness) research project by House et al. (2004) started a comprehensive cross-cultural research initiative to add nuance to cultural dimensions and their impact on leadership and organizational behaviours in different societies. They used a different methodological strategy as they did not focus on employees within a single firm but sampled different firms across 62 countries. They built on the concepts of Hofstede's model to some extent but extended it in two ways. First, they explored culture across nine (instead of six) dimensions, by splitting some of Hofstede's original dimensions. The dimensions of uncertainty avoidance, power distance, institutional collectivism, in-group collectivism, gender egalitarianism, and assertiveness relate strongly to Hofstede's. Second, they measured not only cultural values across the dimension, but also cultural practices ('should be' vs 'as is'). The nine dimensions (see also Figure 4.3) of the study are as follows.

1. 'Performance orientation' measures the degree to which a collective encourages, and should encourage and reward, group members for performance improvement, achievement, and excellence. High performance orientation cultures emphasize success and outcomes, while low performance orientation cultures tend to focus on effort and participation. In high performance orientation cultures, businesses tend to incentivize employees for achieving performance targets, while in low performance orientation cultures, traditional ways of doing things might be preferred.
2. 'Assertiveness' covers the extent to which individuals are assertive, confrontational, and aggressive in their relationship with others. High assertiveness cultures value competitiveness and direct communication, while low assertiveness cultures emphasize cooperation and harmony. In high assertiveness cultures, negotiations tend to be more direct and competitive, while in low assertiveness cultures, negotiations might focus on finding consensus and maintaining harmony.
3. 'Future orientation' reflects the extent to which individuals engage in future-oriented behaviours such as long-term planning, investing in the future, and delaying

gratification. Cultures with high future orientation prioritize investment in the future and are willing to delay rewards for long-term gains. In high future orientation cultures, businesses tend to invest in research and development for future success, whereas in low future orientation cultures, immediate profits tend to be prioritized.

4 'Humane orientation' expresses the degree to which a collective encourages and rewards individuals for being fair, altruistic, generous, caring, and kind to others. Cultures with high humane orientation value compassion and concern for others. In high humane orientation cultures, corporate social responsibility and community involvement tend to be be highly valued, whereas in low humane orientation cultures, individual success tend to be prioritized over community welfare.

5 'Institutional collectivism' measures the degree to which organizational and societal institutional practices encourage and reward collective action and distribution of resources. Individualistic cultures prioritize self-interest whereas collectivist cultures prioritize group interests. In high institutional collectivism cultures, companies tend to prioritize teamwork and group achievements, whereas in low institutional collectivism cultures, individual contributions tend to be emphasized.

6 'In-group collectivism' refers to the degree to which individuals express pride, loyalty, and cohesiveness in their organizations, families, or friends. High in-group collectivism cultures value loyalty and support within their groups. In high in-group collectivism cultures, employees tend to have strong loyalty to their work teams, while in low in-group collectivism cultures, individual goals tend to be more prominent.

7 'Gender egalitarianism' reflects the degree to which a society minimizes gender inequality. Societies with high gender egalitarianism minimize gender-based discrimination and value equal opportunities for men and women. In high gender egalitarianism cultures, there tends to be equal representation of men and women in leadership roles, whereas in low gender egalitarianism cultures, traditional gender roles tend to be more prevalent.

8 'Power distance' measures the extent to which the community accepts and endorses authority, power differences, and status privileges. High power distance cultures emphasize hierarchical relationships and centralized decision-making, while low power distance cultures promote more egalitarian and participatory leadership styles. In a high power distance culture, employees tend to hesitate voicing opinions in front of their superiors. In contrast, in a low power distance culture, the expectation is that there will be open communication between employees and managers.

9 'Uncertainty avoidance' deals with a society's tolerance to ambiguity, uncertainty, and risk. It measures the extent to which a society, organization, or group relies on social norms, rules, and procedures to alleviate the unpredictability of future events. Cultures with a stronger desire to avoid uncertainty tend to seek order, consistency, structure, formal procedures, and laws. In a high uncertainty avoidance culture, there tend to be detailed procedures for handling situations, whereas in a low uncertainty avoidance culture, flexibility and adaptability tend to be more valued.

Spotlight: Uncertainty Avoidance and Corporate Website Recruiting

The use of technology in personnel recruiting has increased tremendously over recent decades, with corporate website recruiting becoming increasingly important. The conventional wisdom is that corporate website recruiting will not replace the full recruitment process because neither the company nor the job applicant can generate sufficient valid information. Nevertheless, pre-screening via online games, CV screening supported by artificial intelligence (AI), and feedback from automated online chats are now frequent elements in the selection process. It seems reasonable to assume that companies from societies with high uncertainty avoidance would be first to employ new technologies to reduce uncertainty and human bias in the selection process. Interestingly, however, empirical evidence suggests that companies from these cultures are late adopters of corporate website recruiting. One interpretation is that uncertainty about the usefulness of the methods (e.g. because they are still relatively new) outweighs their potential in reducing uncertainty in the process.

Source: Puck, Mohr & Holtbrügge (2006)

Despite the newer GLOBE study, some of the criticism of the Hofstede model is still relevant. It uses the same etic approach to culture and mostly neglects diversity within cultures. That the study works with respondents from different companies in different countries addresses the criticism that Hofstede's study was based on a single firm but is open to the challenge that the results are driven by the corporate cultures of the different companies in the sample as well as the national context.

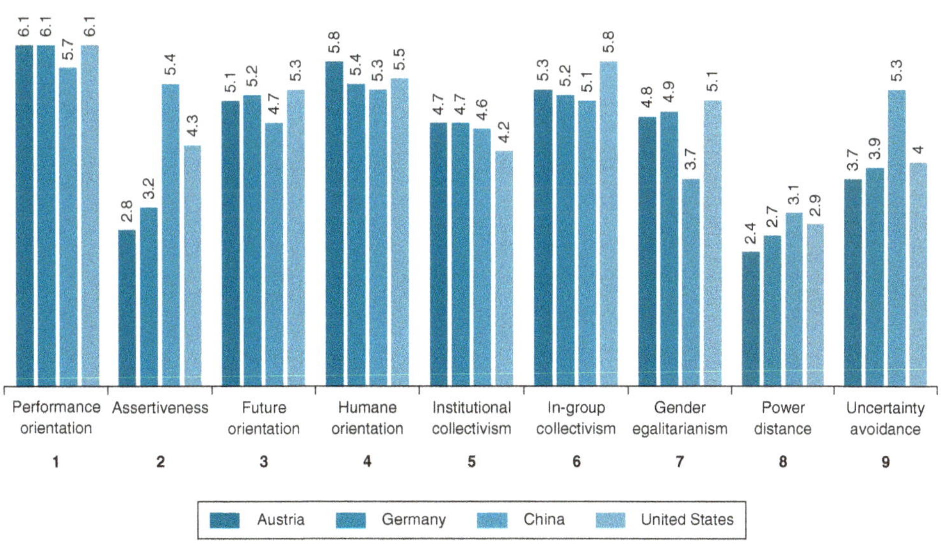

Figure 4.3 Examples of cultural dimensions according to the GLOBE project

Source: Based on data from www.globeproject.com

4.3.2.3 Hall's Study and Model of Culture

Another relevant concept of culture has been developed by Edward T. Hall. Hall's series of monographs, originating in the mid-twentieth century, progressively formulated an extensive cultural framework. His initial notable work, *The Silent Language* (1959), drawing on Freudian psychoanalytic theory, posits that individuals are not fully conscious of their non-verbal communication behaviours. Hall's seminal publication addresses three primary dimensions: time, space, and context.

- *Time* delineates how diverse cultures orient themselves temporally, perceiving time as either monochronic or polychronic.
- *Space* encompasses various cultural constructs in defining and organizing space, ingrained unconsciously in individuals.
- *Context* refers to the differing methods by which cultures construct meaning, employing varying ratios of context and information.

Hall expands on these three cultural dimensions in subsequent works. Although he tended to emphasize one dimension in each of his early monographs (1966, 1976, 1983), he consistently interrelates the three dimensions. For instance, while discussing one dimension in detail, he invariably references the other two, illustrating their interconnectedness.

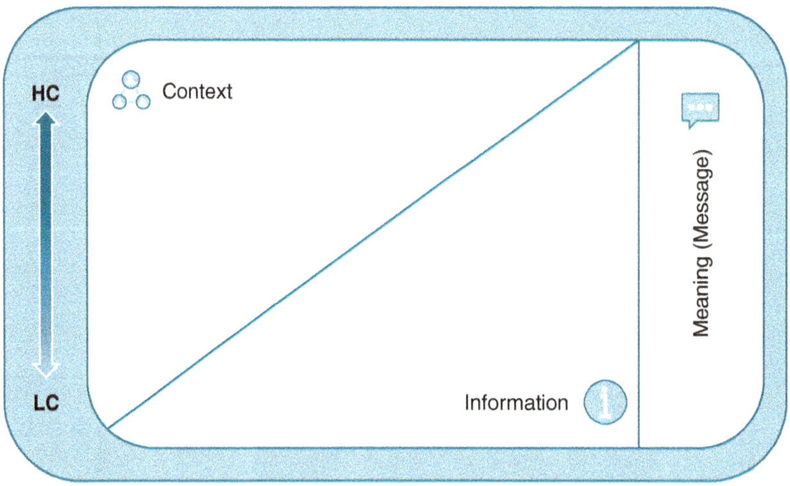

Figure 4.4 Hall's concept of context

Source: Based on Hall (1976: 102)

Hall's strongest contribution to cultural research has often been claimed to be his focus on the role of communication: 'culture is communication and no communication by humans can be divorced from culture' (Hall, 1992: 212). He developed a concept that proposes that the way humans create meaning by combining information and context varies across cultures (Figure 4.4). In low-context cultures, people communicate their intended messages very directly and clearly through verbal expression. In high-context cultures, the intended message can only be decoded by combining the verbal expression with the context in which the communication took place. As outlined earlier, context when discussing language can refer to non-verbal elements (posture, gestures, etc.), as well as para-verbal (tone, rhythm of speech, etc.) and extra-verbal (time, location, etc.) elements of communication. Communication between members of high- and low-context cultures is therefore challenging. A member of a low-context culture would be at risk of misinterpreting communication from a member of a high-context culture as the relevance of the context might be underrated. The other way around, members of high-context cultures might overemphasize the context in communication from members of low-context cultures.

In summary, Hall's model differs from those of Hofstede and GLOBE as it is much more focused. It relates to only three dimensions of culture (time, space, and context) with a strong focus on the role of communication. It has been very influential as it provides a deep understanding of language in the context of culture. However, it too has been criticized. Like Hofstede's work, Hall's model suffers from the shortcomings of the etic approach. Two important additional points of criticism are the omission of other relevant dimensions of culture and the empirical background of his work.

4.3.2.4 Trompenaars' Study and Model of Culture

Fons Trompenaars is a Dutch consultant who works on cross-cultural communication topics. With his colleague Charles Hampden-Turner, he developed a model of culture (Trompenaars & Hampden-Turner, 2011) that is partially based on Hofstede's work.

To gather the necessary data, Trompenaars and Hampden-Turner conducted a large-scale survey involving over 15,000 managers and employees from more than 50 countries. The survey was designed to reveal cultural preferences and values related to the dimensions they aimed to explore. The questionnaire included situational questions and scenarios to elicit responses highlighting cultural preferences. For instance, respondents were asked how they would handle specific business dilemmas or interpersonal situations. Trompenaars' model identifies seven dimensions of culture, each of which addresses a different aspect of how societies are organized and how they function.

1. In the universalism vs particularism dimension, cultures with a universalist orientation emphasize rules, laws, and general principles, applying the same standards to everyone, regardless of the situation or relationship. In particularist cultures, relationships and unique circumstances take precedence over rules. People believe that context and personal relationships should guide behaviour.
2. The individualism vs communitarianism dimension to some extent relates to the individualism vs collectivism dimensions in the studies by Hofstede and GLOBE. Individualist cultures value personal freedom, autonomy, and individual achievement. People see themselves as independent and prioritize their own goals.

In communitarian cultures, the group's well-being is considered more important than individual success. People see themselves as part of a community and prioritize collective goals.

3 The model introduces the specific vs diffuse dimension. In specific-oriented cultures, people compartmentalize their lives, separating work and personal relationships. Interactions are direct and to the point, focusing on specific issues. Diffuse cultures see life as integrated and interconnected. Work and personal relationships overlap, and interactions are more holistic, considering various contexts.
4 Trompenaars also distinguishes neutral vs affective cultures. In neutral cultures, emotions are controlled and restrained. People do not readily express their feelings, maintaining a level of formality in interactions. Affective cultures are more expressive, and people openly show their emotions and feelings. Interactions are more animated and spontaneous.
5 This dimension considers achievement vs ascription. Achievement-oriented cultures value performance and what individuals have accomplished. Status is earned based on one's achievements and skills. In ascription cultures, status is attributed based on factors such as age, gender, social connections, and family background. It is about who you are rather than what you have done.
6 The sequential time vs synchronous time dimension focuses on a culture's perception of time. Cultures with a sequential approach to time see it as linear and segmented. Punctuality, planning, and schedules are important, and tasks are performed one after the other. Synchronous cultures view time as more fluid and flexible. People often do several things at once and are more comfortable with interruptions and changes in plans. This dimension is similar to the time-dimension in Hall's model.
7 The last dimension considers internal direction vs outer direction. Cultures with an internal locus of control believe that individuals can control their environment and their fate. They emphasize self-determination and personal agency. Outer-directed cultures see the environment and external forces as more influential in shaping events. People adapt to circumstances and focus on harmony with nature and others.

Geert Hofstede was very critical of Trompenaars' model. In 'Riding the waves of commerce: A test of Trompenaars' "model" of national culture differences' (Hofstede, 1996) he raised significant concerns about the study's conclusions and methodology, arguing that the theory in the book was not supported by the data. Nevertheless, it is used frequently in applied intercultural management and training.

4.3.2.5 Kluckhohn and Strodtbeck's Study and Model of Culture

The model developed by Florence Kluckhohn and Fred Strodtbeck (1961) – the Kluckhohn and Strodtbeck value orientation framework – posits that all societies must answer a limited number of universal problems, and the manner in which they do so reflects their cultural values. The framework is based on the premise that while these problems are common to all human groups, the solutions vary widely across cultures. Kluckhohn and Strodtbeck identified six fundamental dimensions of cultural values that differentiate societies and tested the model in five communities in the United States.

1 *The first dimension is human nature orientation*, which considers the inherent nature of humans. Cultures can perceive humans as inherently good, inherently evil, or a mixture of both. This orientation influences societal norms and behaviours, such as trust and approaches to crime and punishment.
2 *The second dimension is man–nature orientation*, which explores the relationship between humans and nature. Some cultures view humans as subjugated by nature, others see humans as existing in harmony with nature, and still others believe humans can exert control over nature. This dimension affects attitudes towards environmental conservation and technological development.
3 *The third dimension is time orientation*, which examines how cultures perceive and value time. Time can be viewed in a linear fashion, emphasizing the past, present, or future. Some cultures prioritize traditions and historical continuity, while others focus on present enjoyment or future planning and progress.
4 *The fourth dimension is activity orientation*, which deals with the preferred mode of human activity. Cultures may value being (emphasizing personal development and enjoying life), doing (focusing on action and achievement), or becoming (emphasizing continual growth and improvement). This orientation influences work ethics, leisure activities, and personal goals.
5 *The fifth dimension is relational orientation*, which looks at the preferred ways of structuring social relationships. This includes how societies prioritize individualism vs collectivism, the importance of family ties, and the hierarchy within social structures. It affects social behaviour, organizational practices, and political systems.
6 *The sixth and final dimension is space orientation*, which addresses the use and perception of physical space. Cultures can differ in their preference for personal space, territoriality, and the organization of space in homes, workplaces, and public areas. This orientation can influence architectural styles, office layouts, and social interaction.

The model represents an early model in intercultural research and created an important impetus to further studies. At the same time, it is often criticized for the rather small-scale empirical study that was used to test the model. However, it is important to interpret this criticism in the light of the technological and statistical status of the 1950s and 1960s. From our perspective, it remains one of the core models of early intercultural research.

Spotlight: An Emerging Global Digital Culture

The last twenty years have seen the emergence of a digital culture that is specifically shared among a younger demographic around the world. This phenomenon is driven by the widespread adoption of digital technologies, social media platforms, and the internet, which facilitate instant and borderless communication.

A key characteristic of this global digital culture is the homogenization of entertainment preferences. Young people across the world increasingly consume the same movies, TV shows, music, and video games, often popularized through streaming services like Netflix, Spotify, and YouTube. These platforms offer global access to content, enabling trends and viral phenomena to spread rapidly across different regions. As a result, the cultural consumption of younger generations is becoming more synchronized globally, often overshadowing traditional, localized forms of entertainment.

Fashion and lifestyle trends are a significant aspect of this digital culture. Social media influencers and celebrities with a global following set trends that are quickly adopted by their audiences worldwide. Platforms such as Instagram, TikTok, and X (previously Twitter) play a crucial role in disseminating these trends, creating a shared sense of style and lifestyle among young people from diverse backgrounds. This has led to a more uniform fashion sense and lifestyle choices, from clothing brands to fitness routines.

Another characteristic is a shared digital language and communication styles. The use of emojis, memes, and internet slang transcends linguistic and cultural barriers, creating a universal mode of online expression. Memes, in particular, act as cultural touchstones that resonate globally, often reflecting shared experiences and humour.

Moreover, values and attitudes are also aligning globally among the younger generation. Issues like environmental sustainability, social justice, and mental health are prominent topics of concern and advocacy. Digital platforms facilitate the exchange of ideas and activism, fostering a sense of global citizenship and collective responsibility.

However, this global digital culture is not without its challenges. The dominance of certain cultural products, primarily from the West, can lead to cultural homogenization and the erosion of local traditions and identities. Additionally, the digital divide means that access to this global culture is not uniform, with disparities in internet access and digital literacy affecting participation.

4.4 RELIGION

Religion is a complex and multifaceted aspect of human life that encompasses a wide range of beliefs, practices, rituals, values, and moral codes. It is a fundamental part of human culture and society, often involving belief in the existence of a higher power or powers, the supernatural, and the creation of a moral framework guiding individual and collective behaviour. Many religious beliefs are deeply grounded in cultures and often invisible and unknown to outsiders and sometimes even insiders of a culture. Usually, people are unable to spell out the basic assumptions underlying their belief systems. Religion, thus, strongly connects with the basic assumptions of a culture as illustrated on the third level of the Iceberg Model.

The leading religions in the world, based on the number of adherents, are Christianity, Islam, Hinduism, and Buddhism. Christianity, with approximately 2.3 billion adherents, encompasses various denominations such as Catholicism, Protestantism, Eastern Orthodoxy, and others. Islam has an estimated 1.9 to 2.2 billion adherents, divided primarily into Sunni Islam and Shia Islam, with the majority following the Sunni branch. Hinduism counts approximately 1.2 billion adherents, predominantly concentrated in India and Nepal. Buddhism, with around 520 million adherents, includes diverse traditions like Theravada, Mahayana, and Vajrayana, mainly practised in Asian regions. It is important to note that all figures on adherents are approximate and vary somewhat depending on the source. Further, not all adherents actively practise a religion but may, like for example many Christians, only go to church for the major holidays like Christmas or Easter.

Religions are important for MNCs in many ways. As highlighted earlier, religions are often connected to some of the most basic and central beliefs and assumptions of a culture. Religion often provides a framework for understanding the world, life's purpose, and the nature of existence. It shapes people's perceptions about the origin of life, the afterlife, morality, and human destiny, influencing their view of the world. Religious teachings and scriptures often contain ethical guidelines and moral codes that drive behaviour, decision-making, and interpersonal relationships within a society. These teachings form the basis for the moral compass of adherents. Religious beliefs and rituals thus become integral parts of a culture's customs, traditions, and rituals. They shape daily life, ceremonies, festivals, and social practices, influencing cultural expression, art, music, and literature. In other words, almost all national cultures are strongly connected to the religious beliefs of the nation. That's why it is important to understand religion as a core element of culture.

Religious festivals and routines often bear very explicit implications for MNCs. For example, the weekly day of faithful worship usually is a different day across the three monotheistic religions: Friday for Muslims, Saturday for Jews, and Sunday for Christians. Similarly, Christmas is celebrated on different days in the year in different Christian denominations. This requires coordination in an MNC to ensure functioning communication and operations across different cultural and religious settings.

Though religion influences culture in almost all countries of the world, the role of religion in society varies across countries. In secular societies, the government, institutions, and laws are designed to be separate from religious institutions and principles. This separation exists to ensure that the state does not officially endorse or promote any specific religion or religious belief, and it allows individuals the freedom to practise their religion or beliefs without interference from the government. A secular state maintains neutrality in matters of religion. It treats all religions and beliefs equally under the law, ensuring that no single religion receives preferential treatment or discrimination.

In theocratic societies, religious principles, doctrines, and laws strongly influence or control the government, legal system, social norms, and public life. In such societies, the government derives its authority from religious teachings, and religious leaders or clerics often hold significant positions of power or influence in the state. Legal codes and laws are (partially) based on religious scriptures or teachings and religious beliefs directly influence various aspects of the legal system, including civil laws, criminal justice, and social regulations. Historically, various societies and civilizations have been theocratic, with governance based on religious principles. Examples include ancient Egypt, parts of medieval Europe during the rule of the Catholic Church, theocratic states like Vatican City, and contemporary nations like Iran or Saudi Arabia, which have elements of theocratic governance based on Islamic principles. It is important to note that theocratic societies can vary significantly in their interpretation and implementation of religious governance. Some societies may embrace more moderate or flexible interpretations, while others might have more rigid and authoritarian systems based on religious laws.

4.5 CURRENT DEVELOPMENTS IN INFORMAL INSTITUTIONAL ENVIRONMENTS

Compared to formal institutions, informal institutions change rather slowly. However, we still observe informal institutional change and have seen some interesting trends in recent years, and research continuously introduces new perspectives on the role and relevance of informal institutions.

4.5.1 Adaptive Informal Institutions

Local actors often develop informal coping strategies to navigate and circumvent the constraints imposed by formal institutions. Over time, these strategies can gain traction and become institutionalized, forming what can be termed adaptive informal institutions. These new norms and practices arise as creative responses to overly restrictive formal environments. As they become widespread, they can drive formal institutional reforms. This process is evident in China's private sector evolution since the late 1970s, exemplified by three significant changes: the legalization of private enterprises, the inclusion of capitalists in the Chinese Communist Party, and constitutional amendments supporting the private economy (Tsai, 2006). This highlights the strong interconnectedness and mutual influence of formal and informal institutions.

4.5.2 Informal Institutions, Environmental, Social and Governance Performance and Financial Performance

A recent study (Jiyoung Shin et al., 2023) examines how national cultural aspects, measured using Hofstede's six cultural dimensions, moderate the relationship between environmental, social, and governance (ESG) performance and financial performance. The study found that national culture affects the financial returns of ESG activities significantly. In countries with high levels of individualism and masculinity, such as the United States and the United Kingdom, there is a positive relationship between ESG performance and financial returns. Firms in these cultures benefit economically from their ESG activities to a greater extent than societies characterized by high power distance, uncertainty avoidance, short-term orientation, and indulgence.

4.5.3 Family-Controlled Firms and Informal Institutions

Another recent study (Berrone et al., 2022) clarifies the complex narrative around family-controlled firms, revealing that national cultural contexts, particularly family business legitimacy, have a significant and beneficial influence on their strategic behaviours and performance. In contrast, countries with weak family business legitimacy see less differentiation and performance benefits for family-controlled firms. This study, using meta-analytic tools, challenges the notion that family-controlled firms thrive principally by compensating for weak formal institutions, and emphasizes instead the critical role of supportive informal institutions. These insights underscore the importance of understanding cultural contexts for family-controlled firms, leaders, and policymakers to optimize strategies and improve family business outcomes.

4.5.4 Public Sentiment as a Relevant Informal Institution

In the contemporary landscape shaped by intense scrutiny of public governance, international relations tensions, geopolitical shifts, and the burgeoning influence of social movements and activism within the global economy, multinational companies (MNCs) face mounting pressure from public sentiment. Focusing on China as a research context and analysing more than 100,000 blog posts, a recent study by Yiu et al. (2022) provides evidence for how public sentiment shapes firms' international strategies, specifically the share of ownership in foreign acquisitions. This study advances our understanding of informal institutions by introducing public sentiment as a novel form, one characterized by its normative–cognitive aspects intertwined with affective elements. This sentiment, disseminated through the public sphere, serves to confer social, political, and cognitive legitimacy upon MNCs, thus highlighting its pivotal role in shaping contemporary corporate landscapes.

SUMMARY

This chapter introduced the informal national environment and the iceberg model as a way of recognizing the structure of the informal environment. We discussed the role of language in the informal environment and introduced the phenomenon of national culture and several models to help us understand and compare different (national) cultures. Lastly, we discussed the role of religion in the informal environment.

We used the iceberg model to divide the informal institutional environment into three levels: artefacts and visible behaviours, values and social norms, and basic assumptions. The visible aspects, like clothing and rituals, are the 'tip of the iceberg', while deeper levels include values and norms guiding behaviour, and basic, often unconscious assumptions that shape our worldview. Language plays a crucial role in the informal institutional environment, as it has an impact on communication at multiple levels: verbal, non-verbal, paraverbal, and extraverbal. Effective communication within multinational companies (MNCs) and with external stakeholders is often challenged by language barriers, which can lead to misinterpretation and misunderstanding. Language diversity in MNCs may, however, foster unique corporate cultures and cohesion, though this can be hindered by differing levels of language proficiency, semantic interpretation, and norms of communication. Overall, understanding language is essential for navigating and managing communication complexities in International Business contexts.

Culture is defined by Hofstede as the collective mental programming distinguishing one group from another, encompassing shared values, rituals, heroes, and symbols. Culture acts as an orientation system for group members, integrating observable actions, language, artefacts, and imperceptible values, norms, and attitudes. Researchers use both emic (insider) and etic (outsider) approaches to study cultures. Various models of culture include Hofstede's model, the GLOBE study, Hall's focus on communication dimensions (time, space, and context), Trompenaars' seven dimensions addressing societal organization, and Kluckhohn and Strodtbeck's value orientation framework. All models can help to provide a deeper and structured analysis of different national cultures for MNCs.

Religion is a complex and integral aspect of human life, encompassing beliefs, practices, rituals, values, and moral codes that guide individual and collective behaviour. Major world religions include Christianity, Islam, Hinduism, and Buddhism, each with significant numbers of adherents and diverse traditions. Religion has a strong influence on cultural customs, daily life, ceremonies, and social practices, making it essential for multinational companies to understand religious contexts in order to operate effectively. The role of religion varies from country to country, with secular societies maintaining a separation between religion and state, while theocratic societies integrate religious principles into governance and legal systems.

5

SUPRANATIONAL INSTITUTIONS AND INSTITUTIONAL DISTANCE

CHAPTER INTRODUCTION

Supranational institutions have emerged to complement national and subnational institutions. From the middle of the twentieth century, supranational institutions began to play a major role in the global economy. The establishment of bodies such as the United Nations, the predecessor organizations of the European Union and the World Trade Organization brought about the role that supranational institutions now play in the economy. The majority of legal initiatives for many European countries are created by the European Commission, and economic blocs such as USMCA (the United States–Mexico–Canada Agreement), ASEAN (the Association of South-East Asian Nations), and the European Union have substantial influence on how global business is conducted. This chapter highlights how the supranational layer co-creates the institutional environment firms work in, and how differences between countries can be characterized by institutional distance. Bringing these components together, the chapter closes by discussing economic integration.

LEARNING OUTCOMES

After reading this chapter you should be able to:

1 Describe what supranational institutions are and distinguish between supranational institutions and supranational organizations
2 Critically reflect on the interaction between supranational and national institutions

3. Outline the role of multinational companies in co-creating supranational and national institutions
4. Use institutional distance to understand differences between institutional environments
5. Explain the role of economic integration in fostering the integration of national economies.

Case Study: How ASEAN Helped Thai Union to Expand

Thai Union Group was established in 1977 and has been a regional and global leader for seafood-based products since the 1990s. Today, Thai Union Group is one of the world's largest seafood processors and exporters, known for its brands like Chicken of the Sea, John West, and Petit Navire. The ASEAN Economic Community (AEC) initiatives and the ASEAN Free Trade Area (AFTA) have played a significant role in the company's expansion across the ASEAN region.

Under AFTA, Thai Union Group enjoys reduced or zero tariffs when exporting its seafood products, such as canned tuna, to other ASEAN member states, which include Vietnam, Indonesia, and the Philippines. These preferential tariff rates make Thai Union's products more competitive in these markets than non-ASEAN competitors.

Moreover, the harmonization of trade regulations and standards through AEC initiatives helps Thai Union Group navigate diverse regulatory environments across ASEAN countries. By aligning product standards and certification, the company can streamline its manufacturing processes to meet the required specifications for each market, reducing barriers to entry and ensuring compliance with local regulations.

Additionally, the ASEAN Single Window (ASW) facilitates smoother customs procedures for Thai Union Group. This electronic platform simplifies and expedites documentation processes, enabling quicker customs clearance for the company's seafood exports within the ASEAN region. This enhances efficiency in shipping and distribution, reducing logistical complexities and costs.

By leveraging these ASEAN-driven facilitative measures, Thai Union Group has expanded its market presence within the region. The company has established partnerships, distribution networks, and supply chains that cater to the diverse consumer preferences across ASEAN countries. This expansion has contributed to Thai Union's continued growth and success in penetrating and serving markets within the ASEAN community.

Source: Chakravarthy & Pallivathukkal (2017)

Case Study Questions

1. What are the potential downsides of supranational involvement in national legislation?
2. How has the political landscape in Southeast Asia changed as a result of the emergence of ASEAN?
3. How does ASEAN fit into the architecture of bilateral and supranational agreements in Southeast Asia?

5.1 THE LANDSCAPE OF SUPRANATIONAL INSTITUTIONS

Like national institutions, supranational institutions provide dispute resolution mechanisms and foster coordination among nations. These processes reduce uncertainty and promote stability in International Business (IB). The term 'supranational institutions' refers to the rules, norms, and shared beliefs that provide the 'rules of the game' for global business. The creation and maintenance of supranational institutions resides with international organizations, some of which have substantial influence on business, which we discuss later in the chapter. First, we need to understand the interplay between national institutions, MNCs, and supranational institutions, whose characteristics are outlined below (Hartmann et al., 2022).

1. *Supraterritoriality*: Supranational institutions possess the power to influence multinational companies (MNCs) beyond their national boundaries, even without direct political legitimization. This is contingent upon enforcement mechanisms, which can be both formal (coercive legal means) and informal (global activist campaigns). Supraterritoriality implies that, to understand how the global business environment works, we need to consider the impact of relevant formal and informal supranational institutions on MNCs worldwide.
2. *Co-existence*: The relationship between supranational institutions and national institutions can bridge or magnify institutional differences, which raises questions for MNCs about how best to navigate the relationship which they are also party to.
3. *Contextuality*: The effectiveness of supranational institutions depends on the context, including national institutional environments. MNCs are exposed to the same supranational pressures in a variety of ways by different national institutions. National governments might, for example, shield companies from supranational norms or promote opposing values. IB research therefore needs to consider specific country-level contingencies.
4. *Selectivity*: Supranational institutions have an impact on firms within national settings, which advantages (and disadvantages) some more than others. International investment agreements, for example, might discriminate geographically, potentially disadvantaging domestic firms. Selectivity can also lead to 'jurisdiction shopping', whereby MNCs use supranational institutions to gain an edge over competitors – by, for example, having a case heard in a more sympathetic jurisdiction.
5. *Consensuality*: Supranational institutions require the consent of agents with sufficient authority to enforce decisions or agreements. This might mean two national players agreeing on a nationally ratified supranational institution. In other circumstances it could be consensus among several parties capable of pressuring MNCs. The concept of mutually agreed supranational institutions, like a lingua franca, demonstrates this consensual aspect.

6 *Co-evolution*: There is a mutuality in the way that supranational institutions, national institutions, and MNCs evolve. MNCs can be constrained by and contribute to the development of supranational institutions simultaneously. This co-evolution applies to national institutions as well, although the mechanisms differ. MNCs play a vital role in shaping supranational institutions through both collaboration and lobbying.

Like national institutions, supranational institutions have formal and informal components. Formal components include rules and laws which lay the foundations for the European Union or the UN Charter on Human Rights. Informal components include the shared linguistic heritage of countries with a common predecessor as a nation state, such as the Balkan countries in southeastern Europe, or shared religious beliefs in countries across the Middle East and North Africa. On the supranational level, even more than the national level, the organizations that fill supranational institutions with life are particularly important in maintaining and developing supranational institutions.

Figure 5.1 illustrates the interplay of supranational institutions, national institutions, and organizations, the most prominent of which are MNCs (Hartmann et al., 2022: 1296). The three-way relationship is complemented by institutional distance (which we discuss later in the chapter). The figure also distinguishes between the norms and beliefs that characterize formal and informal institutions (on the left) and the players that interpret, develop, and to some extent ensure the effective operation of formal institutions (on the right).

In the next section, we discuss some of the major players that bring supranational institutions to life.

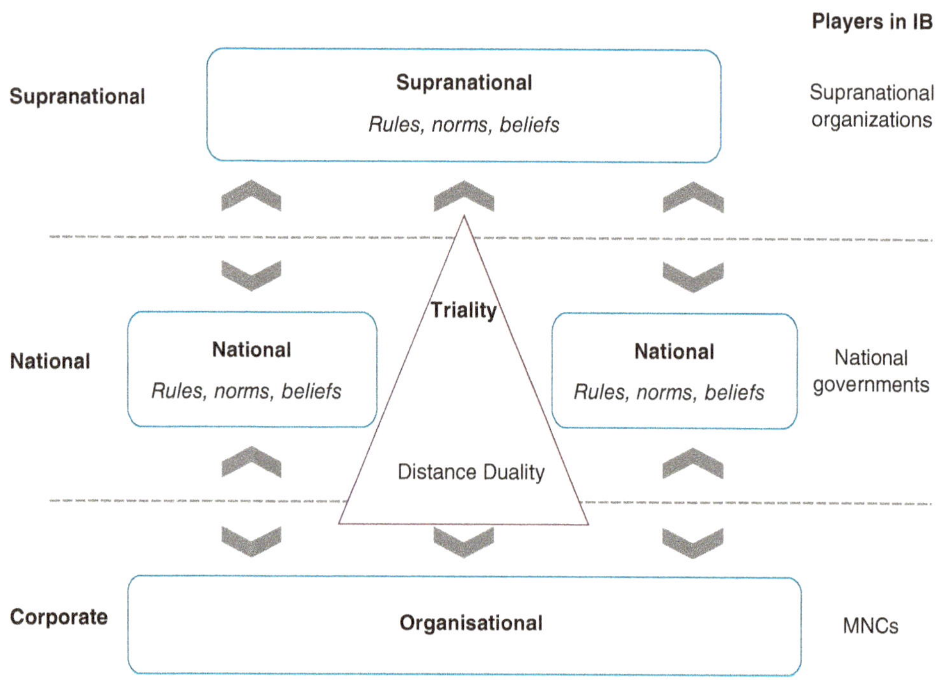

Figure 5.1 Institutional triality

Source: Based on Hartmann et al. (2022: 1296). CC BY 4.0

5.2 ORGANIZATIONS IN THE SUPRANATIONAL LANDSCAPE

5.2.1 Civil Society Organizations

There is growing recognition of the regulatory role that civil society organizations (CSOs) play in IB. CSOs encompass a wide range of non-governmental entities, including non-governmental organizations (NGOs), charities, trusts, foundations, advocacy groups, and national and international non-state associations. Examples range from Greenpeace and the Catholic Church to the British Medical Association. These organizations operate with autonomy and independence from the state, fostering public trust in their civic initiatives. Their primary objective is to influence governmental and corporate agenda-setting to incorporate and promote regulatory objectives. Operating as non-state actors on the international stage, they transcend national borders, exerting influence on various global issues. Their engagement in IB entails both collaboration and monitoring activities, positioning them as essential stakeholders in the global arena.

Over recent decades, the role of CSOs has gained prominence, driven by criticismof state dominance and the public's desire for more opportunities to participate. The collapse of communism, for example, created space for democratic norms, heightening expectations of transparency in international organizations. This is also reflected in the substantial increase in the number of CSOs, actively engaging in a wide range of topics, from environmental regulations to human rights. While CSOs historically faced difficulties in cooperating with governments and firms, attitudes have generally shifted positively. CSOs are now better connected and involved in policy debates, and MNCs are more willing to collaborate with them to improve sustainability practices and brand reputation, and to foster long-term stakeholder trust.

CSOs have been particularly active and involved in political debates and often act as influencers and monitors of laws and treaties. As supranational regulatory institutions, CSOs possess core competencies that make a significant contribution to shaping a responsible and sustainable business landscape:

- *Information gathering*: CSOs provide valuable information and analyses to influence both governments and firms. Through lobbying and advocacy, they encourage governments to implement stricter and more sustainable regulations, while also urging firms to adopt ethical and sustainable practices. Additionally, CSOs engage in monitoring and auditing activities, scrutinizing the effectiveness of state regulations and exposing instances of corporate misconduct through impactful reports and campaigns. This way, they shape public opinion and raise awareness of pressing issues.
- *Standard setting*: CSOs are actively involved in standard setting, contributing to the development and promotion of international standards and certification for responsible business conduct. Notable examples include Fair Trade certification

for ethical sourcing, Forest Stewardship Council certification for sustainable forestry, and certification related to labour, human rights, and environmental protection.

- *Behaviour modification*: CSOs engage in civil actions such as protests, press conferences, demonstrations, or organized petitions to modify behaviour and influence business and corporate agendas. In some cases, CSOs may resort to formal legal action to address instances of non-compliance with regulations.

Spotlight: The Role of CSOs in the Creation of Sustainability Reporting Standards

The discussion surrounding the reporting and control of international investment by MNCs offers valuable insights into the co-evolution of regulation, which has both national and supranational components and has to a large extent been driven by civil society organizations. ESG (environmental, social, and governance) investment gained traction in the early 2000s, notably with Unibanco in Brazil and Jupiter Asset Management in the UK, which provided ESG-focused investment services. While socially responsible investing (SRI) and avoiding 'sin-stocks' have historical roots dating back to the Quakers in the 1700s, the modern ESG discussion began with Unibanco and Jupiter Asset Management's activities in 2001 and 2002. Initially, the focus was on governance and social aspects, driven by pressure from industry pension funds, particularly in sectors like mining, which emphasized labour security standards and governance criteria.

In subsequent years, mainstream finance research and policy makers acknowledged the ESG trend, making the alignment of financial and ESG objectives a subject of active research in business studies. Up to this point, civil society organizations, private investors, and MNCs were instrumental in defining the standards and requirements that determined which investments were considered 'responsible' within the ESG framework.

As the urgency of climate action increased, the European Union (EU) took a leading role in formulating policies aimed at harnessing investment and MNC activities to achieve socially desirable outcomes. The EU's Non-Financial Reporting Directive in 2014 set the policy direction by outlining legally binding standards for ESG-related disclosures. This directive was soon followed by the United Nations' 2015 resolution on sustainable development, which enshrined the UN Sustainable Development Goals (SDGs) and the 2016 Paris Agreement. The EU commission recognized the need for the further development of reporting requirements and the definition of ecological sustainability, leading to the current central focus on the ecological dimension of ESG investments.

With the introduction of the EU taxonomy for sustainable activities, the European Commission outlined what qualifies as sustainable investment and adjusted reporting requirements accordingly. This taxonomy directive was collaboratively created by a technical expert group, which included industry representatives from the earlier ESG initiatives.

As these discussions unfolded, the investment community continued its shift towards sustainable investment. While mainstream investors still prioritize ESG factors, a significant subset of the financial market, as well as several investor networks and shared-interest communities, have transitioned to impact investing, which goes beyond the 'do-no-harm' perspective of ESG to a 'do-good' perspective. Impact investors see investment as a tool to drive positive change and are willing to forego a portion of their profits to achieve their impact goals. They criticize the EU's legalistic approach for being slow to implement changes and lagging behind market trends.

While it remains to be seen how effective the ESG perspective (or impact perspective) are in aligning social and financial interests, it is clear that for the way forward we will need supranationally valid rules and norms, and it will require initiatives that come not from top-down regulation via policy but from bottom-up initiatives for self-regulation to obtain sufficient momentum to find answers that are useful for MNCs while still focusing on the necessary social goals.

Sources: IBM (www.ibm.com/blog/environmental-social-and-governance-history); Forbes (www.forbes.com/sites/betsyatkins/2020/06/08/demystifying-esgits-history--current-status); European Parliamentary Research Service (www.europarl.europa.eu/RegData/etudes/BRIE/2021/654213/EPRS_BRI%282021%29654213_EN.pdf)

Despite their potential to foster ethical development and norms of citizenship, CSOs also face certain concerns. For instance, there is a geographical disparity, with a majority of CSOs located in the north and west, while their activities are often focused on poorer nations in the south and east. Moreover, the regulation of CSOs raises questions, as they are generally less subject to public scrutiny than government bodies. The source of funding can pose a conflict of interest for CSOs, particularly when funding comes from public authorities or large corporations, potentially affecting their independence and positive impact. Furthermore, CSOs are connected to the disruption of business activities, which damages society's trust in them. For instance, protests and demonstrations might disrupt supply chains or transportation routes, which can create challenges for some industries and society more generally.

5.2.2 International Economic Organizations: the World Trade Organization, the International Monetary Fund, and the World Bank

There are supranational institutions that play a key role in underpinning the world trading system by reducing trade barriers, promoting fair competition, and resolving trade disputes. Here we shed light on three of the most important international economic organizations, namely the World Trade Organization (WTO), the International Monetary Fund (IMF), and the World Bank. These institutions help ensure that businesses can access foreign markets and compete on a level playing field.

The WTO is an internationally active organization that deals with the global rules of trade between nations. In 1995, it updated the General Agreement on Tariffs and Trade (GATT). At the end of August 2024 the WTO had 166 members, accounting for more than 90% of world trade value. Like the GATT, the WTO provides a forum for member countries to negotiate and set trade agreements, resolve disputes, and promote fair and open international trade with the objective of raising living standards in member states. The WTO's key principles are non-discrimination (i.e., trading advantages need to become multilateral via extension to all nations), progressive reduction in tariff and non-tariff barriers, and solving of trade disputes through consultation rather than retaliation (i.e., sanctions). Moreover, it aims to ensure that trade rules are transparent and predictable, fostering a stable and conducive environment for businesses to engage in cross-border trade. The WTO has the ability to enforce compliance, using a streamlined disputes procedure with provision for appeals and binding arbitration. In summary, the WTO is the primary international organization responsible for regulating global trade and promoting open, fair, and predictable trade practices among its member countries.

Since 1946, the IMF has been an international financial institution that aims to promote financial stability and global monetary cooperation. While it had only 39 members at the outset, the organization had grown to 191 member states by November 2024. Its role is to provide financial assistance and economic policy advice to member countries that face economic crises or balance of payment problems. It lends to countries in temporary financial difficulties, monitors the global economy, and provides technical assistance to developing countries. The IMF plays a key role in stabilizing exchange rates via foreign currency provision and other sources of world liquidity, targeting international trade and payments growth. They have also helped restore market confidence in struggling countries via standby credits. Interestingly, there are two new financial institutions competing with the IMF: the New Development Bank (NDB) created by the BRIC economies and the Contingent Reserve Arrangement (CRA), which can be seen as a challenge to US and European dominance in establishing rules for global trade.

Lastly, the World Bank is an international financial organization that provides financial and technical assistance to large development projects in developing countries with the goal of reducing poverty. Its primary focus is on funding projects related to transportation infrastructure, agricultural irrigation, education, healthcare, and other key areas of economic development. The World Bank consists of the International Bank for Reconstruction and Development, the International Development Association, and the International Finance Corporation. While the World Bank traditionally had a public sector focus (i.e., governments), it has recently also shifted towards the private sector. For instance, it creates new investment opportunities for businesses to access new markets by giving grants that improve financial services to small- and medium-sized enterprises (SMEs) in the world's poorest countries.

Such international financial organizations play a vital role in stabilizing exchange rates, managing currency crises, and providing financial assistance to countries in need. However, criticism has been levelled at the disproportionate benefits for developed countries, which lead to global economic imbalances. Free trade areas may result in trade from efficient external suppliers being diverted to less competitive internal suppliers, hampering global competitiveness. Concerns also arise over the impact on national sovereignty due to trade rules limiting a country's regulatory autonomy. Furthermore, civil society organizations question the lack of transparency and accountability in international trade institutions, especially regarding environmental issues, and this results in protests and resistance.

5.3 REGIONAL ECONOMIC INTEGRATION

Economic integration can be defined as an agreement whereby two or more countries remove economic barriers and provide reciprocal preferential access to their markets. Trade agreements are the simplest form of economic integration, reducing tariffs on specific products between participating countries and opening new possibilities for trade and investment. When more than two countries (but not all countries) engage in economic integration, we consider the initiative a step towards regional integration. Countries have a variety of reasons for engaging in a higher level of regional economic integration, often economic and political.

5.3.1 Economic Reasons

Economic reasons include:

- Stimulating trade with integration partners through the free flow of goods, capital, people, and ideas
- Increasing the export competitiveness of domestic producers
- Attracting more investors through increased credibility and a better investment climate
- Establishing new value chains among partners for regionally sourced goods.

5.3.2 Political Reasons

Political reasons include:

- Building trust among countries that have been involved in wars or conflicts
- Tackling common challenges, such as threats to the environment, migration, and organised crime
- Countries with large market sizes (e.g. USA, Japan) rewarding their key strategic partners
- Providing alternatives to address difficulties in negotiating global agreements
- Increasing the bargaining power of countries by enabling them to speak with one voice.

As integration between the countries progresses, economic, social, monetary, and fiscal policies become interlinked as well. However, there is still a large difference between countries and regions in terms of their level of integration. For example, in Europe integration has already been achieved to a large extent and most factors of production move freely between countries. However, in other regions, especially in the developing world, integration is not yet as advanced, and economies are less interlinked.

MNCs are some of the key drivers of regional economic integration, as they can produce more efficiently for a regional than a domestic market, taking advantage of economies of scale and scope effects. A higher level of regional integration may thus increase the number of potential customers they can reach. At the same time, MNCs can act as a push factor for advancing integration through government lobbying to remove barriers between the home country and markets where their principal manufacturing plants and suppliers are located.

International managers must understand the regional context in which their business is embedded and adapt their strategy to the impact that various levels of economic integration have on their competitive advantage. For example, when companies face high tariffs in a market where competitors enter duty free because of the existence of trade agreements, this may impact the location choice of supply chains or manufacturing.

At the same time, firms have to be familiar with the 'rules of the game' defined by supranational organizations such as the WTO, which set out the boundaries for regional economic integration and trade. WTO agreements have achieved significant progress in recent years to reduce barriers to trade, yet this is not the case for all sectors, such as agriculture. Additionally, recent disagreements between countries have caused trade wars and spikes in trade protectionism can have a wide-ranging impact on firms.

5.4 THEORY OF REGIONAL INTEGRATION

Economic integration develops in distinct stages, from a loose connection between countries and economies towards closer economic union. These stages can be classified as a hierarchy, whereby each level incorporates all the provisions of the lower level of integration. However, it is not always the case that relationships between partners start at the lowest level or that they will eventually progress to more integration (Balassa, 1961).

- A free trade area is created in an agreement to remove or reduce tariffs on goods and services traded among countries (see Figure 5.2). Members retain their autonomy to conduct trade with countries outside of the agreement and join other free trade areas.

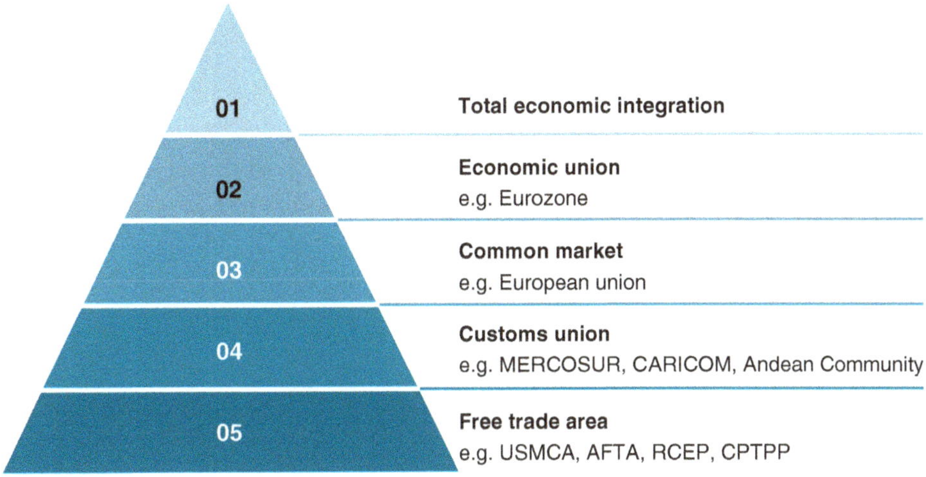

Figure 5.2 The degrees of regional integration

- A customs union regulates trade policies with respect to imports from non-member countries. Countries within the customs union define a common level of external tariffs on all non-member products.
- A common market permits free movement of people and capital across member states, which requires additional collaboration among countries through inter-governmental institutions.
- An economic union harmonises economic policies among member states, eliminating discrimination and removing regulatory differences between them.
- Total economic integration is reached when supranational institutions replace national ministries and can take binding decisions on behalf of all member states.

The original model by Balassa (1961) has since been expanded to include additional stages of economic integration, which can be hierarchically integrated interchangeably (Molle, 1997; Robson, 1998; Crowley, 2006).

- A monetary union uses a common currency which is controlled by a single, supranational central bank.
- A fiscal union includes the harmonisation of taxes among members and the fiscal sovereignty of a supranational body.
- A political union includes an effective and democratic body at a supranational level.

To advance in the integration process, the relationship between countries has to be cohesive, which means that there is a shared interest in achieving a common goal through integration. The more converging interests there are, the more ambitious an integration project can become. On the other hand, when there is little cohesion between states, countries are likely to agree on a lower level of integration instead. This may be because of strong domestic pressures against integration by groups who feel disadvantaged. Additionally, regional integration also inevitably leads to a loss of autonomy, which is often unpopular with domestic voters and represents another barrier for closer collaboration.

5.4.1 Free Trade Area

The free trade area is the most commonly used economic integration instrument. It is achieved by signing trade agreements. There are two types of trade agreement.

- **Regional trade agreements (RTAs)** are reciprocal trade agreements between two or more parties to liberalize trade in goods or services.
- **Preferential trade agreements (PTAs)** are unilateral trade agreements where developed countries can provide favourable market access to imports from developing and less developed countries.

In addition, mega-regional trade agreements have emerged with several unique characteristics as a distinct form of RTA. Characteristics of mega-RTAs include:

- Countries from more than one geographical region
- Member economies that account for a significant share of global trade
- Rules and content that go substantially beyond what countries have committed to in the WTO.

As of July 2023, there were 360 RTAs and PTAs in force, representing a fourfold growth since 2001 (WTO, 2023a). The reasons for this increase can firstly be attributed to the failure to reform the multilateral trade system that has remained largely unchanged since 1995 because of the failure to agree on the closing of the WTO Doha Round and all subsequent negotiations. This has directed countries to seek new forms of collaboration on trade liberalization. This recent shift has also been driven by multinational firms becoming increasingly dissatisfied with the way in which GATT and WTO agreements address the new reality of global value chains. As goods and components are increasingly produced and sourced across the world, under the existing rules they still need to be certified simultaneously in multiple countries, which increases administrative burdens (Bown, 2017). Many of the more recent RTAs therefore seek to unify regulatory requirements among like-minded countries. This is because it would be much more difficult to find a consensus on these aspects in the multilateral WTO context where all member states need to agree.

Case Study: The United States-Mexico-Canada Agreement

The United States-Mexico-Canada Agreement (USMCA) came into force in 2020 and replaced the North American Free Trade Agreement (NAFTA). It was negotiated to modernize and update NAFTA, addressing various issues relating to trade and commerce among the three countries. It preserves the majority of NAFTA's structure that permits North American manufacturers to compete in international markets effectively and supports the digital economy through protection of intellectual property and copyright (Gantz, 2018). The agreement was signed by the leaders of the three countries on 30 November 2018 and was subsequently ratified by each country's legislature, coming into force on 1 July 2020.

Among the significant achievements of the USMCA is the enhancement of labour rights, particularly in Mexico, through provisions aimed at improving worker conditions and wages. The agreement also includes stronger environmental protection and more stringent intellectual property rules. The USMCA has facilitated smoother trade and investment flows among the three countries, contributing to economic growth and stability in the region. Another notable achievement is the successful implementation of automotive rules of origin, which require a higher percentage of North American-made parts in vehicles to qualify for tariff-free status. This has encouraged the development of the regional automotive industry and secured jobs.

However, the USMCA has faced several challenges. Supply chain disruptions, exacerbated by the Covid-19 pandemic, have posed significant hurdles, impacting the flow of goods and services. Disputes over dairy market access between the US and Canada, as well as disagreements on labour rights enforcement and digital trade, have also arisen. Additionally, concerns about the environmental impact of increased trade and ongoing adjustments to the new rules have created friction among the member countries. Despite these challenges, the USMCA remains a critical framework for North American trade relations.

Sources: Brookings (www.brookings.edu/articles/strengthening-usmca-and-north-americas-economic-cooperation) and Office of the United States Trade Representative (https://ustr.gov/trade-agreements/free-trade-agreements/united-states-mexico-canada-agreement/agreement-between)

Spotlight: Mega-RTA

Taking effect in 2018, the Comprehensive and Progressive Agreement for Trans-Pacific Partnership (CPTPP) is a free trade agreement signed by seven Asia-Pacific countries and four countries from the Americas plus the United Kingdom. Members seek to eliminate almost all tariff and import charges on each other's products. It includes obligations on food, environmental protection, the digital economy, financial services, and other sectors.

(Continued)

The Regional Comprehensive Economic Partnership (RCEP) is the world's largest free trade area, launched in January 2022. The signatory states include the 10 AFTA member countries, in addition to Australia, New Zealand, Japan, South Korea, and China. In total, they account for over 30% of global GDP. Under the agreement, members are required to phase out tariffs on determined goods, but requirements are not as comprehensive as under the CPTPP. Additionally, RCEP does not include regulations on the support of state-owned enterprises, labour issues and environmental protection (Schott, 2023).

Sources: United States Trade Representative (https://ustr.gov/tpp/overview-of-the-TPP) and Australian Government Department of Foreign Affairs and Trade (www.dfat.gov.au/trade/agreements/in-force/rcep)

The Transatlantic Trade and Investment Partnership (TTIP) is a trade and investment agreement being negotiated between the European Union and the United States. Negotiations began in 2013. However, since the withdrawal of the US by the Trump administration, there have been no new rounds of negotiations, and TTIP's future looks uncertain.

Spotlight: PTA

The Organization of African, Caribbean and Pacific States (OACPS) comprises 79 countries and strives to achieve sustainable development of its members and advance their integration into the world economy. The OACPS preferential trade agreement (PTA) with the European Union is one of the most comprehensive partnerships for cooperation between developed and developing countries, covering 1.5 billion people over four continents.

The relationship between the EU and the (formerly named) African, Caribbean, and Pacific Group, goes back to 1975 and includes many former European colonies. In April 2021, both parties signed a new agreement covering a wide range of issues, from sustainable development and growth to human rights, peace, and security. The agreement is built on highly preferential trade access to the EU market around three key areas: political dialogue, development cooperation, and regional integration and trade. OACPS countries also receive development aid entitlements to eradicate poverty and strengthen their industrialization and economic development.

Source: OACPS (www.oacps.org/about-us)

5.4.2 Customs Union

Customs unions go beyond the removal of tariffs, as countries adopt a common set of rules. Additionally, trade agreements between customs unions and third countries are not negotiated individually, but as a block. This comes at the cost of autonomy in establishing their own foreign economic policies and such agreements are therefore often more difficult to negotiate than RTAs or PTAs as diverse special interests have to be accommodated. This is a reason why by August 2023 only 18 customs unions had been notified to the

WTO (WTO, 2023b). Additionally, in many of the existing agreements, countries had difficulties finding consensus on a common set of external tariffs, which is why custom unions do not always apply to all of its members' products.

Examples of Customs Unions

The Mercado Común del Sur (MERCOSUR) is the largest trade bloc in Latin America. It was founded in 1991 with the intention of creating a common market, strengthening democracy and spurring economic development. Member states include Argentina, Brazil, Paraguay, and Uruguay. Its highest decision-making body is the Common Market Council, which provides a forum for economic and foreign ministries of the member states, with the presidency rotating every six months among its members. It also has one permanent institution with limited authority, the administrative secretariat located in Montevideo, Uruguay. MERCOSUR has signed several trade agreements with outside countries, for example India, and the European Union.

The Andean Community includes the South American countries Bolivia, Colombia, Ecuador, and Peru and seeks to foster the development of the region. A free trade area was formed in 1992 which evolved into an imperfect customs union. Since 1997, the council of Presidents and Foreign Ministers has had a critical role in decision making and strengthening the integration of the bloc (Communidad Andina, 2021).

The Caribbean Community (CARICOM) is one of the oldest surviving regional integration movements including developing countries and stretches from the Bahamas to Suriname, the majority of its members being island states with relatively small populations. The objectives of the grouping include economic integration, the coordination of foreign policy mechanisms, human and social development as well as cooperation on security matters (CARICOM, 2023).

5.4.3 Common Market and Economic Union

Spotlight: GDPR and Global Data Protection

The General Data Protection Regulation (GDPR), implemented by the European Union (EU) in May 2018, is a comprehensive framework designed to protect the personal data and privacy of individuals within the EU. The GDPR sets strict guidelines for how personal data should be collected, processed, stored, and transferred. Key provisions include the requirement for explicit consent for data processing, the right for individuals to access and delete their data, mandatory data breach notifications, and significant penalties for non-compliance.

Although the GDPR technically applies only within Europe, its impact has been global. The regulation applies to any company, regardless of location, that processes

(Continued)

the personal data of EU residents. This extraterritorial reach means that businesses worldwide must comply with GDPR if they handle the data of EU citizens. As a result, many multinational companies have adopted GDPR standards across all their operations to avoid the complexity of maintaining different data protection regimes.

GDPR has effectively set a high benchmark for data protection, influencing legislation in other jurisdictions. For instance, the California Consumer Privacy Act (CCPA) in the United States, which grants similar rights to California residents, was inspired by GDPR principles. Other countries, including Brazil, Japan, and South Korea, have also enacted or updated their data protection laws to align more closely with GDPR standards, recognizing the need for robust data privacy frameworks in a globally connected economy.

The introduction of GDPR has led to increased awareness and prioritization of data protection and privacy issues. Organizations have invested in enhancing their data governance practices, improving transparency, and ensuring better security measures to protect personal data. The GDPR has also encouraged the development of new technologies and services aimed at ensuring compliance, such as privacy management software and data protection consultancy services.

Sources: European Union (https://gdpr.eu/what-is-gdpr) and State of California Department of Justice (https://oag.ca.gov/privacy/ccpa)

The EU is so far the only regional organization that has advanced to the third and fourth stage of regional economic integration. It is currently an economic and monetary union (EMU) with its single market characterized by the four freedoms of movement, namely goods, services, labour, and capital. A majority of members are part of the area of free movement of people (Schengen) and have adopted the Euro as a common currency. A common budget is in place that finances a substantial number of programmes, for example in joint research, agriculture and promoting economic, social and territorial cohesion among member states. Similar to nation-state institutions, the European Council has the capacity to decide on laws and the European Parliament is composed of citizen-elected representatives. Additionally, the EU Commission has the right to propose legislation and acts as a guardian of EU treaties.

In terms of trade policy, the EU has sole competence over the customs union and also represents member states' interests at the WTO and in trade agreement negotiations. While there is complete integration in economic terms, it remains an incomplete Union in a number of respects, such as foreign and security policy. What limits European integration is a combination of resistance from EU members and concerns about democratic legitimacy.

Case Study: The EU's Agricultural Policy

The European Union's Common Agricultural Policy (CAP) has been in place since 1962 with the aim of improving agricultural productivity and securing a stable supply of affordable food for consumers. Additionally, it seeks to help tackle issues relating to climate change, the management of sustainable resources, and promoting jobs in the rural economy. The CAP is an example of the harmonization of economic policies among EU members, as it is managed and funded at European level from the resources of the EU's budget. In 2019, EU support for farmers amounted to 57 billion euros, approximately 35% of its total budget. The CAP budget is directed to three main areas:

1. Direct financial support for farmers to ensure income stability and remunerate environmentally friendly farming and the provision of public services, such as taking care of the countryside.
2. Market measures to stabilize prices of staple food and prevent sudden drops in demand due to a health scare or temporary oversupply.
3. National and regional rural development programmes to address specific challenges that rural areas are facing.

The EU is also the world's largest agricultural food exporter and importer and plays an important role in international agricultural markets. In this respect, its geographical indicators (GI) quality scheme is an important instrument, which aims to protect the names and origins of agricultural products and promote their unique characteristics and the traditional know-how of agricultural producers. The recognition enables consumers to trust and distinguish quality products. Additionally, producers can better market their products with the use of protected indicators, taking advantage of the reputation linked to the production territory. Its registry includes over 3,600 food, wine, and spirit products that are protected under this scheme.

In international trade, indicators are treated as intellectual property and are therefore legally protected against imitation and misuse within the EU and in non-EU countries where a protection agreement has been signed. On a multilateral level, the EU is also active in improving the protection of GIs globally. Names of products from countries outside of the EU, such as Colombia or South Africa have also been protected under this scheme. In summary, GIs are an important tool, alongside the CAP, for the EU to strengthen the role of the agricultural sector in its member states and beyond as well as secure the sector's future competitiveness.

Sources: European Commission (n.d.)

Case Study Questions

1. What are the different political reasons underlying strong support for farmers in the EU?
2. What is the role of specialization and exporting for small subsistence farmers in the Global South?
3. How do other countries or supranational institutions support farming?

5.4.4 Non-Hierarchical Integration

There are several other regional integration mechanisms located outside of the pyramid presented in Figure 5.2. These are mostly non-binding forums and organizations that serve as a platform for countries with like-minded interests to meet and interact regularly.

Spotlight: APEC and OPEC

Asia-Pacific Economic Cooperation (APEC) is a minimalist economic and trade forum for the Pacific Rim countries and among others includes Australia, China, the United States, and Russia. Commitments are undertaken on a voluntary basis and there are no binding treaties or obligations. Leaders of APEC member countries meet annually to set the vision for overarching initiatives. Its goals are to ensure that goods, services, investment, and people can move more easily across borders, a favourable business climate is maintained and regulations as well as standards are aligned. It also serves as a forum to allow members to deal with important new challenges to the region's economic well-being such as pandemics and disaster resilience.

The Organisation of the Petroleum Exporting Countries (OPEC) is a bloc of thirteen oil-rich member states in the Middle East, Africa, and South America, headquartered in Vienna. It controls close to 40% of global oil production, which has made it possible for the bloc to act as a cartel and coordinate production levels among members to influence global oil prices. Delegations meet at regular and emergency meetings, usually led by the oil minister of each member country. At the same time, a secretary-general is appointed to lead the organisation's day-to-day management.

Sources: Asia-Pacific Economic Cooperation (www.apec.org/about-us/about-apec) and Organisation of the Petroleum Exporting Countries (www.opec.org/opec_web/en/about_ us/24.htm)

5.5 COSTS AND BENEFITS OF REGIONAL ECONOMIC INTEGRATION

Trade agreements provide several challenges and opportunities to the multilateral trading system. The economics literature argues that two distinct trade effects can occur as a result of deeper economic integration between countries (Viner, 1950; IMF, 1992):

1 *Trade creation*: Imports of goods from a regional partner displace goods previously produced domestically at a relatively higher cost, and can no longer compete once tariffs are removed.

2 *Trade diversion*: Imports of goods from a regional partner displace those previously sourced from outside the regional agreement. Companies in non-member countries are no longer competitive when tariffs on trade between members are applied.

The larger the regional group, the higher the chance that it can divert substantial amounts of trade from suppliers outside the region and create positive effects for all members. However, regional integration and the increasing number of RTAs also draws criticism from various sides:

- Trade agreements are discriminatory in nature as they create winners and losers, providing preferences to insiders at the expense of outsiders (Bown, 2017).
- Trade agreements and the creation of distinct blocs distort the global economy, often at the expense of developing countries (Bown, 2017).
- Trade agreements lead to a 'race to the bottom' in terms of wages and employment conditions, with labour-intensive manufacturing jobs in high-wage countries being threatened, exploiting low-paid workers in developing countries.
- Trade agreements mark the declining importance of a universal, rules-based system while many of the twenty-first century's challenges cannot be solved by unilateral actions.
- Trade agreements lead to more complexity – trade increases, but with a 'spaghetti bowl' effect as countries are part of numerous agreements, all with their own set of tariffs, rules, and regulations (Bhagwati, 1995).
- Trade agreements increase protectionism, artificially making companies within regionally integrated areas more competitive than they would be in free markets where the same rules apply to all countries.

5.6 TRADE BARRIERS AND RULES

The WTO sets the 'rules of the game' for regional economic integration through a rules-based system for trade between countries as well as the settlement of disputes. A key article that governs the barriers to trade is the WTO's most favoured nation (MFN) principle (Article I, GATT). The article enforces non-discrimination between foreign and domestic producers where goods produced abroad are not to be treated less favourably than those of national origin. Thus, in principle, every time a country lowers a trade barrier, it has to do so for all other WTO members as well. Some important exceptions are in place that cover the establishment of economic integration and free trade areas to which the MFN principle does not apply:

- Article XXIV of the GATT establishes conditions for the creation of free trade agreements and customs unions for trade in goods.
- The GATT Enabling Clause is the legal basis for the establishment of preferential trade agreements (PTA) where developed countries can establish non-reciprocal preferential treatment with zero or low duties on imports.

International trade has largely been liberalized owing to the reduction of trade barriers under the MFN principle and the increasing numbers of regional and preferential trade agreements. However, there are still three major types of restriction (Figure 5.3) that companies face when trading internationally:

- *Tariffs*: Custom duties on merchandise imports providing a price advantage to domestic producers over foreign ones and raising taxes for governments
- *Non-tariff measures (NTMs)*: Policy measures other than tariffs that can potentially affect international trade, changing quantities traded, or prices, or both
- Rules of origin: Criteria for preferential market access based on the geographical origin of a product.

Tariffs are applied to a substantial share of trade. Tariff barriers differ substantially across countries and even within the same region. Many developing countries' exports, especially in Latin America and Africa, face relatively high tariffs because often they are agricultural products, which are excluded from most MFN tariff agreements (UNCTAD, 2022).

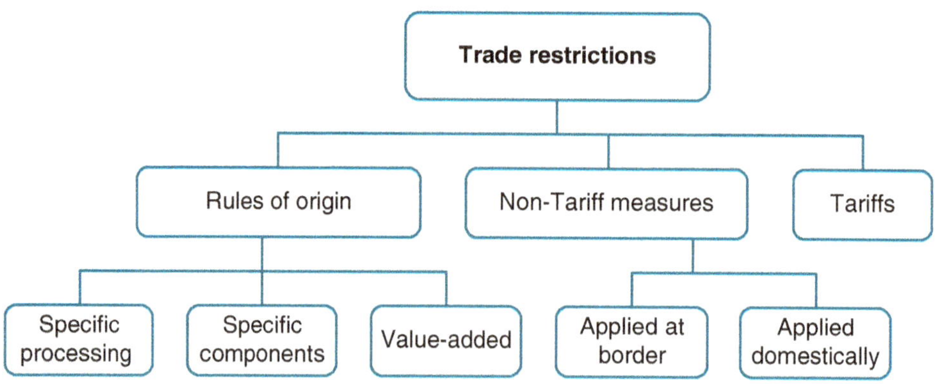

Figure 5.3 Trade restrictions

The use of non-tariff measures (NTMs)can in practice take several forms. Firstly, they can be applied at the border through imports and exports of products. They might include quotas, prohibitions, export subsidies or burdensome custom procedures and administration fees. A second category of NTMs are those applied in the domestic economy through domestic legislation covering health, technical, product, labour, or environmental standards or internal taxes or charges and domestic subsidies (Staiger, 2012).

The measurement of NTMs is much more complex than tariffs due to differences between countries and the difficulty of establishing their practical impact. Another difference is that the NTMs do not necessarily have a negative impact on international trade. They are also important regulatory and quality assurance instruments, whose importance has increased in recent years, because of growing consumer concerns about food safety and environmental protection.

For example, sanitary and phytosanitary measures (SPS) are intended to protect the health of humans, animals, and plant populations in a country or region. They can positively affect consumer demand, as they guarantee the quality of a product, and enhance trust in both foreign and domestic producers (Disdier & Fugazza, 2019).

Rules of origin determine whether products qualify for reduced tariffs in a free trade area or receive MFN treatment. They are therefore a critical component of all RTAs and PTAs to enable trade diversion to the members that are part of a free trade area. Because free trade areas do not have a common external tariff, countries do not want non-members to exploit benefits provided by the agreement. For example, non-member countries could send goods into the free trade area through the country with the lowest tariff and subsequently exploit the provisions of the agreement to access other members' markets. This would lead to a loss of tariff revenue for economies with higher tariffs. Rules of origin in practice can take several forms:

- *Value-added criterion*: A pre-determined percentage of the export value of a product must have been generated within the free trade area.
- *Specific components criterion*: Pre-determined parts of a finished good must have been manufactured within the free trade area for reduced tariffs to apply.
- *Specific processing criterion*: A pre-determined number of stages of the production process of an exported good must have been undertaken within the free trade area.

Case Study: The Automotive Sector in Mexico and USMCA

The automotive industry is one of the sectors most dependent on highly complex global value chains with extended flows of intermediate goods, information, and knowledge between production locations. It is currently being transformed by new technologies and consumer preferences, such as autonomous driving and electric vehicles (EVs).

Mexico is the largest car producer in Latin America and has unique advantages to benefit from these trends that could make it central to the transition to EVs and help countries achieve their climate goals and reduce greenhouse gas emissions. In this

(Continued)

respect, it benefits from its proximity to the US, one of the largest car consumer markets in the world, with a comparatively well-established transportation and communication infrastructure and existing automotive clusters, especially in the north of the country.

The advanced level of regional integration between the three North American countries through the USMCA agreement has also played an important role in the industry's success and is a key driver for companies deciding to invest in the automotive sector. With the implementation of the USMCA trade agreement, new rules of origin require a specific amount of North American content in the final vehicle to qualify for duty-free treatment. The regional value-added criterion was raised to 75% for passenger vehicles and light trucks. Specific component criteria are also in place, as a majority of steel and aluminium purchases have to originate in North America.

To avoid paying tariffs, car makers must thus reconfigure the region's models and range of cars, which increases investment in Mexico. As a result, parallel supplier networks are also being created, from mining of critical minerals, to battery cell and microchip production.

In this respect, the president of Stellantis, a leading global carmaker, mentioned that 'Mexico is unique, because we already have a developed market providing electrification, that is the United States (...) this is a time of decisions regarding how to expand the manufacturing sector of batteries assembly and electric motors.' Furthermore, the CEO of General Motors Mexico highlighted that 'while the combustion engine is currently driving the automotive industry, in the next few years it will be electric vehicles under the USMCA'. During the Tesla investor day in early 2023, CEO Elon Musk announced that 'the next Tesla gigafactory will be in Mexico, near Monterrey (...) this comes at the heels of the US Inflation Reduction Act, which grants tax credits for EV purchases'.

The opportunities brought along by the transformation of the automotive sector are therefore a significant opportunity for Mexico to replace inexpensive labour and a devalued currency as the main reasons to invest in the country. Investment in research and development and infrastructure will be necessary to ride this new wave of technological change and create an innovative economy. The country can then not only be a model for other developing countries seeking to upgrade their manufacturing capabilities, but also for the positive effects brought about by regional integration.

Sources: Flores, 2022; USTR, 2022; UBS, 2023

Case Study Questions

1. How do trade restrictions affect the investment patterns of multinational companies?
2. How have companies from outside the USMCA reacted to the agreement in terms of locating their investment?
3. Do you think the creation of USMCA will lead to deeper regional integration in North America?

5.7 DISPUTE SETTLEMENT

In order to enforce the MFN principle and other WTO rules in the context of disagreement among members, there is a dispute settlement mechanism. It represents the central pillar of the multilateral trade system and provides a unique stability mechanism for trade and economic integration, where common rules can be enforced. It has a similar function to a tribunal – if a country believes that a fellow member is violating a WTO agreement, they have to settle under this system. This prevents countries from taking action unilaterally, with unpredictable consequences for world trade. The dispute settlement consists of several stages (WTO, 2023c):

1. Countries enter into consultation to see if they can settle the dispute among themselves.
2. An ad hoc panel of independent trade experts is appointed to rule on the case.
3. The panel issues its findings, each side being able to appeal.
4. The standing WTO Appellate Body issues a final verdict on the case, upholding, modifying, or reversing the panel's findings.
5. The losing member of the dispute is given a reasonable amount of time to implement the verdict or agree to financial compensation.
6. If consensus cannot be reached, the complaining side can retaliate, usually by raising import tariffs on products from the country that is in breach of agreements.

Case Study: US-China Trade War

In June 2015, the Chinese government published its new industrial strategy named 'Made in China 2025' (MIC 2025) to massively upgrade the country's manufacturing capabilities and technology-intensive industries. After launching a wide range of investigations on MIC 2025 as well as other Chinese schemes, and with the political will to reduce the large trade deficit between the two countries, the United States decided to react by increasing tariffs on Chinese products in various sectors.

Battleground 1, Solar Panels and Washing Machines

The US concluded that imports of solar panels and washing machines caused injury to its domestic manufacturers worth US$8.5 billion. In response to the allegations of harming US manufacturers, China self-initiated anti-dumping duty investigations on US sorghum exports and introduced retaliatory tariffs of 178%.

(Continued)

Battleground 2, Steel and Aluminium

The US regarded deficits from imports of steel and aluminium as threatening its national security and imposed tariffs on all trading partners of 25% on steel and 15% on aluminium. China responded with retaliatory tariffs on US aluminium waste, pork, fruits, and nuts worth US$2.4 billion.

Battleground 3, Technology and Intellectual Property

Because of what the US perceived as unfair trade practices in technology transfer, intellectual property, and innovation, it imposed 25% tariffs on intermediate inputs from China of up to US$34 billion. In response, China introduced tariffs of US$34 billion on goods including soya beans and vehicles. The US then announced that it would subsidise its farmers with up to US$12 billion to compensate for lost sales.

Consequences

Because neither side can win a trade war, the strategy is often to inflict greater losses on the other side. In this respect, China is in a more vulnerable position due to its large trade surpluses with the US. In 2018 and 2019 alone, the US imposed tariffs on about US$350 billion worth of Chinese imports and China retaliated, in accordance with WTO rules, by levying tariffs on an additional US$100 billion worth of imports.

Higher steel prices (Battleground 2) raised the taxable earnings of steel firms by US$2.4 billion but also pushed up costs by US$5.6 billion. The import restrictions added 8,700 jobs in the US steel industry, but each additional job cost steel consumers an extra US$650,000. If the steel companies had used their extra earnings on investment into new technologies it would have increased productivity and allowed them to sustain the creation of new jobs. History shows that protected industries do not tend to prosper and often fail to become more competitive in the market.

The trade war eased and some of the tariffs were lifted after 2022. However, in 2022 US tariffs on imports from China remained well below pre-trade war levels, as China was then the source of only 18% of US imports, compared to 22% before the trade war. With the second Trump administration, the trade war has flared up again and it remains to be seen where the role of global trade for the global economy is heading.

Sources: CSIS (www.csis.org/analysis/made-china-2025) and Peterson Institute for International Economics (www.piie.com/blogs/trade-and-investment-policy-watch/2018/trumps-trade-war-timeline-date-guide)

Case Study Questions

1 What role do companies from the EU play in the US-China trade war?
2 How much influence do you think Chinese and US companies respectively have on policy decisions in the two countries?
3 Do you think the trade war will increase or decrease innovation in the two countries? Why?

5.8 INSTITUTIONAL DISTANCE

To complete the 'institutional triality' in which MNCs operate, we also need to look into institutional distance. The idea underlying institutional distance is that differences in national institutions, which are not bridged by supranational institutions, will create difficulties for MNCs, because bridging such differences will be costly. The cultural differences we mentioned earlier, including language differences, provide good examples of why it is a challenge, even for some of the largest and most successful MNCs in the world, to operate in two (or more) areas that are substantially different.

There are several approaches to categorizing institutional distance. The CAGE framework is maybe the most prominent in business schools. It analyses distances between an organization's home country and the focal host country along cultural, administrative, geographic, and economic dimensions. The framework was developed by Pankaj Ghemawat (2001) and helps organizations improve their understanding of the foreign market and identify opportunities for adaptation, localization, or international expansion strategies:

- *Cultural distance* refers to differences in language, ethnicity, religion, and social norms and values between two countries. The lack of connective ethnic or social networks may result in difficulties conducting business abroad due to miscommunication, misunderstanding, and difficulty in building trusting relationships with local stakeholders.
- *Administrative and political distance* involves differences in regulatory practices and legal systems, levels of corruption, and political stability. Often, such variations stem from a lack of shared colonial connections, religious links, or free trade agreements. Political hostilities and the absence of shared monetary or political association may increase the distance between two countries and thus create complexities and uncertainties for companies trying to navigate a foreign market.
- *Geographic distance* refers to the physical aspects of the distance between countries. Physical remoteness may mean a lack of common borders and waterway access, resulting in higher logistical costs and difficulties in communication. It also includes variations in time zones, climate, and market size.
- *Economic distance* relates to different household incomes, different levels of economic development and market knowledge, and different costs and quality of natural, financial, and human resources.

While the CAGE dimensions are still used a lot in business school teaching, academic research has recently made a lot of progress in understanding institutional distance, and in providing new data sources that academics and practitioners can use. The following two perspectives are particularly useful, and they come with data that is available at no cost through the respective research teams.

Heather Berry and colleagues (Berry et al., 2010) developed a set of nine dimensions of institutional distance, which together capture a lot of the variation that is relevant for global business. These dimensions draw on three theoretical perspectives that are central to cross-national distance.

The first theoretical perspective on cross-national distance, introduced by management scholar Richard Whitley in 1992, centres on the concept of 'national business systems'. This framework focuses on the particular arrangements of hierarchy–market relations that become institutionalized and relatively successful in specific contexts. Countries exhibit varying degrees of difference in terms of the characteristics of their business systems, encompassing economic, financial, and administrative practices. These differences have their origins in demographic, geographic, cultural, and political institutions, rendering some countries more distinct or distant from a given focal country. Such distinctions significantly influence managerial decisions.

The second important thrust in the literature on cross-national institutions relates to governance. National governance systems encompass the set of incentives, safeguards, and dispute-resolution processes used to regulate the activities of various corporate stakeholders, including owners (shareholders), managers, workers, creditors, suppliers, and customers. These governance systems trace their roots to administrative, legal, and political institutions that historically endow specific stakeholders with greater influence in particular countries. This tradition emphasizes a more limited set of institutional dimensions than the theory of business systems, but it shares the underlying logic of institutional variation that results in greater distances between countries. Governance dimensions also hold relevance for managerial decisions as firms need to establish relationships with stakeholders when operating in a specific country.

The third facet of the institutional approach to cross-national distance concerns national innovation systems, which represent configurations of institutions fostering the development of technology and innovation. A key tenet substantiated by this literature is that countries exhibit differences in their capacity to generate knowledge and their ability to leverage that knowledge through connections with other nations. These disparities in knowledge production and utilization impact managerial decisions and strategies, as they influence the potential for innovation and technological advancement within a given country.

From these theoretical perspectives Berry et al. (2010) developed nine dimensions of cross-national distance, which include a number of metrics for each of the dimensions (see Table 5.1).

The theory-grounded perspective in Berry et al. (2010) develops the discussion from the CAGE dimensions discussed above. The data they compute from their dimensions are available for free (upon registration) from the website: https://mgmt.wharton.upenn.edu/distance-data-downloads-guillen

Apart from drilling down into the respective dimensions of distance, research has also recently begun to search for an easily manageable and holistic measure of institutional distance. This remains a challenge, because aggregating the data necessary to obtain a holistic measure of institutional distance remains difficult. A recent publication made the first suggestion on how to solve the challenge. Lindner & Puck (2024) use machine learning methods to analyse financial markets and apply information theory to obtain a holistic measure of institutional distance, which uses

Table 5.1 Dimensions and components of institutional distance according to Berry et al. (2010)

Dimension of distance	Definition	Component variables
Economic	Differences in economic development and macroeconomic characteristics	• GDP per capita (2000 US$) • GDP deflator (% GDP) • Exports of goods and services (% GDP) • Imports of goods and services (% GDP)
Financial	Differences in financial sector development	• Domestic credit to private sector (% GDP) • Market capitalization of listed companies (% GDP) • Number of listed companies (per 1 million population)
Political	Differences in political stability, democracy, and trade bloc membership	• Policy-making uncertainty (political stability measured by considering independent institutional actors with the power to veto) • Democratic character (democracy score) • Size of the state (government consumption (% GDP)) • WTO member (membership of WTO (GATT before 1993)) • Regional trade agreement (dyadic membership in the same trade bloc)
Administrative	Differences in colonial ties, language, religion, and legal system	• Colonizer–colonized link (whether dyad shares a colonial tie) • Common language (% population that speak the same language in the dyad) • Common religion (% population that share the same religion in the dyad) • Legal system (whether dyad shares the same legal system)
Cultural	Differences in attitudes towards authority, trust, individuality, and importance of work and family	• Power distance (World Value Survey (WVS) questions on obedience and respect for authority) • Uncertainty avoidance (WVS questions on trusting people and job security) • Individualism (WVS questions on independence and the role of government in providing for its citizens) • Masculinity (WVS questions on the importance of family and work)
Demographic	Differences in demographic characteristics	• Life expectancy (life expectancy at birth, total (years)) • Birth rate (birth rate, crude (per 1000 people)) Population under 14 (population ages 0–14 (% of total)) • Population under 65 (population ages 65 and above (% of total))
Knowledge	Differences in patents and scientific production	• Patents (number of patents per 1 million population) • Scientific articles (number of scientific articles per 1 million population)
Connectedness	Differences in tourism and internet use	• International tourism expenditure (international tourism, expenditures (% GDP)) • International tourism receipts (international tourism, receipts (% GDP)) • Internet use (internet users per 1000 people)
Geographic	Great circle distance between geographic centre of countries	• Great circle distance (great circle distance between two countries according to the coordinates of the geographic centre of the countries)

financial markets as a means of aggregating the data on institutional distance that is relevant to MNCs. The measure they suggest – 'information distance' – measures the amount of information necessary to understand one economy if all information on another economy is available. Data on information distance is available at www.thomaslindner.info

5.9 CURRENT DEVELOPMENTS IN SUPRANATIONAL INSTITUTIONAL ENVIRONMENTS

5.9.1 Sustainable Development

For most of its history, the WTO focused discussions solely on the liberalization of trade, its members having little interest in issues of climate change and economic development. However, with countries having committed to climate targets, future regional integration agreements will play an important role in how countries can achieve sustainable development.

Much of the current debate in the WTO about sustainability focuses on 'policy space'. This can be described as the tension between economic integration and the need for countries to manage their economies' green transition so that it benefits their own producers, is sustainable, and creates local jobs. While countries may have good intentions – for example, to increase their share of renewable energy production – the most favoured nation principle and other WTO rules limit the subsidies that governments can issue to incentivize domestic 'green' products at the expense of limiting imports from abroad. Developing countries in particular may therefore be unable to make a transition to a greener economy and rely on cheaper, but more polluting technologies instead.

While some RTAs already include provisions to increase sustainability, these issues can only be dealt with effectively by multilateral organizations such as the WTO. Currently, WTO law does not make any distinction between sustainable and polluting industries. Additionally, common pool resources that are becoming scarce – for example, fisheries – are not adequately protected.

5.9.2 Digital Trade

Digital technologies have transformed how people communicate, learn, work, and shop. They also affect the scope of economic activity and integration between countries. Digital industries have been driving much of the global services trade, especially since the transformation brought about by the Covid-19 pandemic. However, in order to exploit their full potential, a higher level of integration between countries is needed. Domestic regulatory barriers account for more than 55% of the trade costs of services, which is twice as high as for manufactured goods. Additionally, the WTO currently does not have a functioning e-commerce regime, which shows the difficulties it has in keeping up with digital transformation (WTO, 2022).

On an RTA level, trade facilitation agreements have already been implemented under RTAs such as the USMCA. Approaches to data governance in these agreements have increasingly supported restrictions of data flows, considering them to be like any other trade barriers. Specific chapters also include the protection of personal data, electronic signatures, and paperless trading.

What makes governing data through trade agreements difficult is that, unlike manufactured goods, it is not linked to any trade flow between countries. Users generate cross-border data flows through the use of social media or search engines that the provider can monetize without engaging in any trade transaction. However, current trade rules were generally developed for goods and services that are produced and cease to exist when they are consumed.

Additionally, many countries, especially in the developing world, do not have processes in place to address competition issues about who can store, process, and use personal data. With no agreements between countries in place, data can be appropriated by multinational companies, leaving little benefit to local economies where it is generated. Regional cooperation on capacity development with the creation of digital infrastructure and data-sharing mechanisms between countries could play a crucial role in investment and competition policies.

SUMMARY

In this chapter we have analysed supranational institutions and institutional distance. Together with (formal and informal) national institutions they build what we call the 'institutional triality' relevant to MNCs. The institutional triality highlights the intricate web of governance and decision-making structures that shape the modern world. National institutions, rooted in historical, cultural, and political contexts, play a pivotal role in guiding a country's policies, economy, and societal norms. These institutions not only reflect the unique identity of each nation but also influence the dynamics of international relations. Supranational institutions, rules, norms, and shared beliefs provide structure to the international collaboration of MNCs and countries. These supranational institutions require organizations to bring them to life. Such organizations include the European Union, the United Nations, and civil society organizations, which represent collaborative efforts to address global challenges and harmonize policies among sovereign states.

The chapter has also drawn attention to the delicate balance between sovereignty and cooperation that characterizes the interactions between MNCs and national and supranational entities. While national institutions guard a nation's autonomy and preserve its cultural identity, they must also adapt to a globalized world where complex issues call for collective solutions. Supranational institutions embody the goal of multilateral collaboration and rule-based international order. However, their effectiveness depends on the consent and engagement of nation states, MNCs, civil society, and international organizations, reflecting the delicate dance of power and diplomacy.

Lastly, we also investigated institutional distance – the challenges multinational companies (MNCs) face due to differences in national institutions that are not bridged by supranational entities, leading to higher costs and complexities. The CAGE framework, developed by Pankaj Ghemawat, categorizes these distances across cultural, administrative, geographic, and economic dimensions, highlighting factors like language, regulatory practices, physical proximity, and economic disparities. Recent advancements in research, such as the nine dimensions by Berry et al. (2010) and the 'information distance' measure by Lindner and Puck (2024), offer deeper insights into institutional variations and their impact on MNC strategies.

6

COUNTRY-LEVEL THEORIES OF INTERNATIONAL ECONOMIC EXCHANGE

CHAPTER INTRODUCTION

This chapter introduces the main theories of international economic exchange at country level, building on insights into the business environment that we have discussed and developed on formal, informal, and supranational institutions in Chapters 3, 4 and 5 respectively. This combination of perspectives enables us to understand decisions that firms make in the context of country-level international trade and investment.

Traditional economic theories in the field of International Business (IB) offer valuable insights into the reasons behind nations engaging in trade. As global business activities become increasingly complex and challenging, understanding the underlying principles of international trade becomes more important. Trade is often seen as a catalyst for growth and prosperity in the world economy, facilitating the efficient use of local resources through specialization, which helps maintain low product costs by each nation specializing in the production of certain goods and services and trading with other nations to acquire products in which it does not specialize. Eighteenth-century mercantilism provided an initial explanation of the reasons for nations engaging in trade, suggesting that governments can increase a country's economic well-being by promoting exports and restricting imports, resulting in a positive balance of trade.

Earlier chapters, covering content such as economic systems, national and supranational institutions, and regional economic integration provide foundational knowledge, insights, and a framework for understanding theories of economic exchange at both country and firm level, the complexity of IB operations, and factors that determine economic interactions. Subsequent chapters explore important aspects of IB, such as internationalization, managing a global firm, international finance and marketing, human resources, international supply chain management, digitalization, and sustainability. These chapters build on the theoretical foundations and address specific areas and challenges within the field of IB, progressively expanding and deepening our understanding of IB theories.

This chapter presents a number of relevant traditional theories in the field of IB. It covers various international trade theories, including absolute and comparative advantage, factor endowment (also known as Heckscher-Ohlin theory), international product life cycle (IPLC), the Leontief paradox, Linder's income-preference similarity, and new trade (NTT). Firm-level theories like the resource-based view (RBV), transaction cost theory (TCT) and the institution-based view (IBV) will be presented and discussed in Chapter 7.

Theories of international trade enhance our understanding of patterns of global trade by explaining the factors that influence International Business activities, the role that countries' resources play, and the ability of countries to compete in international markets. They offer insights into a firm's competitive advantages based on its unique resources and capabilities, and decision-making processes related to outsourcing, alliances, and other governance structures that are critical for multinational companies (MNCs).

The chapter also explores how institutional factors influence business operations across borders, impacting market entry strategies and overall business success in diverse contexts.

Research from the developed and developing world plays a crucial role in advancing our understanding of IB theories, providing diverse perspectives and empirical evidence that contribute to the validation and refinement of the theories discussed in this chapter. It does so by highlighting well-established and highly competitive markets, as well as emerging markets. Finally, we discuss the economic rationale for free trade and provide explanations to better comprehend the dynamics of international trade and its impact on global economies. By considering research findings from different countries, scholars and practitioners are able to gain a more holistic understanding of the nuances of international trade, investment, and business strategies, leading to more informed and effective decision-making in the global business economy.

LEARNING OUTCOMES

After reading this chapter you should be able to:

1. Demonstrate understanding of the main country-level theories of international trade and investment
2. Critically reflect on traditional theories of trade and investment
3. Apply the basic theories of International Business
4. Analyse decisions in the light of major theories of trade and investment.

Case Study: National Interest and the Consequences for Agricultural Firms

The influence of the European Union's (EU) agricultural policy, notably the Common Agricultural Policy (CAP), on trade in agricultural products between the EU and Africa has a variety of implications for different companies. Large multinational agribusinesses based in the EU, such as Cargill and Nestlé, benefit from reduced input costs thanks to subsidies. However, this advantage can create challenges for African agricultural producers, impacting companies like Olam International and OCP Group in Africa's agribusiness sector, limiting their potential for growth.

Stringent standards imposed by the EU for food safety, quality, and sustainability affect companies across the board. European retailers such as Tesco and Carrefour may face difficulties in sourcing certain products from Africa, impacting African firms such as Kenyan horticultural exporters or Ethiopian coffee producers, restricting their access to the European market. Equally, African companies involved in sustainable agriculture, such as those in organic farming like Organically Grown Company or Eco Farms, may find increased opportunities in line with the EU's emphasis on sustainability.

The impact extends to small-scale enterprises as well. Local African cooperatives, such as coffee or cocoa farmers' cooperatives, may find it challenging to comply with EU standards or compete against heavily subsidized European products. Initiatives like Fairtrade International, supporting small-scale producers in meeting these standards, play a crucial role in facilitating access to EU markets in a more equitable manner.

In summary, the EU's agricultural policy, particularly the CAP, shapes trade dynamics between the EU and Africa, affecting a wide range of companies. While large multinational companies navigate the complexities of subsidies and standards, African agribusinesses and cooperatives face challenges but also find opportunities through sustainable practices. Ongoing discussions on policy reforms and trade initiatives remain essential for fostering a more balanced and mutually beneficial agricultural trade relationship between the EU and Africa.

Sources: European Commission (https://agriculture.ec.europa.eu/international/international-cooperation/africa/eu-africa-partnership_en) and *The Farmer's Journal Africa* (https://thefarmersjournal.com/opportunities-and-challenges-for-african-farmers-understanding-the-impact-of-the-eus-common-agricultural-policy)

6.1 ABSOLUTE ADVANTAGE THEORY

In his famous work *An Inquiry into the Nature and Causes of the Wealth of Nations*, Scottish political economist Adam Smith introduced the concept of laissez-faire to the field of international trade in 1776 (Smith, 1937/1776), building on the principle of freedom of trade.

This theory is known as the absolute advantage theory, which states that a nation should import goods that can be produced more efficiently abroad while focusing on exporting goods that can be produced more efficiently in the domestic market. Smith (1937/1776) held that unrestricted free trade would benefit all nations involved because individual countries could specialize in the production of goods in which they had advantages. According to absolute advantage theory, the market would naturally achieve optimum efficiency without government intervention in a nation's economic affairs or in trade relations between nations. He discusses his theory mathematically in a two-country example.

Table 6.1 illustrates the gains derived from free trade, using the example of Italy and Colombia. Italy demonstrates an absolute advantage in producing olive oil, requiring four labour hours per unit compared to Colombia's twenty hours. Conversely, Colombia has an absolute advantage in producing coffee, requiring only three labour hours per unit compared to Italy's twenty hours. By specializing in their respective areas of advantage and engaging in trade, both countries benefit, leading to increased global production.

Table 6.1 An illustration of absolute advantage

Country	Olive oil (labour hours per unit unit)	Coffee (labour hours per unit)
Italy	4	20
Colombia	20	3

6.2 COMPARATIVE ADVANTAGE THEORY

David Ricardo, a nineteenth-century British political economist, addressed the question of whether it is beneficial for countries to engage in trade when one country is more efficient in producing all goods than another. In *On the Principles of Political Economy and Taxation*, Ricardo (1948) argued that international trade remains beneficial for both countries, even when one country is more efficient in all goods, as comparative advantage determines trade flows.

To illustrate this concept, Ricardo presented an example involving England and Portugal in which the labour cost of producing a gallon of wine and a yard of cloth is lower in Portugal than in England. Portugal, therefore, holds an absolute advantage in both wine and cloth production. However, when considering opportunity cost, Portugal is found to have a lower opportunity cost in wine production, while England has a lower opportunity cost in cloth production. The opportunity cost of producing one unit of a good is the quantity of other goods that must be sacrificed. This establishes Portugal's comparative advantage in wine production and England's comparative advantage in cloth production, as shown in Table 6.2. When opportunity costs for the same goods are different in each country, open trade leads to advantages through specialization, allowing each country to focus on producing the good in which it has a comparative advantage over its trading partner.

The absolute and comparative advantage theories have both strengths and weaknesses. The absolute advantage theory is regarded as marking the birth of modern economics and plays a crucial role in shaping economic thought, as it serves as a forerunner of the free trade movement, promoting the idea of unrestricted trade between nations. However, a significant limitation is that when one nation is inferior to another in terms of productivity or resources, the theory fails to offer any guidance on how to address the imbalance. It has also frequently been criticized for its rather simplistic assumptions. Criticism focuses, for example, on the model of a world with only two countries and two goods, which does not reflect the complexity of the real global economy. Further, the theory unrealistically assumes that resources are immobile internationally but fully mobile within a country. Simplistic too is the theory's assumption that countries can specialize on the basis of advantages – this restricts job opportunities to certain industries and does not reflect the realities of today's labour markets.

Table 6.2 An illustration of comparative advantage

Country	Wine (labour hours per gallon)	Cloth (labour hours per yard)
England	120	100
Portugal	80	90

Country	Opportunity cost for wine	Opportunity cost for cloth
England	120/100 = 12/10	100/120 = 10/12
Portugal	80/90 = 8/9	90/80 = 9/8

The comparative advantage theory does, however, provide more practical guidance to nations seeking to engage in trade, especially when they lack absolute advantages in producing certain goods or services. By focusing on relative efficiencies, it helps countries identify areas in which they can specialize and benefit from trade. A major criticism is its relatively static nature, assuming as it does that comparative advantages remain constant over time. In reality, economies and industries undergo transformations, and comparative advantages may shift as technology, skills, and market conditions change. In addition, many of the assumptions of comparative advantage theory are just as simplistic as those in absolute advantage theory.

Case Study: Comparative Advantage and International Investment at Dell

Dell, founded in 1984 by Michael Dell, is as one of the leading global technology companies, specializing in the design, manufacture, and sale of personal computers, laptops, servers, and other electronic devices. Renowned for its innovative business model that initially emphasized direct sales to consumers, Dell has evolved into a multinational company with a commitment to delivering cutting-edge technology solutions, continually adapting to the dynamic landscape of the technology industry.

(Continued)

Dell's expansion into international markets, particularly its strategic move into China, has been a pivotal aspect of the company's global growth strategy. Recognizing the vast potential of the Chinese market, Dell established a presence in the country to capitalize on its skilled labour force, cost-effective manufacturing capabilities, and a burgeoning consumer base. Over the years, Dell has not only positioned manufacturing and assembly operations in China, but it has also actively engaged with local expertise, forming partnerships, establishing research and development centres, and contributing to the development of the Chinese workforce.

Dell's engagement with local expertise and labour in China is a crucial aspect of its strategy, showcasing how the company has effectively harnessed comparative advantage. One notable example is Dell's collaboration with Chinese manufacturing partners, such as Foxconn and Quanta Computer. These partnerships allow Dell to tap into the specialized knowledge and experience of these local firms in electronics manufacturing. By leveraging the proficiency of these Chinese partners, Dell benefits from streamlined production processes, improved quality control, and access to the latest technological advances.

Moreover, Dell has established research and development (R&D) centres in China, reflecting a commitment to harnessing local innovation and talent. These centres, located in cities like Shanghai and Chengdu, serve as hubs for developing cutting-edge technologies and solutions tailored to the preferences and needs of the Chinese market. By actively involving Chinese engineers and researchers, Dell gains insights into the local consumer landscape, ensuring that its products are not only cost effective but also resonate with the preferences of the Chinese clientele.

In the realm of customer support and services, Dell has invested in building a robust network of call centres and service facilities in China. This localization of support services allows Dell to provide timely and culturally sensitive assistance to its Chinese customers. By employing local staff who understand the nuances of the Chinese market, language, and consumer expectations, Dell can offer a more personalized and effective customer service experience.

Dell's recruitment of local talent for managerial and leadership positions further exemplifies its commitment to leveraging local expertise. The company has appointed Chinese executives to key positions, recognizing the importance of understanding and navigating the complexities of the Chinese business environment. This approach not only aligns with the principles of comparative advantage but also fosters a deeper connection with the local market, facilitating better decision-making and adaptability to regional dynamics.

Additionally, Dell has actively participated in initiatives to promote technology education and skill development in China. Through collaboration with educational institutions and programmes, Dell contributes to the development of a skilled workforce in the country. By investing in the education and training of local talent, Dell ensures a sustainable pipeline of skilled professionals who can contribute to the company's growth and innovation.

Sources: Dell (www.dell.com/en-us/dt/it-transformation/esg-interactive-report-the-dell-technologies-global-alliances-story.htm) and *China Daily* (www.chinadaily.com.cn/a/202308/22/WS64e4119fa31035260b81d83c.html)

Case Study Questions

1 How does the global distribution of R&D activities influence Dell's overall global strategy?
2 Which part of Dell's value chain activities do you think faces most pressure for global integration or local responsiveness?
3 How has the comparative advantage proposition in China shifted over the last 20 years?

6.3 FACTOR ENDOWMENT THEORY

In the 1920s, Swedish economists Eli Heckscher and Bertil Ohlin developed the factor endowment theory, also known as the Heckscher-Ohlin theory. It suggests that countries will participate in producing and exporting goods that require abundant utilization of available production factors, and import goods that require substantial quantities of production factors that are lacking (Ohlin, 1933; Heckscher, 1949). This theoretical framework enhances our understanding of comparative advantage by incorporating considerations of endowment and production factor costs and sheds light on why nations, depending on their size and characteristics, tend to focus on the production of labour-intensive or capital-intensive goods (Costinot, 2009).

The factor endowment theory can be exemplified by considering climatic conditions as a central factor. For instance, Caribbean countries possess favourable climates, while US firms possess capital. This difference in endowments leads to foreign direct investment (FDI), such as the case of US firms investing in the Caribbean for agricultural purposes. Additionally, extractive industries and tourism also illustrate the role of endowments. Countries with abundant natural resources and desirable destinations may lack the capital necessary to fully exploit them, resulting in the involvement of foreign investors in these industries.

Spotlight: Rare Earths

China has long dominated the global market in rare earth elements (REEs), which are critical components in various high-tech applications, including electronics, renewable energy, and defence systems. Since the 1980s, China has leveraged its substantial rare earth reserves and lower production costs to become the world's leading producer and exporter of these essential materials. By the early 2000s, China accounted for more than 80% of the global rare earth supply, effectively establishing a near monopoly.

(Continued)

Several factors contributed to China's dominance in the rare earth market. The country invested heavily in mining and processing infrastructure, benefiting from economies of scale. Additionally, lax environmental regulations and lower labour costs allowed China to produce REEs more cheaply than other countries. China also strategically restricted rare earth exports to ensure a steady domestic supply and to exert geopolitical influence.

However, this dominance has come under pressure in recent years due to significant rare earth discoveries in other parts of the world and growing concerns about supply chain security. Several countries, including the United States, Australia, and Canada, have ramped up efforts to explore and develop their own rare earth deposits. Notable discoveries and developments include:

- *United States*: The Mountain Pass mine in California, one of the richest rare earth deposits outside China, has resumed production. The US government has also prioritized rare earth independence as a national security issue.
- *Australia*: Australia is home to significant rare earth reserves, with major projects like the Lynas Corporation's Mount Weld mine contributing to a growing share of global supply.
- *Canada*: Canada has identified numerous rare earth deposits, with companies like Neo Performance Materials and others actively developing these resources.
- *Africa*: Countries such as Burundi, Madagascar, and South Africa have reported promising rare earth deposits, attracting investment and exploration.

These developments are part of a broader effort to diversify the global rare earth supply chain and reduce dependence on China. Governments and industries worldwide are investing in research and development to improve rare earth extraction and processing technologies, aiming to make production more economically viable and environmentally sustainable.

Sources: The Oxford Institute for Energy Studies (www.oxfordenergy.org/publications/chinas-rare-earths-dominance-and-policy-responses) and Foreign Policy Research Institute (www.fpri.org/article/2022/03/chinas-rare-earth-metals-consolidation-and-market-power)

Although the theory clearly explains trade patterns, it is not without limitations. It raises concerns about trade imbalances and shifts in internationalization patterns. A notable weakness lies in the presence of minimum wage laws in certain countries, which can lead to increasing labour prices even in economies abundant in this factor of production. Consequently, these nations may discover that importing certain goods becomes a more cost-effective option compared to domestic production. Furthermore, another weakness of the theory emerges when considering countries such as the United States, which exhibit a pattern of exporting a relatively higher proportion of labour-intensive goods while simultaneously importing capital-intensive goods (Collinson et al., 2020).

Case Study: Toyota and the Product Life Cycle

Toyota Motor Corporation, a global automotive giant, exemplifies a strategic approach to introducing products across various stages of the product life cycle in both developed and developing countries, with a commitment to innovation, sustainability, and market adaptability.

In developed countries like the United States and Japan, Toyota focuses on introducing advanced technologies, such as hybrid and electric vehicles (EVs), to appeal to environmentally conscious consumers. As a pioneer in hybrid technology with models like the Prius, Toyota positions itself as a leader in sustainable mobility. During the introduction phase, the company invested heavily in research and development to ensure cutting-edge features, safety standards, and environmental performance.

Toyota's strategy includes comprehensive marketing campaigns that emphasize the efficiency, reliability, and eco-friendly nature of its hybrid and electric models. Collaboration with local governments, utility companies, and technology partners contributes to building the necessary infrastructure, such as charging stations, to support the growth of electric transport.

In contrast, in developing countries such as India and parts of Southeast Asia, Toyota tailors its product offerings to suit evolving automotive markets. Recognizing the predominance of traditional internal combustion engine (ICE) vehicles and the importance of affordability, Toyota introduces entry-level models with a focus on fuel efficiency, durability, and ease of maintenance.

To address the specific needs of consumers in these markets, Toyota often collaborates with local manufacturers, sources materials locally, and adapts vehicle designs to suit regional preferences. The company also engages in community initiatives, such as skill development programmes and road safety campaigns, to integrate with the local environment and foster brand trust.

Managing different product life cycles presents Toyota with challenges that require strategic adaptation. In developed countries, where rapid technological advances drive consumer preferences, Toyota navigates the complexities by continuously innovating and staying at the forefront of automotive technology. Addressing concerns about charging infrastructure and consumer education on electric vehicles remains a priority.

In developing countries, Toyota grapples with economic constraints, infrastructure limitations, and diverse regulatory environments. The company adapts by offering financing options, localizing production to control costs, and engaging in collaborative efforts with local governments and communities to align its products with the needs of the market.

By aligning strategies with the unique demands of each market segment, Toyota successfully manages the challenges posed by varying consumer preferences, economic conditions, and regulatory landscapes. This approach allows Toyota to maintain a global presence, driving innovation in mature markets while contributing to automotive development and accessibility in emerging economies.

Sources: Toyota (https://global.toyota/en/newsroom/corporate/39288520.html) and University of Louisville (https://business.louisville.edu/cob_mediawiki/Product_Life_Cycle_Theory)

6.4 INTERNATIONAL PRODUCT LIFE CYCLE THEORY

The international product life cycle theory (IPLC), proposed by Raymond Vernon, offers valuable insights into the field of international trade, directing attention to the distinct stages of a product's life cycle. Vernon's (1992) model highlights the changes in input requirements and market standardization as a new product becomes established. According to his theory, as the product cycle progresses, the cost advantage associated with the product changes, potentially offsetting the comparative advantage gained through innovative capacity. Specifically, Vernon focused on US exports of manufactured goods and developed a four-stage model to explain the behaviour of these exports.

In the first stage, the United States holds a monopoly in exporting a new product. However, in the second stage, foreign production of the same product begins. As the cycle advances to the third stage, foreign production becomes competitive in the export market. Finally, in the fourth stage, the United States transitions from being an exporter of the once-new product to becoming an importer of it, as the product is no longer considered new. The theory places emphasis on fundamental aspects often overlooked by comparative advantage theory, namely the influence of market size and expansion in determining trade patterns and the role of technological innovation.

Figure 6.1 shows the product cycle model for an innovating country (e.g., the US) and an imitating country (e.g., Germany). It links the product's life cycle to distinct stages: new-product stage, growth-product stage, and mature-product stage. Each stage represents different aspects of production, competition, and market dynamics in the context of international trade. The new-product stage corresponds to the initial production of the product within the innovating country, as well as the early phase of the export monopoly stage. As the cycle progresses, the growth-product stage emerges, encompassing the latter part of the export monopoly stage and the commencement of foreign production. Ultimately, the mature-product stage aligns with the third and fourth stages of the product cycle model in international trade. This stage is characterized by the production of standardized products and intense price competition (Rink & Swan, 1979).

At the initial point in time (A), the innovating country begins exporting the newly innovated product, while foreign production in the imitating country starts (B) to compete with the innovator's exports. Consequently, the innovating country's exports begin to decline. As time progresses, the innovating country reaches a stage where it no longer produces the new product and becomes an importer of it (C). Meanwhile, the imitating country starts importing the new product from the innovating country (A') when the local markets grow sufficiently large and cost conditions favour local production instead of imports (B'). In the case of an advanced country like Germany, there will be a period of overlapping time between the innovating country's initial exports (A) and the imitating country's imports (A'), as well as between the start of foreign production (B) and local production (B'). Eventually, local production in the imitating country surpasses domestic consumption (C'), leading to a shift from being an importer to an exporter of the product.

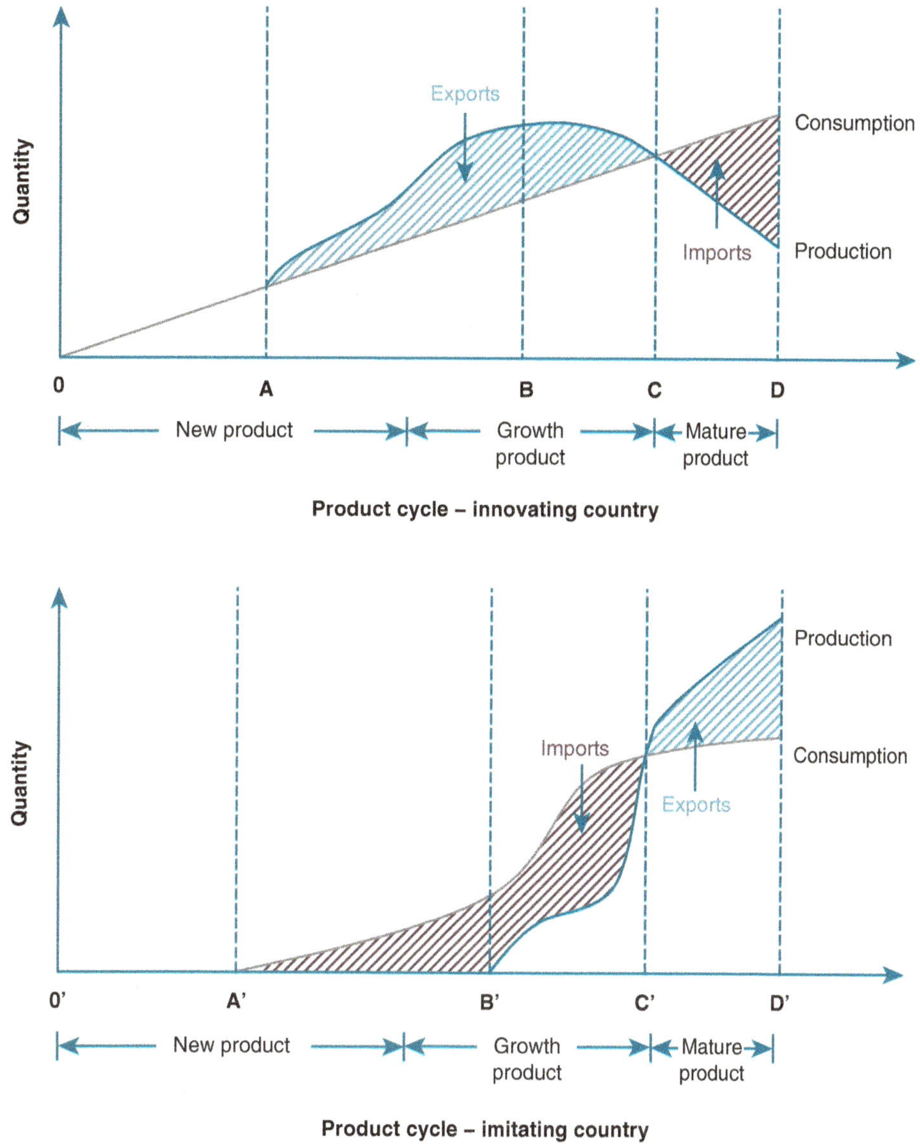

Figure 6.1 Illustration of the international product life cycle

6.5 THE LEONTIEF PARADOX

The Leontief paradox, initially identified by Nobel-Prize-winning economist Wassily Leontief (1953), addresses considerations beyond labour hours, specifically including the quality of labour input. In regard to the United States, it is observed that the country produces and exports technology-intensive goods that require a highly educated workforce. However, the Leontief paradox revealed that countries can successfully export products that use less abundant resources – for example, the US often exports labour-intensive goods. Consequently, the Leontief paradox not only exposes a limitation within the factor endowment theory but also deepens our understanding of the inadequacy of any one theory in fully explaining the role of economic factors within trade theory.

The Leontief paradox also explains why intraregional trade remains significant in the global economy. This phenomenon occurs because countries within the same region tend to have similar income levels, demand patterns, and operational efficiencies, which reduces uncertainty and transaction costs, making trade within regions a substantial component of world trade. However, a weakness of the theory lies in its inability to fully explain how trade activities would occur between two nations with similar income levels but different consumption preferences. As a result, it struggles to account for the increasing trade observed between developed countries and industrialized markets, where inequalities in consumption patterns exist (Minabe, 1966; Leamer, 1980).

6.6 LINDER'S INCOME-PREFERENCE SIMILARITY THEORY

The framework of renowned Swedish economist Staffan B. Linder (1961) introduces a classification of international trade and distinguishes between primary products and manufactured products. He posits that factor endowments explain trade in natural resource-intensive products but not in manufactured ones. Instead, Linder argues that a country's range of manufactured exports is primarily determined by domestic demand and contends that trade in manufactured products is influenced by domestic demand, with preference similarity between countries driving increased trade.

Additionally, he asserts that average per capita income is a crucial determinant of a country's demand structure, which influences demand for types of goods and how sophisticated they are. Countries with higher per capita income tend to demand higher-quality consumer goods and advanced capital goods. In contrast, countries with lower per capita income primarily demand lower-quality consumer goods.

6.7 NEW TRADE THEORY

In the 1970s, economists, including Paul Krugman, observed a remarkable trend in international trade – it was growing fastest between industrialized countries that shared similar factors of production. This observation led to the development of the new trade theory, which argued that increasing returns to scale played a significant role in determining superior international performance for industries that boomed as their production volume increased (Krugman, 1979). This theory highlights the significance of exports and gaining access to the global marketplace, particularly for firms unable to sell products in large quantities.

New trade theory addresses the phenomenon of different product varieties being produced in different countries. Consequently, when one country exports a product to another country, it often imports a similar product class from that country. This mutual exchange of products within the same industry is known as intra-industry trade and challenges the traditional notion of trade being solely based on absolute advantages (Markusen & Venables, 1998). Intra-firm trade involves trade within a unified firm, which allows the involved MNCs and their affiliates to exercise some discretion over the transfer prices charged for goods and services. This strategic approach can help address financial barriers that otherwise hinder trade between countries.

New trade theory has enriched our understanding of international trade dynamics, particularly in the context of industrialized countries with similar factors of production. By emphasizing the importance of increasing returns to scale and the potential of intra-industry trade, this theory offers valuable insights for policymakers and businesses aiming to enhance their global performance. Furthermore, the concept of intra-firm trade provides a means of overcoming financial challenges between economies, fostering greater economic cooperation in the interconnected global market (Markusen & Venables, 1998).

Spotlight: Within-MNC Trade and Its Role in Sustainability Policy

Trade within multinational companies (MNCs) is a significant component of global trade. Such intra-firm trade occurs when different branches or subsidiaries of the same multinational company exchange goods, services, or resources across international borders. This form of trade is estimated to account for a substantial portion of global trade flows, underscoring the pivotal role MNCs play in the global economy.

MNCs manage complex and extensive supply chains that span multiple countries, allowing them to optimize production and distribution processes to reduce costs and increase efficiency. These companies often control various stages of production, from raw materials to finished goods, leveraging their global networks to source inputs from the most cost-effective locations. This intricate management of global supply chains enables MNCs to maintain competitive advantages and exert considerable influence over international trade patterns.

The power that MNCs wield over supply chains can serve as a crucial lever for enforcing global sustainability policies. Given their scale and reach, MNCs have the capacity to implement and propagate sustainable practices across their entire supply chain. By adopting sustainability standards, MNCs can ensure that their suppliers comply with environmental, social, and governance (ESG) criteria, which might include reducing carbon emissions, minimizing waste, ensuring fair labour practices, and promoting resource efficiency.

MNCs can also drive sustainability through their procurement policies. By prioritizing suppliers that adhere to sustainable practices, they can create market incentives for other

(Continued)

businesses to adopt similar standards. Additionally, MNCs can invest in sustainable technologies and innovation, further driving the adoption of green practices across industries.

Furthermore, MNCs' influence extends beyond their immediate supply chains. They can collaborate with governments, NGOs, and international organizations to promote global sustainability initiatives. Through partnerships and advocacy, MNCs can help shape regulatory frameworks and industry standards that support sustainable development goals.

Sources: US Bureau of Economic Analysis (www.bea.gov/research/papers/2003/trade-goods-within-multinational-companies-survey-based-data-and-findings) and Trade Finance Global (www.tradefinanceglobal.com/posts/influential-factors-on-global-trade)

6.8 CURRENT DEVELOPMENTS IN COUNTRY-LEVEL THEORIES OF ECONOMIC EXCHANGE

Finally, let us look at some more recent developments in the foundational theories of International Business. Bellino and Fratini's (2022) study 'Absolute advantages and capital mobility in international trade theory' explores the role of absolute advantages in international specialization, particularly in relation to the phenomenon of capital mobility. The paper challenges widely accepted conclusions about the mutual benefits of international trade and country specialization. One of the key arguments discussed in the paper is the theoretical possibility of exclusion from trade. This means that under certain conditions, a country might be excluded from participating in international trade due to factors such as a lower rate of remuneration from capital. The authors also discuss the implications of exclusion and its effects on the country's unemployment, trade balance, and potential measures like wage adjustments and capital mobility restrictions (Bellino & Fratini, 2022). By challenging traditional assumptions about the unequivocal benefits of international trade and specialization, the paper provides insights into the potential risks and complexities associated with capital mobility in a globalized economy.

A recently published study compares the Heckscher-Ohlin theory and the modern trade theory when explaining global trade flows (Kunroo & Ahmad, 2023). The authors use the trade complementarity index and per capita income variables in an empirical examination, supporting the Heckscher-Ohlin theory and indicating that countries trade based on their factor endowments rather than engaging in intra-industry trade. The study also reveals significant export potential, suggesting the importance of trade cooperation and infrastructure investment for economic growth. Inter-industry trade occurs more in capital-intensive commodities, while imports are luxury oriented, highlighting the need for further development to achieve intra-industry trade dominance. This paper has significant relevance for the development of IB by emphasizing the importance of countries leveraging their factor endowments in international trade.

The dynamic landscape of IB theories has involved significant developments through various insightful studies. These studies contribute to a more comprehensive understanding of the challenges in the field of IB and provide new perspectives and potential policy implications for global economic relations, trade, and firm strategies. From re-examining the role of absolute advantages in international specialization to comparing different trade theories, researchers have shed light on the tasks and potential risks in the global economy. Moreover, exploring the applicability of the resource-based view (e.g., Alexy et al., 2018; Arda et al., 2023) and the implications of institutional distance on subsidiary performance enriches our understanding of how firms can gain a competitive advantage. As the field of IB continues to evolve, these findings offer valuable guidance and serve as a foundation for future research, driving further developments in theory and practice.

SUMMARY

The country-level theories presented in this chapter offer valuable insights into the complex and dynamic nature of global trade and economic interactions. Starting with traditional economic theories that laid the groundwork for understanding the reasons behind nations engaging in trade, various international trade theories and their implications for International Business activities were presented. These theories, such as absolute and comparative advantage, factor endowment, international product life cycle, and others, shed light on how nations can use their resources efficiently through specialization and trade, driving growth and prosperity in the world economy. Real-life scenarios, industry examples, and case studies provided insights into how theoretical concepts apply in business operations, enriching our understanding of these theoretical frameworks.

7

FIRM-LEVEL INTERNATIONALIZATION THEORIES AND STRATEGIES

CHAPTER INTRODUCTION

The previous chapter looked at the reasons why international business activity happens from a country-level perspective. This chapter builds on our understanding of the environment developed in Chapters 2–5 and country-level theories in Chapter 6 to consider strategic questions about international expansion – why, when, where, and how firms internationalize.

International expansion has different dimensions and requires firms to make a number of important decisions. In analysing those dimensions sequentially, it is important to keep in mind that in practice such decisions are often considered alongside each other by firms considering international activity. The first decision is to define the objectives of internationalization and analyse the extent to which the firm has the resources and capability to achieve these objectives. The second decision addresses the timing of internationalization: when should a firm take a specific step and how many steps should it take at the same point in time? The third relates to the locus of internationalization and the fourth is multifaceted, considering how to internationalize from a strategic perspective.

Research differentiates three dimensions of this decision. The first analyses the extent to which ownership in a foreign activity provides the most value. The second is about how to establish a presence in a foreign market. And the third considers what elements of the value chain should be transferred to the new market. Exploring these dimensions not only helps us build an understanding of the options that firms have when internationalizing, but the rationale behind the choices that are made.

Lastly, we introduce a theory that combines a number (but not all) of the decisions in the internationalization process: the eclectic paradigm or OLI framework by John Dunning.

Across all the strategic steps, we discuss relevant International Business theories, such as the resource-based view (RBV), transaction cost theory (TCT), the institution-based view (IBV), the Uppsala internationalization model, and Porter's diamond. In addition, we provide case studies to illustrate the real-life relevance of the content and application of the theories. We highlight topics associated with digitalization and sustainability as in the previous chapters, and continue to present a global perspective on the internationalization process supported by novel research findings.

LEARNING OUTCOMES

After reading this chapter you should be able to:

1. Demonstrate understanding of the nature of the internationalization process
2. Identify the strategic options that firms have in the internationalization process
3. Apply relevant theories to support decision making in the internationalization process
4. Analyse decisions in the light of major theories of International Business.

Case Study: The Internationalization of Siemens

Siemens, founded in 1847 by Werner von Siemens and Johann Georg Halske in Berlin, Germany, has a long and storied history of internationalization. Over the years, Siemens has evolved from a small telegraph company to one of the world's largest conglomerates, operating in various sectors such as energy, healthcare, infrastructure, and industrial automation.

Siemens began its internationalization journey by expanding its telegraph business across Europe in the mid-nineteenth century. The company capitalized on the increasing demand for telecommunication infrastructure and, besides exporting, established subsidiaries and partnerships in key European markets. By establishing a presence in countries such as England, Russia, Austria-Hungary, and others, Siemens laid the foundation for its future global expansion and established its reputation as a leading provider of electrical engineering solutions.

In the twentieth century, Siemens diversified its product portfolio beyond telegraphy and ventured into new industries such as power generation, transportation, healthcare, and industrial automation. The company expanded its global footprint through greenfield and brownfield investments, establishing manufacturing facilities, research centres, and sales offices in key markets worldwide. Siemens became a truly global company, with operations spanning multiple continents and industries, serving diverse customers and markets around the world.

In response to changing market dynamics, technological advances, and geopolitical shifts, Siemens underwent significant restructuring and transformation during the late twentieth century. The company reorganized its operations, divested non-core assets, and focused on high-growth sectors such as renewable energy, digitalization, and smart infrastructure. Siemens also expanded its global reach through strategic alliances, joint ventures, and partnerships with local companies and governments, strengthening its market position and innovation capabilities in emerging markets.

In the twenty-first century, Siemens intensified its focus on innovation, sustainability, and digital transformation to address global challenges and capitalize on emerging opportunities. The company invested heavily in research and development, fostering collaboration with universities, startups, and industry partners to drive technological innovation and develop solutions for sustainable infrastructure, energy efficiency, and healthcare advances. Siemens has embraced digitalization and Industry 4.0 principles, leveraging data analytics, artificial intelligence, and automation to enhance productivity, efficiency, and connectivity across its businesses and value chains.

Today, Siemens maintains a strong global presence with operations in over 200 countries and territories, employing hundreds of thousands of people worldwide. The company continues to expand its international footprint through strategic investments, partnerships, and collaborations.

Sources: Siemens (www.siemens.com/global/en/company/about/history.html); https://press.siemens.com/global/en/pressrelease/siemens-accelerate-high-value-growth-focused-technology-company) and Politico (www.politico.eu/article/germany-china-siemens-representative-of-globalization-economy)

Case Study Questions

1 What are the main business activities, in terms of geographies and industries, that Siemens pursues today?
2 What is the role of government relationships in internationalization at Siemens?
3 In which business segments was Siemens not successful in? Why was this?

7.1 WHY FIRMS INTERNATIONALIZE

The primary driver for firms to internationalize is the pursuit of increased profits. In basic terms, profit can be maximized in two ways: by increasing revenues, or by reducing costs. Consequently, a simple differentiation of firms' motives to internationalize separates efficiency-based and market-based motives of internationalization. However, both objectives can be achieved either by exploiting existing advantages or by exploring new ones, and can be realized through strategic foci (e.g., resources vs markets). International Business researchers have identified four main categories of motivation depending on how the firm intends to achieve the underlying profit motive. The first three aim to exploit existing advantages while the fourth seeks to create new ones (Dunning & Lundan, 2008):

1. Market seeking internationalization involves firms expanding their operations to cater to specific foreign markets. As domestic markets become saturated or competitive, firms often look abroad for new growth opportunities. By entering foreign markets, companies can tap into new customer bases, diversify their revenue streams, and extend the lifecycle of their products or services. Additionally, international markets might offer different consumer preferences, allowing firms to diversify their product lines and cater to a broader range of tastes and demands.
2. Resource seeking internationalization involves firms venturing abroad to gain access to natural resources, unskilled labour, or commodities that might be scarce, of superior quality, or more affordable than in their home country.
3. Efficiency seeking internationalization involves firms entering other countries with the goal of promoting a more efficient division of labour or specialization, thereby reaping economies of scale and scope. By distributing different parts of their production process across various countries, firms can optimize costs and efficiencies. This is often seen in global supply chain strategies, where each location specializes in a specific part of the production based on its comparative advantage.
4. Strategic asset-seeking internationalization involves firms looking to access resources that either enhance an existing competitive edge or diminish a competitor's advantage. This motivation goes beyond immediate financial gains and looks at the long-term strategic positioning of the firm. Companies might seek to acquire unique technologies, intellectual property, or specific competencies that are present in foreign markets. Alternatively, a company might enter a foreign market to directly compete with a rival, aiming to reduce the competitor's market share and global influence. This strategy can also involve forming alliances or joint ventures with local firms to tap into their established networks and market knowledge.

From a modern perspective it is evident that the four motives overlap. For example, in many cases access to superior resources for lower cost will also lead to greater efficiency. Further, in an increasingly globalized world, the reasons for internationalization can seem as straightforward as the reasons a company might expand from one city to another. The delineation of these motives becomes clearer when contextualized in the late 1970s and early 1980s – when this classification was made – a period marked by the emergent predominance of multinational companies and a dominant neoliberal economic perspective. A modern understanding would be that firms internationalize to achieve their instrumental goals of boosting revenues, cutting costs, or enhancing their products, operations, or competitive stance. Yet even this modern classification is not without its challenges. Managers often cite a combination of the four motives above when justifying their internationalization decisions, highlighting the multifaceted nature of such strategic choices (Cuervo-Cazura & Narula, 2015).

Spotlight: Investing in Africa for Data

Multinational companies from developed countries are increasingly investing in Africa to collect data that can be used to train machine learning (ML) models, which are subsequently applied globally. This investment is, among other aspects, driven by the unique and diverse datasets that African markets offer, which are valuable for developing robust and versatile ML applications.

One major area of focus is the collection of diverse data that encompasses various languages, cultural practices, and economic activities. Africa's diverse demographic and environmental conditions provide rich, varied datasets that enhance the training of ML models, making them more adaptable and effective in different global contexts. This diversity is crucial for building AI systems that are inclusive and representative of a wide range of users.

Companies from developed countries invest in data collection through various means, including establishing research centres, partnering with local institutions, and launching pilot projects. These initiatives help gather data on consumer behaviour, health, agriculture, and financial transactions, among other areas. For instance, data from mobile phone usage and financial transactions can improve models for financial inclusion, while agricultural data can enhance predictive analytics for crop yields and weather patterns.

One example is Kenya, which has seen significant investment from multinational companies. Companies such as IBM and Vodafone have established research labs and innovation centres in Kenya to collect and analyse data. For instance, IBM's research lab in Nairobi focuses on using data to develop AI solutions for agriculture, healthcare, and urban planning. Vodafone's M-Pesa platform, a mobile banking service, collects extensive financial data that helps train ML models to improve financial inclusion and service delivery in similar markets worldwide.

Once collected, this data is used to train ML models in developed countries, leveraging advanced computational resources and expertise. The resulting models benefit from the rich, diverse data inputs, making them more accurate and generalizable across different regions and applications. These ML models are then deployed globally, enhancing the performance of AI applications in various sectors such as healthcare, agriculture, finance, and logistics.

Sources: African Infrastructure Investment Managers (https://aiimafrica.com/media/media-centre/how-we-made-it-in-africa) and Mantralabs (www.mantralabsglobal.com/blog/ai-in-africa-artificial-intelligence-africa)

7.1.1 Why Firms Internationalize - Firm-Specific Assets

Imagine a world where every firm, regardless of its country or industry of origin, has exactly the same access to resources and capabilities. In such a scenario, as posited by theories of economic exchange (see Chapter 6), the incremental costs associated with conducting business across borders would render International Business unfeasible. Hence, any firm considering venturing beyond its home territory requires a competitive edge to ensure its offerings remain enticing even after factoring in the complexities and costs of cross-border activities.

Identifying the source of a firm's competitive advantage is pivotal in the study of strategic management. Broadly, competitive advantage springs from two key factors:

1. *Resources and capabilities*: At the heart of a firm's competitive prowess lies its unique blend of resources and capabilities. But what sets one firm apart from its competitors? The resource-based view (RBV) of the firm (see below for more detail) is concerned with this very question, contending that a firm's internal resources and capabilities are the bedrock of its competitive advantage. International Business scholars have long argued that those resources and capabilities are at the core of a firm's firm-specific assets (FSAs).
2. *Competitive positioning*: Rooted in the industrial organization tradition, the structure of an industry can have a strong influence on a firm's competitive position. Here the size of the companies within the industry, and the bargaining power of their suppliers and customers, as well as the threat of other companies entering the industry or substituting its products are the central determinants of competitive advantage. These industrial factors have enjoyed much scholarly attention in early International Business research, but more recently the focus has shifted away from them, mirroring a similar trend in strategic management research overall.

However, for these competitive advantages to be relevant in the context of International Business, they need an essential attribute: transferability. An FSA, no matter how potent in its home market, must have the capacity to be transferred and adapted to diverse international contexts. If an advantage lacks this ability, its relevance diminishes in the global arena.

In conclusion, firm-specific advantages provide a nuanced understanding of why certain firms compete successfully in the international arena while others falter. In this way they provide an understanding of what type of firm should internationalize and what type should not. By examining the origins, nature, and transferability of these advantages, businesses can derive strategies that not only leverage their unique strengths but also navigate the intricacies of the global market effectively.

Spotlight: Liabilities of Foreignness

Liabilities of foreignness (LOFs) (Zaheer, 1995), refer to the disadvantages or challenges that foreign firms may face when operating in unfamiliar or foreign markets. These liabilities might arise from cultural differences between the firm's home country and the host country, institutional and regulatory challenges, intense competition from local competitors that have a deeper understanding of the market, resource constraints, or challenges to establish trust and credibility with local stakeholders, including customers, suppliers, investors, and government authorities. Essentially, liabilities of foreignness represent the costs and obstacles associated with being an outsider or foreign entity in a particular market.

An important consequence of the existence of LOFs is that to be able to successfully internationalize firms must hold a sustainable competitive advantage over local firms. Otherwise the cost disadvantage may outweigh the potential benefits of internationalization.

Source: Oxford Research Encyclopedia (https://oxfordre.com/business/display/10.1093/acrefore/9780190224851.001.0001/acrefore-9780190224851-e-402)

7.1.2 Why Firms Internationalize - The Resource-Based View

The resource-based view (RBV) provides a more detailed conceptual perspective on firm internationalization. It posits that a firm's competitive advantage lies in its unique and firm-specific advantages (FSAs). These FSAs are the key to a firm's success and need to be continuously upgraded, necessitating a culture of innovation within the organization that considers the accumulation of knowledge and technology. To comprehend how FSAs can provide a competitive advantage, the RBV directs our attention to the internal sources of competitive advantage within a firm. The key implication of the RBV is that a firm must maintain and control certain resources and capabilities to achieve a state of sustainable competitive advantage (SCA), as opposed to the institutional perspective, which emphasizes the firm's external environment. The resource-based view (RBV) assumes that a firm's competitive advantage derives from its exclusive and inimitable strategic assets that are owned or controlled by it (Penrose, 1959).

Superior resources allow firms not only to outperform rivals in the domestic market but also to gain a competitive edge in foreign markets. The core questions addressed by the RBV revolve around how firms can effectively manage and develop their resources to create value. Resources can be classified into primary resources, which are the productive assets of a firm, and capabilities, which represent a firm's ability to utilize these resources effectively. Primary resources encompass both tangible and intangible assets that can be acquired through open markets and customized to suit the firm's needs. Tangible resources include financial and physical assets, as well as human capital, which comprises knowledge and skills. Intangible resources encompass intellectual property, reputation, and the values and norms within the organization. By strategically leveraging these valuable and rare resources that are imperfectly imitable and organized (Valuable, Rare, Imperfectly Imitable, and Organized are the so-called VRIO criteria), a firm can enhance its efficiency and effectiveness, thereby developing value-creating strategies (Barney, 1991. A resource is considered to be valuable (V) if it enables a firm to exploit opportunities or neutralize threats in the environment, contributing to efficiency or effectiveness. If a resource does not add value, it cannot be a source of competitive advantage. A resource is considered rare (R) if it is not widely possessed by competitors. When few or no other firms have the resource, it can help the firm gain a temporary competitive advantage. A resource is costly to imitate (I) if competitors cannot easily duplicate it due to unique historical conditions, causal ambiguity, or social complexity. Difficult-to-imitate resources help sustain competitive advantage over time. Lastly, the firm must be organized (O) to fully exploit its valuable, rare, and hard-to-imitate resources. This includes appropriate structures, processes, policies, and culture that support strategic deployment of these resources.

Tangible resources consist of:

- *Financial assets*, such as securities, cash and stocks
- *Physical assets*, such as land, buildings and equipment
- *Human capital*, such as knowledge, skills and know-how.

Intangible resources consist of:

- *Intellectual property*, such as patents, trademarks and copyrighted work
- *Reputation*, such as brands, corporate goodwill and relationships
- *Organizational culture*, such as values, tradition and norms.

Capabilities, in the context of the RBV, refer to firm-specific abilities to use resources in achieving organizational objectives effectively. These capabilities involve creating, modifying, reconfiguring, and leveraging resources and are often developed internally and based on tacit knowledge specific to the firm. Although capabilities are challenging to quantify, they can be illustrated through the firm's value chain, showcasing different activities where the firm possesses distinctive competencies. Additionally, examining the firm's outcomes can reveal capabilities that emerge from managing various functions and stages of the value chain effectively. Some crucial capabilities can be found in the innovation process, such as research and development and business model innovation (BMI), while others may occur in operational, marketing, sales, corporate management functions, and dynamic capabilities. Table 7.1 provides an overview of crucial capabilities.

Table 7.1 An overview of capabilities

Department	Responsibility
R&D/innovation	New product development, design, BMI
Operations	Product quality, lean management, manufacturing efficiency
Marketing	Consumer brands, reputation for quality and luxury, responsiveness to trends
Sales/service	Sales know-how, sales channels, distribution management, service platforms
Corporate management	Risk management, talent development, government relations and strategy management
Dynamic capabilities	Respond, sense, reconfigure, adjust to internal and external changes

The internal focus enables firms to leverage their unique strengths to gain a sustainable advantage over competitors and contributes to an understanding of the durability of competitive advantages and the importance of valuable resources. One of the major strengths of the RBV is its emphasis on analysing a firm's internal resources and capabilities to explain competitive advantage. This approach has brought increasing rigour and precision to the strategy field, enabling a deeper understanding of the sources of the heterogeneity and performance of firms (Foss, 1998). The RBV has offered fresh perspectives on, and novel ways of addressing, fundamental questions of strategy. By focusing on the uniqueness of resources, the RBV has shed light on how firms can achieve sustainable competitive advantages.

Further, the RBV can help us to explain under what conditions internationalization helps firms to maintain or improve their competitiveness. Simply stated, firms should only internationalize if this helps them to maintain or develop their VRIO resources. Firms without VRIO resources, or if a specific internationalization strategy puts VRIO resources at substantial risk, they should consider alternative investments to develop or maintain their competitive assets.

Like any theory, the RBV is not without limitations. In real life, it can be difficult to determine whether a firm's resources are truly unique. It is also difficult to know whether a competitor's product or service using the same resources is equivalent or inferior. Firms often lack objective information about their competitors' tangible and intangible assets, as competitors' resources are frequently embedded in routines, brands, and individual expertise. Further, it can be problematic to assess the superiority of a firm's technology or knowledge assets in comparison to a competitor's. Critics of the RBV claim that it offers a limited understanding of a firm's sustainable competitive advantage because the concepts of resources and value in the RBV are indeterminate. This limited view results from the RBV's alignment with neoclassical economic rationality, which neglects the importance of resource pooling and the role of human engagement in the process of value creation (Kraaijenbrink et al., 2010).

Spotlight: Sustainability and the RBV

Over the years, more attention has been paid to the RBV because of its relevance to, and rigour in, addressing sustainability challenges faced by businesses worldwide. The RBV provides a framework to identify and harness resources that contribute to environmental, social, and economic sustainability, thus contributing to long-term sustainability. By emphasizing the importance of valuable and rare resources, the RBV encourages firms to invest in environmentally friendly technologies, sustainable supply chain practices, and socially responsible initiatives. Moreover, the RBV's focus on inimitable resources demands continuous innovation and adaptation to changing market conditions, encouraging firms to embrace sustainable practices as part of their core competencies.

(Continued)

A recent study by Arda et al. (2023) exemplifies the relationship between the RBV and sustainability, aiming to achieve a better understanding of sustainability in corporations by applying a resource-based view of sustainable supply chain management. The researchers examine whether environmental and social performance act as mediators in the relationship between environmental management practices and operational performance. The results reveal a positive mediating effect, aligning with the principles of the resource-based view. This suggests that enhancing capabilities and resources through environmental management practices positively influences all dimensions of sustainability and enhances the financial performance of the firm.

Another study in this research stream explores how green innovation can be a valuable resource for competitive advantage and sustainable development. It uses the resource-based view to address the dilemma of resource consumption and preservation and identifies key contributors and four thematic areas: green supply chain management, green product design, corporate environmental responsibility, and social sustainability. The study provides insights into current research and considers the direction of future research into green innovation. As the examples earlier in the chapter show, RBV contributes to sustainability by promoting strategic alignment, encouraging innovation, and creating sustainable competitive advantage. Businesses continue to face increasing pressure to adopt sustainable practices, which is why the RBV remains a robust and useful framework for shaping a more sustainable and responsible future in International Business.

Sources: Arda et al. (2023) and Ullah et al. (2021)

Case Sudy: Unilever and Sustainability as a Source of Competitive Advantage

Unilever is a compelling example of a company that has successfully leveraged sustainability to create a competitive advantage, aligning with the principles of the resource-based view (RBV) of the firm. Unilever, a multinational consumer goods company, has strategically integrated sustainability practices into its business model, emphasizing the importance of environmental and social responsibility. This approach has enhanced Unilever's reputation and contributed to a sustainable competitive advantage.

One key resource that Unilever has developed is its Sustainable Living Plan (SLP), a comprehensive strategy aimed at decoupling the company's growth from environmental impact and increasing its positive social impact. The SLP focuses on three main goals: improving health and well-being, reducing its environmental footprint, and enhancing livelihoods. By embedding sustainability into its core business activities, Unilever has created a unique set of resources that are valuable, rare, and difficult to imitate.

For example, Unilever has invested in developing sustainable sourcing practices for its raw materials, such as palm oil, tea, and soy. Through initiatives such as the Sustainable

Agriculture Code and Rainforest Alliance certification, Unilever ensures that its supply chain is environmentally friendly and socially responsible. This not only secures a consistent supply of resources but also appeals to an increasingly environmentally conscious consumer base.

Furthermore, Unilever's commitment to reducing its environmental impact extends to its product development and manufacturing processes. The company has set ambitious targets to improve the environmental performance of its products, including reducing water and energy usage in its production facilities. These initiatives not only contribute to cost savings but also position Unilever as a responsible and sustainable choice for consumers.

From the RBV perspective, Unilever's sustainability efforts can be seen as valuable, as they contribute to the company's financial performance, enhance its brand image, and meet the evolving preferences of consumers. These sustainability-focused resources are also rare, as not all competitors have adopted such comprehensive and integrated sustainability strategies. Lastly, these resources are difficult to imitate, as they are deeply embedded in Unilever's organizational culture and business processes.

Sources: Unilever (www.unilever.com/news/press-and-media/press-releases/2020/unilever-celebrates-10-years-of-the-sustainable-living-plan; www.unilever.com/news/news-search/2023/leading-and-delivering-on-sustainability-through-our-compass-commitments)

Case Study Questions

1. How can Unilever balance its sustainability efforts with the sometimes environmentally difficult products it offers?
2. How does Unilever's sustainability strategy differ from that of major competitors, such as Procter & Gamble and Henkel?
3. What are the limits of Unilever's sustainability focus?

7.1.3 Why Firms Internationalize – Summary

Firms generally internationalize to increase profits, either to reduce costs or to increase revenue. Building on this differentiation Dunning (2000) discusses four different motives for internationalization: efficiency-seeking, resource-seeking, market-seeking, and strategic asset seeking. To internationalize successfully, firms need firm-specific assets – bundles of capabilities and resources or a specific competitive positioning that differentiates the firm sustainably from competition. The resource-based view (RBV) provides a fitting theory to explain and analyse to what extent a firm holds such firm-specific assets. Once a firm holds a strong firm-specific asset, it can benefit significantly from internationalization but must make sure that its firms-specific assets remain valuable, rare, hard to imitate, and organized (VRIO).

7.2 WHEN TO INTERNATIONALIZE: FIRST MOVER ADVANTAGES, THE SPEED OF INTERNATIONALIZATION, AND BORN GLOBAL FIRMS

Deciding when to enter a foreign market is crucial for MNCs as it can have a significant effect on their performance. In this respect, the literature mostly discusses three (partially overlapping) phenomena: the first analyses the timing of a firm's entry into a foreign market in comparison to the firm's competitors. The second looks at the pace of the expansion process, analysing how quickly the steps in the internationalization process are taken. The third considers how long it takes firms to have a 'global' presence, in particular the phenomenon of firms that operate globally from when, or soon after, they were founded.

The speed of entry into a single market can categorize firms as first movers, early followers, or late movers (Kerin et al., 1992). Pioneering firms – first movers and early followers – often enjoy several advantages. They can select the most lucrative business opportunities, establish robust distribution networks, shape consumer preferences, and accumulate valuable location experience. By pre-emptively securing distribution channels, engaging in aggressive marketing, and promoting their brand, these pioneers can create barriers to entry for subsequent entrants. The absence of significant competition during their initial phase further strengthens their position. These advantages can pose formidable challenges for late movers, making it difficult for them to establish a strong foothold.

However, being the first to enter is not without its drawbacks. First movers and early followers often grapple with heightened market and regulatory uncertainties. They bear the costs associated with pioneering a new market, which can be intensive in terms of time and resources. In contrast, late movers can capitalize on the groundwork laid by pioneers. They benefit from lower uncertainty, can leverage market insights gained by early entrants, and might even poach lucrative opportunities and partners from them. Additionally, late entrants often have the advantage of refining their offerings based on the market's evolved preferences, allowing them to allocate resources more efficiently.

Case Study: Blockbuster – Challenges for a First Mover

Blockbuster was a dominant force in the home entertainment industry throughout the 1990s and early 2000s. The company pioneered the concept of video rental stores, offering customers a wide selection of movies and video games for rent on VHS tapes and DVDs. Blockbuster's extensive network of bricks-and-mortar stores, coupled with its aggressive marketing and branding efforts, made it synonymous with video rental for millions of consumers worldwide.

However, despite its early success and market dominance, Blockbuster failed to adapt to the changing dynamics of the home entertainment industry, particularly the shift towards digital distribution and online streaming.

Blockbuster was slow to recognize the growing popularity of digital technologies and the impact they would have on the home entertainment landscape. While competitors like Netflix embraced the emerging trend of online DVD rental and streaming services, Blockbuster remained focused on its traditional bricks-and-mortar business model. The company underestimated the disruptive potential of digital distribution and failed to invest adequately in technology and online platforms to stay ahead of the curve.

Despite being approached by Netflix in the early 2000s for a potential partnership or acquisition, Blockbuster declined the opportunity, dismissing online streaming as a niche market with limited growth potential. This decision proved to be a costly mistake, as Netflix went on to become a formidable competitor in the streaming industry, eventually surpassing Blockbuster in market value and subscriber base. Blockbuster's reluctance to embrace online streaming and invest in digital innovation allowed Netflix to gain a significant competitive advantage and erode Blockbuster's market share.

As consumer preferences shifted towards convenience and on-demand access to content, Blockbuster struggled to innovate its customer experience and adapt its business model accordingly. The company's reliance on late fees and rigid rental policies alienated customers and deterred them from patronizing Blockbuster stores. In contrast, Netflix introduced subscription-based pricing plans, unlimited rentals, and personalized recommendations, offering consumers greater flexibility and value for their money.

Blockbuster's rapid expansion and aggressive store growth strategy in the 1990s led to overexpansion and a substantial debt burden. The company invested heavily in opening new stores and acquiring competitors, such as Hollywood Video, to maintain its market dominance. However, the high costs associated with store operations, real estate leases, and inventory management strained Blockbuster's financial resources and limited its ability to invest in digital innovation and strategic initiatives.

With the rise of digital streaming platforms and the decline of physical media formats such as DVDs, Blockbuster's core business model became increasingly obsolete. The shift towards digital content consumption rendered Blockbuster's vast network of rental stores less relevant and economically viable. Despite attempts to diversify its offerings and introduce digital rental kiosks and streaming services, Blockbuster could not compete effectively with online streaming giants like Netflix, Amazon Prime Video, and Hulu.

In 2010, Blockbuster filed for bankruptcy and began closing its remaining stores, marking the end of an era for the once-dominant video rental chain. The failure of Blockbuster as a first mover provides a good example of the importance of adaptability, innovation, and strategic foresight in navigating evolving market trends and technological disruptions. Despite its early success and market leadership, Blockbuster's inability to anticipate and respond effectively to digital transformation ultimately led to its downfall - and the late movers, like, for example, Netflix, are still successful in the market.

Sources: Business Insider (www.businessinsider.com/rise-and-fall-of-blockbuster) and Wikipedia (https://en.wikipedia.org/wiki/Blockbuster_(retailer))

Regarding the second phenomenon associated with timing – the pace of the internationalization process – most research analysing this aspect conceptualizes it as the time between two consecutive foreign expansions, or the number of foreign expansions per year. However, it can also consider the speed of expansion within a specific host country – for example, the time to increase investment, the time to upgrade from export to investment, or the time to set up a second or third investment. In other words, we can differentiate two types of speed in the internationalization process: the speed of expansion across markets, and the speed of expansion within markets.

The pace of international expansion is strongly driven by the strategic objectives of the internationalizing firm. Some companies prefer to take a cautious and methodical approach to international expansion, focusing on thorough market research, strategic planning, and risk assessment before entering new markets. In contrast, other companies may pursue an aggressive and ambitious expansion strategy, seeking to capture market share quickly and establish a global presence. These companies may enter multiple markets simultaneously or in rapid succession through organic growth, mergers and acquisitions, joint ventures, or licensing agreements. Aggressive expansion strategies require significant financial investment, operational resources, and the organizational capacity to support simultaneous market entries and scale operations efficiently. While aggressive expansion can accelerate growth and competitive advantage, it also entails higher risks, greater complexity, and more management challenges, including cultural integration, regulatory compliance, and brand consistency across diverse markets.

Beyond strategic objectives, the speed of expansion may also be influenced by external factors such as market conditions, economic trends, political stability, and industry dynamics (for a more detailed understanding of the environment see Chapters 2–5). Companies may accelerate or decelerate their expansion plans in response to changing market conditions, emerging opportunities, or unforeseen challenges. For example, companies may expedite expansion into high-growth or underserved markets to capitalize on favourable economic conditions or competitive advantages. Conversely, companies may delay or scale back expansion in response to economic downturns, political instability, regulatory barriers, or market saturation in certain regions.

The born global firm is the third phenomenon frequently discussed in the literature. Born global firms started to be discussed in the literature in the late 1990s as a new phenomenon that supposedly challenged many assumptions in existing research (Knight & Cavusgil, 1996). The term refers to a company characterized by rapid internationalization and global orientation from the outset of its operations, or shortly after, rather than more traditional businesses that start their operations in a single domestic market and gradually expand internationally over time.

To do so, they often utilize advanced technologies, digital platforms, and communication tools to facilitate International Business operations and reach global customers. Technologies such as the internet, e-commerce platforms, social media, and digital marketing enable them to overcome geographic barriers and connect with customers, suppliers, and partners worldwide.

Examples of born global firms include technology startups, software companies, biotech firms, and creative industries that are able to leverage digital technologies, intellectual property, and global networks to achieve rapid internationalization and success. Revolut is a good example. Founded in the United Kingdom in 2015 by Nikolay Storonsky and Vlad Yatsenko, Revolut disrupted the banking industry by offering a digital banking app with features such as currency exchange, money transfers, and cryptocurrency trading. Revolut adopted an aggressive international expansion strategy, launching its services in multiple European countries and beyond within a short period. By leveraging technological enablers and network relationships with regulatory authorities and financial partners, Revolut rapidly grew its user base and became one of the leading fintech companies globally.

7.3 WHERE TO INTERNATIONALIZE - COUNTRY MARKET SELECTION

Internationalisation is a bundle of strategies where, among other questions, firms juggle the choice of 'if' they should expand beyond borders with the question of 'where' they should set their footprint. If firm-specific advantages answer the former, then country-specific advantages or location advantages shine light on the latter. Simply put, the core motivation for firms to sell or relocate activities to another country lies in the prospect of enhanced profitability. Such enhanced profitability can only be achieved in the long run if countries possess a specific location advantage that helps a firm to operate more successfully.

7.3.1 Location Advantages

Location advantages – advantages that help specific firms to operate more successfully in one country rather than another – can have different sources. One source lies in the concept of agglomeration economies. For a long time, geographic economists have tried to answer the question of why economic activity happens where it does. One of the most successful theories – agglomeration economies – emphasizes the benefits of proximity to other enterprises, such as in cities. The benefits are multifaceted, including superior infrastructure, lower operational costs owing to ample service providers, and a vast pool of potential recruits. On an industry-specific level, the benefits comprise knowledge spillovers, specialized labour pools, lower costs of doing business, and easy access to critical resources. However, agglomeration also has its downsides. The very factors that are advantageous can, under excessive concentration, morph into diseconomies of agglomeration. Think of surging prices due to heightened competition for resources or the palpable congestion strangling a city's infrastructure. Agglomeration economies are, therefore, a frequent source of location advantages and country-specific advantages.

A second source is connected to the institutional environment that we analysed in Chapters 2–5. Institutions play an indispensable role in shaping the geographical dispersion of commercial activities. Douglass North defines institutions as 'the humanly devised constraints that structure political, economic, and social interaction. They consist of both informal constraints (sanctions, taboos, customs, traditions, and codes of conduct), and formal rules (constitutions, laws, property rights)' (North, 1990: 97). In essence, institutions are 'the rules of the game' in society, shaping our choices and interactions. Institutions differ from one country to another and encompass a wide range of factors such as the overarching economic organization, the developmental stage of a system, the constraints on political decision-makers. Institutions play a major role in shaping economic outcomes. Thus, they are also critical in a firm's decisions about where to locate international operations.

A third source consists of macro factors. Trade theory suggests factors that influence location advantages, including exchange rates, the size of markets, the availability of resources, and favourable corporate tax regimes. While the theoretical impact of those factors is firmly rooted in formal economic models, many of those factors have a patchy empirical record. Corporate tax rates and wage levels in particular do not consistently determine firms' location choices, contrary to neoliberal economic thought. A likely explanation for such surprising findings is that wages and tax rates are representations of the quality of labour and public services a firm receives in a location. Consequently, higher taxes and wages may also indicate higher purchasing power or higher quality in production.

From a practical point of view, it would be almost impossible for firms to analyse all the countries in the world as potential markets. To streamline this process, managers frequently turn to a sequential scoring model when considering international expansion. Initially, firms must identify the key success factors vital for their international activities. These success factors are subsequently grouped based on their overarching significance. Using this established hierarchy, markets that do not meet the criteria of the most essential factors are filtered out during the first selection step. The markets that pass this initial phase are then subjected to a more detailed analysis based on the next set of factors. This systematic process of filtering and subsequent more detailed analysis is repeated until the desired number of markets is selected. Throughout this method, there's a trade-off between the impact of the information and its availability. In some instances, it is more economical to utilize easily accessible data for an initial market pruning, reserving in-depth and potentially costlier market research for a select group of markets.

7.3.2 Country-Market Selection: Institution-Based View

The institution-based view (IBV) has emerged as a prominent perspective in the field of IB, shaped by the works of Nobel Prize laureate Douglass North (1990) and other influential scholars, and helps us to understand country characteristics in the market selection process. As highlighted in previous chapters, the view emphasizes the crucial role of institutions in governing human interactions and shaping firm behaviour in various contexts and underscores the significance of formal and informal institutions in reducing uncertainty and providing a framework for decision-making in International Business settings. North defines institutions as the humanly devised constraints that structure human interaction and which encompass the formal and informal rules governing individual and firm behaviour. The ability of firms to comprehend and capitalize on the diverse rules of the game has a significant influence on their success (see Chapters 2–5 for more details on institutions).

The IBV revolves around two fundamental ideas. Initially, it posits that managers and firms act rationally, pursuing their interests while adhering to institutional limitations. For instance, in certain countries, labour laws shield workers from unemployment risks. Secondly, firm conduct is shaped by institutions; however, when formal constraints are ambiguous or ineffective, informal constraints become more influential. Figure 7.1 shows the institutional framework based on Peng (2002).

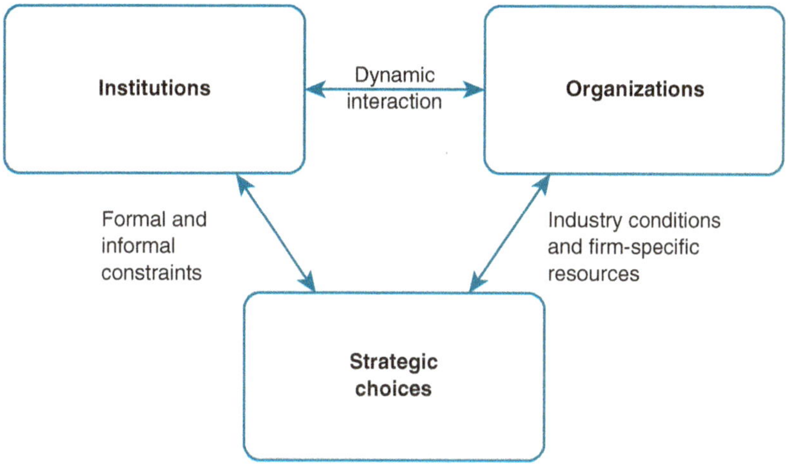

Figure 7.1 Institutions, organizations, and strategic choices

Source: Based on Peng (2022: 253). Adapted with permission of Springer Nature

North highlighted the importance of informal and formal institutions. Informal institutions, such as norms and values, dictate morally right and wrong behaviours and what is deemed important within a society. These informal norms are deeply embedded and change slowly over time. Formal institutions encompass laws, regulations, and rules established by authorized bodies, such as national governments or the European Union, to govern business activities while informal institutions encompass ethics, norms, and cultures.

The IBV places significant emphasis on understanding and navigating the complex interplay between formal and informal institutions in various markets. By grasping the influence of these institutional constraints, firms can make informed decisions, reduce uncertainty, and enhance their chances of success in the global business landscape.

The IBV acknowledges the context-specific nature of institutional environments in different countries and allows for a nuanced analysis of how firms must adapt their strategies to align with unique institutional characteristics in various host countries. A strength of the institutional view is that when strategy is aligned with the big picture, it provides a clear link between broad institutional issues, corporate strategy, and performance.

However, Peng (2002) also had some criticisms of the IBV. Most existing research focuses on static relationships and fails to explore the dynamic aspects of complex relationships, such as the potentially negative effects of close supplier relations and diversification on firm flexibility and coordination. Moreover, the extent to which further diversification might be disadvantageous remains unclear and requires further investigation in a dynamic institutional environment. He further argues that the interaction between national cultures and institutional frameworks in shaping strategic choices needs more in-depth exploration, as it is unlikely that all companies in non-Western countries will follow exactly the same strategies as Western companies, but they might become more similar over time as they develop similar institutions.

7.3.3 Country Market Selection - Porter's Diamond Model

Another conceptual model that helps to analyse potential advantages in a country market is Porter's diamond model (Porter, 2011). This framework evaluates the competitiveness of an industry within a particular nation by identifying four primary determinants that enable firms in that industry to compete on an international scale (see Figure 7.2):

- *Factor conditions*: This determinant focuses on the availability, price, and quality of inputs essential for the production process. Advanced and specialized factors are given more emphasis over simple and generic ones, as they play a pivotal role in fostering competitive advantage.
- *Demand conditions*: This aspect considers the nature and characteristics of market demand. A substantial local demand or a demand for diversified or high-quality products drives local firms to innovate and enhance their offerings, thereby serving as a potential source of competitive advantage.
- *Related and supporting industries*: The existence of industries that are either related or provide support to the focal industry can bolster competitive advantage. This is through the accumulation of agglomeration effects and the emergence of stable and profitable inter-firm relationships.
- *Firm strategy, structure, and rivalry*: This component encompasses the strategies employed, the organizational structures in place, and the managerial systems adopted by firms within an industry in a specific country. Additionally, it sheds light on the intensity of rivalry within the industry. A heightened level of rivalry can amplify a firm's capacity to compete on a global scale.

While these four determinants are central to the diamond model, Porter also underscores two supplementary elements that influence a country's attractiveness:

- *Governments*: In Porter's view, the government's role is ancillary, a viewpoint that has been extensively debated in contemporary scholarship. In this subsidiary capacity, governments can mould market attractiveness by influencing the primary four determinants (see Chapter 3 for a detailed analysis of formal national institutions).
- *Chance*: Occasionally, external events, which are beyond the control of firms – such as groundbreaking innovations, global supply disruptions, wars, or climate change – can have a significant impact on one or more of the primary determinants.

A salient feature of Porter's diamond model is the interplay and mutual reinforcement among the four primary determinants. When these determinants synergistically bolster each other, creating a virtuous cycle, the likelihood of a country possessing location advantages for a specific industry is heightened.

7.3.4 Country Market Selection – The Uppsala Model Part 1

The Uppsala internationalization model emerged from the observations of Jan Johanson and Jan-Erik Vahlne (1977), scholars based at the University of Uppsala in Sweden. They discerned that traditional economic theories did not entirely explain the internationalization behaviours of the small- and medium-sized Swedish firms they studied. Instead of making substantial foreign investments straight away, these firms adopted an incremental approach to international expansion, in terms of both geographical reach and commitment level.

Johanson and Vahlne's research spanned diverse sectors, including specialty steel, pulp and paper, engineering, and pharmaceuticals. A consistent internationalization pattern emerged across these industries. Initially, companies would receive recurring orders from abroad. To better cater to this foreign demand, they would appoint a sales agency in the respective country. As the market's significance grew or if challenges arose with the agency, the company would then establish a subsidiary, either by acquiring the agency or recruiting its former employees. This subsidiary often laid the groundwork for local production, should the demand necessitate it in the future. This entire process highlighted a gradual and adaptive approach to internationalization, contrasting with the more deterministic views of traditional economic theories. To explain those observations, Johanson and Vahlne developed a behavioural theory of internationalization based on organizational learning, now known as the Uppsala model.

At the core of the Uppsala model is the idea that internationalization decisions are not solely about optimizing resource allocations, but are instead beholden to the incentives, behaviours, and biases of managers. In this view, internationalization decisions are incremental responses to emerging challenges or newfound opportunities. Managers make

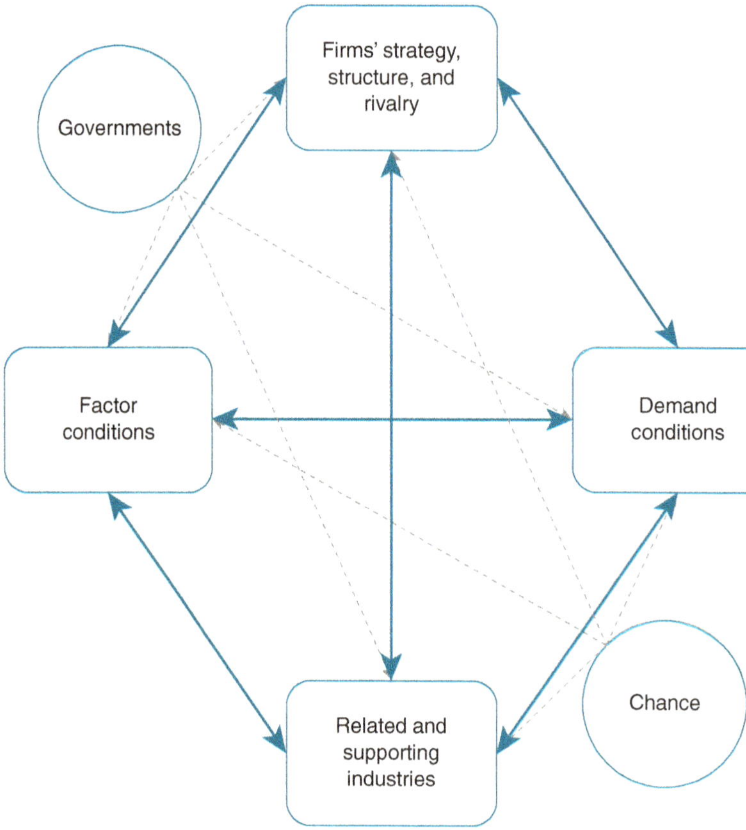

Figure 7.2 The diamond model of country market selection

Source: Based on Porter (2011)

decisions with the dual aim of maximizing company growth while concurrently minimizing associated risks (Cyert & March, 1963). Each internationalization decision is made independently, without necessarily adhering to a predetermined strategic blueprint. These individual decisions offer the firm organizational learning experiences. As managers become more familiar with the local market, their understanding deepens, leading to a lower perception of risk in subsequent decisions and, consequently, greater commitments.

This behavioural perspective serves as the basis for the process model Johanson and Vahlne propose as an explanation of firm internationalization. In their suggested process, firms' international activities are constrained by how risky managers perceive them to be. This risk is partly economic and partly due to the 'psychic distance' of managers to the market. However, the international activities a firm does engage in provide market knowledge, which in turn reduces the perceived uncertainty of future international activities. This enables firms to engage in more and higher commitment internationalization, further increasing market knowledge and thereby decreasing perceived uncertainty. This iterative process of knowledge acquisition and reduction of perceived risk forms the essence of the Uppsala model's logic, emphasizing the evolutionary nature of International Business strategies.

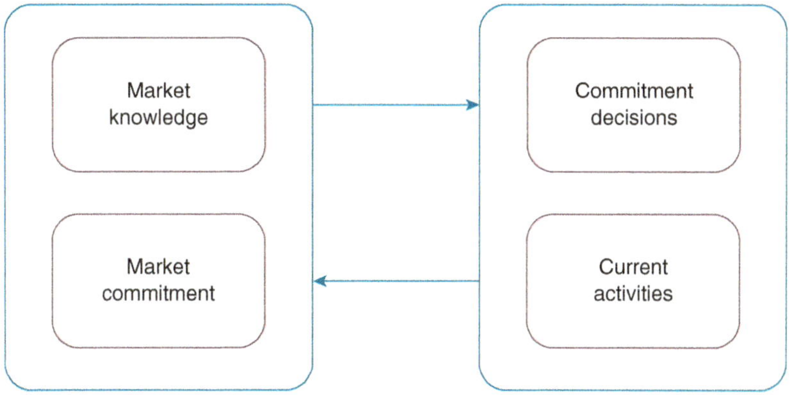

Figure 7.3 The relationship between knowledge, decisions, commitment, and activities according to the Uppsala model

The process model is made up of two state aspects – market commitment and market knowledge – and two change aspects – commitment decisions and current activities. As depicted in Figure 7.3, they are mutually dependent.

7.3.4.1 Market Commitment

Market commitment refers to the extent and nature of resources that a firm dedicates to a specific market. This commitment is not solely determined by the volume of resources allocated but also by the challenge associated with repurposing these resources for alternative uses. It is important to note that these committed resources aren't necessarily physically present in the target market. They could encompass investments made in different locations that indirectly support the market in question.

The depth of a firm's market commitment can be gauged by considering the potential value of alternative applications for the committed resources. For instance, a horizontally integrated firm, with a business unit abroad that does not directly relate to its core operations, might find it relatively easy to divest from that unit with minimal losses. In contrast, a firm that's more intricately integrated internationally would face significant challenges if it decided to withdraw from a market. Such a firm would likely need to re-establish key functions in alternative markets, reflecting a deeper level of commitment to its initial market of operation.

7.3.4.2 Market Knowledge

Market knowledge encompasses a comprehensive understanding of various facets of a market. According to Carlson (1974), market knowledge can be understood as present and future demand, supply, and competition as well as about channels for distribution, payment conditions, and the transferability of money. This knowledge is bifurcated into two categories: explicit and tacit. Explicit knowledge is readily communicable and can be shared by one individual with another. In contrast, tacit knowledge is more elusive and challenging to convey. It is often rooted in personal experiences or ingrained within organizational routines and processes. Market knowledge is, to a large degree, of the latter kind.

Another distinctive feature of market knowledge is its market-specific nature. It is tailored to a particular market and does not seamlessly apply to other markets. This characteristic establishes a symbiotic relationship between market knowledge and market commitment. A firm with profound market knowledge can more effectively deploy its resources in that market. However, since this knowledge is not universally applicable, it diminishes the potential value of those resources in different contexts. Consequently, this deepens the firm's commitment to the market in question.

7.3.4.3 Current Business Activities

Current business activities play a pivotal role in shaping both market commitment and market knowledge. These activities, whether they involve sales, marketing, production, or other operations, do not instantly yield their intended outcomes. There is inherently a time lag between the initiation of an activity and the realization of its results. The more extended this delay, the more resources a firm needs to allocate and keep engaged in that specific market, leading to an increased market commitment.

Furthermore, these ongoing business activities serve as the primary source of tacit market knowledge. As employees immerse themselves in these activities, they accumulate context-specific experience that goes beyond textbook knowledge. Their day-to-day interactions, challenges, and problem-solving endeavours equip them with insights that are hard to document but crucial for effective market operations. Over time, these insights shape and refine organizational procedures, ensuring that the company becomes more adept and responsive to the market's unique demands and nuances.

7.3.4.4 Commitment Decisions

Commitment decisions are strategic choices made by firms in response to identified challenges and opportunities within a market. The identification of both is largely dependent on market knowledge. A profound understanding of the market enables managers to discern potential problems and lucrative opportunities.

When faced with challenges, managers typically seek solutions that are closely aligned with the nature and context of the problem. Similarly, when they spot opportunities, frequently their response is to expand operations within the market in order to capitalize on them. This means that most decisions, whether they address problems or leverage opportunities, lead to actions that are tied to the market. These decisions often result in an expansion of the firm's existing activities, thereby amplifying its commitment to that market.

There is also a reciprocal relationship between market commitment and opportunities. As a firm deepens its commitment to a market, it not only increases its internal footprint but also increases its interactions with external entities. This heightened engagement with the external environment often leads to new opportunities being presented to the firm, leading to further commitment decisions. In essence, the more committed a firm is to a market, the more it becomes a magnet for external opportunities, creating a virtuous cycle of growth and investment.

The Uppsala internationalization model provides explanations for two strategic decisions in firm internationalization: how much does a firm commit to a foreign market, and how does a firm select new country markets? The first is a 'how' question and will be explained later in this chapter; the latter relates explicitly to the mechanisms of country-market selection.

To explain how firms decide to commit to a specific market, we look to the concept of psychic distance, which was introduced by Beckermann (1956: 40):

> a special problem is posed by the existence of 'psychic' distance. It is probable that the manner in which the purchases of raw materials by a firm are distributed geographically will depend partly on the extent to which foreign sources have been personally contacted and cultivated. While the transport costs paid … by an Italian entrepreneur on a raw material supplied by Turkey may be no greater … than the same material supplied by Switzerland, he is more likely to have contacts with Swiss suppliers, since Switzerland will be 'nearer' to him in a psychic evaluation (fewer language difficulties, and so on) …

Psychic distance, thus, can be thought of as the perceived differences between the home country and a foreign market as a result of differences in culture, language, business practices, legal systems, and other factors. The greater the psychic distance between the home country and the foreign market, the higher the perceived uncertainty and risk for the firm because of information asymmetry between the home market and the foreign market. Managers, thus, tend to invest in markets that they know more about and that they perceive as less psychically distant. It is important to keep in mind that we can understand the model as an explanatory theory (it explains how firms behave), rather than a normative theory that recommends how firms should behave.

7.3.5 Summary - Country Market Selection

Country market selection is a core strategic decision in the internationalization process. An important starting point is that firms decide for or against country markets based on location advantages that markets present for their operations. Such location advantages can develop through agglomeration economies, institutional factors, or macro factors. The institution-based view provides a detailed understanding of the relevance of institutions to the development of location advantages. Porter's diamond model can help to structure and assess the attractiveness of a specific industry in a specific market by analysing factor conditions, demand conditions, firms' strategy, structure, and rivalry, as well as the role of governments and chance. This highlights that the attractiveness of one specific market varies for different firms and industries. While one company might be able to find location advantages in a market, others may not.

The Uppsala model provides a rationale for firms' country market selection, specifically for the observation that many firms prefer to invest in psychically close markets. The theory is based on the idea that decision-makers are risk averse and prefer to commit to markets they are familiar with. Decision-makers thus act with bounded-rationality and are not considered purely rational decision-makers. It is important therefore to understand that the theory is explanatory, that it helps us to understand firms' country market selection – it is not a normative theory that makes recommendations.

7.4 HOW TO INTERNATIONALIZE: MARKET ENTRY DECISIONS

Market entry decisions are strategic decisions associated with the question of 'how' to internationalize. In the literature on International Business, this usually includes decisions on ownership (how much ownership do I want in a foreign activity?), establishment (do I invest in an existing bundle of resources abroad or do I set up a new one?), and value chain activities (which value chain activities do I set up abroad?) (see Figure 7.4). It is important to understand that these decisions are not independent from each other; a decision on ownership, for example, has significant consequences for the other two dimensions as some options may become impossible to pursue while others may have a better strategic fit. In addition, the motives of internationalization, the intended speed of internationalization, and the country market will also influence decisions on entry mode. Consequently, firms need to develop and find the perfect bundle of decisions for entry into a certain market at a certain point in time.

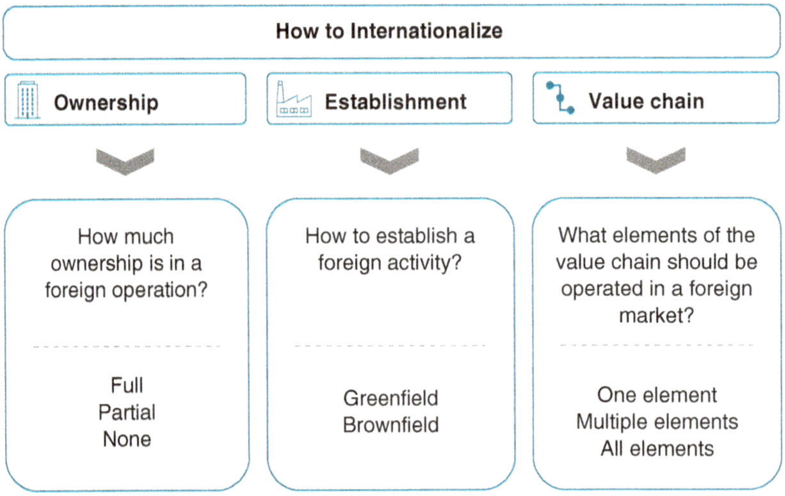

Figure 7.4 Strategies in entry mode decisions

7.4.1 Ownership Mode Decisions - Strategic Options

Firms have multiple options of ownership in entering foreign markets (see Figure 7.5). Initially, we might differentiate between entries with ownership in a foreign market (foreign direct investments) and entries without ownership. The distinction is crucial, as equity-based modes require firms to conduct operations directly in the foreign nation. This often introduces complexities, given the challenges of managing activities across vast geographical distances, navigating different political and administrative systems, adapting to particular cultures, and operating within diverse socio-economic landscapes.

Non-equity entry modes offer firms various strategies to penetrate international markets without significant capital investment in foreign territories. Two of the most prevalent non-equity entry modes are exporting and importing. Exporting allows firms to sell their surplus production and gauge the compatibility of their products with foreign markets. Exporting can be direct, where firms sell directly to foreign customers, or indirect, where agents or distributors handle sales and potentially logistics to and within the foreign country. While indirect exporting offers convenience, especially for firms without established processes for international orders, it limits their direct experience and understanding of the target market. Importing refers to the process of purchasing goods or services from foreign countries for sale or use in the domestic market. It plays a crucial role in firms' global value chains and allows access to a wide range of products, raw materials, and resources that may not be available domestically or are more cost effective to procure from overseas suppliers.

Another prominent non-equity entry mode is licensing and franchising. Licensing entails granting rights – to intangible property, such as patents, trademarks, or technology – to a foreign partner in exchange for royalties. This allows companies to generate revenue from their intellectual property without significant capital expenditure. However, licensors have limited control over how licensees use the licensed property, risking brand reputation or intellectual property infringement. Franchising, on the other hand, involves granting rights to use a complete business model, including branding and operational processes, to franchisees. This facilitates rapid expansion into foreign markets by leveraging the resources and efforts of franchisees. However, maintaining consistent quality and customer experience across franchise outlets can be challenging. A classic example is McDonald's, which does not run most global McDonald's restaurants directly. Instead, it provides operational guidelines to local franchisees, who, in turn, share a portion of their revenues with the parent company.

Opting for non-equity entry modes presents firms with both advantages and challenges. On the upside, these modes are generally less risky, demanding fewer resources and less in-depth market knowledge. However, they may not be as efficient for larger-scale operations. Moreover, specifically in licensing and franchising, firms relinquish a degree of control over their intellectual property, which can lead to brand dilution, intellectual property theft, or even inadvertently fostering new competitors in the market.

Equity entry modes involve internationalizing companies establishing their operations directly in a foreign country. Unlike non-equity modes, they require firms to invest their assets and resources directly into the foreign market, inherently exposing them to greater risks. This is due to the challenges of navigating unfamiliar political, cultural, and socio-economic landscapes. The degree of ownership in the foreign subsidiary further categorizes FDI into distinct types, each with its unique set of advantages and challenges (see Figure 7.5).

One prevalent equity entry mode is the joint venture (JV). In a JV, firms partner with a local entity to either establish or acquire a co-owned company in the foreign market. This collaboration often arises from the need to share or mitigate the risks associated with international operations or to comply with patricular legal mandates. While the idealistic perspective is that JVs ensure better adaptation to local markets and equitable profit-sharing, sceptics argue that such measures are designed to create involuntary technology transfers or even foster the emergence of local competitors. In one type of JV, one firm brings technological expertise, while the other offers market insights. However, given the mutual learning opportunities, which can render one partner redundant over time, and the limits to creating synergies in the long run, many JVs tend to have a finite lifetime.

Another significant equity entry mode is the wholly owned subsidiary (WOS). As the name implies, a WOS is entirely owned by the internationalizing firm, offering it complete control over its foreign operations. This ownership mode offers full control over operations, marketing, and decision-making, providing protection for intellectual property and proprietary technology. However, setting up and operating wholly owned subsidiaries requires significant upfront investment in infrastructure, facilities, and personnel. Companies must also navigate local regulations, compliance requirements, and cultural differences, which can be time-consuming and costly.

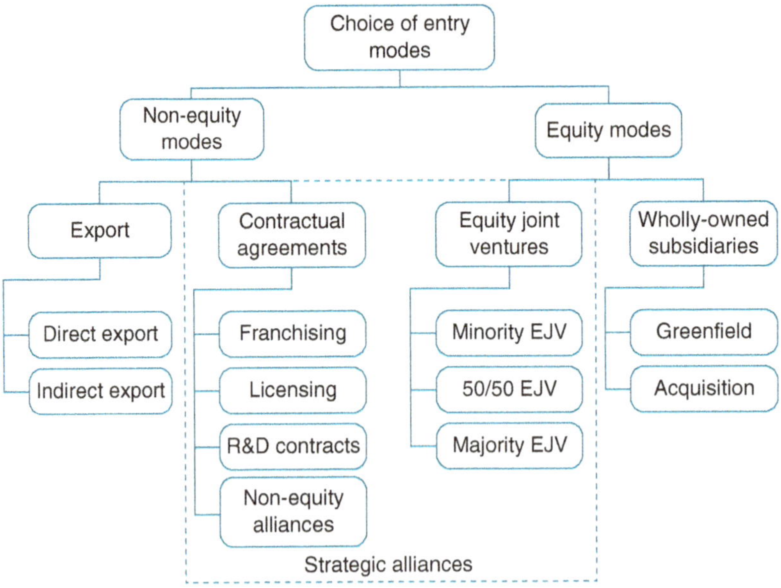

Figure 7.5 Mode strategies in a foreign entry

Source: Adapted from Pan & Tse (2000)

Spotlight: Outsourcing and Offshoring

Offshoring and outsourcing are two terms frequently used in today's media, but also in the academic world. While both appear to be similar, it is important to be able to differentiate between the two.

Offshoring is a business strategy in which a company relocates some of its business operations or processes from one country to another, typically to lower-cost locations abroad. The primary motivation behind offshoring is to reduce production costs, increase efficiency, and remain competitive in the global marketplace. Offshoring can involve various types of business activity, including manufacturing, services, and support functions.

Outsourcing is a business strategy in which a company contracts out certain business functions, processes, or services to external service providers or third-party vendors, rather than handling them in-house. The primary objective of outsourcing is to leverage external expertise, resources, and efficiencies to improve operational efficiency, reduce costs, and focus on core business activities.

Consequently, offshoring is a question associated with country-market selection, and outsourcing is a question associated with the ownership decisions of a firm. Firms can pursue each strategy individually but can also pursue both options jointly. Figure 7.6 highlights the options.

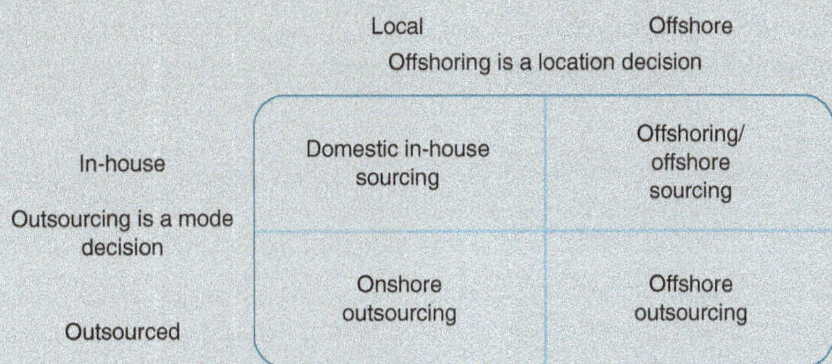

Figure 7.6 Outsourcing and offshoring

7.4.2 Ownership Mode Decisions – Transaction Cost Theory

A theory that is frequently used to decide between different degrees of ownership in a foreign activity is transaction cost theory (TCT), which offers insights into how organizational actors optimize gains from interdependence by choosing appropriate governance structures. When a firm engages in a market, it incurs transaction costs, defined as the costs of organizing transactions. These transaction costs emerge from various transaction-related activities, including partner search, monitoring, product quality assurance, contract enforcement, and sub-optimal resource allocation due to unrealized transactions. Developed by Oliver Williamson in 1985, the theory postulates that transactions are assigned to different governance structures based on three key attributes – asset specificity, uncertainty, and frequency (Williamson, 1985). Markets are an attractive choice for transactions. However, TCT acknowledges that under certain conditions transactions can be more efficiently organized within hierarchical relations (i.e. within organizations. Hierarchies facilitate the coordination of investments that would be difficult to manage through markets alone, thus reducing the risk of opportunistic behaviour and fostering cooperation (Cuypers et al., 2021). Over time, TCT has given rise to hybrid governance modes, which seek to leverage the advantages of both approaches, as for example in the form of alliances (Williamson, 1991).

For MNCs, managing disparities between the home and host countries is crucial as these variations can increase coordination costs. The primary concern for managers facing the make-or-buy decision lies in evaluating the transaction costs associated with any supply relationship. This evaluation involves considering the implications of two companies collaborating while safeguarding their respective interests. TCT highlights the advantages of FDI, necessitating an understanding of the factors influencing transaction costs and the strategic management of internalization advantages. MNCs must carefully assess the costs and benefits of different organizational forms to optimize their global operations effectively. TCT offers significant strengths in minimizing the drawbacks of relying on external partners and intermediaries and in reducing the risk of losing knowledge and proprietary assets to competitors.

Spotlight: TCT and the Blockchain

A recent study explores the application of TCT to blockchain technology in supply chain relationships. It posits six theses that blockchain reduces opportunistic behaviour, environmental uncertainty, and transaction costs, while increasing transaction transparency and validity (Schmidt & Wagner, 2019). The study highlights how TCT contributes to understanding the impact of blockchain on the digitization of International Business. In another paper, Nagle et al. (2020) focus on the application of TCT in the context of the digital economy. Given the increasing prevalence of digitally mediated transactions, the study explores how TCT applies in the digital world and identifies three key characteristics of digitally mediated transactions: reputation mechanisms, private information, and non-pecuniary transactions. The paper also outlines a research agenda, emphasizing the importance of exploring boundary conditions of TCT through digitization and highlighting the evolving usefulness of TCT, particularly in areas such as personal information markets and data portability (Nagle et al., 2020).

Sources: Schmidt & Wager (2019); Nagle et al. (2020) and Chen et al. (2022)

Anderson and Gatignon (1986) used TCT logic to develop a framework to guide MNCs in selecting optimal entry modes for international activities. When MNCs decide on an entry mode, the central objective is to optimize risk-adjusted returns. The degree of control that an entry mode provides is a crucial factor in this decision-making process, as it profoundly influences both the returns and the associated risks. High control enables MNCs to coordinate actions effectively, implement strategies, and resolve disputes in a manner that aligns with their interests. It also usually entitles MNCs to a more substantial share of the foreign enterprise's profits. However, high control is a double-edged sword. It brings with it increased responsibility and is often accompanied by higher direct costs, necessitating more significant resource commitment and administrative overheads. Additionally, it imposes larger switching costs, creating a form of lock-in, and exposing the MNC to heightened risk.

The choice of ownership in an entry mode decision represents a delicate trade-off between acquiring control and managing the costs of resource commitments, particularly in environments characterized by risk and uncertainty. The control that entry modes afford can be conceptualized along a spectrum of integration, ranging from arm's length marketing contracts to complete integration into the company hierarchies via ownership.

TCT provides insights into the level of integration and control MNCs should seek. According to TCT, market solutions should be the default option. When competition is robust, it aligns incentives due to competitive pressure and keeps the cost of replacing unsatisfactory partners, such as unreliable distributors, low. In such scenarios, the overhead of managing market contracts is minimal, allowing the MNC to specialize further in its core business model.

However, the logic of market solutions breaks down as competition erodes and the number of potential partners diminishes. This erosion is driven by the accumulation of transaction-specific assets, which are valuable only in a narrow range of transactions. These assets can be tangible, like specialized machinery, or intangible, like trust and knowledge about the other firm. As these assets accumulate over time in an ongoing business relationship, competition erodes, and replacing partners becomes more expensive. In situations where competition is eroding, MNCs are advised to increase control over the transaction by integrating it into the firm or by redesigning the task to prevent the accumulation of transaction-specificity. Integration changes the governance mode from arm's length contracting to hierarchical authority in an employer–employee relationship. A high degree of control is particularly suitable for transactions involving highly proprietary, unstructured, or poorly understood products and processes, customized products, and new products.

Uncertainty, both internal and external, is a critical factor determining the optimal degree of control. External uncertainty, arising from country risk, exacerbates the effects of transaction-specificity of assets, necessitating higher control. Conversely, internal uncertainty, stemming from the firm's unfamiliarity with the new environment, usually favours a lower degree of control. As firms gain experience, thereby reducing internal uncertainty, they become more adept at leveraging a higher degree of control. Sociocultural differences also have an impact on the degree of control, where firms need to decide on either giving the local enterprise more leeway through lower control or implementing the MNC's modus operandi via a high degree of control.

Finally, the threat of opportunistic behaviour or freeriding is a decisive factor in determining the optimal degree of control. When local partners have incentives to benefit from the MNC's efforts without contributing equivalently, a higher degree of control is advisable to prevent such freeriding, which can occur, for example, when a local partner leverages the MNC's brand name without maintaining its quality standards.

According to TCT, equity joint ventures become an effective mode of transaction when markets for resources held by each participating party are failing, and replicating or acquiring those resources is more costly than accessing them through a joint venture. When these conditions are met, market solutions become less viable, leading firms to opt for co-ownership as it minimizes the risks associated with opportunistic behaviours (Hennart, 1988). In the international arena, joint ventures offer MNCs the advantage of tapping into local market knowledge and are therefore a good strategy for firms that are new to a market. However, international joint ventures (IJVs) come with their own set of challenges. Factors that increase the costs and complexities of IJVs include the necessity for frequent intra-firm resource transfers, the presence of export conflicts, and significant cultural distance between the partnering entities. These factors can make the establishment of IJVs less likely, emphasizing the need for firms to weigh the benefits carefully against the potential challenges when considering this mode of entry (Hennart, 1988).

However, the theory also has some shortcomings. Existing TCT literature has primarily focused on explaining strategic choices, leaving limited exploration of the performance implications of these decisions (Cuypers et al., 2021). To further enhance our understanding, scholars should engage in empirical research to evaluate the actual impact of governance choices on firm performance. Additionally, Cuypers et al. (2021) call for research with a more dynamic approach, changing environments and evolving phenomena, such as technological advances. In the paper 'Bad for practice: A critique of the transaction cost theory' Ghoshal and Moran (1996) argue that the theory's prescriptions for practice are dangerous for corporate managers, as TCT oversimplifies organizational advantages, neglects the unique logic of organizations, and fails to recognize the distinctive mechanisms that organizations possess for coordinating economic activities. The authors emphasize the need for a different theory that considers the specific strengths and attributes of organizations. However, despite this criticism, the theory remains one of the most influential theories in International Business and beyond.

Case Study: BSH Household Appliances

Established in 1967, Bosch Siemens Household Appliances (BSH) was a 50:50 joint venture between two renowned German engineering giants, Robert Bosch GmbH and Siemens AG, to manufacture and market household appliances worldwide.

The BSH joint venture was founded at a time when both Bosch and Siemens recognized the potential for growth in the household appliances market and at the same time started to face competition from lower-cost competitors, particularly from Asia. By pooling their expertise in engineering, technology, and manufacturing to reduce costs and increase revenue, the two companies wanted to become a leading global player in the home appliance industry. In 1967, BSH was officially established with its headquarters in Munich, Germany.

From its inception, BSH focused on strategic expansion into key markets around the world. Leveraging the strong brand reputation and distribution networks of Bosch and Siemens, the joint venture quickly expanded its presence in Europe and established subsidiaries in North America, Asia, and other regions. BSH introduced innovative and high-quality appliances tailored to the needs and preferences of consumers in different markets, driving growth and market share gains.

BSH has a long history of product innovation and differentiation, introducing groundbreaking technologies and features that set its appliances apart in the market. The company invested heavily in research and development, collaborating with leading universities, research institutions, and industry partners to drive technological advances in areas such as energy efficiency, connectivity, and user convenience. BSH's portfolio includes a wide range of appliances, including refrigerators, dishwashers, washing machines, dryers, ovens, and cooktops, designed to meet the diverse needs of consumers worldwide.

At the same time, BSH was also able to develop and sustain synergies in the production process. BSH operates a global manufacturing and supply chain network, with production facilities located in multiple countries to serve local and regional markets efficiently. The company's manufacturing plants adhere to high quality and sustainability standards, employing state-of-the-art production technologies and processes to ensure product excellence and environmental responsibility. BSH's global footprint enables it to optimize production, logistics, and distribution, minimizing costs and lead times while maximizing responsiveness to customer demand.

Over the years, BSH has established itself as a market leader in the household appliances industry, known for its innovative products, superior quality, and customer-centric approach. The company remains committed to sustainability and corporate social responsibility, integrating environmentally friendly practices into its operations, products, and supply chain. BSH invests in energy-efficient technologies, eco-friendly materials, and

(Continued)

recycling initiatives to minimize its environmental footprint and contribute to a more sustainable future.

Despite its success, Siemens decided to sell its shares in the JV. In 2014, both companies announced that Bosch would buy all Siemens shares in the company, a decision finalized in 2015 after receiving all relevant institutional approvals.

Sources: Siemens (https://press.siemens.com/global/en/pressrelease/bosch-acquire-siemens-stake-bsh-bosch-und-siemens-hausgerate-gmbh) and BSH-Group (https://wiki.bsh-group.com/de/wiki/Hauptseite)

Case Study Questions

1 Why do joint ventures frequently become unstable after a period of time?
2 What are the resources that joint venture partners in International Business usually bring to the table?
3 Why do governments sometimes stop joint ventures from happening? Or, the other way around, why do governments sometimes implement minimum requirements for local content in joint ventures?

7.4.3 Establishment Mode Decisions

Following the question regarding the ownership mode, the second relavant question when entering a foreign market is how to establish a foreign activity. Generally, firms can decide between greenfield and brownfield investments. Greenfield FDI involves establishing new operations or facilities in a foreign country from the ground up. This approach entails building factories, offices, or other infrastructure and initiating operations from scratch. Companies opting for greenfield FDI directly invest in new physical assets, technology, and human resources in the host country. For example, a multinational automobile manufacturer may decide to build a new production plant in a foreign country to meet growing demand in that market, investing in land, buildings, machinery, and hiring local workers. Brownfield FDI, also known as acquisitions, entails acquiring existing businesses, assets, or subsidiaries in a foreign country. This approach allows the investing company to gain immediate access to established market presence, infrastructure, customer base, distribution networks, and operational capabilities. For instance, a global retail chain may acquire a local supermarket chain in a foreign market to quickly establish its brand presence and expand its retail footprint.

Greenfield FDI offers the advantage of full control over the design, location, and operation of the new facility, enabling alignment with strategic objectives and preferences. However, it also involves significant upfront costs, risks, and uncertainties, including land acquisition, construction, regulatory approvals, and market development expenses. Despite the challenges, greenfield FDI allows companies to build operations tailored to local market conditions and preferences, fostering long-term growth and sustainability.

Brownfield FDI provides immediate access to established market presence, distribution networks, customer relationships, and revenue streams, accelerating market entry and expansion, yet it may encounter integration challenges, cultural differences, and overpayment risks during the acquisition process. Despite these challenges, Brownfield FDI allows companies to leverage existing market infrastructure and operational capabilities to drive synergies, cost efficiencies, and revenue growth in the acquired business.

Case Study: Microsoft Acquires Nokia's Devices and Services Division

In 2013, Microsoft made headlines with its acquisition of Nokia's devices and services division for approximately US$7.2 billion. The move was seen as Microsoft's ambitious attempt to bolster its position in the fiercely competitive mobile phone market and challenge dominant players like Apple and Samsung. With this acquisition, Microsoft aimed to leverage Nokia's extensive experience and expertise in hardware manufacturing and design, combining it with its own software and services capabilities to create a formidable presence in the smartphone industry.

However, the acquisition failed to deliver the anticipated results, and Microsoft faced numerous challenges integrating Nokia's mobile phone business into its global operations. The transition was marred by management conflicts, cultural clashes, and organizational restructuring, which impeded collaboration and innovation within the combined entity. Despite substantial investment in marketing and product development, Nokia's market share continued to decline in the face of stiff competition, particularly from Android-based smartphones.

Strategically, the acquisition was questioned by industry analysts and shareholders, as it diverted Microsoft's focus and resources away from its core software and services businesses. The company found itself grappling with the conflicting priorities of hardware manufacturing and mobile devices, which did not align with its broader vision of transitioning towards cloud computing, productivity software, and enterprise services. Ultimately, the acquisition of Nokia's mobile phone business represented a misstep in Microsoft's strategy, as it failed to yield the desired results and instead led to significant financial losses.

In 2015, Microsoft announced a massive write-down of US$7.6 billion related to its Nokia acquisition, acknowledging the diminished value of Nokia's mobile phone business. The write-down underscored the challenges of integrating disparate businesses in the fast-paced and competitive technology industry. Following this setback, Microsoft underwent a strategic shift and decided to exit the mobile hardware business altogether. The company scaled back its smartphone operations, discontinued certain product lines, and refocused its efforts on its core strengths in software, cloud services, and productivity solutions.

(Continued)

The failed acquisition of Nokia's mobile phone business serves as a cautionary tale in the world of corporate mergers and acquisitions, highlighting the importance of strategic alignment, effective integration, and market dynamics. Despite its initial aspirations, Microsoft's foray into the mobile phone market ultimately ended in disappointment, underscoring the complexities and risks involved in brownfield investments and the need for careful consideration of strategic objectives and industry.

Source: Computerworld (www.computerworld.com/article/1620732/microsoft-writes-off-76b-admits-failure-of-nokia-acquisition-2.html)

7.4.4 Value Chain Decisions – Strategic Options

Firms need to decide not only about the level of ownership in a foreign activity or establishment strategy, but the value chain elements that should be set up in a foreign market. To understand the options that firms have, Porter's value chain framework provides a strong starting point.

The value chain model is a strategic management framework developed by Michael Porter (2001). The model helps analyse and identify the activities that create value for customers and ultimately contribute to a company's competitive advantage. The value chain model divides a company's activities into two categories: primary activities and support activities.

Primary activities are directly involved in the production, marketing, delivery, and support of a product or service. Porter identified five primary activities within the value chain:

- *Inbound logistics*: This involves the reception, warehousing, and inventory management of raw materials or components needed for production. Efficient inbound logistics contribute to cost savings and supply chain optimization.
- *Operations*: Operations encompass the processes of converting raw materials or inputs into finished products or services. This includes manufacturing, assembly, packaging, and quality control. Efficient operations can lead to improved product quality, faster production cycles, and cost reductions.
- *Outbound logistics*: Outbound logistics involve the storage, distribution, and transportation of finished products to customers. Effective outbound logistics ensure timely delivery, accurate order fulfilment, and customer satisfaction.
- *Marketing and sales*: Marketing and sales activities involve promoting and selling products or services to target customers. This includes market research, advertising, pricing, sales channels, and customer relationship management. Effective marketing and sales efforts drive demand, customer acquisition, and revenue growth.
- *Service*: Service activities encompass the support and assistance provided to customers after the sale of a product or service. This includes customer support, technical assistance, warranty services, and maintenance. Quality service enhances customer satisfaction, loyalty, and retention.

The first two elements, inbound logistics and operations, are usually labelled as upstream activities, and the remaining activities are labelled downstream activities. Support activities provide the necessary infrastructure and resources to support the primary activities and overall operations of the business. Porter identified four support activities within the value chain:

- *Firm infrastructure*: Firm infrastructure refers to the organizational structure, management systems, and support functions that enable the operation of the business. This includes strategic planning, finance, accounting, legal, and corporate governance.
- *Human resource management*: Human resource management involves the recruitment, training, development, and management of employees. Effective HR practices ensure a skilled and motivated workforce capable of contributing to the company's objectives and competitive advantage.
- *Technology development*: Technology development encompasses research, development, and innovation activities aimed at enhancing products, processes, and capabilities. This includes investments in technology, R&D, intellectual property, and innovation management.
- *Procurement*: Procurement involves the sourcing, negotiation, and management of external suppliers and vendors. This includes supplier selection, contract management, and supplier relationship management. Efficient procurement practices ensure reliable and cost-effective access to inputs and resources.

Porter's value chain model emphasizes the importance of analysing each activity within the value chain to identify opportunities for cost reduction, differentiation, and value creation. By understanding the value-creating activities and their interrelationships, companies can develop strategies to optimize their value chain, enhance their competitive position, and achieve sustainable competitive advantage in the marketplace. One of the opportunities for optimization is the internationalization of parts of the value chain. In the internationalization process, firms need to decide where to locate each element of the value chain geographically, and whether elements should only be operated at one location or at multiple locations.

7.4.5 Value Chain Decisions - The Uppsala Model Part 2

Based on the Uppsala internationalization model (see also Section 7.3.4; Johanson & Vahlne, 1977), firms adopt a gradual approach to internationalization as managers are risk averse. Initially, they venture into countries with a low psychic distance, as these nations present lower perceived uncertainties. Such countries are typically geographically closer, share similar economic development stages, have similar institutions, and resonate with the home country's culture. This is what we discussed earlier, in Section 7.3.4.

However, the Uppsala internationalization model focuses not only on country-market selection, but also explains the commitment a firm makes to a market by setting up particular elements of the value chain. While the authors of the model call this the establishment chain, it is not related to the establishment dimension of the entry mode decision, but to the value chain dimension.

In each country, firms begin with entry modes that require minimal commitment, progressively learning about the new environment and transitioning to modes demanding higher commitment. For instance, a firm's journey might start by exporting. With increasing market knowledge this might progress to licensing or franchising agreements. Later it might consider equity-based modes, such as joint ventures or wholly owned subsidiaries. This incremental approach extends to the value chain elements they internationalize. Sales, which require lower commitment, are typically the first to be internationalized, followed by more commitment-intensive elements like production and R&D at later stages. An idealized version of such a chain of internationalization steps is depicted in Figure 7.7.

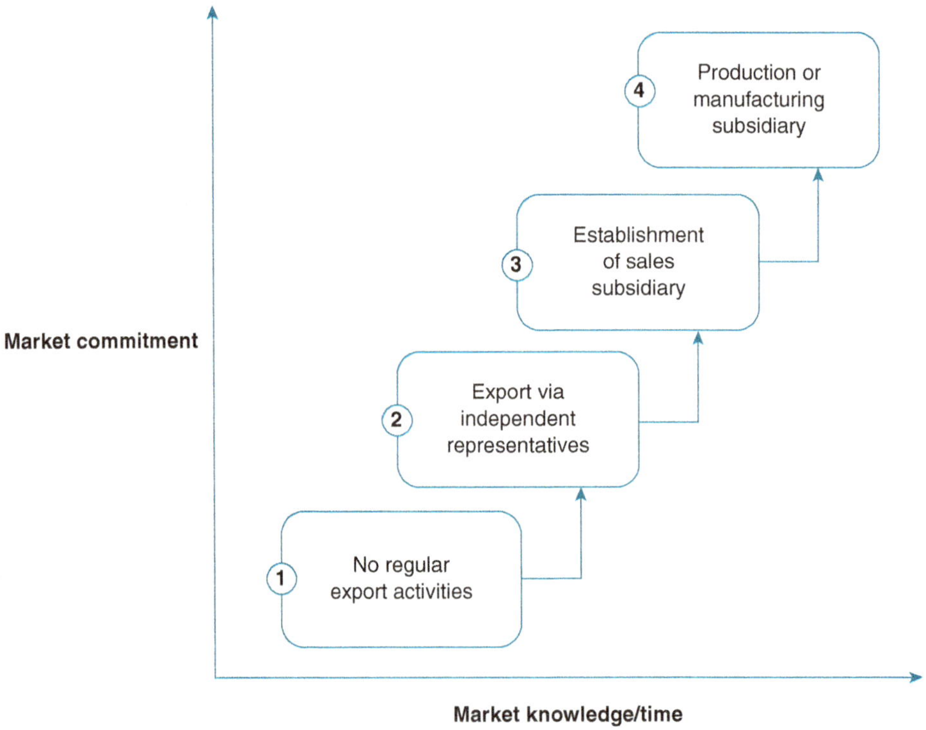

Figure 7.7 The establishment chain

Source: Based on Johanson & Vahlne (1977)

7.4.6 Summary - Market Entry Decisions

Market entry decisions refer to three decisions that are often interdependent in the internationalization process: ownership in a foreign market, establishment strategies, and decisions on value chain activities in a foreign market. With regard to ownership strategies, we can differentiate equity and non-equity modes of entry. Transaction cost theory can help when making deciisons about different ownership strategies. Greenfield and brownfield investment are the two alternatives for establishment strategies, both associated with particular opportunities and challenges. When it comes to the value chain decision, Porter's value chain model helps to improve understanding of the structure of value creation in a company, while the Uppsala internationalization model helps develop an understanding of why firms operate with increasing commitment over time in a particular market.

7.5 THE ECLECTIC PARADIGM OF INTERNATIONALIZATION: AN INTEGRATIVE MODEL

The eclectic paradigm, also known as the OLI framework, developed by John H. Dunning (1979), offers a somewhat integrative perspective on the internationalization process. The model aims to connect a number of theories and suggests that for a company to internationalize with production in a particular country, it must satisfy three interrelated conditions: ownership, location, and internalization advantages (see Figure 7.8).

At the core of the paradigm is the recognition that irrespective of their motivations, only firms that possess some form of competitive edge in the foreign market can succeed internationally – having a so-called ownership advantage. An ownership advantage can stem from proprietary technology, brand reputation, managerial expertise, access to distribution networks, or superior production processes, among others. The underlying assumption of the ownership aspect of the OLI framework is that firms engage in FDI to leverage their unique ownership advantages to exploit opportunities in foreign markets. Essentially, firms invest abroad because they possess particular assets or capabilities that give them a competitive edge over local competitors.

Possessing an ownership advantage is essential. Why? Because when companies enter a foreign market, they are at a natural disadvantage to local firms, which are adept at navigating the intricacies of their home turf – from understanding the cultural nuances to having the right local connections and being deeply rooted in local institutions. In such an environment, the ownership advantage acts as a levelling tool, giving the internationalizing firm a fighting chance. We refer to the disadvantages that foreign firms experience as the liabilities of foreignness (LOF) (see Spotlight in Section 7.1.2).

One way to test if a firm has an ownership advantage is to apply the resource-based view, particularly the VRIO characteristics (see Section 7.1.3). If a firm possesses capabilities and resources that are valuable to the customer, are rare, hard to imitate, and organized in the firm, one can assume that an ownership advantage exists. If a firm does not possess an ownership advantage, the model recommends not going ahead with internationalization.

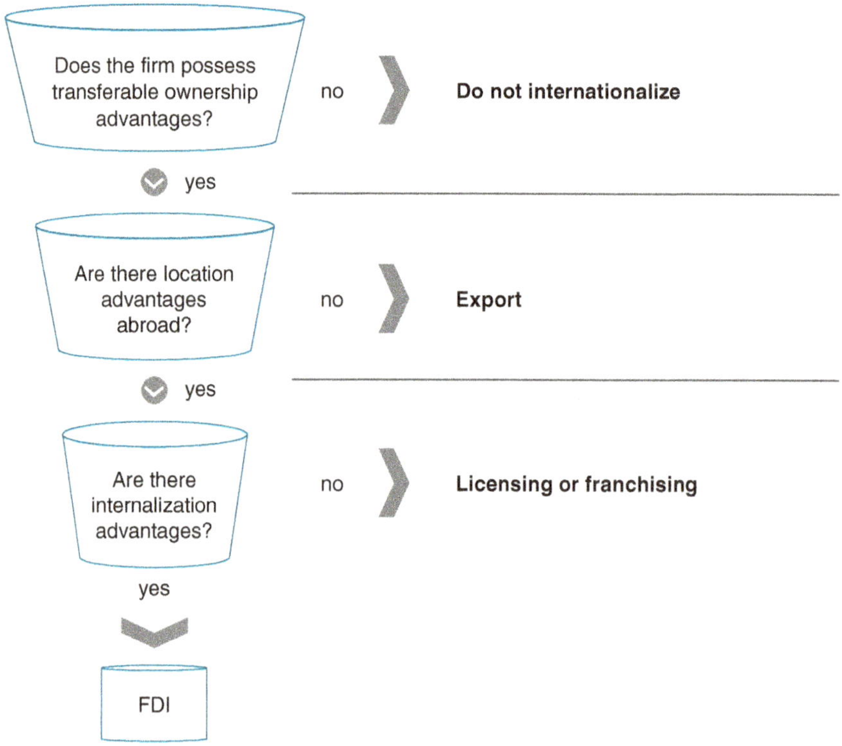

Figure 7.8 The OLI paradigm

However, having an ownership advantage alone isn't sufficient. Dunning's eclectic paradigm argues that the chosen foreign country must also offer *location advantages* conducive to the company's business. The location advantage refers to the attributes or characteristics of a foreign market that make it an attractive destination for FDI. These attributes might include factors such as market size, growth potential, resource availability, infrastructure, labour costs, regulatory environment, political stability, and proximity to suppliers or customers. Tools such as Porter's diamond (see Section 7.3.3), PESTEL analysis (see Chapter 3, Section 3.5), or sequential scoring models (see Section 7.3.1) can help in this process. If the foreign location does not offer benefits that outweigh the costs of establishing facilities there, or if it negates potential economies of scale, firms might opt to export rather than set up local production.

The final question the OLI framework attempts to answer is why a company should conduct international operations itself, or in different words, why it should *internalize* them. The answer depends on whether the relevant firm advantages can be sold efficiently or contracted. Economists call inefficiencies arising during such transactions 'transaction costs' (see Section 7.4.2). If the transaction costs of the critical assets would be lower than the costs arising from the liabilities of foreignness a firm would face when conducting its international operations itself, the firm might consider selling or licensing its assets to a local partner. This local partner could realize the full potential of the firm's competitive advantage without incurring liabilities of foreignness due to its familiarity with the local market. Thus, a firm will only conduct international operations itself if the transaction costs of contracting or selling the assets outweigh the liabilities of foreignness it faces in the foreign market. As can be seen in the section on transaction cost theory (Section 7.4.2), transactions associated with high asset specificity and fairly low uncertainty should be internalized, while transactions associated with fairly low asset specificity and high uncertainty should be transacted on the market (e.g., by licensing or franchising).

In essence, Dunning's eclectic paradigm elegantly intertwines these three pillars – ownership, location, and internalization – to offer a holistic view of the strategic decisions firms make in their internationalization journeys. It emphasizes that to successfully produce abroad, a competitive advantage is not enough – firms also need to decide where and how to leverage it effectively. While this is an important contribution, the model has also been criticized in the literature, principally because it is 'multi-theoretical' – it combines multiple theories, each based on different assumptions.

7.6 CURRENT DEVELOPMENTS IN INTERNATIONALIZATION THEORIES AND STRATEGIES

Research questions associated with the internationalization process and the different decisions within the process are among the most researched field in IB research. As such, this field can be considered as very mature; thus Shaver (2013) has asked the question, 'Do we really need more entry mode studies?' as he perceived the potential knowledge gains from further studies to be incremental. Nevertheless, we do see several studies being published that have made a significant contribution to our knowledge about internationalization processes and decisions.

One example is a stream of research that focuses on internationalization decisions after market entry. This shows that firms' internationalization does not stop after entering a specific market but continues with new and additional investments, elevations of existing investments, or divestments. This stream of research adds substantially to our understanding of the temporal nature of international expansion.

We have also seen more research on the internationalization of digital economy firms. Stallkamp & Schotter (2021) theorize on the internationalization strategies of platform businesses and argue that network externalities – the conception that a platform becomes more valuable to each user as more users join – influence the international expansion strategies of these firms and influence country-market selection and market entry strategies. Kim (2020) and Kim and Cavusgil (2020) also focus on platform businesses and show that the specific platform risks are a key driver for internationalization decisions of such firms, too. We feel that substantial further research in this domain will develop given the strong relevance of the phenomenon.

Understanding and measurement of between-country information asymmetry, a core element of many theories, especially of the Uppsala internationalization model, have also been the focus of relevant research. Dow and Karunaratna (2006), for example, provide a better conceptualization of psychic distance by differentiating between the perceived psychic distance of decision-makers and the psychic distance stimuli that drive such perceptions of distance. They also maintain a homepage (http://dow.net.au) that provides access to the psychic distance stimuli scales for many countries for free. Lindner and Puck (2024) have also developed a measure of information distance based on information theory, signal analysis, and financial market information that can be related to the model. Data is freely available at https://thomaslindner.info

Another study by Chatzoglou et al. (2018) on the role of firm-specific factors in the strategy-performance relationship, revisits the resource-based view of the firm and the VRIO framework by exploring the relationship between strategic orientation and firm performance in the context of two firm-specific factors – distinct manufacturing capabilities and organizational structure. The major findings of the paper include the identification of three distinct categories of effects on firm performance: strategy effects, firm-specific effects, and organizational effects (Chatzoglou et al., 2018). The authors highlight the mediating role of strategic orientation and the complementary role of organizational structure. Furthermore, the paper supports the notion that strategy follows structure, challenging the traditional belief that structure follows strategy.

Given the growing interest in understanding the implications of the RBV, a further study explores the applicability and relevance of this theoretical framework in the field of IB. The paper by Alexy et al. (2018) analyses the paradox of strategic openness and the resource-based view of the firm and demonstrates when and how firms can gain a competitive advantage by opening parts of their resource base. The authors show that under specific circumstances, strategic openness can lead to a significant improvement in performance by considering key conditions such as increasing demand for remaining proprietary resources.

Konara and Shirodkar (2018) investigate the impact of regulatory institutional distance on the performance of MNCs' foreign subsidiaries. The authors introduce the concept of an institutional ladder to distinguish between upward institutional distance (subsidiary operating in a stronger institutional environment than the parent-firm's home country) and downward institutional distance (subsidiary operating in a weaker institutional environment). The major contribution of the paper lies in highlighting the asymmetric effect of institutional distance on subsidiary performance, depending on the direction of that distance (Konara & Shirodkar, 2018). The study draws on institutional theory, organizational imprinting, and learning perspectives to propose that the implications of institutional distance are more positive when MNCs' subsidiaries climb down the institutional ladder rather than climbing up.

SUMMARY

In this chapter we have discussed firm-level internationalization theories and strategies. Internationalization strategies are driven by firms' objectives to enhance profitability through cost reduction or revenue expansion. Dunning (2000) identifies four motives: efficiency-seeking, resource-seeking, market-seeking, and strategic asset-seeking, which necessitate firm-specific assets that are valuable, rare, difficult to imitate, and organized. We also highlighted that timing is crucial in international market entry strategies, categorized into first mover, early follower, and late mover strategies, each carrying distinct advantages and challenges such as pioneering costs vs market uncertainties. The pace of international expansion, whether across multiple markets or within a single host country, varies depending on firms' strategic goals, influenced by factors like market conditions and industry dynamics. Born global firms exemplify rapid internationalization from inception, often leveraging digital technologies to access global markets early and strategically.

Country market selection involves evaluating location advantages driven by agglomeration economies, institutions, and macro factors, essential for competitive positioning analysed, for example, through the institution-based view and Porter's diamond model. The Uppsala model explains the preference firms have for proximate markets, guided by risk aversion and familiarity rather than purely rational decision-making. Market entry decisions are associated with the 'how to internationalize' question and encompass ownership choices (equity vs non-equity), establishment strategies (greenfield vs brownfield), and optimizing value chain activities, all critical in achieving sustainable competitive advantage and navigating complexities across international markets. The eclectic paradigm, or OLI framework developed by Dunning (1979), integrates various perspectives on internationalization. It posits that successful international production requires firms to possess competitive advantages in ownership (such as technology or brand reputation), capitalize on location advantages (such as market size or regulatory environment), and determine when to internalize operations to minimize transaction costs compared to the liabilities of foreignness. This framework integrates multiple conceptual and theoretical perspectives and underscores the importance of aligning firm-specific advantages with favourable foreign market conditions and transaction efficiencies for effective global expansion strategies.

8

STRUCTURE AND STRATEGY IN THE MULTINATIONAL COMPANY

CHAPTER INTRODUCTION

In this chapter, we will discuss strategic management in global firms. This chapter covers firms that have undergone extensive internationalization (see Chapter 7) and have a substantial international presence. Such firms, multinational companies (MNCs), are the behemoths of the modern economy, and include some of best-known organizations such as Apple, Microsoft, VW, Tesco, LVMH, Unicredit, Procter & Gamble, and Unilever. The strategic choices those companies make frequently influence not only their customers, suppliers, and employees, but have a bearing on broader society. How to manage such a global company strategically is therefore an important challenge. We will build our understanding from a strategic perspective.

Business strategy is a relatively new field that emerged in the twentieth century. There is a long history of strategic thinking, relevant mostly in the context of military strategy and dating back at least to ancient Greece. Renowned military leaders such as Sun Tzu and Thucydides laid the groundwork for strategic thinking, emphasizing the importance of planning, adaptability, and understanding the competitive landscape. These principles, initially formulated on the battlefield, soon found application in various domains of human endeavour.

Fast forward to the modern era, and the similarities between the evolution of (global) business and military strategy become evident in terms of the competitive dynamics, allocation of resources, and the need for long-term planning. Businesses, like armies, have to navigate a complex environment, anticipating competitors' moves, exploiting opportunities, and mitigating risks. The parallels extend to the organizational structure, where hierarchies, divisions of labour, and effective communication are critical components of success.

A key aspect common to business and military strategy is the notion of competitive advantage. In warfare, gaining the upper hand over adversaries is essential for victory. Similarly, businesses strive to outperform competitors by identifying and leveraging distinctive capabilities, whether through innovation, cost leadership, or other strategic differentiators. The importance of intelligence, another common element, is evident in both contexts as accurate and timely information is crucial for decision-making. Moreover, the concept of manoeuvring is significant in both military and business strategy. In the military context, manoeuvring involves positioning forces strategically to gain a favourable position over the enemy; in business, it translates to adaptability and the ability to navigate changing market conditions successfully.

The advent of globalization and technological advances underlines the similarities. The business landscape is often described as a battlefield, where companies compete for market share and dominance. The principles of speed, surprise, and flexibility, inherited from military strategy, find application in today's fast-paced and dynamic business environment. In this chapter we outline the basics of strategic management of global firms.

LEARNING OUTCOMES

After reading this chapter you should be able to:

1 Describe the relationship between global business strategy and generic strategies
2 Demonstrate an understanding of how pressures in the global business environment influence the global strategy of firms
3 Explain how global value chains and strategy are related
4 Identify the characteristics of competitive strategy.

Case Study: Positioning at Lidl

Lidl, a prominent international supermarket chain, faces challenges due to its positioning in the competitive spectrum, often referred to as being stuck in the middle. This strategic challenge arises when a company fails to differentiate itself sufficiently from competitors, leaving it in a precarious position between low-cost providers and those offering premium products or services.

At its core, being stuck in the middle implies a lack of a clear and compelling strategic focus. Lidl, known for its emphasis on providing quality products at competitive prices, risks falling into this middle ground where it neither excels in "lead to offering premium products nor stands out as a low-cost leader. This can be problematic for several reasons.

One key issue is the intense competition in the supermarket industry. Lidl competes with traditional low-cost retailers like Aldi, which are known for their relentless focus on cost efficiency and providing budget-friendly options. Simultaneously, Lidl faces competition from higher-end supermarkets that emphasize premium products, quality, and a more upscale shopping experience. Lidl's failure to establish a distinct identity in either of these categories leaves it vulnerable to losing customers to competitors that offer a more compelling value proposition.

The middle ground also poses challenges in terms of brand perception. Consumers may perceive Lidl as lacking the prestige and quality associated with premium supermarkets while not providing the rock-bottom prices offered by budget-focused competitors. This can result in a weaker brand image and customer loyalty compared to brands that excel in one specific dimension. Operational challenges may arise from attempting to cater to a broad customer base with varying preferences. Stocking both low-cost essentials and higher-quality products necessitates a more complex supply chain and inventory management system. This complexity can lead to inefficiencies and increased operational costs, putting additional strain on profit margins. Furthermore, marketing becomes a delicate balancing act for companies stuck in the middle. Lidl must communicate its value proposition effectively, but without a clear strategic focus, it may struggle to create a compelling and consistent brand message. This can lead to confusion among consumers who may find it challenging to understand what sets Lidl apart from other supermarkets.

To overcome the challenges of being stuck in the middle, Lidl may need to reassess its strategic positioning. One option is to shift towards a more clearly defined low-cost strategy, emphasizing even greater cost efficiency and appealing to budget-conscious consumers. Alternatively, Lidl could explore avenues to enhance its premium image, focusing on higher-quality products, a superior shopping experience, and exclusive offerings.

In conclusion, Lidl's positioning in the middle of the competitive spectrum presents strategic challenges that require careful consideration. The supermarket chain must address issues related to differentiation, operational efficiency, brand perception, and marketing to avoid being squeezed by competitors on both ends of the spectrum. By reevaluating its strategic focus and possibly moving towards a more defined low-cost or premium strategy, Lidl can position itself more effectively in the highly competitive supermarket industry.

Sources: The Strategy Story (https://thestrategystory.com/blog/lidl-swot-analysis) and The Telegraph (www.telegraph.co.uk/business/2024/03/30/end-of-cheap-money-brought-lidls-expansion-to-halt)

Case Study Questions

1. What does the strategic positioning of a political party in the USA look like? How does avoiding being stuck in the middle relate to political polarization?
2. In a market with five or more competitors, how can companies position themselves if it is impossible to be at the highest or lowest end of the pricing spectrum?
3. How can Lidl manage to position its products more clearly on a dimension other than price?

8.1 GENERIC STRATEGIES

Porter's generic strategies and basic military strategies share striking similarities, particularly in the parallels between force and guile (Porter, 2008). In Porter's model, the generic strategies of cost leadership and differentiation closely align with military principles. Cost leadership corresponds to the use of force in military strategy, emphasizing efficiency, economies of scale, and overpowering competition through sheer cost advantages. On the other hand, differentiation strategy mirrors the concept of guile in military strategy, focusing on outsmarting adversaries through unique offerings, innovation, and a distinctive market position. Both force and guile highlight the importance of creating a sustainable advantage, whether through superior resources and efficiency or through clever, strategic manoeuvring in the face of competition or conflict. The resonance between these business and military strategies underscores the universality of certain principles across diverse domains of strategy and competition.

Porter's generic strategies are fundamental strategic approaches that businesses can adopt to gain a competitive advantage within their industry. These strategies provide a framework for companies to position themselves effectively in the market and achieve sustainable profitability.

The cost leadership strategy focuses on achieving the lowest cost of production and operation in the industry. Cost leadership can be achieved through economies of scale, efficient processes, volume production, and supply chain optimization. However, the challenge lies in maintaining quality while keeping costs low. The differentiation strategy emphasizes creating unique and distinctive products or services that stand out in the market: it allows businesses to charge premium prices for their offerings, attracting customers who value these unique attributes. Successful implementation requires continuous innovation, strong brand management, and effective communication of the unique value proposition to customers. The focus strategy narrows the scope of the target market to a specific niche or segment. Within this type of strategy, there are two sub-strategies: cost focus and differentiation focus. Cost focus entails offering products or services to a narrow market segment at the lowest cost, while differentiation focus involves catering to the specific preferences and needs of a niche market through unique offerings. Focus strategies allow businesses to compete effectively in small market segments where they can establish a strong market position.

Following this theoretical foundation, the biggest mistHeake for a firm would be to attempt to employ all these strategies, and as a result, to find itself in a situation of being neither here nor there. In essence, being stuck in the middle implies that the company lacks a clear strategic direction and fails to create a sustainable competitive position, since each generic strategy represents a radically different approach.

8.2 STRATEGY ANALYSIS

To develop a global strategy, companies need to understand the environment in which they operate as well as their internal strengths. It is the application of internal strengths in a way that exploits the external opportunities that makes good strategy. We will explore a key tool of internal and external analysis below and go on to introduce five components of corporate strategy. Building on these insights, we will look into the specifics of global strategy.

8.2.1 Internal Analysis: The Resource-Based View

The resource-based view (RBV) (see Chapter 7) is a strategic management framework that emphasizes the internal resources and capabilities of a firm as the primary sources of sustainable competitive advantage. This perspective contends that not all resources are equal, and firms must possess valuable, rare, and difficult-to-imitate resources to gain a competitive edge (the VRIO criteria). To realize the competitive edge, companies need to embed those resources within the organization. The RBV provides a means by which organizations can identify and leverage their distinctive competencies to create and maintain a strong position in the market.

Central to the RBV is the concept of resources, which encompass tangible and intangible assets such as physical assets, human capital, organizational culture, patents, and relationships. The first criterion for a resource to contribute to competitive advantage is value. For a resource to be a source of competitive advantage, it must enable the firm to exploit opportunities or neutralize threats. Valuable resources contribute to a firm's ability to meet customer needs effectively, enhance product quality, and reduce costs. Identifying and leveraging resources that add value to the customer proposition are crucial for sustained competitive advantage.

Rarity is the second criterion. Resources that are rare or scarce in the industry are more likely to provide a competitive advantage. If a resource is readily available to all competitors, it becomes a common denominator and does not contribute significantly to differentiation. Rarity enhances the uniqueness and value of a resource, making it a source of sustained competitive advantage.

The third criterion is the difficulty of imitation. Resources that are difficult for competitors to replicate or substitute are crucial for sustained competitive advantage. This can result from unique historical conditions, proprietary technology, or complex organizational processes. If competitors can easily imitate a resource, any initial advantage gained will be short-lived.

Finally, resources need to be organizationally embedded or 'owned' in order to be a source of sustainable competitive advantage. Figure 8.1 provides an overview of resource types and how the presence of the respective criteria transforms resources into different types of competitive advantage.

Table 8.1 The sources of exploited sustainable advantage: VRIO

Type of advantage	Valuable	Rare	Inimitable	Organizationally embedded
Disadvantage	No			
Parity	Yes	No		
Temporary advantage	Yes	Yes	No	
Unexploited sustainable advantage	Yes	Yes	Yes	No
Exploited sustainable advantage	Yes	Yes	Yes	Yes

The RBV also recognizes the importance of organizational capabilities, which represent the firm's capacity to deploy, manage, and integrate its resources effectively. Capabilities often involve dynamic and complex processes that allow a firm to adapt to changing market conditions, innovate, and continuously improve. The ability to leverage resources through effective organizational capabilities enhances the likelihood of maintaining a competitive edge over time.

Applying the RBV involves a thorough internal analysis to identify and evaluate the firm's resources and capabilities. This introspective examination helps categorize resources as unique, valuable, rare, or difficult to imitate. These resources can then be leveraged to form the basis of the firm's competitive strategy.

Case Study: The Sources of Competitive Advantage at Mercedes-Benz

Applying the VRIO concept to Mercedes-Benz provides insights into the key factors contributing to its competitive edge in the automotive industry.

Value: Mercedes-Benz is renowned for delivering high-quality and technologically advanced vehicles that cater to a premium market segment. The brand's commitment to innovation, safety, and luxury adds significant value to its products. Cutting-edge features, superior performance, and a strong focus on customer experience contribute to the perceived value of Mercedes-Benz vehicles. This commitment to delivering value is a crucial element in sustaining the brand's competitive advantage.

Rarity: Mercedes-Benz has a history of introducing groundbreaking technologies and designs that set its vehicles apart from competitors. The brand's emphasis is on exclusivity and luxury image. Features such as advanced safety systems, state-of-the-art infotainment, and iconic design elements contribute to the rarity perception of Mercedes Benz products, as well as the resources needed to produce them.

Imitability: While other automakers may attempt to replicate certain features or design elements, Mercedes-Benz has successfully established a reputation for innovation and engineering excellence that is challenging to imitate fully. The brand's commitment to research and development, coupled with a strong focus on proprietary technologies, creates barriers for competitors looking to replicate its success.

Organizational embeddedness: The effective organization of resources and capabilities is a critical aspect of the VRIO framework. Mercedes-Benz benefits from a well-established and globally recognized brand, a sophisticated global supply chain, and a network of skilled professionals. The company's organizational structure and processes contribute to its ability to consistently deliver high-quality vehicles with advanced features. The emphasis on quality control, manufacturing excellence, and a strong distribution network enhances the overall organization of Mercedes-Benz, supporting its competitive advantage.

The VRIO analysis applied to Mercedes-Benz reveals that the company possesses valuable, rare, and difficult-to-imitate resources and capabilities that contribute to its sustained competitive advantage in the automotive industry. The brand's commitment to delivering value through innovation, the rarity of its offerings, limited imitability, and the effective organization of its resources position Mercedes-Benz as a leader in the premium automobile market. This strategic alignment with the VRIO framework underscores the importance of a holistic approach to assessing and leveraging key factors that contribute to a firm's competitive advantage in a dynamic business environment.

Sources: Mercedes-Benz (https://group.mercedes-benz.com/company/strategy; https://media.mbusa.com/releases/release-391299d8b45791ed364add967110229d-mercedes-benz-sets-out-long-term-ambitions-as-the-worlds-most-valuable-luxury-car-brand) and Bloomberg (www.bloomberg.com/news/newsletters/2023-09-19/supply-chain-latest-mercedes-benz-and-resilience)

8.2.2 External Analysis: Porter's Five Forces

The external environment of a firm has different levels. We discussed the institutional perspective to analyse the national external environment in Chapters 2–5. Porter's five forces framework is a powerful tool for conducting external analysis on the industry level, offering a structured approach to understanding the competitive forces that shape an industry's attractiveness and potential profitability. The model examines five key forces: the threat of new entrants, the bargaining power of buyers, the bargaining power of suppliers, the threat of substitute products or services, and the intensity of competitive rivalry.

The first force, the threat of new entrants, assesses the ease with which new companies can enter an industry and compete with established players. High entry barriers, such as significant capital requirements, economies of scale, and brand loyalty, can deter new entrants, limiting the threat. Conversely, low entry barriers make it easier for new competitors to enter the market. This analysis helps firms understand the level of competition they may face and take pre-emptive measures to fortify their position.

The bargaining power of buyers, the second force, explores the influence customers have over an industry. If buyers have substantial bargaining power, they can demand lower prices, higher quality, or additional services, potentially squeezing industry profits. Understanding customer dynamics, preferences, and the availability of alternative options is crucial for firms to tailor their offerings and maintain a competitive edge. In industries where buyers have limited choices or are less influential, firms may have more control over pricing and terms.

The third force, the bargaining power of suppliers, examines the influence exerted by those providing inputs to the industry. If suppliers have significant power, they can raise prices, limit quality, or even disrupt the supply chain. Industries heavily reliant on a single supplier or facing challenges in switching suppliers are more susceptible to supplier power. Analysing supplier relationships helps firms develop strategies to mitigate risks and secure favourable terms.

The threat of substitute products or services, the fourth force, focuses on the availability of alternatives that can fulfil the same or similar needs as the products or services offered by the industry. The existence of viable substitutes can limit price flexibility and erode market share. Understanding the dynamics of substitute products, their relative quality, and customer preferences aids firms in developing strategies to differentiate their offerings and enhance brand loyalty.

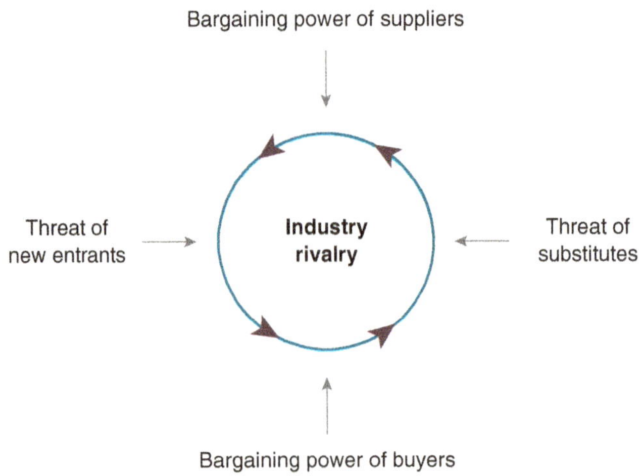

Figure 8.1 Porter's five forces

The fifth force, the intensity of competitive rivalry, assesses the level of competition among existing firms in the industry. High competition often leads to price wars, lower profitability, and increased pressure to innovate. Factors such as the number of competitors, industry growth rate, and differentiation strategies contribute to the intensity of rivalry. By understanding the competitive landscape, firms can position themselves strategically, whether that is by focusing on cost leadership, differentiation, or niche markets. Figure 8.1 summarizes the five forces and shows how they act together.

Porter's five forces can be utilized as a comprehensive external analysis tool in strategy development by guiding firms to assess each force individually and collectively. The framework helps identify the key drivers of industry competition, enabling firms to make informed decisions and formulate effective strategies. It encourages a proactive approach, allowing companies to anticipate and respond to changes in the external environment.

8.2.3 The Components of Strategy

Beyond the choice between cost leadership and differentiation (as well as more focused strategies), companies also need to develop strategy into a more comprehensive plan. Corporate strategy is a comprehensive approach that guides an organization in making choices about the scope of its activities, the industries or markets it competes in, and how it seeks to gain a competitive advantage. The five components of corporate strategy, as outlined by management scholars C. K. Prahalad and Gary Hamel (2009), are arenas, vehicles, differentiators, staging, and economic logic.

The concept of arenas in corporate strategy refers to the specific markets, industries, or segments in which a company chooses to compete. Arenas define the scope of the organization's activities and influence its overall strategic direction. Companies need to carefully select their arenas based on their capabilities, resources, and growth objectives. This component involves making decisions about where to compete geographically, in terms of product or service offerings, and across various customer segments. The selection of arenas is crucial as it determines the range and diversity of the organization's business activities.

Vehicles are the means by which a company enters or participates in a particular arena. These can include mergers, acquisitions, joint ventures, partnerships, strategic alliances, or organic growth through internal development. The choice of vehicles is critical to achieving strategic objectives in the selected arenas. Different vehicles offer varying levels of control, risk, and resource commitment. Companies must carefully evaluate the most suitable vehicles based on their strategic goals and the specific characteristics of the chosen arenas. Effective selection and implementation of vehicles contribute to the successful execution of the overall corporate strategy.

Differentiators in corporate strategy are the unique capabilities, resources, or competitive advantages that set a company apart from its rivals within a chosen arena. Identifying and leveraging differentiators are essential for creating value and sustaining a competitive advantage. Differentiators can take various forms, such as technological expertise, innovative product offerings, superior customer service, or cost leadership. A successful corporate strategy involves aligning the organization's strengths with the requirements of the chosen arenas, allowing it to stand out and excel in the market. The emphasis on differentiators reflects the need for organizations to have a clear understanding of what makes them distinctive and valuable to customers.

Staging involves determining the sequence and timing of a company's moves into different arenas and the allocation of resources over time. This component recognizes that successful corporate strategies often unfold in multiple stages, each requiring distinct approaches and resource commitments. Staging allows companies to manage the pace of expansion, mitigate risks, and learn from experience before moving into new arenas. It involves making strategic decisions about when to enter a market, scale operations, and diversify or refocus. Effective staging helps organizations adapt to changing market conditions and ensures that their expansion is well considered and strategically timed.

Economic logic encompasses the rationale behind a company's corporate strategy, explaining how it aims to achieve superior financial performance and generate value. This component is concerned with the fundamental principles that underpin the organization's ability to capture profits and create a sustainable competitive advantage. Economic logic aligns the chosen arenas, vehicles, differentiators, and staging with the overall goal of maximizing shareholder value. It requires a deep understanding of the economic drivers within each chosen arena and the mechanisms by which the organization intends to generate profits over the long term. The economic logic component serves as the foundation for the entire corporate strategy, providing a coherent and logical framework for decision-making.

In summary, the five components of corporate strategy – arenas, vehicles, differentiators, staging, and economic logic – collectively form a comprehensive framework for organizations to navigate the complexities of the business landscape. Each component addresses a specific aspect of strategic decision-making, guiding companies in defining where to compete, how to enter or participate in chosen arenas, what sets them apart from competitors, when and how to stage their moves, and the economic rationale behind their strategic choices. An effective corporate strategy requires careful integration of these components, ensuring alignment with the organization's overall mission and objectives. By systematically addressing each element, companies can enhance their strategic clarity, improve decision-making, and position themselves for sustained success in the dynamic and competitive business environment.

We focus on the international dimension in the five components of corporate strategy. There is an overarching question that touches on corporate positioning with regard to all five components, which we have not yet covered: how do companies adjust their activities to local characteristics, and to what extent will they standardize rather than differentiate activities as a function of external pressures? This is the topic of the following section.

8.3 GLOBAL INTEGRATION VS LOCAL RESPONSIVENESS

As the world has become more interconnected and globalized, International Business plays a crucial role in shaping the global economy. Trade liberalization, favourable investment policies, removal of regulatory boundaries, and sustained reduction of shipping, travel, and communication costs have led many firms to operate on a global scale and distribute their products across the globe.

Against this backdrop, there are two central questions for MNCs: to what extent should they globalize and where should they draw the line between global standardization and local adaptation? Two fundamental concepts in the field of International Business strategy – global integration and local responsiveness – help corporate management and scholars to find the answers to these questions.

Maintaining the balance between global integration and local responsiveness, also known as I–R balance, is one of the major strategic challenges for MNCs. Global integration refers to the extent to which an MNC seeks to maintain consistency and uniformity in its products, processes, and operations across different countries. The goal of global integration is to capitalize on economies of scale, reduce costs, and create a standardized global brand image. Local responsiveness relates to the degree to which an MNC tailors its products, services, and business operations to suit the specific conditions of individual countries. When this approach dominates, the strategy focuses on local customer needs and their differentiation in various markets.

Managers often face a trade-off between these two strategies. Pursuing a high level of global integration might lead to standardized products that do not resonate well with local customers, potentially resulting in lower market share and customer dissatisfaction. However, prioritizing local responsiveness could lead to higher costs due to customization and a lack of the efficiency that standardized processes provide. Effective International Business strategies aim to strike a balance between these two conflicting demands, and require careful consideration of various factors such as market characteristics, consumer behaviours, cultural differences, regulatory environments, and competitive landscapes in different countries. This global–local dilemma led scholars to develop the integration–responsiveness (IR) framework (Prahalad & Doz, 1987), which illustrates that the conflict between global integration and local adaptability results in three fundamental strategies. When the incentives a business identifies are primarily at the local level, its strategies will mostly be customized for each local market. However, if a company is under pressure to globalize, it will seek to increase central coordination and integrate operations seamlessly across borders. Lastly, when a firm needs to address both global integration and local responsiveness pressures, management will pursue a multifocal business strategy which prioritizes coordinating activities while still being highly responsive to each market (Roth & Morrison, 1990). In this case, balancing operations and strategic decisions is the key to success.

Bartlett and Ghoshal (1989) worked on further development of the IR framework. They advanced the integration–responsiveness balance model by proposing organizational frameworks suited to the different strategies resulting from the convergence of globalizing and localizing forces (Figure 8.2). When the pressure for global integration is high and the pressure for local responsiveness is low, we see a global organization with a standardization strategy – a company that does not differentiate between markets, on the basis that everyone needs the same product or service. When the pressure is reversed, we see a multinational organization with a multidomestic strategy in which products or services are highly customized and businesses trade off the advantages of achieving scale efficiencies in favour of being adaptable to local needs and preferences. When there is little pressure for global integration or local responsiveness, we have an international organization with a strategy whose primary interest is in exporting goods regardless of how global reach is achieved. A new concept in the upgraded IR framework is a transnational organization with a transnational strategy: a company that aims at economies of scale but maintains flexibility regarding local requirements.

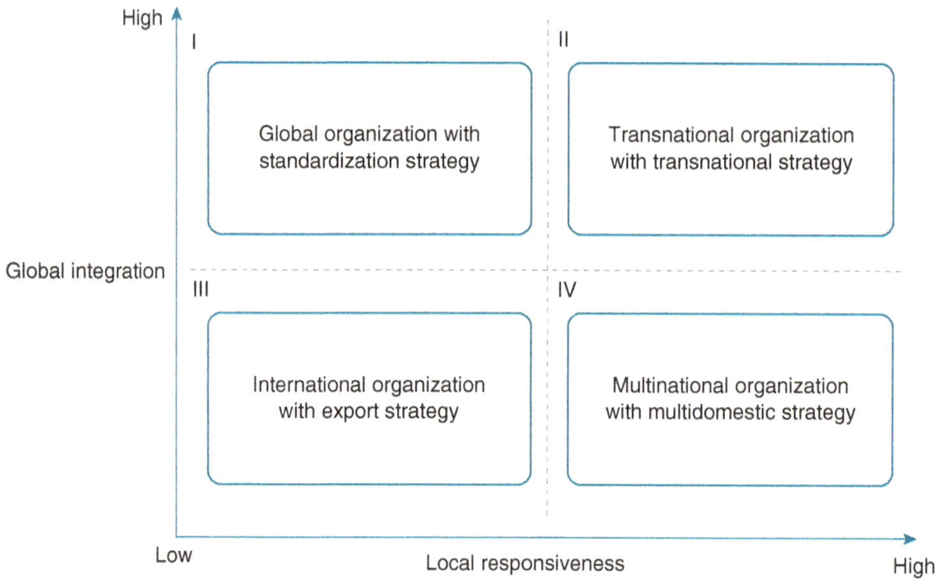

Figure 8.2 The strategies and structures under industry pressures for global integration and local responsiveness

Case Study: Global Operations and Management Strategies at Ford

Ford Motor Company, an American automobile manufacturer, was founded in 1903. Many inventions are associated with the Ford name, including the conveyor belt assembly line. During the twentieth century, Ford introduced a large number of models of vehicles, which by 2000 made the company the second largest car manufacturer in the world with a 12.5% market share. In addition to its brand, Ford was also the primary stakeholder in other car brands such as Aston Martin, Jaguar, Land Rover, and Volvo. By 2000, the car company had dealerships and manufacturing plants in Europe, North and South America, Asia Pacific, and Africa.

However, succeeding in the global arena and maintaining a brand's reputation is complicated. In the early 2000s, Ford pursued a management strategy with a strong emphasis on local responsiveness. Some models were constructed using different parts on different continents and had different exterior designs. The best example of this is the North American and European Ford Focus. Tailoring supply to local needs may be necessary in some cases, but it also means that global integration is left untapped, and the costs are higher. Yet that was not the biggest challenge Ford Motor Company faced in 2006. The US oil crisis, the run-up to the global economic crisis and the massive recession around the world created enormous difficulties for dealers. Bill Ford, Ford's CEO, failed to keep pace with the economic changes, resulting in a US$12.6 billion loss for the company in 2006. A new CEO, Alan Mulally, took over and in a few years his One Ford plan turned the company around and avoided bankruptcy and state ownership.

The company's success can be attributed to its new management system. A key factor in the achievement of the positive financial results was working together as one big team, taking advantage of global economies of scale. As part of the One Ford approach, weekly meetings were held for company executives to discuss plans, implementation, and potential disruptions. This ensured that employees around the world were aware of the goals and the steps needed to achieve them. The restructuring also meant ceasing to investing in brands other than Ford and Lincoln. The sale of Ford's stakes in Aston Martin, Jaguar, Land Rover, and Volvo freed up resources for product development, marketing, and sales of the company's own brands.

The new leadership method sought to reap the benefits of global integration. This was achieved by reducing the number of suppliers and manufacturing plants. In countries where there was overcapacity, plants were shut down and thousands of workers were made redundant. In 2012, for example, three European plants were closed due to the decline in purchasing power in the middle class. At the same time, Ford expanded in countries where the company saw the potential to increase sales significantly. By 2012, 80% of the components of Ford vehicles were the same regardless of where they were assembled, as were 75% of its global suppliers and 100% of its assembly processes. The more efficient development and production of its cars improved the financial balance sheet. In addition, the independence of the company's subsidiaries was reduced and the management system became more stakeholder oriented.

The success of the One Ford plan lay in Alan Mulally's understanding of market needs and his ability to harness the company's strengths through global collaboration. As the culture of the company changed, the mindset of its employees also changed, supporting the transformation of processes and the restructuring of the company. By 2012, Alan Mulally's One Ford plan, with the help of a loan in 2006 and some financial belt-tightening, returned Ford Motor Company to the top of the industry.

Sources: Ingrassia (2013); Caldicott (2014); Mulally & McArthur (2022)

(Continued)

Case Study Questions

1. Which car brands does Ford control today? How do they complement or compete with each other?
2. What is the role of local context in the automotive industry? How much do cars differ across countries?
3. How does Ford's strategy contrast with some of the other major car manufacturers, such as Volkswagen, Toyota, and Tesla?

8.4 STRATEGIC ORIENTATIONS

The process of strategic planning builds on the strategic orientation of an MNC and plays a role in shaping particular choices. Strategic orientations are different approaches that organizations adopt when making decisions related to their international operations and global business activities. These orientations help shape how an MNC manages its operations, marketing, staffing, and overall strategy across different countries and regions. Here we will consider four main strategic orientations: ethnocentric, polycentric, regiocentric, and geocentric (EPRG), which are summarized in Table 8.2.

Where there is an ethnocentric orientation, a company places a strong emphasis on the practices and values of its home country. This approach assumes that the company's way of doing business and its products or services are superior to those of other countries. As a result, key decisions are made at the headquarters, and the company tends to rely on its home-country employees to manage international operations. Since the ethnocentric oriented firm sells the same product for both home and foreign markets, this approach can be effective for maintaining control and consistency but may lead to a lack of adaptation to local markets and cultures.

A polycentric orientation takes a decentralized approach to international operations. In this case, subsidiaries and local managers in different countries have a high degree of autonomy to adapt strategies to local market conditions and cultural differences. This approach recognizes the diversity of markets and aims to tailor products and marketing strategies to each specific region. While this allows for better adaptation, it might lead to inefficiencies due to duplication of effort and a lack of global coordination.

The regiocentric orientation falls between the ethnocentric and polycentric approaches. It divides the world into regions or geographic areas and groups countries with similar characteristics together. Decision-making is done on a regional level, which allows for some adaptation to local market conditions while still maintaining a level of central control. This approach can strike a balance between standardization and adaptation, optimizing resources while responding to regional differences.

Table 8.2 Orientation of the firm under different EPRG profiles

ORIENTATION OF THE FIRM	ETHNOCENTRIC	POLYCENTRIC	REGIOCENTRIC	GEOCENTRIC
1. MISSION	Profitability (viability)	Public acceptance (legitimacy)	Both profitability and public acceptance (viability and legitimacy)	Both profitability and public acceptance (viability and legitimacy)
2. GOVERNANCE: a Direction of goal setting	Top down	Bottom up (each subsidiary decides on local objectives)	Mutually negotiated between region and its subsidiaries	Mutually negotiated at all levels of the corporation
b Communication	Hierarchical, with headquarters giving a high volume of orders, commands and advice	Little communication to and from headquarters and between subsidiaries	Both vertical and lateral communication within region	Both vertical and lateral communication within the company
c Allocation of resources	Investment opportunities decided at headquarters	Self-supporting subsidiaries, no cross-subsidiaries	Regions allocate resources, under guidelines from headquarters	World-wide projects, allocation influenced by local and headquarters' managers
3. STRATEGY	Globally integrated	National responsiveness	Regionally integrated and national responsiveness	Globally integrated and national responsiveness
4. STRUCTURE	Hierarchical product divisions	Hierarchical area divisions, with autonomous national units	Product and regional organizations tied through a matrix	A network of organizations, (including some stakeholders and competitor organizations)
5. CULTURE	Home country	Host country	Regional	Global

Source: Adapted and extended from: Chakravarthy & Perlmutter (1986)

A geocentric orientation seeks to integrate a global perspective into the organization's operations. Focusing on identifying the best talent and resources from around the world regardless of their origin, the company aims to create a truly global approach by blending standardized practices with local adaptation. This approach recognizes that certain functions or expertise might be better located in specific regions, and it encourages a global mindset among employees. It can be challenging to implement due to cultural and operational complexities, but it has the potential to achieve a high level of effectiveness.

The choice of orientation depends on factors such as the company's goals, industry, resources, market characteristics, and overall corporate culture. For instance, some MNCs prioritize short-term profitability and/or expansion, adapting their range of products and services to align with evolving markets; others concentrate on a more extended strategic approach, cultivating expertise in specific brands or technologies that can be capitalized in the long run. Additionally, some MNCs might use a combination of these orientations for different aspects of their global business strategy in order to achieve the best result.

8.5 GLOBAL VALUE CHAINS

When developing a global strategy, it is particularly important for international firms to consider the organization of global value chains (GVCs). A GVC is a set of activities on a global scale performed in the production, distribution, and marketing of goods and services. Effective integration of the value chain can contribute to cutting costs, accessing specialized skills and resources, and paving the way into global markets. Until recently, managers did not strategize value chains to a great extent due to the complexity of the process but digitalization and advances in technology and communication have made it easier for firms and subsidiaries to coordinate and manage activities across borders. In today's interconnected world, companies seek to optimize their production processes by leveraging the comparative advantages of different countries and regions. We are now going to look in detail at some strategically important attributes of global value chain organization: outsourcing/insourcing and offshoring/onshoring.

Outsourcing and insourcing are two contrasting approaches that firms use to manage their business (see Section 7.4.1). These strategic modes have been of interesting to both managers and scholars since the early 1990s.

Outsourcing is the process of delegating specific business tasks or operations to external third-party service providers. Contracting an external IT service agency, for example, can reduce the cost of salaries, training, and infrastructure, etc. when maintaining an internal IT department. The main advantage is that a firm can concentrate on its own expertise and outsource the other chain activities. Outsourcing also increases efficiency and mitigates risks, often enabling the development of competitive advantage.

Insourcing involves bringing tasks or processes that were previously outsourced back in-house and performing them internally. For example, a manufacturer might insource the production of essential components to mitigate supply chain disruptions. Insourcing choices involve both decreasing the amount of work handled by external contracts (and shifting this work to internal management) for a specific value-creating task, and establishing a new governance structure or modifying the current one. Insourcing allows a certain degree of freedom in terms of contracting, increases the flexibility of production processes, and supports a broad array of expertise.

Offshoring and onshoring are two strategies used by companies to manage their business operations in the context of global production. The difference between these two approaches and outsourcing and insourcing is the flexibility of the geographical dimension.

Offshoring involves moving certain business functions or processes abroad, often where labour costs are lower, specific expertise is available, or legal constraints are more flexible. Bals et al. (2013) define offshoring as 'international relocation of disaggregated firm value chain activities in captive, collaborative or outsourced governance modes'. Onshoring is bringing business functions or processes back into the company's home country. This strategy aims to benefit from advantages associated with local control, proximity, and quality assurance.

There are complicated multidimensional decision-making processes behind the configuration of global value chains. Some companies have chosen to bring operations back in-house *and* source locally, while others seek suppliers closer to their customer markets by adjusting their geographic reach while still outsourcing delivery operations (Bals et al., 2016).

Spotlight: Digitalization and Global Value Chains

Digitalization has enhanced the efficiency of global value chains (GVCs) significantly, transforming how businesses operate and compete in the global market. By integrating digital technologies, companies can streamline operations, reduce costs, and improve coordination across geographically dispersed activities.

Enhanced communication and collaboration are major benefits of digitalization. Digital tools such as cloud computing, video conferencing, and collaborative platforms enable seamless communication and real-time collaboration among global teams. This facilitates quicker decision-making, reduces misunderstandings, and ensures that all parts of the value chain are aligned and responsive to market changes.

Supply chain management is another critical area where digitalization has had a profound impact. Technologies like the Internet of Things (IoT), blockchain, and advanced analytics provide greater visibility and traceability throughout the supply chain. IoT devices can monitor the condition and location of goods in transit, while blockchain technologies can support secure and transparent record-keeping. These technologies help in optimizing inventory levels, reducing delays, and ensuring quality control.

Automation and efficiency are boosted by digitalization. Automation technologies, including robotics and artificial intelligence (AI), streamline production processes and reduce the need for manual intervention. AI algorithms optimize everything from production schedules to logistics routes, enhancing operational efficiency. For example, predictive maintenance powered by AI can foresee equipment failures before they occur, minimizing downtime and disruptions.

(Continued)

Data-driven decision-making is another major benefit of digitalization. Big data analytics allows companies to analyse vast amounts of data from various stages of the value chain, gaining insights that drive strategic decisions. By understanding patterns and trends, businesses can forecast demand more accurately, tailor products to customer preferences, and enhance overall supply chain agility.

Digitalization has made global value chains more efficient by enhancing communication, improving supply chain management, enabling automation, and facilitating data-driven decision-making. These advances help businesses optimize operations, reduce costs, and remain competitive in an increasingly interconnected global economy. However, as the Covid-19 pandemic has shown, heightened efficiency in global value chains comes at the cost of lower resilience. As a result, there is an emerging trend away from hyper-efficient supply chains towards resilient supply chains.

Sources: Harvard Business Review (https://hbr.org/2014/07/how-the-internet-of-things-changes-business-models); Deloitte (www.deloitte.com/dk/en/blogs/tech/blog-jesper-kamstrup-unlocking-the-power-of-big-data.html); Forbes (www.forbes.com/sites/bernardmarr/2023/10/12/the-impact-of-digital-transformation-on-business-models-opportunities-and-challenges)

8.6 INTERNATIONAL ORGANIZATION STRUCTURES

International organization structures are the ways in which MNCs arrange their operations, activities, and management across the world. The main purpose of these structures is to facilitate effective coordination, communication, decision-making, and resource allocation in a global business environment. We look at five common international organization structures that companies might adopt depending on their strategic goals, industry, and market conditions.

8.6.1 International Division Structure

The international division structure is a type of organizational arrangement used by MNCs to manage their international operations. In this structure, a separate division is established that is solely responsible for handling all international activities. This division operates independently and is equipped with its own set of resources, personnel, and strategies, distinct from the company's domestic operations. The most substantial benefit of this structure is that it makes possible a clear focus on international operations and facilitation of the company's entry into new markets. While an international division structure offers increased independence in making decisions, it is commonly employed in the initial phases of international expansion, when the foreign-to-domestic sales ratio is relatively low, and there is limited diversity in foreign products and geographic presence.

8.6.2 Global Product Structure

In order to address the growing and diverse requirements of international customers, MNCs need more streamlined and effective organizational frameworks. The global product structure is an organizational arrangement used by MNCs to manage their operations based on product lines. Using this structure, the company groups its activities and resources according to its various product categories, and each product line is managed globally across different markets. Thus, the company focuses on its core products and develops and markets them on a global scale. This type of arrangement is a highly efficient means of implementing product adjustments to fulfil evolving customer demands across the globe. However, the structure has some disadvantages. Global market demand and strategy may receive insufficient attention, with management tending to prioritize currently profitable markets while overlooking those with greater potential. Moreover, discrete product divisions often mean that functional tasks are duplicated and there are more employees than are needed.

8.6.3 Global Area Structure

The global area structure is an organizational design used by MNCs to manage their operations according to geographic regions, each division responsible for managing all aspects of the company's operations within that particular area. Allowing the company to tailor its strategies and operations to the unique characteristics and needs of each geographic market, this multi-domestic approach involves managing national subsidiaries with minimal coordination as though they were independent businesses. This approach is often used by well-established companies with sufficient experience but little variety in their product portfolio. The main advantage of this structure is its strong responsiveness and interconnectivity with local environments and circumstances but it commonly brings with it the disadvantage that some functions (e.g., R&D) are duplicated across the company as a whole, which and can complicate the achievement of economies of scale.

8.6.4 Global Functional Structure

The global functional structure is based on specialized functions or departments (e.g., marketing, finance, production, etc.), regardless of geographic location. Different functional areas are organized globally, and each function is responsible for its activities across all markets. This type of organizational arrangement leverages the specialized knowledge within each functional division and facilitates highly centralized control with a strong international orientation. However, coordination and interconnection between functions and management of multiple product lines can be challenging. In addition, centralized control makes adapting quickly to emerging opportunities and challenges and decision-making slower.

8.6.5 Matrix Structure

Finally, the matrix structure demonstrates joint control over an MNC's functional activities, unlike the forms discussed above. It combines elements of both the functional and product-based structures. Employees report to both functional managers and project or product managers simultaneously, creating a dual reporting relationship. Organizations often use this approach to address the complexities of managing multiple projects, products, or initiatives while still leveraging functional expertise. It is used most often in industries where projects are complex and require input from multiple functional areas. Even though the structure encourages collaboration across functional departments, helps to break down silos and promotes knowledge sharing, it will collapse without careful planning, clear communication, and strong leadership. A matrix structure can similarly combine the global area and product structures. Some companies even organize activities along three or more dimensions, creating more complex reporting relationships.

8.6.6 The Interplay Between Organizational Structure And Strategy

Organizational structure and strategy must align to achieve common goals. The structure should be designed to support the strategy's objectives and ensure that resources and responsibilities are appropriately allocated to meet those goals. Hence, the transnational strategy, which is characterized by a simultaneous focus on global integration and local responsiveness, often finds synergy with the matrix organizational structure. Here, companies aim to achieve a balance between centralized control and decentralized operations, so that the structure reflects the needs of the strategy. A global strategy, where a company seeks economies of scale through standardization, often aligns with a functional organizational structure – departments are organized according to specialized functions to maintain efficiency in resource allocation and to ensure a consistent approach across global markets. When pursuing a multidomestic strategy, which involves tailoring products and marketing strategies to specific regional markets, companies might choose to opt for a region-oriented organizational structure. This particular structure groups operations by geographical region, allowing for localized decision-making and customization. Matching strategy with structure is crucial in order to respond appropriately to the demands of a dynamic global business environment.

8.7 AGENCY CONFLICTS AND REMUNERATION IN GLOBAL COMPANIES

Companies with a global presence invariably have to deal with misalignments in incentives. These misalignments may be the consequence of different cultures, requirements for employee representation as a result of formal institutions, or simply variations in how much risk individuals are ready to take. The dominant perspective through which to understand such misalignments is agency theory, which we introduce briefly below. We will then use agency theory to understand remuneration in multinational companies.

8.7.1 Agency Theory

Agency theory has established itself as a fundamental framework to capture the interactions and conflicts that occur between principals and agents in various organizational contexts. Rooted in both management and economics literature it is one of the first theories to shed light on the complexity of governance structures (Daily et al., 2003). Agency theory can be traced back to Adam Smith's seminal work *The Wealth of Nations* (1937/1776). Smith's foresight regarding the challenges in delegating the management of an organization to individuals who are not the actual owners laid the foundation for what would later become agency theory. Building on this foundation, Berle and Means (1932) went further and examined the ownership dynamics of large US firms. Their analysis revealed that agents appointed by owners exercise significant control over these firms, leading to concerns about possible misappropriation, which may foster conflicts between the interests of principals and agents.

Agency theory has been refined and extended in the field of IB. Eisenhardt (1989) contributed to the theory's evolution by describing two fundamental models: the positivist agency model and the principal–agent model (Harris & Raviv, 1978). The latter model portrays principals as risk-neutral and profit-oriented entities, while agents exhibit risk aversion and rent-seeking behaviour. The positivist agency theory, on the other hand, focuses on the causal factors underpinning agency conflicts and associated costs, according to which contracts based on incentives lead agents to act in the interest of principals, and information available to principals acts as a disciplining mechanism for agent behaviour (Eisenhardt, 1989).

At the heart of agency theory is the principal–agent relationship, in which principals exercise control over economic functions or assets while delegating day-to-day operational control to agents (Jensen & Meckling, 1976). Agency theory places particular emphasis on the flow of information, the challenges posed by information asymmetry, and associated monitoring costs. Agency theory is closely related to the problems arising from the separation of ownership and management in MNCs. The overarching goal of this theory is to overcome this separation, implement governance mechanisms and optimize organizational efficiency and value creation.

Contemporary research has expanded the scope of agency theory to account for the heterogeneous nature of principals. Recent research has shed light on the fact that principals themselves can vary in their incentives and goals (Ramaswamy et al., 2002). Several authors highlight emerging markets, where a dual-principal problem occurs in state-controlled public enterprises owned by both state and non-state shareholders (e.g., Thomsen & Pedersen, 2000).

Traditional agency theory has been criticized for its narrow focus on agents, overlooking potential issues originating from the principal's side. Perrow (1986) raises this concern, suggesting that the theory neglects the possibility that principals might deceive, shirk responsibilities or exploit agents. The critique highlights an imbalance and underlines the need for a holistic view of principal–agent dynamics. Scholars such as Eisenhardt (1989) and Shleifer and Vishny (1997) have drawn attention to its limitations. They argue that the theory's reliance on contractual agreements to mitigate agency problems may encounter hurdles like information asymmetry, rationality challenges, fraud and transaction costs. Moreover, the theory's shareholder-centric focus tends to neglect the interests of broader stakeholders, which can undermine organizational harmony.

8.7.2 Stock Options And Aligning Risk Propensity

Case Study: Starbucks and the Bean Stock Programme

In the early 2000s, Starbucks Corporation, a global leader in the coffeehouse industry, encountered a significant challenge: aligning the incentives of its rapidly expanding global workforce with the company's long-term strategic goals. Recognizing the importance of employee motivation and retention across diverse markets, Starbucks turned to an innovative solution - expanding its stock option programme, known as the Bean Stock plan, to include employees worldwide.

Founded in 1971 in Seattle, Washington, Starbucks had grown exponentially by the early 2000s, with thousands of stores across North America, Europe, Asia, and other regions. As the company expanded, it became increasingly clear that maintaining consistent service quality and operational efficiency across all locations was crucial to sustaining its brand reputation and financial performance. However, the diverse cultural and economic environments in which Starbucks operated presented unique challenges. Employees in different regions had different motivations, expectations, and levels of engagement. The company's leadership realized that to drive performance and commitment globally, they needed to align employees' incentives with the company's success.

Originally launched in 1991, the Bean Stock programme granted stock options to eligible employees, allowing them to purchase Starbucks stock at a set price after a vesting period. This initiative aimed to foster a sense of ownership among employees, motivating them to contribute to the company's growth and success. By the early 2000s, Starbucks decided to extend this programme to its international workforce.

Extending the Bean Stock programme to global employees involved several strategic steps. Starbucks ensured that the programme was inclusive, offering stock options to employees at all levels, from baristas to store managers. The company conducted comprehensive training sessions and workshops to educate employees about the benefits of the programme and how it worked. Clear communication was crucial to ensure that employees understood the value of their stock options and how their efforts could directly impact the company's stock price. Recognizing the diverse economic conditions and regulatory environments in different countries, Starbucks adapted the Bean Stock programme to comply with local laws and norms. This included adjustments in the vesting periods and the structure of stock grants to suit the needs of employees in various regions. The stock options were designed to reward long-term commitment and performance. Employees who stayed with the company and contributed to its success would see the value of their stock options increase, directly linking their financial gain to the company's overall performance.

The expansion of the Bean Stock programme yielded several significant benefits for Starbucks. By giving employees a stake in the company's success, Starbucks fostered a sense of ownership and pride among its global workforce. Employees were more motivated to maintain high standards of customer service and operational efficiency, knowing that their efforts would be rewarded through the stock options. The programme helped reduce turnover rates, particularly in international markets where retaining skilled employees was challenging. The prospect of owning company stock incentivized employees to stay with Starbucks longer, contributing to greater stability and consistency in operations. With their financial interests aligned with the company's success, employees were more likely to go above and beyond in their roles. This alignment of incentives helped drive performance improvements across the board, from sales growth to customer satisfaction.

While the Bean Stock programme was largely successful, it was not without challenges. The complexity of managing a global stock option programme required significant administrative effort and investment. Additionally, fluctuations in the stock market could impact the perceived value of the stock options, potentially affecting employee morale. By giving employees a tangible stake in the company's success, Starbucks was able to enhance motivation, improve retention, and drive performance across its international operations. This case underscores the importance of aligning incentives in a way that fosters long-term commitment and shared success, particularly in a diverse and globalized business environment.

Sources: Starbucks (https://starbucksbeanstock.com/en-us) and Marketscreener (www.marketscreener.com/quote/stock/STARBUCKS-CORPORATION-4905/news/Starbucks-The-Program-that-Turned-Employees-Into-Partners-Continues-to-Change-Lives-18161129)

Case Study Questions

1 What is the role of stock options for managers in general? Is there evidence of stock options overcompensating for managerial risk aversion?
2 Why do shopfloor employees usually not have stock options?

Stock options serve as a powerful tool in mitigating agency conflicts between managers and shareholders by aligning their interests and fostering a sense of ownership among executives. This compensation mechanism grants managers the right to purchase company shares at a predetermined price, typically tied to the stock's current market value.

By doing so, managers are incentivized to act in the best interests of shareholders, as the value of their stock options is directly linked to the company's overall performance and stock price appreciation.

Moreover, stock options create a direct and tangible link between managerial decision-making and shareholder wealth, encouraging executives to make strategic choices that enhance the company's financial health and long-term sustainability. This alignment of interests helps mitigate the principal–agent problem, where managers may prioritize personal gain over shareholder value. Additionally, stock options often have a vesting period, requiring managers to stay with the company for a specified duration to realize the full benefits, further promoting continuity and a focus on the organization's long-term success.

In addition to aligning interests, stock options play a crucial role in encouraging appropriate risk-taking behaviour. The linkage between stock option rewards and the company's stock performance motivates managers to make strategic decisions that balance risk and return. Having a stake in the company's equity makes managers more inclined to pursue initiatives that could lead to long-term value creation, even if those initiatives involve a certain degree of risk. This dynamic fosters a culture of responsible risk-taking, as managers are more likely to engage in ventures that align with shareholders' expectations for sustainable growth. The vesting period associated with stock options further enhances this risk management aspect, ensuring that managers have a vested interest in the outcomes of their decisions over the long term. In this way, stock options not only address agency conflicts but also contribute to a corporate environment where calculated risk-taking is aligned with shareholder interests and the overall success of the organization.

Spotlight: Stock Options and Long-Term Sustainability

The increasing focus on stock options as a major component of executive remuneration has shifted corporate priorities from long-term objectives to short-term gains. This trend has significant implications for environmental sustainability, often leading to decisions that prioritize immediate financial returns over long-term ecological health and corporate responsibility.

Stock options tie a significant portion of executives' compensation to the company's short-term stock performance. This creates strong incentives for executives to boost share prices quickly, often through measures such as cost-cutting, share buybacks, and aggressive marketing strategies. These actions can lead to short-term profitability but may undermine long-term investments essential for sustainable growth and environmental stewardship.

To meet the immediate demands of stockholders, executives might deprioritize or delay investment in sustainable practices that typically require substantial upfront costs and yield benefits over a longer period. For instance, initiatives like transitioning to renewable energy sources, improving energy efficiency, or investing in sustainable supply chains may be postponed or minimized because they do not provide immediate financial returns and can temporarily depress profits.

Moreover, the pressure to deliver short-term results can lead to practices that are detrimental to the environment. Cost-cutting measures might include reducing expenditure on pollution control, waste management, and sustainable resource utilization. Companies may also engage in extractive or environmentally harmful activities that provide quick financial benefits but cause long-term ecological damage.

This short-term focus driven by stock option compensation can also discourage the pursuit of innovation in sustainability. Investments in research and development for green technologies, which could position a company as a leader in the emerging sustainable economy, might be sacrificed for projects that promise quicker returns.

Sources: McGregor (2014) and *Harvard Business Review* (https://hbr.org/2015/10/yes-short-termism-really-is-a-problem)

8.8 GLOBAL COMPETITIVE STRATEGY

Competitive strategy is concerned with strategic moves relative to competitors. Employing a successful competitive strategy is about making strategic choices on how to position the company's products or services, allocate resources, and leverage its strengths to gain a competitive advantage on a global scale. In order to succeed, a firm should consider the diverse cultural, economic, political, and technological factors that influence business operations across different countries and regions. In this section we will consider some attributes of competitive strategy that are useful to consider when managing a global firm.

8.8.1 The Bandwagon Effect

Rooted in the fundamental human need for acceptance and belonging, the bandwagon effect showcases how people often make decisions, adopt beliefs, or follow trends simply because others around them are doing the same. Firms can also become a victim of this psychological phenomenon. In the context of competitive business strategy, the bandwagon effect refers to the phenomenon whereby companies or businesses choose to adopt certain strategies, practices, or trends solely because their competitors are doing the same, rather than making decisions based on a careful analysis of their own strengths, weaknesses, and market conditions.

The reasoning behind strategy imitation can be an attempt to avoid falling behind in the market. However, if the issue is critically assessed, it would become clear that this strategy is rarely successful. When businesses blindly follow competitors, they may miss opportunities to differentiate themselves in the market; it leads to neglect of their own core competencies, missing out on opportunities to leverage their unique strengths for competitive advantage. The bandwagon effect can also exacerbate the overall environment of the global market; lack of innovation, an oversaturated market where all players offer similar products or services, and market instability are some of the most evident consequences of adopting a single strategy. Instead of blindly imitating competitors, businesses should focus on differentiation, sustainable competitive advantages, and innovative approaches that cater to their unique strengths and the evolving needs of their customers.

8.8.2 First Mover Advantage

First mover advantage is a competitive advantage gained by a company that is the first to enter a market, introduce a new product or service, or pioneer a novel business model. In essence, the first mover advantage stems from the idea that the company has the opportunity to establish a strong market presence, build brand recognition, and capture a significant share of the market and profit before competitors enter. Examples of first mover advantage can be seen in various industries, such as Amazon's early entry into the e-commerce market, Apple's introduction of the iPhone, and Google's dominance in online search.

First mover advantages are multi-stage processes (Lieberman & Montgomery, 1988). The first stage creates some sort of asymmetry that allows one firm to benefit from initiating the first move due to acquiring unique resources, a new strategy, or good luck. The employment of tools to reinforce the position leads to higher profits and better market position. These tools encompass elements like patents, proprietary learning effects, securing input resources and strategic locations ahead of competitors, as well as creating buyer loyalty through the imposition of switching costs. Conversely, disadvantages associated with being a first mover may arise due to challenges like free-rider issues, prolonged uncertainty resolution, alterations in technology or consumer demands, and a range of organizational obstacles.

Ultimately, whether management should pursue a first mover advantage depends on the company's appetite for risk, resources, ability to innovate, market understanding, and the competitive environment. Companies that are well positioned to innovate, manage uncertainty, and adapt to changes are more likely to succeed as first movers. However, it is essential to carefully assess the specific circumstances, weigh the pros and cons, and consider alternative strategies before committing.

8.8.3 Attacks And Counterattacks (Pre-Emption)

Attacks and counterattacks are types of competitive strategy that contribute to an advantage over rivals in the market: those actions are taken to outmanoeuvre competitors, capture market share, and establish a stronger position. Competing with the rival, a firm can launch an attack, employing a set of actions to its strategic advantage. A counterattack involves responding to competitive attacks or challenges initiated by rivals: they are strategic manoeuvres designed to protect the company's position and minimize the impact of competitive threats. Let us consider an example of competitive strategy using attacks and counterattacks. Price leadership is achieved by lowering prices, thereby attracting more customers and gaining a bigger share of the market. The response strategy can be price matching, when the 'attacked' firm undercuts the prices as well in order to retain customers.

Is it possible to predict whether a market player will attack or whether a firm will respond to another's aggressive move? It is not always easy to pre-empt a strike, but the awareness–motivation–capability (AMC) framework is a useful supportive tool for predicting a rival's move. The goal of using the AMC framework is to identify behavioural drivers for competitive actions in the best interests of competitor analysis (Chen et al., 2007. Awareness signifies a company's understanding of its competitors and the competitive landscape. Motivation pertains to a company's drive to engage with and counter the competitive moves of specific rivals. Capability relies on a company's available resources and decision-making capacities to effectively compete against its rivals. As the AMC framework contributes to the success of both attacks and counterattacks, it proves useful not only in research and analysis but also in management and practice.

Overall, attacks and counterattacks drive the dynamics of competition in the business world. They encourage companies to continuously improve, innovate, and strive for excellence, ultimately benefiting customers by offering better products, services, and value. However, it is important for companies to employ these strategies ethically and responsibly to maintain healthy and constructive competition within the market.

8.8.4 Why do Firms Like to Collude Sometimes?

Spotlight: Antitrust Legislation in the USA

Antitrust regulation in the USA emerged in response to the growing power of large corporations and monopolies during the late nineteenth and early twentieth centuries. The primary aims were to promote fair competition, protect consumers, and prevent the formation of monopolies and anti-competitive practices.

The roots of antitrust regulation can be traced back to the decades following the US Civil War, a period of rapid industrialization and economic expansion. This period saw the rise of powerful trusts and monopolies, such as Standard Oil and the railroads, which dominated their respective industries. These entities often engaged in practices that stifled competition, manipulated prices, and exploited consumers and small businesses.

The public outcry against these monopolistic practices led to the enactment of the first federal antitrust law, the Sherman Antitrust Act of 1890. Sponsored by Senator John Sherman, this landmark legislation aimed to curb concentrations of power that interfered

(Continued)

with trade and reduced economic competition. The Sherman Act made it illegal to form contracts, combinations, or conspiracies that restrained trade and to monopolize or attempt to monopolize any part of trade or commerce.

Enforcement of the Sherman Act initially faced challenges due to vague language and judicial interpretation. However, significant progress was made with the establishment of the Bureau of Corporations in 1903 and the subsequent creation of the Federal Trade Commission (FTC) in 1914. The Clayton Antitrust Act of 1914 further strengthened antitrust regulation by addressing specific practices that the Sherman Act did not explicitly prohibit, such as price discrimination, exclusive dealing agreements, and mergers that substantially lessened competition.

Over the years, antitrust enforcement evolved, adapting to the changing economic landscape and business practices. Landmark cases, such as the breakup of Standard Oil in 1911 and AT&T in 1982, underscored the government's commitment to maintaining competitive markets. The role of antitrust regulation expanded to address issues in various sectors, including technology, pharmaceuticals, and telecommunications.

Sources: Federal Trade Commission - The Antitrust Laws (www.ftc.gov/advice-guidance/competition-guidance/guide-antitrust-laws/antitrust-laws) and National Archives (www.archives.gov/milestone-documents/sherman-anti-trust-act#:~:text=Approved%20July%202%2C%201890%2C%20The,U.S.%20Congress%20to%20prohibit%20trusts)

In a competitive market, multiple companies offer similar products or services, and they strive to differentiate themselves through different channels. Healthy competition benefits consumers by promoting better products, lower prices, and greater choices. However, sometimes rivals resort to collusion, which implies secret or illegal agreements between competitors to manipulate the market in their favour. Colluding companies may work together to fix prices, limit production, allocate customers, or engage in other anticompetitive behaviours. As a result, competition is stifled, consumer choice is limited, prices rise, and quality falls.

Collusion usually consists of three stages. First, there is tacit collusion, which is characterized by a pattern of behaviour that suggests cooperation even though there is no explicit communication between the companies involved. The companies may observe each other's actions and reactions in the market and adjust their strategies accordingly to maintain higher prices or other anticompetitive outcomes. Second, collusion becomes explicit, with discussions, negotiations, or agreements between competitors to manipulate market conditions, prices, production levels, or other competitive factors. Lastly, a cartel is created – that is, a formal agreement or arrangement between competing companies to coordinate their actions and strategies in order to manipulate market conditions, achieve anticompetitive outcomes, and benefit from them. There are a number of conditions that foster collusion: concentration ratio (the percentage of total industry sales accounted for by the top firms); an industry price leader; homogeneous products; high entry barriers; and high market commonality.

While firms might be enticed by the short-term gains of collusion such as increased profits and reduced uncertainty, it is important to recognize that the negative consequences far outweigh any potential benefits; fair competition stimulates innovation, consumer welfare, and economic growth, making collusion harmful to the overall health of the economy.

Case Study: The Book-Publishing Industry

Giant international corporations are often allegedly involved in some form of collusion. Even one of the world's most valuable companies, Apple, has dark episodes in its history. In 2015, a federal judge in the USA determined that the company collaborated with major publishers to increase the prices of e-books. The court uncovered evidence indicating that Apple, in order to eradicate competition in retail pricing, was involved in collusion with a group resembling an oligopoly (a market dominated by a few large players), comprising Harper Collins, Penguin, Simon & Schuster, Hachette, and Macmillan. The court concluded that Apple's actions unequivocally violated antitrust regulations. Apple contended that the agreement with the publishers was essential to counterbalance Amazon's control over the e-book market; however, the appeals court did not accept this reasoning mainly because major publishers weren't interested in price competition. They aimed to uphold the existing favourable price structure, which allowed them to profit from high-priced hardcover versions of new books before releasing cheaper editions.

It was noted that the publishers, even before Apple's involvement, operated as a close-knit industry, frequently discussed joint strategies, and colluded. Apple's entry provided an opportunity to leverage their influence over Amazon's pricing terms. Once Apple joined, the publishers forced Amazon to accept the 'agency pricing' model, whereby publishers set book prices. This resulted in higher prices for newly released and bestselling books, achieving what the industry desired. According to the US Justice Department, the price of new books grew by an average of 24%, reaching 40% in some cases.

Apple aimed to present itself as an innocent business partner amid allegations of price-fixing collusion by book publishers. Its argument was that its uniform deals with publishers were coincidental. Rather than relying on publishing partners' market positions, Apple tied its e-book prospects to an industry with inflexible pricing and resistance to change. This approach backfired, resulting in Apple suffering the consequences.

Sources: Fortune (https://fortune.com/2015/06/30/apple-court-books) and Reuters (www.reuters.com/article/us-apple-ebooks-idUSBRE9690GE20130710)

(Continued)

Case Study Questions

1. Which industries work like oligopolies?
2. In what ways are oligopolistic competition and competitive advantage via differentiation related?
3. How does technology disrupt pricing in the publishing industry more broadly?

8.9 REAL OPTIONS

Myers (1977) established the term 'real options' and conceived the idea of applying the principles of financial options to the domain of strategic decision-making. Real options were perceived as opportunities to acquire tangible assets under potentially advantageous conditions. So, real options are opportunities a business has to make decisions regarding assets, investments, or projects in an uncertain environment. They are called 'real' because they usually involve tangible assets such as land, real estate, and inventory, rather than being a financial instrument.

Nevertheless, real options theory is basically enhanced FDI theory: a firm can derive advantages from uncertainty because it can contain downside risks and maintain favourable opportunities. According to the theory, a firm operating in uncertain conditions must create real options to be flexible and seize such opportunities as they arise in order to adapt to changing circumstances (Li & Rugman, 2007). Moreover, real options theory recognizes that investment decisions are not one-time commitments but rather ongoing choices that organizations can make as new information emerges. Contrary to other International Business theories like internationalization theory, which perceive uncertainty as a detrimental factor (Johanson & Vahlne, 1977), real options theory argues that uncertainty does not have only negative consequences. Firms can leverage uncertainty by generating real options that provide them with the adaptability to navigate new information and maintain flexibility in their responses.

There are a number of real option types. The most basic are options to abandon (to stop operations), expand, wait, contract (to close a project or a subsidiary), and switch. By considering real options, companies can make more informed and agile decisions that align with their strategic objectives and maximize long-term value in the context of International Business.

8.10 RECENT DEVELOPMENTS IN MNC STRUCTURE AND STRATEGY

Research on MNC structure and strategy is in frequent flux because of ongoing changes in external and internal environments. We highlight three recent topics: platform MNCs, de-globalization and the MNC, and MNC political strategies.

A first, rather novel topic in global strategy and structure is platform MNCs. Platform MNCs (Stallkamp & Schotter, 2021) are multinational companies that provide digital platforms or ecosystems through which international users and businesses can connect, interact, and transact. These companies typically operate on a global scale to leverage their vast user base, data analytics capabilities, and technological infrastructure. Examples include social media platforms (e.g., Facebook, X (previously Twitter)), e-commerce platforms (e.g., Amazon, Alibaba), and content-sharing platforms (e.g., YouTube, Netflix). Many of these firms rely heavily on data collection and analysis to personalize user experiences, target advertisements, and improve their services. This data-driven approach helps them optimize their platforms and generate revenue through targeted advertising or subscription models. Their global presence gives them significant influence and impact on digital economies worldwide. At the same time, they often face regulatory scrutiny concerning issues such as user privacy, data security, antitrust concerns, and their impact on traditional industries.

A second emerging topic is MNC structures and strategies as a result of de-globalization pressures. For example, Luo and Witt (2022) examined the challenges posed by de-globalization for emerging market multinational companies (EMNCs), proposing adjustments to their global strategic stance. Ambos et al. (2020) explored how managers' perceptions of risks and returns might differ during periods of de-globalization and periods of globalization. However, how different types of MNCs respond to particular de-globalization pressures has not yet been fully explored.

A third stream addresses the political strategies of MNCs. Corporate political strategies refer to the deliberate actions and tactics that organizations employ to influence government policies, regulations, and decisions to their advantage (Puck et al., 2018). These strategies often involve lobbying, campaign contributions, forming coalitions with other businesses or interest groups, and engaging in public relations efforts to shape public opinion. Research indicates that corporate political strategies are prevalent across various industries and can significantly impact firms' competitive positions and profitability by affecting regulatory outcomes and market conditions. MNCs face particular challenges in this domain as they are confronted with multiple diverse political systems and stakeholders and multiple regulatory systems that regulate MNCs' political involvement.

SUMMARY

This chapter has provided an overview of the challenges associated with strategically managing an MNC. We discussed Porter's framework and outlined three main strategies – cost leadership, differentiation, and focus – each tailored to specific market segments to enhance market positioning and profitability. The strategies involve minimizing costs through efficiencies, offering unique products or services, or targeting niche markets with specialized offerings. The chapter also highlighted the importance of strategic clarity and the risks associated with being stuck in the middle.

Additionally, we introduced the resource-based view (RBV) and Porter's five forces frameworks for analysing internal strengths and external market dynamics, crucial for crafting effective corporate strategies. The integration–responsiveness framework provides insights into global integration vs local responsiveness in International Business strategies, highlighting the challenges and strategic decisions multinational companies face in balancing standardization and adaptation across diverse markets.

Strategies in MNCs are developed based on strategic orientations that guide decision-making in international operations and global business activities. We can differentiate ethnocentric, polycentric, regiocentric, and geocentric strategic orientations. These orientations influence the design of an MNC's global value chain (GVC), and its focus on onshoring vs offshoring and insourcing vs outsourcing. International organization structures, such as the international division, global product, global area, global functional, and matrix structures, facilitate MNC coordination and management along the GVC. Each structure optimizes resource allocation and decision-making based on product lines, geographic regions, functional expertise, and project needs. Within such organizational structures, tasks and processes need to be coordinated. Agency theory helps us to understand the challenges associated with this objective and examines conflicts between principals (owners) and agents (managers) in MNCs, emphasizing governance mechanisms like stock options to align interests and mitigate risks.

Global competitive strategy involves strategically positioning products or services, allocating resources, and leveraging strengths to gain a competitive edge on a global scale. Factors such as cultural, economic, political, and technological influences across different regions must be considered. Key aspects include understanding the bandwagon effect, where firms may imitate competitors' strategies without assessing their own capabilities, potentially missing opportunities for differentiation and innovation. First mover advantage is another critical strategy, offering benefits like market dominance and brand recognition, though it also involves risks such as uncertainty and the need for continuous innovation. Additionally, using attacks and counterattacks allows firms to outmanoeuvre competitors and strengthen their market position, supported by tools such as the awareness–motivation–capability (AMC) framework. These strategies play a crucial role in navigating global markets, shaping competitive dynamics, and sustaining long-term success.

9

INTERNATIONAL FINANCE

CHAPTER INTRODUCTION

This chapter, along with the three chapters that follow, will broaden our discussion of International Business. We will look into four business functions that play an important role in multinational companies: international finance, international marketing, international human resource management, and international supply chain management. We will introduce some basic concepts and then focus on the particular challenges that arise from working in these functions in an international context.

International finance deals largely with how risks can be incorporated into financial planning, and how risk influences a company's finances and investments. We cover these topics as well as some perspectives on international accounting as starting points for more detailed discussion.

LEARNING OUTCOMES

After reading this chapter you should be able to:

1. Demonstrate an understanding of risk and how it relates to International Business
2. Explain how foreign exchange rate markets work, and how to hedge against fluctuations in foreign exchange markets
3. Outline the basic principles of international accounting, particularly transfer pricing
4. Describe how international expansion in foreign investments will influence company financing via capital structure.

Case Study: Doing Business in Argentina

The early 2000s witnessed a severe economic crisis in Argentina, which led to a default on its sovereign debt in 2001. This crisis resulted from a combination of factors, including a fixed exchange rate regime, high levels of public debt, and a fragile financial system. The government's decision to abandon the pegged exchange rate and devalue the Argentine peso led to a sharp contraction of the economy, soaring unemployment rates, and widespread social unrest.

In the aftermath of the crisis, Argentina implemented various economic measures to stabilize its economy, such as debt restructuring, fiscal adjustments, and the adoption of more flexible exchange rate policies. While these measures initially contributed to a period of economic recovery, the country continued to grapple with structural issues, including high inflation and reliance on external financing.

One of the persistent challenges has been inflation, which has remained a significant concern for Argentina. The country has struggled to control inflationary pressures, with rates often surpassing official targets. High inflation erodes the purchasing power of the currency, leading to uncertainties for businesses and consumers alike. It complicates financial planning, wage negotiations, and overall economic decision-making, creating an environment that can be challenging for businesses to navigate.

The issue of public debt has also played a crucial role in Argentina's economic difficulties. Despite debt restructuring efforts, the country has faced challenges in managing its debt levels, leading to periodic bouts of financial stress. The burden of servicing debt obligations diverts resources away from essential public investments and social programmes, impacting the overall economic environment.

Furthermore, political factors have contributed to economic uncertainties in Argentina. Changes in government administrations have often led to shifts in economic policies, creating an unpredictable business environment. Policies related to trade, taxation, and regulatory frameworks have experienced fluctuations, making strategic planning difficult for businesses operating in the country.

In recent years, Argentina has faced additional economic challenges, including the impact of the Covid-19 pandemic. The pandemic exacerbated existing vulnerabilities, leading to a contraction in economic activity and increased fiscal pressures. The government implemented various measures to mitigate the effects of the pandemic, including increased public spending, which further strained fiscal resources.

The cumulative impact of these economic challenges has influenced the risk landscape for businesses operating in Argentina. Volatility in exchange rates, high inflation, and uncertainty regarding government policies have created a challenging environment for investors and entrepreneurs. Businesses must navigate the complexities of the economic landscape, including managing currency risks, adapting to changing regulations, and staying resilient in the face of economic uncertainties. It remains to be seen how the tenure of President Milei (elected in 2023) will influence the risk of doing business in the long run.

Sources: Brookings (www.brookings.edu/wp-content/uploads/2016/06/11_argentina_kiguel.pdf#:~:-text=URL%3A%20https%3A%2F%2Fwww.brookings.edu%2Fwp); United States Congress (www.jec.senate.gov/public/_cache/files/5fbf2f91-6cdf-4e70-8ff2-620ba901fc4c/argentina-s-economic-crisis---06-13-03.pdf#:~:text=URL%3A%20https%3A%2F%2Fwww.jec.senate.gov%2Fpublic%2F_cache%2Ffiles%2F5fbf2f91); International Monetary Fund (www.imf.org/en/Publications/Occasional-Papers/Issues/2016/12/30/Lessons-from-the-Crisis-in-Argentina-17402)

Case Study Questions

1 How does inflation beyond 200% influence the internationalization strategy of firms entering Argentina?
2 How can companies protect themselves against disproportionate government influence on their operations?
3 On which dimensions does Argentina have low risk, and on which dimensions does it have high risk for MNCs?

9.1 COUNTRY RISK

The concept of risk is important when discussing international finance. Historically, risk has been associated with negative outcomes or potential adversities, such as financial diminution or a decrease in investment value (see also Chapter 3.5, Country Risk).

The historical precedents for risk associated with transnational capital flows can be observed through various lenses. For instance, Marco Polo, a Venetian merchant and explorer, documented his commercial expeditions to Asia in his travelogue. While Polo successfully navigated trade with Asian markets, bringing novel commodities back to Europe, not all European merchants were as fortunate. There are numerous accounts of traders being kidnapped, assassinated, or murdered on their journeys, leading to substantial or complete loss of their invested capital.

However, the concept of country risk lacks a uniform and precise definition. Risk relates to the potential barriers posed by the host country's economic, social, and political factors (see Chapters 2–5) that may influence an investor's ability to realize returns on investment. In other words, it encapsulates the various uncertainties that could disrupt the expected return on an investment due to conditions in a particular country (Bouchet et al., 2003). Meldrum (2000: 33) puts it this way: 'All business transactions involve some degree of risk. When business transactions occur across international borders, they carry additional risks not present in domestic transactions. These additional risks, called country risks, typically include risks arising from a variety of national differences in economic structures, policies, socio-political institutions, geography and currencies.'

Understanding country risk isn't just an academic exercise; it has practical implications for international operations and investments. Elevated country risk can deter foreign entities from investing due to the potential of unstable returns. For an MNC, understanding and mitigating country risk is essential to ensure successful and sustainable operations. An inaccurate assessment can result in failure to make a profit, a damaged reputation, and, in extreme cases, total operational failure.

In the realm of risk analysis, two primary categories emerge: systematic and unsystematic risk. Systematic risk refers to factors that impact the whole market, with consequences felt by all market participants. These risks arise from macroeconomic events. Prominent examples include the 2008 financial crisis and the Covid-19 pandemic, both of which had severe effects on global financial systems and markets. Unsystematic risk, also called idiosyncratic risk, manifests at the microeconomic level, influencing a specific subset of market participants, such as a particular company or sector.

Understanding country risk needs to take account of the relationships among a nation's economic, political, and social characteristics. Each factor possesses distinct characteristics and implications for external entities aiming to conduct business within a country's borders. To define the risks included in the term country risk we refer to the framework developed by Bouchet et al. (2003) and use this approach to dig deeper into each type.

1 *Economic risks*: Economic stability is paramount to a country's ability to attract and maintain foreign investment. Economic risks include:

   - *Inflation*: A rapidly rising inflation rate can erode purchasing power, destabilizing economies.
   - *Currency depreciation*: Fluctuating exchange rates can lead to unpredictable operational costs for MNCs.
   - *Fiscal deficits*: These suggest a government's overspending can lead to tax hikes or reduced public services.
   - *Unemployment rates*: High unemployment can lead to reduced consumer spending and increased social unrest.

2 *Political risks*: A country's political climate undeniably influences its attractiveness to foreign investors and businesses. Political risks include:

   - *Policy instability*: Frequent shifts in government policies can make it challenging for businesses to plan long term.
   - *Corruption*: Widespread corruption can lead to unpredictable costs and ethical dilemmas.
   - *Lack of rule of law*: An inconsistent legal environment can result in lack of protection for foreign businesses and their assets.

3 *Social risks*: Beyond the tangible economic and political factors, the social fabric of a country plays a critical role in determining its overall risk. Social risks include:

   - *Strikes*: Workforce strikes can halt production and result in lost revenue.
   - *Civil unrest*: Protests, riots, and other forms of civil discord can disrupt business operations and pose physical risks.
   - *Cultural differences*: A misunderstanding of local customs and traditions can lead to public relations nightmares and potential legal issues.

Given the multifaceted nature of risk, decision-making can be increasingly complex. Consequently, investors must systematically quantify and assess these factors through rigorous country risk analysis to minimize the probability of poor investment choices. In this way, you can get a clearer picture of all the different factors that might impact your investment in a particular country.

9.2 INTERNATIONAL INVESTMENT

International investment has the potential to result in substantial returns for firms investing abroad. However, the quest for returns may sometimes overshadow the need for critical assessment of associated risks. Capital mobilization across countries usually occurs via two primary mechanisms: foreign direct investment (FDI) and foreign portfolio investment (FPI). According to data from the UN FDI Data Explorer, global FDI inflows amounted to approximately US$1.3 trillion in 2022, catalysing numerous technological and innovative advances in various nations (UNCTAD, 2023).

With FDI, investors obtain direct equity ownership and influence over the targeted asset. It involves proactive management by the investor, enabling them to engage in pertinent decision-making activities. According to OECD guidelines, FDI is characterized by a minimum equity ownership of 10% in the respective foreign enterprise or asset (OECD, 1996). Consequently, the definition of FDI includes joint ventures, which are described as collaborative endeavours with ownership distributed among multiple domestic or foreign entities.

FDI categorizes investments into two primary modes: brownfield and greenfield (see Chapter 7, Section 7.4.3). Each mode has a distinct method of investment and can offer economic advantages to host nations. However, potential investors should evaluate the inherent risks associated with each type before finalizing their investment choices.

In a brownfield investment, one entity acquires control of another. Cross-border acquisitions are the most common type of international brownfield investment. This implies that the location of the investment target and foundational elements, such as suppliers, production capacity, and market share, are predetermined. Such an investment allows the parent company instant market penetration via its foreign subsidiary. Brownfield investments demand substantial initial capital and may pose integration challenges. Moreover, such acquisitions might be perceived sceptically, or even adversely, by local stakeholders and governments. The term 'brownfield' is etymologically rooted in the idea that the acquired land may have prior 'contamination' or entrenched practices from previous owners. Empirical data suggests that brownfield investments occur predominantly in developed economies. Furthermore, the Global Investment Competitiveness Report (2019/2020) established a positive relationship between a country's income level, market dimensions, and the proportion of global brownfield investments in developing nations (The World Bank, 2020).

In greenfield investment, an investor introduces a new subsidiary in a target host country, as opposed to acquiring a pre-existing entity, as in brownfield investment. For example, if Volkswagen was to establish a new manufacturing facility in Poland, it would be classified as a greenfield investment. Advantages of greenfield investments include freedom to select the location, lower initial capital requirements (although they may increase over time), potential tax benefits, subsidies, and possibly a favourable reception by local entities and governments. Conversely, challenges may arise from negligible initial market share, or hurdles in market entry and supplier identification.

Foreign portfolio investment, as opposed to FDI, represents investments in financial instruments. Such instruments encompass bonds (both corporate and governmental), mutual funds, exchange traded funds, and equities, which typically do not demand active investor management. For illustration, equity holders can attend annual shareholder meetings, receive dividends, and possess the right to liquidate their holdings as needed. Equities mark a stakeholder's proportionate ownership in a company publicly listed on stock exchanges, facilitating buy–sell transactions predominantly via digital platforms. As of January 2025 the most important global stock exchanges, ranked by market capitalization, were:

1 New York Stock Exchange (US$26 trillion)
2 NASDAQ (US$21 trillion)
3 Shanghai Stock Exchange (US$6 trillion)
4 Euronext (US$6 trillion)
5 Japan Stock Exchange (US$6 trillion)

Equity valuations are largely driven by the market forces of supply and demand. Elevated demand may, for instance, be attributed to optimistic investor projections. Dividends, a distribution of profits to shareholders, are determined by the company's board of directors, which includes key executives such as the chief executive officer (CEO), chief financial officer (CFO), and chief information officer (CIO). Alternatively, corporations may opt to reinvest profits in forthcoming ventures, leveraging internal financing mechanisms.

Separately, bonds represent debt instruments whereby the bondholder essentially extends a loan to the issuer. The predominant bond categories are government and corporate bonds. Bondholders typically receive annual interest payments, or coupons, and upon bond maturity, are repaid the principal amount alongside the final interest instalment. Generally perceived as less volatile than equities, bonds offer a more secure investment avenue. Moreover, in liquidation scenarios, bondholders (secured creditors) hold precedence in claims over equity stakeholders.

9.3 INTERNATIONAL CAPITAL MARKETS

Spotlight: ESG in Financial Markets

The emergence of environmental, social, and governance (ESG; see also Chapter 14) criteria in financial markets marks a significant shift in how investors evaluate companies and their potential for long-term success. ESG factors encompass a broad range of issues: environmental concerns like climate change and resource management, social factors such as labour practices and community engagement, and governance aspects including board diversity and corporate ethics.

The roots of ESG can be traced back to socially responsible investing (SRI) movements in the 1960s and 1970s, when investors sought to align their portfolios with their ethical values, often excluding industries like tobacco, arms, and gambling. The formal integration of ESG into mainstream finance began to take shape in the early 2000s, particularly with the launch of the United Nations Principles for Responsible Investment (PRI) in 2006. The PRI provided a framework for incorporating ESG issues into investment decisions, garnering significant support from institutional investors worldwide.

Over the past two decades, ESG investing has gained momentum as evidence mounted showing that companies with strong ESG performance often exhibit better long-term financial performance. This is attributed to factors like lower regulatory risks, better resource efficiency, and enhanced corporate reputation. Investors increasingly view ESG as a means to identify risks and opportunities that traditional financial analysis might overlook. More recently, research has shown that many of these potential benefits of ESG investments are not material.

The rise of ESG investing has also attracted criticism, a major one being the lack of standardized metrics and reporting, which can lead to inconsistencies and challenges in comparing ESG performance across companies. Critics argue that this lack of standardization can result in 'greenwashing', whereby companies exaggerate or misrepresent their ESG efforts to appear more sustainable than they are.

Another criticism focuses on the potential for ESG factors to distract from the primary goal of financial performance. Some investors worry that an overemphasis on ESG might lead to suboptimal investment decisions or reduced returns. Additionally, there are concerns about the actual impact of ESG investing on social and environmental outcomes. Sceptics argue that without substantial regulatory frameworks and enforcement, ESG investing alone may not drive the systemic changes needed to address global challenges such as climate change and social inequality.

Moreover, the recent political backlash against ESG investing, particularly in the United States, has highlighted the divisive nature of this trend. Some view ESG as politicization of investing, arguing that it imposes a particular set of values on investors and companies.

Sources: United Nations (www.unpri.org/about-us/what-are-the-principles-for-responsible-investment) and Acuity Knowledge Partners (www.acuitykp.com/blog/the-rise-of-esg-investing/#:~:text=Environmental%2C%20social%20and%20governance%20(ESG,while%20generating%20superior%20financial%20returns)

International capital markets represent a vast network in which participants trade financial instruments, such as bonds, equities, and derivatives, across borders. These markets act as the bloodstream of the global economy. By offering diverse investment opportunities and sources of funding, they enable nations to achieve economic growth, stabilize their financial systems, and weather economic downturns. Efficient functioning of these markets can influence global financial health, while their failures, as seen during financial crises, can have severe ripple effects. One of the chief roles of capital markets is providing liquidity.

International bond markets are places where foreign governments or companies issue, purchase, or sell bonds. These markets have grown because international bonds offer benefits not found in domestic bonds. One reason for this growth has been differences in tax laws between countries. For instance, until 1984, foreign investors buying US-issued bonds faced a significant withholding tax, but tax treaties and changes in the law reduced this tax, increasing the appeal of US bonds for foreign investors. In the international bond markets, a group of investment banks usually underwrite the bonds. In the Eurobond market, where bonds are issued in a currency different from the country's own, many underwriters are offshoots of US banks. This is because they historically couldn't underwrite corporate bonds in the US due to regulations like the Glass-Steagall Act. Some of the big names issuing bonds in the Eurobond market include Daimler Financial, Citicorp, General Motors Acceptance Corp., and the World Bank. For instance, during Daimler and Chrysler's partnership from 1995 to 2007, DaimlerChrysler Financial Corp. sourced around 25% of its funding from the Eurobond market in various currencies. Similarly, Citicorp now raises about half of its funding from international sources.

Case Study: Argentina's Century Bond

In 2017, Argentina shocked the financial world by issuing a hundred-year bond, known as the 'Century Bond'. This was surprising, given Argentina's tumultuous history with debt and having defaulted on its external debt eight times since independence. Argentina raised US$2.75 billion in June 2017 by selling these Century Bonds with an annual yield of 7.9%.

Argentina had recently emerged from the status of financial pariah, having settled long-standing issues with bondholders that refused to participate in its debt restructurings after its 2001 default. The Century Bond issue was seen as a strong statement of international investor confidence in the economic policies of then President Mauricio Macri and his finance team. It wasn't the first time a country had issued a hundred-year bond. Mexico, Ireland, Belgium, and some other nations had previously done so. However, Argentina's case was notable because of its checkered debt history. Unfortunately, the confidence that led to the Century Bond's success didn't last long. By 2019, Argentina was in the midst of economic difficulties again, with rising inflation, a falling currency, and growing fears of another default. Investors who had initially taken a gamble on Argentina's Century Bond saw its value drop significantly.

Lessons learned:

- The international bond market can often be driven by short-term optimism, overlooking long-term fundamentals. In Argentina's case, investors were lured by the high yields despite the country's economic record.

- Sovereign debt, especially in emerging markets, can be highly volatile. Factors such as political instability, global economic conditions, and local economic policies can all significantly influence a country's ability to meet its debt obligations.
- Investors need to be cautious and conduct thorough due diligence before investing in high-yield, long-term instruments, especially from countries with histories of defaults.

Sources: Spears (https://spearswms.com/wealth/argentina-marks-new-era-landmark-century-bond-launch) and Oxford Business Group (https://oxfordbusinessgroup.com/reports/argentina/2018-report/economy/back-at-the-table-following-a-return-to-international-markets-in-2016-the-country-is-confronting-the-challenges-of-global-interconnectedness)

International stock markets refer to platforms where companies list and trade their stocks on foreign stock exchanges. For instance, Sweden's Spotify lists its stock on the New York Stock Exchange (NYSE). By tapping into foreign markets, firms can secure additional funding without oversaturating their local market, thereby preserving their share value. Many multinational companies also opt for foreign listings due to different regulations across markets, and in the belief that a global listing can boost their brand image. Listing overseas can also offer better liquidity, improved perceived financial stature, and as a defence against hostile takeovers. Daimler-Benz AG, for instance, saw a substantial surge in its share price after announcing its NYSE listing.

Emerging economies with less stable equity markets sometimes list in developed countries to benefit from a more robust regulatory framework. An example is the Chinese e-commerce giant Alibaba, which made a historic initial public offering (IPO) on the NYSE in 2014, raising US$21.8 billion. Analysts suggested this move aimed at ensuring stock price stability, which might have been hard to achieve on the more fluctuating Chinese exchanges.

International loan markets consist of major commercial banks and financial entities offering loans to overseas companies. While international money markets focus on short-term liquidity, international loan markets offer long-term debt capital. With standardized regulations in places like Europe, Japan, and the US, financial services, including loans, are becoming more interconnected globally. Consequently, various financial institutions aim to maximize the services they provide through scale benefits. Even those not eyeing global expansion face heightened foreign competition in domestic markets. US banks, in particular, have shown a keen interest in overseas markets.

Many banks worldwide view international lending as a diversification strategy. By granting loans across different countries, banks can insulate themselves from potential downturns in their home economies. Furthermore, such lending facilitates deeper relationships with foreign corporations, subsequently generating demand for other banking services. A significant chunk of international lending also supports international acquisitions. Both commercial and investment banks often play a dual role as advisors and financial intermediaries, facilitating stock and bond placements or granting loans. A prevalent form of engagement is direct loans, particularly for management-led leveraged buyouts (LBOs). Since LBOs typically have high debt ratios, they boost the demand for loanable funds significantly. International syndicates of banks often back many LBOs, enabling each bank to minimize its risk exposure. Given the diversified nature of LBO-involved firms, challenges in a single industry do not necessarily translate into a larger lending issue. Moreover, the loan amounts for individual firms are often manageable, ensuring borrowers have limited leverage in renegotiating debt schedules. Hence, from a risk perspective, banks often consider financing LBOs safer than offering loans to developing nations, another primary borrower group in global loan markets.

9.4 EXCHANGE RATES AND FOREIGN EXCHANGE RISK MANAGEMENT

The value of a country's currency can be unstable, leading to fluctuations in exchange rates with other currencies. However, the extent and nature of these fluctuations depend on the country's exchange rate system and its macroeconomic management. To manage foreign exchange risk effectively, one must first grasp the workings of the international monetary system and related concepts, including crawling peg policies, and the distinction between nominal and real exchange rates.

The international monetary system primarily consists of policies, institutions, regulations, and mechanisms that determine foreign exchange rates. It includes individual currencies, monetary unions like the Eurozone, and composite currency units like the special drawing right (SDR). The international monetary system has evolved over time, including periods like the gold standard, the Bretton Woods system, and the present floating exchange rate system. The use of gold as a medium of exchange, for instance, dates back to around 3000 BCE in Egypt and was carried forward by the Greeks and Romans through the mercantile era into the nineteenth century. The late nineteenth century surge in trade prompted the need for a formalized system to settle international trade balances. This led to the development of the 'gold standard', whereby countries set a fixed value for their currency in terms of gold. For instance, the US set the dollar's value at US$20.67 per ounce of gold, while the British pound was pegged at £4.2474 per ounce of gold, resulting in a dollar/pound exchange rate of US$4.8665/£. This simple system gained acceptance in Western Europe during the 1870s. Various agreements and economic events have shaped the system's dynamics, affecting global currency markets. Within these evolutionary phases, it is essential to recognize the significance of the formation of the International Monetary Fund (IMF) following the Bretton Woods conference. In 1944, as World War II was nearing its end, the Allied Powers convened at Bretton Woods, New Hampshire, with the objective of establishing a new international monetary system for the post-war era (Moffett et al., 2021). Through the implementation of the Bretton Woods Agreements, the world witnessed the emergence of a US dollar-based international monetary system and the establishment of two new institutions: the IMF and the World Bank. The primary mission of the IMF was to assist nations facing challenges related to their balance of payments and exchange rates, while the World Bank, also known as the International Bank for Reconstruction and Development, played a crucial role in financing post-war reconstruction efforts and has since been dedicated to supporting overall economic development. Table 9.1 summarizes the key developments and characteristics of the international monetary system during different historical periods in order to understand the strengths and weaknesses of the current monetary system.

Table 9.1 Exchange rate regimes

Period	Key characteristics
Gold standard (1876–1914)	Gold used as medium of exchange and store of value
	Each country pegged its money to gold
	Governments maintained fixed parity rates
	Gold reserves were crucial to support currency's value
	Suspended during World War I
The World Wars and the years between (1914–44)	Currencies fluctuated widely, affecting speculators
	Contributed to the Great Depression in the 1930s
	US returned to a modified gold standard in 1934
	Exchange rates tied to gold values
Bretton Woods system (1944–73)	Fixed exchange rate system
	Government commitment to maintain fixed rates
	US dollar as the primary reserve currency
	Persistent US balance of payments deficits
	Ended with the inconvertibility of the US dollar in 1971
Post-Bretton Woods (1973–present)	Floating exchange rate system
	Exchange rates more volatile and less predictable
	Oil crisis in the 1970s increased volatility
	Various currency crises in the 1990s (Asian, EMS, peso)
	Global financial crisis in 2008 and Eurozone crisis
	China's currency reforms and inclusion in 2016
	Impact of the Covid-19 pandemic on currency markets
	EU's efforts to strengthen the euro relative to the dollar

Foreign exchange refers to the currency of another country. Firms in countries with soft currencies often use hard foreign currencies for export businesses. A soft currency is expected to devalue or depreciate relative to major trading currencies, while a hard currency is anticipated to revalue or appreciate. Exchange rates represent the price of one currency in terms of another. They can be nominal or real: nominal exchange rates are observed rates, while real exchange rates consider the impact of inflation differentials between currencies.

Countries can adopt different exchange rate systems as fixed, floating or pegged. In a fixed-rate system, maintaining a currency's par value involves two main approaches: foreign exchange control and market intervention. Foreign exchange control, primarily seen in centrally planned economies like the former Soviet Union, mandated that all importers and exporters conduct foreign exchange transactions through a designated bank, usually the central bank, at the exact established fixed exchange rate. The primary objective of exchange control was to allow the government to preserve limited foreign reserves and allocate them to state-owned entities based on governmental priorities. However, most countries utilizing a fixed-rate system tend not to enforce strict foreign exchange control. Typically, the central bank intervenes in the foreign exchange market, buying and selling its currency when exchange rates deviate from the specified par values due to demand and supply fluctuations. But determining the correct par value, influenced by political pressures from domestic and international sources, can be complex, and an incorrect par value can lead to resource misallocation and trade distortions. Divergent monetary policies among countries can cause inflation disparities, and high economic uncertainty can trigger speculative currency trading, which results in extreme exchange rate volatility, as seen in Argentina in April 2002.

The floating exchange rate, which is employed by approximately half of the IMF member countries and nearly all major global economies, represents the prevailing exchange rate system. It offers a more adaptable means of addressing trade imbalances than fixed exchange rates and prevents countries from sustaining substantial and persistent deficits. Unlike fixed-rate systems that often necessitate economic recessions to reduce real income or prices during trade deficits, flexible exchange rates naturally lead to currency depreciation, aiding in the restoration of balance. A significant advantage of the flexible exchange rate system is that exchange rates adjust automatically in response to changes in supply and demand conditions, eliminating concerns about the government breaking its exchange rate commitment. This system reduces the need for central banks to maintain large foreign exchange reserves, as there is typically no requirement for intervention in the foreign exchange market. Countries can therefore reserve their foreign exchange reserves as a defence against speculative bubbles and assure foreign creditors that the central bank has adequate reserves to meet short-term debts, thus mitigating any creditor panic.

The crawling peg system falls between the fixed-rate and floating exchange rate systems and is primarily characterized by two key features: a fixed initial value of the currency, which is frequently updated and modified in response to market conditions like inflation, and a predetermined range of exchange rates within which the currency is allowed to fluctuate.

As described by the International Monetary Fund (IMF), in a crawling peg system, 'the currency is adjusted periodically in small amounts at a fixed rate or in response to changes in selective quantitative indicators' (IMF, 2003). These indicators may include past differences in inflation rates compared to major trading partners or variations between the targeted inflation rate and expected inflation in those trading partners. The crawling rate can be determined retrospectively, considering factors like inflation or other metrics, or prospectively, based on a pre-announced fixed rate and projected inflation. This type of exchange rate system is commonly utilized with 'vulnerable' or less robust currencies. Latin American nations are often associated with employing the crawling peg exchange system against the United States dollar, where, in some instances, devaluation may occur on a daily basis.

It is essential to understand that maintaining a crawling peg constrains the ability to conduct monetary policy, similar to target zone arrangements.

Target zone arrangements are used as a middle ground between fixed exchange rate systems (where the exchange rate is rigidly pegged to another currency) and floating exchange rate systems (where the exchange rate is determined solely by market forces). They provide some exchange rate stability while allowing for adjustments in response to economic conditions. However, maintaining a target zone arrangement can be challenging, as it requires frequent central bank interventions and foreign exchange market operations to keep the currency within the specified range (Shenkar et al., 2021: 340). Table 9.2 gives an overview over exchange rate regimes.

Table 9.2 Examples of exchange rate regimes

Independent float	Managed float	Target zone	Crawling peg	Fixed
Australia	Afghanistan	EMS (before 1992)	Algeria	Brunei
Canada	Angola		Bangladesh	Djibouti
Chile	China		Botswana	Egypt
Eurozone	Gambia		Burundi	Grenada
Japan	Kenya		Ethiopia	Hong Kong
Mexico	Mongolia		Honduras	Iraq
Norway	Myanmar		Nicaragua	Jordan
Poland	Pakistan		Papua New	Morocco
Russia	Sierra Leone		Guinea	Nigeria
Sweden	Vanuatu		Rwanda	Saudi Arabia
UK			Singapore	Vietnam
US			Sri Lanka	
Uruguay			Tanzania	
			Uzbekistan	

Source: Based on International Monetary Fund (2020) IMF Annual Report on Exchange Arrangements and Exchange Restrictions 2019

The current international monetary system exhibits a combination of various exchange rate regimes, including free floating, managed floating, crawling peg, and fixed rates. There isn't a single comprehensive theory that can consistently predict exchange rates in all circumstances.

The purchasing power parity (PPP) principle provides insights into both the absolute levels of exchange rates and their relative changes over the long term. The PPP approach emphasizes the significance of price levels for goods and services in influencing exchange rates, while interest rate parity focuses on the role of capital flows. As per the interest rate parity theory, any disparity between a currency's forward and spot rates arises from variations in interest rates across two nations. Interest arbitrage triggers short-term shifts in capital flows, and over time, the forward rate discount or premium corrects itself, restoring equilibrium between the currencies. The Fisher effect, named after economist Irving Fisher, posits that a nation's future currency direction can be indicated by its inflation rate, which, in turn, can be predicted by comparing interest rates among countries (Mishkin & Simon, 1995). The international Fisher effect posits that differences in interest rates between two countries lead to opposite movements in exchange rates. For instance, when comparing Australia and the United States, if Australia has a higher interest rate, it will result in the long-term appreciation of the US dollar. In the short term, the effect may be in the other direction. Higher interest rates, such as those in Australia, attract foreign capital inflows, leading to short-term currency appreciation. The Reserve Bank of Australia observed this short-term effect when the Australian dollar rose in 1998 following an interest rate hike announcement. Although these approaches alone may not fully elucidate the intricate dynamics of exchange rates, they serve as valuable foundational concepts for understanding the factors influencing foreign exchange rate determination.

Spotlight: High-Frequency Trading and Digital Transmission of Information

High-frequency automated trading (HFT) in the exchange rate market represents a sophisticated, technology-driven approach to trading currencies, leveraging algorithms and powerful computing systems to execute large volumes of trades at extremely high speeds. This type of trading exploits minute price discrepancies and market inefficiencies that are often imperceptible to human traders. HFT relies on advanced algorithms that can analyse vast amounts of market data in real time to identify trading opportunities. These algorithms are designed to execute trades within fractions of a second, capitalizing on small price movements. The speed at which these trades are executed is crucial, as the window of opportunity for profit in HFT is typically very short. HFT firms invest heavily in technology, including low-latency trading infrastructure and direct market access (DMA).

They use high-speed data feeds and co-location services, where trading servers are placed in close proximity to the exchange's servers, minimizing the time it takes for data to travel. Common HFT strategies in the exchange rate market include arbitrage, where traders exploit price differences between different markets or instruments; liquidity provision, where firms act as market makers by providing buy and sell quotes; and statistical arbitrage, which uses quantitative models to predict and exploit price movements based on historical data and correlations.

Financial centres such as New York, London, Tokyo, and Hong Kong play a pivotal role in the HFT ecosystem. These centres are home to major currency exchanges and offer robust financial infrastructure, legal frameworks, and access to large pools of liquidity. The concentration of financial institutions and technological infrastructure in these hubs facilitates efficient trading and quick execution of HFT strategies. Additionally, these financial centres provide the necessary regulatory environment to govern trading activities, ensuring market integrity and fair competition, which are critical for the smooth functioning of HFT operations. The combination of advanced infrastructure, legal support, and liquidity makes these financial centres ideal locations for HFT firms to operate effectively.

Success in HFT depends heavily on the ability to process and react to market information in real time. Traders use real-time data feeds to monitor currency prices, news events, economic indicators, and other relevant information that might impact the market. The faster a trader can receive and act on this information, the greater the potential for profit. HFT firms continuously seek to reduce latency, the time delay between receiving information and executing trades. This includes optimizing algorithms, upgrading hardware, and using cutting-edge communication technologies like microwave and fibre-optic networks to ensure the quickest possible data transmission. The interconnectedness of financial markets means that events in one part of the world can have immediate effects elsewhere. For instance, economic news from the United States can quickly influence currency markets globally. Maintaining a global network of information and trading capabilities is therefore crucial for HFT firms to capitalize on these rapid market changes.

Sources: Financial Times (www.ft.com/content/9941bba6-00f0-11df-a4cb-00144feabdc0) and Financial Conduct Authority (www.fca.org.uk/publications/research-articles/role-high-frequency-traders-fx-markets)

International businesses face a currency risk due to the global economy's interconnectedness. This risk primarily involves exchange rate fluctuations and can be categorized into two main types: transaction risk and translation risk. Transaction risk refers to unexpected exchange rate changes impacting cash flow from contractual agreements. In contrast, translation risk relates to fluctuations in an asset's value when converting it from a foreign currency to the domestic currency (Solnik & McLeavey, 2004).

Translation risk can also be defined as changes in the book value of assets and liabilities (excluding stockholders' equity) resulting from foreign exchange rate shifts. Companies trading and earning revenue in foreign currencies are susceptible to translation risk. A common scenario involves overseas subsidiaries translating their financial statements into the parent company's functional currency for reporting, as required by regulations (Homaifar, 2004). During this process, exchange rate movements can lead to accounting gains or losses affecting stockholders' equity. Multinational companies adopt strategic responses to manage FOREX risk by spreading operations across currencies and countries to mitigate risk or hedging,

Hedging is a protective strategy employed by investors and companies to safeguard their portfolios from unfavourable currency, interest rate, or price fluctuations. It entails taking an opposing position in a derivative instrument, such as forward, futures, options, and money market instruments, to counterbalance potential gains or losses in the original portfolio. The ultimate goal of hedging is to create a 'seesaw effect' where one movement offsets another. While hedging shields against losses resulting from adverse market conditions, it can also limit potential gains if the market moves in favour of the hedging party. In essence, hedging serves as a risk management tool, offering protection at the cost of potentially foregoing some gains in favourable market scenarios (Jüttner, 2000).

9.5 ACCOUNTING, TAXATION, AND REPORTING IN THE MULTINATIONAL FIRM

International accounting plays a pivotal role in facilitating global business and investment activities. It is divided into two main categories: financial accounting, which focuses on the external reporting of financial information to external stakeholders such as investors, creditors, regulators and the public; and management accounting, also known as cost accounting, which focuses on providing financial information and analysis to internal stakeholders, primarily management, for decision-making, budgeting, and performance evaluation.

The primary purpose of international accounting is to provide a common framework for organizations across different countries to prepare and present their financial information in a standardized and comparable manner. This ensures transparency, enhances the credibility of financial statements, and enables international investors and stakeholders to make informed decisions. Enterprises worldwide prepare financial statements in a regular manner and depending on their size and reporting standards, include the following core elements:

1 Balance sheet (or statement of financial position): Provides a snapshot of a company's financial position at a specific point in time, listing its assets, liabilities, and equity
2 Income statement (or statement of comprehensive income): Summarizes a company's revenues, expenses, gains, and losses over a specific period, resulting in net income or loss

3 Cash flow statement: Details the cash inflows and outflows from operating, investing, and financing activities during a particular period, helping assess a company's cash management
4 Statement of changes in equity: Shows how a company's equity has changed over time due to transactions with shareholders, including dividends, stock issuances, and retained earnings

In general, the creation of financial information is guided by four fundamental principles: the 'going concern' principle, which assumes a business will continue to operate in the foreseeable future, the 'accruals or matching principle', which associates revenues and costs with the period in which they occur, the 'prudence or conservatism' principle, designed to prevent overly optimistic views by recognizing revenue upon realization and accounting for expenses and losses when they become known, and finally, the 'consistency' principle, which ensures uniformity in asset valuation and cost allocation to facilitate meaningful comparisons over time.

Various fundamental accounting conventions (such as the 'objectivity' convention based on verifiable, measurable facts, the 'separate entity' convention recognizing the legal distinction between a company and its managers and owners, the 'money measurement' convention quantifying all assets and liabilities in monetary terms, and the 'historic cost' convention valuing assets at their original cost while considering depreciation or write-downs for value declines) are employed, and the 'double entry' convention is also applied to ensure that transactions encompass both giving and receiving, as exemplified by the double-entry bookkeeping system that balances sources of funds with their uses (Wall et al., 2015: 342).

Debates surrounding these principles, conventions, and legal requirements have intensified due to recent corporate scandals. The regulatory framework and the target of harmonizing accounting standards globally has become a crucial concern for businesses.

9.5.1 Regulatory Frameworks Governing International Accounting

The regulatory framework for international accounting is primarily governed by the International Financial Reporting Standards (IFRS) developed by the International Accounting Standards Board (IASB). IFRS is a set of global accounting standards used in over 150 countries, promoting consistency and comparability of financial statements. In contrast, the United States follows generally accepted accounting principles (GAAP), governed by the Financial Accounting Standards Board (FASB). While there are similarities between IFRS and GAAP, differences exist in areas such as revenue recognition, financial statement presentation, and accounting for specific transactions. Although there is a growing move to harmonize accounting standards, challenges remain in achieving complete harmonization due to differences in regulatory philosophies and specific industry practices.

In the preceding section we explored the pivotal role that accounting plays in ensuring that organizations maintain accurate financial records and make informed financial decisions. However, the journey into the financial management landscape does not stop here. Accounting and taxation are intricately connected, and understanding this relationship is vital. Taxation, the process by which governments collect revenue to fund public services and infrastructure, relies heavily on the financial information provided by accounting. In the following section we will dive deeper into the world of taxation and explore tax planning strategies like transfer pricing.

Spotlight: Fair Value Accounting and Market Bubbles

International Financial Reporting Standards (IFRS) and fair-value accounting have introduced significant volatility, particularly for real estate companies that mark up the value of rented-out buildings. IFRS requires assets, including real estate, to be reported at their fair value, reflecting current market conditions rather than historical cost. This method aims to provide a more accurate and timely representation of a company's financial position.

For real estate companies, this means regularly revaluing their properties based on market fluctuations. When the real estate market is booming, this can lead to substantial increases in reported asset values and corresponding boosts to equity and profit. However, during market downturns, the same assets must be marked down, potentially leading to significant losses on the balance sheet and in reported earnings.

Such volatility can create instability for real estate companies. Investors and stakeholders may react strongly to large swings in asset valuations, which can affect stock prices and access to capital. Additionally, fluctuations in reported earnings due to fair-value adjustments can obscure the company's underlying operating performance, making it challenging for investors to assess long-term profitability and financial health accurately.

Moreover, reliance on fair-value accounting can incentivize management to focus on short-term market conditions rather than long-term strategic planning. Companies might engage in behaviour aimed at temporarily boosting property values to improve financial statements, which can be detrimental to long-term stability and growth.

In summary, while IFRS and fair-value accounting aim to provide a transparent and current view of a company's financial status, they can introduce significant instability for real estate companies. The frequent revaluation of rented-out buildings based on market conditions can lead to considerable volatility in reported asset values and earnings, affecting investor perceptions and company stability.

Sources: PwC Austria (www.pwc.at/de/newsletter/ifrs/in-brief-in-depth/2019/ifrs13-european-real-estate-survey-2018-update-in-depth.pdf) and IFRS (www.ifrs.org/issued-standards/list-of-standards/ifrs-13-fair-value-measurement)

9.5.2 Taxation

Taxation policies have gained importance, especially in light of multinational companies (MNCs) exploiting tax discrepancies between nations, as discussed below in the paragraphs on transfer pricing. Tax havens, characterized by their minimal or non-existent tax rates, offer a favourable environment for MNCs aiming to reduce their global tax burdens through strategic tax planning. While legitimate tax planning is permissible, the use of aggressive tax avoidance strategies exploiting tax havens has come under increased scrutiny. Governments are responding by implementing measures to counter the use of tax havens and promote fair taxation. The US, for example, introduced the Stop Tax Haven Abuse Act in 2007 and the Incorporation Transparency and Law Enforcement Assistance Act in 2008 to improve transparency in corporate ownership and prevent the flow of offshore funds with uncertain origins, bypassing anti-money-laundering measures. Simultaneously, many countries have introduced country-by-country reporting requirements, obligating MNCs to disclose financial and tax-related data for each jurisdiction they operate in. However, MNCs are well placed to take advantage of any differences in national tax and subsidy regimes. A particularly significant element that can shape pricing strategies revolves around endeavours to alleviate the corporate tax responsibility through a practice known as 'transfer pricing'.

Transfer pricing is motivated by the practical reality that MNCs frequently operate through multiple subsidiaries situated in different countries, engaging in various transactions like selling goods, providing services, licensing intellectual property, and resource sharing. The pricing of these transactions significantly affects how costs, revenues, and ultimately, taxable profits are distributed among the involved entities. The core objective of transfer pricing is to ensure that these transactions among related MNC entities adhere to the arm's length principle. This principle necessitates that such transactions be priced as if they were conducted between independent parties, reflecting fair market value.

Here is a simple example to explain transfer pricing. A multinational company, GlobalMD, operates in two countries, Country A and Country B. GlobalMD produces medical devices in Country A and sells them to its retail division in Country B.

For GlobalMD to determine the price at which it sells these components to its retail division, it must establish a transfer price. The transfer price is the amount charged for the goods or services exchanged between different parts of the same company, particularly when they are in different countries. This price is essential for several reasons:

- *Taxation*: Country A may have a lower corporate tax rate than Country B. GlobalMD might be tempted to set a high transfer price (selling the components at a high cost to its retail division in Country B) to shift profits from high-tax Country B to low-tax Country A, reducing GlobalMD's overall tax liability.

- *Performance evaluation*: If the retail division in Country B pays a high price for the components, its profits might appear lower, impacting the division's performance evaluation.
- *Customs and regulations*: A high transfer price might trigger higher import duties in Country B.

Transfer pricing therefore aims to strike a balance between minimizing tax liabilities, ensuring fair divisional performance evaluations, and complying with international tax laws and regulations. It must align with the arm's length principle, meaning the transfer price should be similar to the price unrelated companies would charge for the same product or service in an open market. This principle helps prevent tax avoidance and ensures fairness in financial reporting within MNCs.

Case Study: Apple and the 'Double Irish with a Dutch Sandwich'

The 'Double Irish with a Dutch Sandwich' is a tax strategy that gained notoriety for being employed by several multinational companies, including Apple, to minimize their corporate tax obligations. This approach involves complex corporate structures and takes advantage of differences in tax laws between countries, allowing companies to make a significant reduction in their tax liabilities.

The term 'Double Irish with a Dutch Sandwich' refers to a series of transactions that involve Irish and Dutch subsidiaries. Here's a more detailed explanation of how this tax strategy works and its implications, particularly for Apple:

- *Irish incorporation*: The first step in the Double Irish strategy involves incorporating two Irish subsidiaries. The first subsidiary is incorporated in Ireland and is intended to become the legal owner of the company's intellectual property (IP), such as patents, trademarks, and copyrights. Ireland is chosen for its relatively low corporate tax rate, which has been especially attractive for multinational companies seeking to minimize their tax burden.
- *Intellectual property transfer*: The company then transfers the rights to its intellectual property to the Irish subsidiary. This transfer allows the company to attribute a significant portion of its profits to the subsidiary in Ireland, where the corporate tax rate is lower than in many other jurisdictions.
- *Tax residency outside Ireland*: The second Irish subsidiary is established in Ireland but is not tax-resident in Ireland. Instead, it is registered in a tax haven or a jurisdiction with minimal corporate taxes. This subsidiary licenses the intellectual property from the first Irish subsidiary and pays royalties for its use. The payment of royalties results in a deductible expense for the second subsidiary, further reducing its taxable income.

- *Dutch Sandwich*: The Dutch Sandwich comes into play by introducing a Dutch subsidiary. The second Irish subsidiary, which is not tax-resident in Ireland, makes its royalty payments to the Dutch subsidiary. The Dutch tax laws, combined with specific structures in place, allow the company to further reduce its tax liability. The Dutch Sandwich involves routing funds through the Netherlands, taking advantage of favourable tax treatment for certain transactions.
- *Profit shifting*: Through these intricate transactions, the company effectively shifts a significant portion of its global profits to Ireland and the Netherlands, where corporate tax rates are comparatively lower. This profit-shifting mechanism allows companies like Apple to reduce their overall tax obligations in the countries where they generate substantial revenues.

While the Double Irish with a Dutch Sandwich strategy was legal under the tax laws of the jurisdictions involved, it faced criticism for enabling large multinational companies to exploit loopholes and avoid paying what many considered their fair share of taxes. In response to growing international scrutiny and efforts to combat tax avoidance, Ireland announced in 2014 that it would phase out the Double Irish tax arrangement. New rules were introduced to prevent companies from establishing such structures for tax purposes.

Apple, being a prominent user of the Double Irish with a Dutch Sandwich strategy, faced criticism and investigations from various governments and regulatory bodies. In 2016, the European Union ruled that Ireland had provided illegal state aid to Apple by allowing the company to pay substantially lower taxes than other businesses. The EU ordered Ireland to recover €13 billion in unpaid taxes from Apple. Both Apple and the Irish government appealed the decision, arguing against the characterization of the tax arrangement as illegal state aid.

The Double Irish with a Dutch Sandwich approach exemplifies the challenges and controversies surrounding corporate taxation in a globalized economy. While multinational companies seek to optimize their tax positions within the bounds of existing laws, these practices have prompted calls for international tax reforms to ensure a fair and equitable distribution of tax burdens among countries. In recent years, there has been a growing push for global initiatives to address tax avoidance and establish more transparent and standardized tax regulations across borders.

Source: Supermoney (www.supermoney.com/encyclopedia/double-irish-with-a-dutch-sandwich)

Case Study Questions

1. What challenges does Apple face when it comes to putting the money it has moved into offshore destinations to use?
2. Why do the Irish and Dutch governments support the Double Irish with a Dutch Sandwich tax management technique?
3. How has the government in the USA influenced the repatriation of offshore funds?

9.6 INTERNATIONAL CAPITAL STRUCTURE

Companies that invest abroad via FDI need to finance those investments by raising external debt or equity, or by generating sufficient capital internally. Because FDI typically are large-scale strategic investments, MNCs usually have to raise external capital. When raising debt or equity capital, companies have to consider conflicting incentives. On the one hand, companies can use the interest payable on debt to reduce their tax bill, because most countries allow deducting interest payments from the tax base. On the other hand, when raising debt capital, companies need to be aware that having to repay interest and the principal introduces a substantial drain on company funds in the future. Because FDI (as well as other money-generating activities) is fundamentally uncertain, having to pay high interest rates increases the risk of a company facing financial distress in the future. How to manage these two effects is addressed in one of the major theories of how companies finance themselves: the trade-off theory of capital structure.

The theory is a financial concept suggesting that companies aim to strike a balance between the benefits and costs associated with debt and equity financing. According to this theory, there is an optimal capital structure in which the tax advantages of debt, such as interest deductions, are set against the potential costs, including financial distress, bankruptcy, and agency conflicts between shareholders and debt holders.

Firms consider leveraging debt to benefit from tax shields, as interest payments are typically tax-deductible, enhancing overall financial performance. However, they also recognize the risks and costs associated with higher debt levels. The trade-off theory acknowledges that as a company increases its debt, the probability of financial distress rises, impacting its creditworthiness and potentially leading to bankruptcy. Ultimately, the trade-off theory provides a framework enabling companies to make informed decisions about their capital structure by assessing the trade-offs between tax advantages and the associated financial risks, in order to establish the optimal mix of debt and equity that maximizes shareholder value.

Because doing business abroad increases risk more than an otherwise equivalent domestic business initiative (because of liabilities of foreignness, which we discussed in Chapter 7, Section 7.1.2), FDI is typically financed with less debt than other business activities. This is because, in order to buffer the extra business risk that comes from international activity, firms cannot also accept the high financial risk that comes from substantial debt. As a result, internationally active companies tend to have lower debt than equivalent domestic companies (Lindner et al., 2018).

Case Study: How Apple Uses The Complexities of International Finance to Its Advantage

As a global technology giant, Apple Inc. provides a compelling case study illustrating the intricate interplay between foreign direct investment (FDI) and financing strategies.

One facet of Apple's FDI and financing strategy involves tapping into foreign debt markets. Apple has strategically issued bonds in various currencies to fund its international operations. By doing so, Apple not only diversifies its sources of capital but also takes advantage of favourable interest rates in different regions. Apple's ability to access foreign debt markets allows it to optimize its capital structure by securing cost-effective financing tailored to the specific conditions of each market.

Apple's financing decisions are influenced to a significant degree by tax considerations (as seen in the 'Apple and the "Double Irish with a Dutch Sandwich"' case study above). The company has leveraged debt to optimize its global tax position. By borrowing funds and incurring interest expenses, Apple benefits from interest deductions, effectively reducing its taxable income. This tax optimization strategy, while legally compliant, showcases how multinational companies navigate tax rules in different jurisdictions to their advantage.

Apple's substantial cash reserves, often held offshore, play a crucial role in its financing strategy. While Apple uses debt strategically, the company retains significant liquidity to ensure flexibility for operational needs, strategic investment, and unforeseen challenges. This balance between leveraging debt for efficiency and maintaining financial reserves exemplifies the nuanced decision-making inherent in optimizing capital structure within the global landscape.

Operating in numerous countries exposes Apple to currency risks, a factor it addresses in its financing strategy. The company's choice of financing instruments and its cash management practices demonstrate a keen awareness of the potential impact of exchange rate fluctuations. Apple may use debt denominated in local currencies to match cash flows up to US$75 billion, reducing exposure to currency risk.

Apple's financing decisions are also influenced by market conditions in the countries where it operates. The company assesses the attractiveness of debt vs equity financing based on prevailing interest rates, investor preferences, and the overall stability of financial markets. Adapting its financing strategy to local market conditions allows Apple to optimize its financing costs.

Sources: Apple Insider (https://appleinsider.com/articles/12/01/22/apples_overseas_manufacturing_operations_offer_much_needed_flexibility_not_just_savings)

9.7 RECENT DEVELOPMENTS IN INTERNATIONAL FINANCE

In 2015 the United Nations General Assembly (UNGA) defined seventeen Sustainable Development Goals (SDGs) which are often referred to as a central orientation for environmental, social, and governance (ESG) factors. These are key criteria used to assess and measure the sustainability and ethical impact of a company's operations and business practices. As countries set ambitious targets to decarbonize their economies, the need to finance the right projects is growing.

Project finance is a vital tool in addressing those global challenges of climate change and sustainability. It is a specialized financial approach used to fund and manage large-scale infrastructure or development projects, where the project's cash flows and assets serve as collateral for securing financing, and the project operates as a separate legal entity, a so-called special purpose vehicle (SPV). Its roots trace back to the eighteenth and nineteenth centuries in England and the 1880s in Russia when project-generated cash flows were used as collateral, and since then it has evolved and expanded across various sectors and regions (Yescombe, 2014; Gatti, 2023).

The basic stakeholder structure in project finance consists of five different parties (see Figure 9.1). First, the sponsors, which can be a single entity or a group, provide equity to the project company. Subsidiaries of these sponsors may also play various roles, such as subcontractors or suppliers of raw materials. Second, a public body may provide contractual guarantees or credit support for a project. Third are the contractors who are responsible for the construction and operation of the project, typically through project-execution contracts. Fourth are the lenders, which typically include commercial banks, international agencies, export credit agencies, or bond investors. Finally, there are the consultants, who are specialists and provide advisory services to both project sponsors and lenders (Rossi & Stepic, 2015).

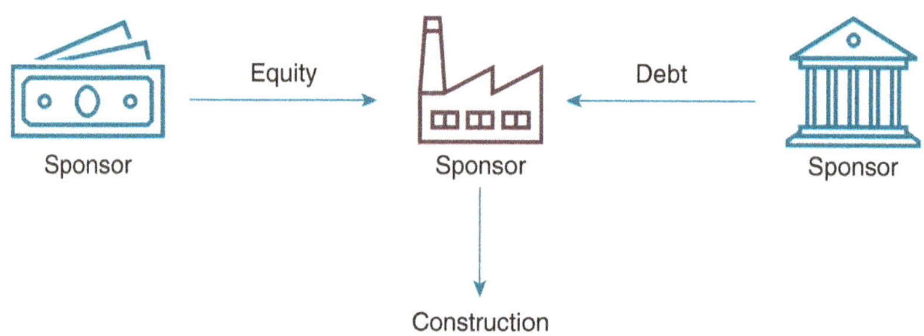

Figure 9.1 Project finance

Project finance leverages financial engineering to secure long-term debt financing from diverse lenders and investors, with repayment solely reliant on project-generated cash flows (Yescombe, 2014), which sets it apart from traditional project financing. This approach is often used in emerging markets, particularly in asset-intensive industries such as commodities. It is particularly attractive where the country's economy is unstable, political risk is high and banks have significant influence over national policy. Recent years saw a significant increase in project finance deals, with growth driven by Europe and emerging markets (see Table 9.3). However, crises such as the Russian invasion of Ukraine, high inflation, and energy prices in 2022 have resulted in less investment (UNCTAD, 2023).

Currently, economic trends are reshaping the landscape of project financing. The shift from fossil fuels to renewable energy sources, the rise of carbon capture and storage technologies, and the increasing prominence of green hydrogen and battery technologies are notable global trends. The combination of project finance and ESG principles represents a promising way to finance large-scale projects and contribute to sustainable development while offering attractive returns for investors.

Table 9.3 Example sectors with project finance activity

	Deal volume (USD BN)			Number of deals		
Sectors	**2020**	**2021**	**2022**	**2020**	**2021**	**2022**
Renewable energy	211	705	411	844	1301	1238
Industrial real estate	54	187	161	60	186	257
Residential commercial real estate	22	43	47	62	190	209
Telecommunication	40	82	65	49	93	110
Oil and gas	54	151	62	72	123	97
Power	29	51	48	56	101	93
Transportation infrastructure	42	54	40	55	99	87
Mining	33	42	49	72	125	78
Petrochemicals	15	33	38	23	51	49
Waste and recycling	3	4	8	13	16	49
Totals	500	1377	948	1342	2349	2343

Source: Based on the UNCTAD World Investment Report (2023); the totals include other sectors not listed in the table.

SUMMARY

International finance emphasizes the integration of risk into financial planning, highlighting its impact on company finances and investments. Understanding risk is crucial, especially country risk, which includes economic, political, and social factors that may affect investment returns. Country risk is vital for MNCs as it can hinder foreign investments and influence business strategies. Both systematic risks, like economic crises, and unsystematic risks, such as company-specific issues, necessitate rigorous country risk analysis for informed investment decisions.

International capital markets, encompassing bond, stock, and loan markets, are vital for global economic growth and financial stability by facilitating cross-border trade in financial instruments like bonds, equities, and derivatives. These markets provide liquidity, diversify investments, and bridge capital gaps, enabling efficient financial resource allocation. International money markets deal with foreign currencies, offering cost savings and profit opportunities despite currency risks. International bond markets, benefiting from tax law differences, involve foreign bond transactions, often underwritten by global banks. International stock markets allow firms to list and trade stocks on foreign exchanges, enhancing liquidity and funding. International loan markets, including major commercial banks, offer cross-border loans, supporting international acquisitions and leveraged buy-outs, thus fostering global financial interconnections and diversification.

The value of a country's currency can fluctuate significantly based on its exchange rate system and macroeconomic management. The international monetary system, which has evolved from the gold standard to the present floating exchange rate system, includes policies, institutions, and mechanisms that determine foreign exchange rates, impacting global financial health. This system encompasses various regimes like fixed, floating, and crawling peg exchange rates, each with its own methods for maintaining currency value. Understanding concepts like nominal and real exchange rates, interest rate parity, and the Fisher effect is crucial for managing foreign exchange risk. International businesses face transaction and translation risks due to exchange rate fluctuations, which they manage through strategic responses such as hedging. The creation of the IMF and the World Bank after World War II has played a pivotal role in stabilizing international finance, aiding countries with balance of payments and exchange rate challenges.

International accounting is crucial for global business and investment activities, divided into financial accounting for external stakeholders and management accounting for internal stakeholders. The primary aim is to standardize financial information across countries, ensuring transparency and comparability, thus aiding international investors and stakeholders in making informed decisions. Financial statements, including the balance sheet, income statement, cash flow statement, and statement of changes in equity, are prepared regularly following fundamental principles like going concern, accruals, prudence, and consistency. The International Financial Reporting Standards (IFRS) and generally accepted accounting principles (GAAP) govern international accounting, promoting consistency and comparability despite some differences. Recent corporate scandals have intensified debates over these principles, emphasizing the need for global harmonization. Additionally, accounting significantly intersects with taxation, influencing strategies like transfer pricing to manage tax liabilities across multinational companies (MNCs).

Companies investing abroad via foreign direct investment (FDI) often need to raise external capital due to the large-scale nature of these investments. They must consider the trade-off between the tax advantages of debt financing, where interest payments are tax-deductible, and the risks associated with future financial obligations and potential financial distress. This balance is central to the trade-off theory of capital structure, which suggests that firms strive to optimize their mix of debt and equity to maximize shareholder value. Given the heightened risks of International Business activities, such as liabilities of foreignness, firms typically finance FDI with less debt than domestic investments to mitigate these additional risks. This cautious approach helps internationally active companies maintain financial stability despite the complexities of operating in foreign markets.

10

INTERNATIONAL MARKETING

CHAPTER INTRODUCTION

Marketing can be defined as the process of promoting, selling, and distributing products or services to consumers. It includes understanding customer needs and wants, creating products or services that satisfy those needs, and communicating their value to potential customers. A firm active on a single uniform market needs to develop a single marketing strategy to be executed within the firm. Every internationally active firm selling a product or service, however, faces the challenge of developing multiple successful marketing strategies because international marketing requires a market-by-market approach taking account of the environmental specifics that differ from country to country. These differences include formal and informal institutional conditions such as legal, cultural, economic, and political dimensions that need to be respected when finding suitable sales opportunities for the product or service.

As a result of those differences in the institutional environment it is common for MNCs to modify their marketing strategy when entering the international marketplace. However, developing such country-specific strategies does not come without costs, and firms need to balance these additional costs with the expected increases in earnings from adaptation. The literature proposes that developing country-specific marketing strategies involves decisions on seven dimensions: the product to be sold, how it is to be promoted, the price at which it is sold, where it is made available to consumers, the people bringing the product/service to customers, how a company brings its goods to the end consumer, and the physical evidence surrounding the sales process.

These aspects are the '7 Ps' of the marketing mix, a typical approach that coordinates marketing activities into one marketing strategy. Introduced by Jerome McCarthy in 1960, the marketing mix initially comprised only the first 4 Ps (product, price, place, and promotion). Three more Ps (people, process, and physical evidence) were added by Booms and Bittner (1981) who realized that in the service context especially the first four Ps needed expansion to formulate successful marketing strategies.

This chapter highlights the fundamentals of international marketing strategies based on the 7 Ps marketing mix. Each one is discussed and explained with examples to illustrate the differences in international marketing strategies.

LEARNING OUTCOMES

After reading this chapter you should be able to:

1. Demonstrate an understanding of the meaning and structure of the 7 Ps of international marketing
2. Explain phenomena involved in the 7 Ps of international marketing
3. Identify connections between the learning from Chapters 2, 3, and 4 and the development of an international marketing strategy
4. Discuss how specific issues associated with sustainability and digitalization connect with an international marketing strategy.

Case Study: International Marketing at MUJI

MUJI, a Japanese retail company known for its minimalist, no-brand products, has a unique international marketing strategy that emphasizes simplicity, quality, and sustainability. It revolves around maintaining its core philosophy of minimalism and quality while carefully adapting to local markets. This approach allows MUJI to leverage economies of scale and provide a uniform brand experience worldwide, appealing to consumers who value these principles.

To cater to diverse international markets, MUJI employs strategic adaptations without compromising its brand identity. For instance, the company modifies its product sizes and types to fit local living spaces and preferences, such as offering smaller furniture items in European markets. Additionally, MUJI tailors its food products to match regional tastes and dietary habits, ensuring relevance and appeal in each market it enters. These subtle adaptations help MUJI resonate with local consumers while maintaining its distinct no-brand, minimalist ethos.

MUJI's international expansion strategy focuses on establishing flagship stores in major cities and affluent neighbourhoods, targeting consumers likely to appreciate its unique value proposition. The brand enhances its global presence through collaborations with local designers and artists, creating region-specific products that foster community connections. Coupled with a strong online presence and an omnichannel approach, MUJI ensures accessibility and convenience for its international customer base, reinforcing its brand identity and expanding its loyal following globally.

Source: Foscht et al. (2011)

Case Study Questions

1 Use the dimensions of the 7 Ps to analyse the international marketing strategy of MUJI.
2 Discuss the elements of the 7 Ps that MUJI has attuned to local context and those that are globally standardized.

10.1 PRODUCT: GLOBAL PRODUCT STANDARDIZATION OR ADAPTATION

The product dimension in the 7 Ps refers to the goods or services a company provides. The international product life cycle by Raymond Vernon (1966) is applicable not only to an understanding of why countries engage in economic exchange (see Chapter 6, Section 6.4), but also to an understanding of the modifications a product undergoes over time. From an international marketing perspective, the model describes the different stages a product goes through once it enters the market, from introduction to growth to maturity, and then to standardization and finally decline.

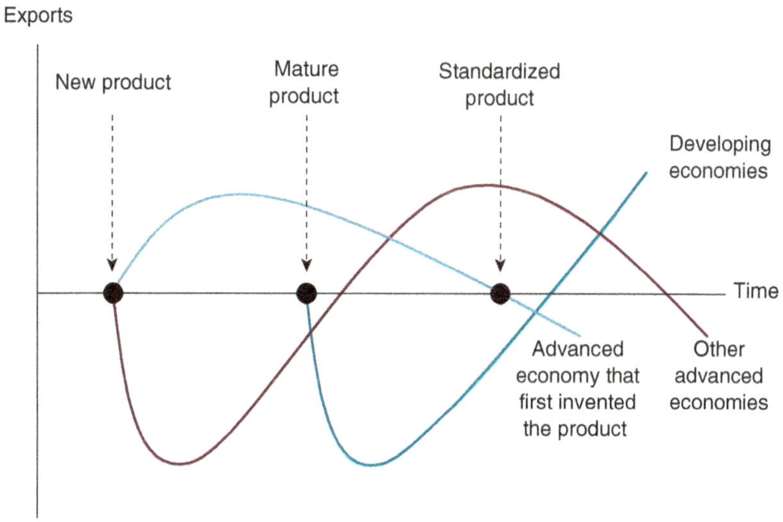

Figure 10.1 The international product life cycle

In the introductory phase, the product experiences low sales. The primary focus of product management is to increase sales through product diffusion. This includes strategies such as special introductory prices, a free trial period or samples to encourage customers to the try the new product.

Historically, new products were typically invented in advanced economies (e.g., Germany or the US) as they had more resources such as research and development (R&D) capabilities and high-income consumers who were more willing to try new products.

In the first phase, the product is produced where it was invented, resulting in a temporary monopoly for the inventing country.

When the product is adopted by customers, sales and profits begin to increase. But growth does not last forever and sales of the product reach a point of saturation in the home market (i.e., the maturity state). The inventors of the product now start to export it to other countries with advanced economies. This is the end of the monopoly for the inventing country, as foreign companies begin to produce competitive products and the inventor's profit margin decreases.

Once knowledge about how to produce the product is widespread, the product reaches the standardization/decline phase. When the product was being developed, skilled workers in R&D were required to drive production. However, once this process has been standardized, mass production in foreign countries becomes the norm in order to save labour and material costs. The country that invented the product and other advanced economies often then become net importers. Once the product's underlying technology has been exported, it becomes widely known and standardized around the world.

The international product life cycle illustrates the phases a product goes through after its invention, but it also shows that monopolies do not last forever. New products are constantly being invented – and imitated. For a long time, it was assumed that the cycle would progress slowly enough to create a disparity in access and use of the technology between the country where the product was invented and other countries. This is often no longer the case. The circle has become much smaller as new products emerge more quickly and customers adopt new technologies when they become available. This limits opportunities for inventors to generate income from a monopoly.

Case Study: The Product Life Cycle of Smartphones

An invention from Europe that illustrates the international product life cycle well is the smartphone, a mobile device that combines the functions of a traditional mobile phone with those of a computer. It typically features a touchscreen interface for user interaction, allowing users to access a wide range of applications, including communication tools (such as calls, text messaging, and email), web browsing, social media, multimedia playback (such as photos, videos, and music), gaming, productivity tools (such as calendars, notes, and document editing), and more. The smartphone, as we know it today, has its roots in Europe, with key contributions from companies such as Nokia and Ericsson.

Introduction (growth in Europe): The first smartphones emerged in the early 2000s, with companies such as Nokia and Ericsson pioneering the integration of mobile phone capabilities with personal digital assistants (PDAs). The R380 Ericsson was probably the first mobile device to be marketed as a 'smartphone'. These early smartphones gained popularity primarily in Europe, where there was significant demand for mobile communication technology.

Growth (expansion into global markets): As smartphones became more advanced and affordable, they began to penetrate global markets, particularly in North America and Asia. Companies such as Apple with its iPhone and various Android manufacturers, including those from Europe, expanded their reach, capturing market share in different regions. This phase saw rapid technological advances, increasing competition, and a growing consumer base.

Maturity (global saturation): By the mid to late 2010s, smartphones reached maturity, with widespread adoption and saturation in global markets. Multiple manufacturers from Europe, Asia, and North America competed fiercely for market share, driving innovation and pushing the boundaries of smartphone capabilities. During this phase, product differentiation became crucial as companies focused on features, design, and user experience to maintain or increase their market share.

Decline (competition and commoditization): In recent years, the smartphone market has entered a phase of maturity and saturation, leading to intense competition and price pressures. With most consumers owning smartphones and fewer innovations driving upgrades, the market has become saturated, leading to slower growth and declining profitability for some manufacturers. Additionally, commoditization of smartphones has made it challenging for companies to maintain high margins, leading to consolidation and strategic shifts in the industry. Throughout this product life cycle, the smartphone has evolved from a niche product in Europe to a ubiquitous technology with global reach, experiencing different stages of growth, maturity, and decline.

Sources: ThoughtCo (www.thoughtco.com/history-of-smartphones-4096585); Wikipedia (https://en.wikipedia.org/wiki/History_of_Nokia); Ercan et al. (2016)

Case Study Questions

1. How has the increasing versatility of smartphones changed the product life cycle from the time when phones were mostly tools for direct communication only?
2. Which smartphone features include are the most profitable for the companies that make them?
3. How has the product life cycle changed for smartphones since software providers have taken over much of the feature development?

One way to counteract the more limited opportunities to generate income from a monopoly product is to shorten the life of the product by regularly modifying goods and services before demand for the initial product drops significantly. Product adaptions enable companies to retain and capture a large market share: either by extending the maturity phase in finding new markets for the existing product (extended life cycle) or shortening the life cycle by offering a new product (short life cycles). The latter is achieved by launching a new product and modifying it before competitors have the chance to launch a copied version.

Product modifications are also often the result of pressures from informal institutions, particularly cultural pressures (see Chapter 5). Some products are used worldwide – for example, photocopiers and hairdryers – and only minor adaptions (e.g., voltage, language used in the instructions) are required for them to be sold in different nations. However, some other products are used very differently around the globe. Consider washing machines. While the French prefer to have washers loaded from the top, the British use front-loading devices. The Germans want high-speed washer-dryers, whereas the Italians want to line-dry their laundry outside. This means that a manufacturer has to offer several adaptations of the product to meet all customer needs and to sell in different nations. Probably the best-known example of a company selling cultural varieties of products is McDonalds. The food not only differs in taste, but the choice is adapted nationally. In Jerusalem for example, kosher meat is demanded whereas in India, vegetarian options are served because cows are sacred. McDonalds offers local options and yet is perceived as a global brand which can be found in multiple nations (Fischer, 2016).

Cultural influences also determine purchase decisions – for example, the meaning of some colours differs from region to region. In the United States black, for example, is worn as a sign of mourning; in other nations white is the colour of mourning and is therefore not used for consumer goods.

However, it is not only informal institutions that need to be considered when selling products globally. Formal institutional requirements, such as national laws and regulations, also often require firms to adapt products and services. For example, ingredients must match local laws, and intellectual property rights need to be respected. When Burger King entered the Australian market in 1971, its name presented a problem because an American immigrant had already registered the trademark 'Burger King' in 1966. Unable to buy the rights, the original owner used the name 'Hungry Jacks' instead. Since then, the burger restaurant has operated successfully under this name in Australia (Terry & Forrest, 2007).

10.2 PROMOTION: VARIATIONS IN ADVERTISING STRATEGIES

Spotlight: Social Media Marketing

Social media marketing has profoundly transformed the landscape of global advertising, absorbing significant advertisement spending from traditional local news outlets such as magazines and newspapers. This shift has been driven by the unparalleled reach, targeting capabilities, and engagement potential offered by social media platforms, which have made them indispensable tools for modern marketers.

One of the primary factors contributing to the globalization of marketing through social media is its vast and diverse audience. Platforms like Facebook, Instagram, X (previously Twitter), and LinkedIn boast billions of active users worldwide, enabling brands to reach a global audience from a single platform. Unlike traditional local news outlets, which are geographically constrained, social media allows marketers to connect with potential customers across borders, time zones, and cultures. This broad reach has led many companies to reallocate their advertising budgets from local to digital platforms to maximize their exposure and impact.

Another significant advantage of social media marketing is its sophisticated targeting capabilities. Social media platforms collect extensive data on user behaviours, preferences, and demographics, allowing advertisers to create highly personalized and effective campaigns. Brands can target specific segments of the population based on factors such as age, location, interests, and online activity. This precision targeting ensures that advertisements reach the most relevant audience, improving the return on investment (ROI) compared to traditional media, which often relies on broader, less precise demographic data.

Engagement and interaction are also crucial components of social media's appeal. Unlike static advertisements in magazines or newspapers, social media ads can be interactive, encouraging users to like, share, comment, and engage with the content. This interactivity not only increases the visibility of the ads through viral sharing but also fosters a sense of community and loyalty among customers. The ability to interact directly with consumers allows brands to build relationships, gather feedback, and refine their marketing strategies in real time.

Furthermore, social media marketing offers detailed analytics and performance metrics, providing insights into the effectiveness of campaigns. Marketers can track engagement rates, click-through rates, conversion rates, and other key performance indicators (KPIs) to assess the success of their efforts and make data-driven decisions. This level of transparency and accountability is often lacking in traditional advertising media, where measuring the direct impact of an ad can be challenging.

The shift to social media marketing has also been fuelled by cost considerations. Advertising on social media can be more cost effective than traditional media, allowing brands to reach a larger audience with smaller budgets. Small and medium-sized enterprises (SMEs), in particular, benefit from the affordability and scalability of social media ads, enabling them to compete with larger companies on a global stage.

However, this shift has had significant implications for local news outlets, which have seen a decline in advertising revenue. Magazines and newspapers, once the primary channels for local advertising, are struggling to compete with the reach and efficiency of social media platforms. This reduction in ad spending has led to financial challenges for many traditional media outlets, affecting their ability to produce quality journalism and maintain operations.

Sources: Forbes (www.forbes.com/sites/forbesagencycouncil/2022/08/25/how-social-media-marketing-can-help-with-business-growth) and MIT Sloan Management Review (https://sloanreview.mit.edu/article/where-influencer-marketing-goes-wrong-and-how-to-fix-it)

Promotion is the process whereby a company tries to stimulate demand for a product or service. This is mainly achieved through advertising to make consumers aware of the product. The most effective way to promote a product depends on the nature of the product. As with all other Ps, standardizing the promotion strategy globally reduces expense and complexity. At the same time, environmental pressures frequently force firms to adapt their promotional strategy to national conditions.

The first dimension of an international advertising strategy we are going to look at is the advertising message –the content conveyed by an advertiser to a target audience through a media channel or channels to promote a product, service, or idea. It is the core element of an advertising campaign and aims to capture the attention of the audience, communicate the key benefits or features of the advertised offering, and persuade them to take a desired action, such as making a purchase, requesting more information, or changing their behaviour.

Many MNCs apply a standardized advertising message worldwide and build on the promotion of the same (or at least a very similar) message across countries. This is easiest when target groups and their characteristics are very similar across markets. However, national differences in the institutional environment must be considered as well. For example, some countries prohibit comparative advertising, comparing a product to the competition. Some countries do not allow particular products (such as sweets or cigarettes) to be advertised at all. Whether to adapt or standardize a message is also related to similar decisions at the product level. Considering both perspectives, we can outline four different strategic approaches to the standardization of the advertising message:

- *Identical product and identical message*: This approach is applied when both the product and the advertisement strategy can be used worldwide. Both product and advertising preferences need to be very similar to follow such a strategy. Examples include luxury products like Rolex watches or Luis Vuitton Bags.
- *Identical product but different message*: When the product addresses diverse needs in different markets, there is no need for product modification, only the advertising message. In the United States, for example, many car companies point out the luxury and convenience of their vehicle, whereas in other countries more value is set on fuel efficiency and basic transportation needs (Jamal, 2014). The car that is sold, however, is very much the same in both cases.
- *Modified product but same message*: This strategy is used when the local market requires a variation of the product, but the customer needs are similar. Consider the washing machine example above: the French load their washing machines from the top while the British prefer front-loading machines. The consumer needs are the same and therefore can be addressed very similarly.
- *Modified product and modified message*: Sometimes both the product and the message need to be adjusted to a local market. This is not a common strategy as it reduces opportunities stemming from standardization on both dimensions. One

example is Red Bull. In Europe it is marketed as a fashionable drink for young to middle-aged consumers and is sold in stylish cans. In Thailand, however, energy drinks have a long tradition and are more often consumed by long-distance lorry drivers needing to stay awake. This requires a different advertising message. In addition, the energy drink is usually sold in glass bottles to resemble old-fashioned cough medicine. We therefore see variations at both product and message levels.

When considering the channels of advertising, the literature identifies the following communication or promotion mix:

- *Classical advertising*: Classical advertising involves paid, non-personal communication through various media channels such as television, radio, print (newspapers, magazines), outdoors (billboards, posters), online (websites, social media), and mobile (apps, SMS). Advertising allows companies to reach a large audience and build brand awareness, as well as convey detailed product information and persuasive messages.
- *Sales promotion*: Sales promotion includes short-term incentives designed to stimulate immediate sales or action from consumers or trade partners. Examples of sales promotion tactics include discounts, coupons, rebates, free samples, contests, sweepstakes, loyalty programmes, and point-of-purchase displays. Sales promotions are often used to encourage trials, increase purchase frequency, and generate excitement around a product or service.
- *Public relations (PR)*: Public relations focuses on managing the reputation and image of a company or brand through media coverage and communication with various stakeholders, including the media, investors, employees, customers, and the general public. PR activities may include media relations, press releases, publicity events, sponsorships, community relations, crisis management, and influencer partnerships. PR helps to build credibility, trust, and positive associations with the brand.
- *Direct marketing*: Direct marketing involves communicating directly with individual customers or targeted groups through channels such as direct mail, email, telemarketing, SMS messaging, and personalized online ads. Direct marketing allows companies to tailor messages and offers to specific segments of their audience, increasing relevance and response rates. Direct marketing is often used to generate leads, drive sales, and build customer relationships.
- *Personal selling*: Personal selling involves one-to-one or face-to-face interactions between sales representatives and potential customers. It allows for customized product presentations, demonstrations, and negotiations tailored to the needs and preferences of individual buyers. Personal selling is common in industries with complex or high-value products and services, as well as in business-to-business (B2B) sales.
- *Digital marketing*: Digital marketing encompasses various online tactics aimed at reaching and engaging audiences through digital channels such as websites, social

media, search engines, mobile apps, and online advertising. Digital marketing strategies may include content marketing, social media marketing, search engine optimization (SEO), pay-per-click (PPC) advertising, affiliate marketing, and influencer partnerships. Digital marketing allows companies to target specific audiences, track performance metrics, and optimize campaigns in real-time.

- *Events and experiential marketing*: Events and experiential marketing involve organizing and participating in live events, and experiences to engage consumers and create memorable brand interactions. They include trade shows, conferences, festivals, product launches, pop-up shops, and brand-sponsored experiences. Events and experiential marketing allow companies to connect with consumers in a more immersive and interactive way, fostering emotional connections and brand loyalty.

Use of these channels in international promotion can vary significantly across countries because of differences in their relevance, the extent to which they are developed, regulations on what is or is not allowed, and cultural preferences on how to be contacted and informed about a product or service.

Overall, the less that modification of a product or advertisement is required, the easier the promotion strategy for an MNC. Consequently, there is a trend towards standardization, and the perception of 'global brand' can influence some consumers' purchase decisions. Sometimes, adapting one of the above aspects to local conditions is required, however. Consequently, finding the right balance between globalization and localization is an important task for MNCs.

Case Study: The 'Share a Coke' Campaign by Coca-Cola

One example of an advertising campaign in which the advertising channels varied across countries was the 'Share a Coke' campaign by Coca-Cola. Launched in Australia in 2011, it involved printing common first names on Coca-Cola bottles and cans, and encouraged consumers to share a Coke with friends and family. The campaign was highly successful in Australia, driving increased sales and engagement among consumers who sought out bottles with their own names or the names of friends and family.

As the campaign expanded globally, Coca-Cola faced the challenge of adapting the advertising channels to fit with diverse cultures, regulations, and preferences in different countries. While television commercials, print ads, and outdoor billboards were common advertising media used in many countries, the specific channels and platforms varied depending on local media consumption habits and preferences. For example, in the United States, Coca-Cola launched TV commercials featuring people sharing a Coke and connecting with friends, while in Australia, outdoor billboards and digital displays prominently featured personalized Coke bottles with names.

Coca-Cola tried to leverage digital marketing channels such as social media, websites, and mobile apps to amplify the 'Share a Coke' campaign and engage consumers online.

Social media platforms were used to encourage user-generated content and sharing. In the United States, where Facebook and Twitter (now X) are widely used, Coca-Cola created dedicated Facebook pages and Twitter accounts for the 'Share a Coke' campaign, encouraging users to share photos and stories using the hashtag #ShareACoke. In China, where platforms like WeChat and Weibo dominate, Coca-Cola leveraged these platforms to engage with consumers and promote the campaign through branded accounts, sponsored posts, and interactive content.

In-store promotion and activation also varied across countries based on local retail environments and consumer behaviours. Coca-Cola worked with retailers to create special displays, promotions, and signage featuring personalized Coke bottles with names. In some countries, Coca-Cola organized experiential events and sampling campaigns in shopping malls, supermarkets, and public spaces to encourage consumer participation and drive sales. In other countries, the retail structure did not allow the creation of such events.

Source: Coca-Cola (www.coca-colacompany.com/about-us/history/how-a-campaign-got-its-start-down-under)

10.3 PRICING: PRICE VARIATIONS ACROSS COUNTRIES

Pricing refers to the process of determining the monetary value or cost associated with a product or service that a company offers its customers. Pricing is a critical element of the marketing mix as it directly influences customer perceptions, demand, profitability, and overall business success.

Before setting prices, companies need to establish clear objectives that align with their overall business goals. Common pricing objectives include maximizing profitability, increasing market share, achieving sales targets, maintaining competitiveness, and enhancing brand perception. The choice of pricing objectives will influence the pricing strategies and tactics employed by the company. Just as the objectives of a firm can vary across international markets, so can price and pricing strategies.

Pricing strategies refer to the approach or method used to set prices for products or services. For example, in cost-based pricing, prices are based on production, distribution, and overhead costs, plus a markup to ensure profitability. This can include methods such as cost-plus pricing, where a fixed percentage or amount is added to the cost of production. Market-based pricing is based on market conditions, competitor prices, and customer demand. This might include competitive pricing, where prices are set in line with or slightly below competitors' prices, or value-based pricing, where prices are based on the perceived value of the product or service to the customer. Firms can also follow a skimming pricing strategy and initially set high prices to maximize revenue from the least price-sensitive customers before gradually lowering prices to attract more price-sensitive customers. Alternatively, using a penetration pricing strategy, firms can set low prices initially to gain market share and attract customers quickly, with the intention of increasing prices once a foothold in the market has been established.

International pricing strategies involve determining the pricing strategy and tactics to be used when selling products or services in multiple countries or regions around the world. International pricing requires careful consideration of various factors, including market conditions, a competitive landscape, currency fluctuations, consumer preferences, and regulatory requirements. When it comes to market conditions, the most important driver of differences in pricing is varying purchasing power across markets. Setting a global standard price will significantly reduce sales volume in markets with comparatively low purchasing power. Firms therefore need to consider consumers' willingness to pay before entering markets, or must either accept lower revenues or a lower price. A similar effect can stem from intense competition in a market. Local competition may respond to an international firm's entry in a market with significant price reductions to reduce the profits of the MNC. This again forces the international firm to either reduce the price too or accept lower sales volumes.

Further, an MNC has to consider exchange-rate fluctuations in foreign currencies. Any plan for a specific return on investment will be affected if the foreign currency is devalued. If the dollar, for example, decreases by 10% in relation to the euro, the profit of a company whose home currency is the euro will decline. In this situation, the MNC has to choose between either (1) increasing the price of the product to compensate for the loss, (2) accepting the loss and leaving the price as it is, or (3) accepting part of the loss and increasing the price for the dealer to compensate for the difference. When both countries have the same currency, such as the Euro, these problems do not occur.

Firms also need to consider variations in consumer preferences, particularly because of different cultural characteristics. Taste and demand differ across nations, and sales in some countries will benefit from country-of-origin effects. If the demand for a product in one market is low, MNCs need to consider whether to reducing the price or only address a niche market. German beer is much more expensive in South Korea but only addresses a niche market with lower expectations regarding volume. A good example of a positive country-of-origin effect is that in many countries customers are willing to pay higher prices for German cars as they are perceived to be of very high quality. Japanese customers, interestingly, are unwilling to pay such high prices, thus Mercedes' pricing model is different in Japan.

Spotlight: Pricing of Apple's iPhone

In 2023, Apple sold the same iPhone (15 Pro Max7/1TB) at different prices in different markets (see Table 10.1). It was most expensive in Germany, Australia, Denmark, and Spain and cheapest in the USA, closely followed by Japan. There are several reasons for this, which are influenced by market conditions. Apple argued that the prices result from a mixture of different taxation, purchasing power and mostly currency fluctuations.

Table 10.1 Prices for iPhone 15 Pro Max/1TB in USD

Country	Cost in USD ($)
Australia	1,867.54
Germany	2,078.38
USA	1,599.00
Japan	1,684.65
Denmark	2,256.55
Spain	2,099.71
Thailand	1,863.56
Singapore	1,932.06

Source: iPhone Worldwide (https://iphone-worldwide.com)

Lastly, almost every nation has governmental regulations that specify pricing policies. Sometimes there are requirements for minimum or maximum prices. A minimum price can protect local companies and ensure a profit for local firms. For example, if the minimum price for a TV is US$1,000 and the production cost for the locally produced one is US$800, the company gets US$200 per sold piece. But if a foreign competitor produces a comparable product with production costs of US$600 per piece, the foreign company makes US$400 per sold piece. If there wasn't a minimum price regulation, the foreign firm could sell the TV for US$800 so that the customers buy the imported TV. As a result, the local company would eventually have to close their business and the foreign competitor could raise the price of the TV.

Summing up, internationalizing firms always need to decide between global pricing strategies, where prices are the same across all countries, or local or regional pricing strategies.

A relevant challenge associated with price adaptation are differing consumer perceptions and expectations across countries, but also the risk of grey imports, also known as parallel imports or parallel market goods. These are genuine products imported and sold through unauthorized or unofficial channels without the consent of the manufacturer or authorized distributors. They are typically sourced from a country where the products are sold at a lower price or released earlier than in other markets and then imported and resold in another country where the products are officially distributed by authorized channels. The bigger the price difference between international markets, the higher the risk of grey imports.

Spotlight: Dynamic Pricing in the Airline Industry

Dynamic pricing has revolutionized the airline industry by transforming how airlines set and adjust ticket prices. Powered by advanced algorithms and real-time data analysis, this strategy allows airlines to maximize revenue and optimize seat occupancy by varying prices based on demand, booking patterns, and market conditions.

Historically, airlines used fixed pricing structures with occasional fare adjustments. However, dynamic pricing enables continuous price adjustments in response to various factors such as booking trends, remaining seat availability, competitor pricing, and even external factors like weather conditions and local events. This approach helps airlines capture the highest price customers from different customer segments are willing to pay, thus increasing overall revenue.

The implementation of dynamic pricing relies heavily on sophisticated revenue management systems that analyse vast amounts of data. These systems predict demand fluctuations and adjust prices accordingly, ensuring that flights are sold at the optimal price point at any given time. For instance, prices might be lower during off-peak times or when seats are abundant, attracting price-sensitive customers. Conversely, prices can surge closer to departure dates or during peak travel seasons when demand is high.

Dynamic pricing has introduced greater transparency and flexibility into the market. Customers can see fare variations in real time, prompting many to book tickets earlier to secure lower prices or take advantage of last-minute deals. This transparency has led to a more competitive environment, where airlines continuously adjust their strategies to attract customers.

However, dynamic pricing has also brought challenges. It requires significant investment in technology and data analytics capabilities, which can be a barrier for smaller airlines. Additionally, the constant fluctuation in prices can lead to customer frustration and perceptions of unfairness, especially if passengers find themselves paying significantly different prices for the same flight.

Global variation in airline prices is another consequence of dynamic pricing. Prices can vary widely depending on the region, local economic conditions, competition levels, and regulatory environments. For example, routes in highly competitive markets like Europe and North America might experience more aggressive pricing strategies, leading to frequent fare changes. Conversely, in regions with less competition or stricter regulations, price variations might be less pronounced.

Sources: Betancourt et al. (2022); and Skyscanner (www.skyscanner.net/news/how-does-airline-pricing-work#:~:text=These%20price%20changes%20reflect%20how,numbers%20rather%20than%20search%20volumes) and McKinsey (www.mckinsey.com/industries/travel-logistics-and-infrastructure/our-insights/how-airlines-can-gain-a-competitive-edge-through-pricing)

10.4 PLACE: INTERNATIONAL DISTRIBUTION STRATEGIES

Choosing the right distribution channel is one of the most important aspects to consider in marketing strategy. Distribution is the path a product follows from production to the end consumer, which again differs from country to country. MNCs need to work out the best distribution strategy, and examine local criteria when selecting distributors and channels, as a distribution strategy is rather inflexible once established; while prices and promotion can be adapted relatively easily, distribution decisions are often constrained by expensive commitments and longer-term contracts.

10.4.1 Direct and Indirect Distribution Strategies

MNCs must decide on an appropriate distribution strategy in a particular country. The first choice is whether to sell the product directly or through intermediaries. Intermediaries are firms that mediate between companies and their export markets and support them with logistics, documentation, and related services. A company is likely to adopt a different strategy in its home country than in the international market. In mainland Europe, for example, many people still prefer to shop in physical stores while in some countries it is more common to buy online. Even when products are sold online the company can sell either directly to the end consumer or through online marketplaces. In other words, several distribution channels need to be considered and analysed when being active internationally.

Another major difference between nations is the location in which consumers buy. In more developed countries, people are used to buying a great variety of groceries in one big supermarket. In some other countries, there are more smaller shops which means that the MNC has to deal with several retailers. Additionally, retailers and merchants vary from country to country so that international standardization is frequently difficult.

10.4.2 Choice of Distribution System and Partners

The choice of distribution system and partners often requires a long commitment. Hence, the financial strength of the retailer is important so that a long-lasting business relationship with strong support can be expected. When products are sold that need maintenance or servicing (e.g., cars or electronic devices), the MNC will also be interested in cooperating with firms that can execute those services. Another critical aspect can be how well the foreign distributor has the ability to assist the MNC in navigating foreign bureaucratic processes. To determine whether the distributor is a suitable business partner to promote the product, the exporting firm may review the number and type of products the distributor already sells. However, selecting distributors is not a one-sided choice. If the distributor already sells comparable products and has no demand for additional products, the MNC must provide an incentive offer, such as:

- Offering profitable sales incentives
- Conducting and communicating market research to identify customer niches and sales forecasts, to find out how much of the product the distributor can handle
- Financial support for local marketing campaigns
- Allowing the return of unsold and/or outdated goods with a full refund.

Spotlight: The Carbon Footprint of Retailing

The carbon footprint of e-commerce and traditional store-based commerce differs significantly due to variations in logistics, consumer behaviour, and operational practices. Understanding these differences is crucial in order to assess the environmental impact of each mode of shopping and to develop strategies to minimize carbon emissions in the retail sector.

E-commerce typically involves multiple stages of delivery, including long-distance shipping from centralized warehouses and last-mile delivery to consumers' homes. While bulk shipping to centralized warehouses is generally efficient, last-mile delivery often involves numerous stops, leading to higher emissions per unit compared to bulk deliveries to retail stores. Additionally, e-commerce generates substantial packaging waste due to the use of individual shipping boxes, cushioning materials, and plastic wraps to protect goods during transit. This excess packaging contributes significantly to the carbon footprint, especially when non-recyclable materials are used. Moreover, e-commerce often experiences higher return rates than traditional retail commerce, requiring additional transportation and handling, further increasing carbon emissions.

Traditional store-based commerce involves transporting goods from manufacturers to distribution centres and then to retail stores. While this process is generally efficient due to bulk transportation, consumers' individual car trips to and from stores can significantly increase the carbon footprint, especially in regions where driving is the primary mode of transportation. Physical stores also require energy for lighting, heating, cooling, and other operational needs, contributing to their overall carbon footprint. The energy efficiency of stores varies widely, with older buildings typically being less efficient than newer, green-certified structures. Additionally, the construction and maintenance of retail spaces contribute to the carbon footprint, including the materials used for construction and the ongoing energy consumption associated with maintaining these spaces.

The carbon footprint of e-commerce and traditional store-based commerce depends on various factors, including consumer behaviour, logistics efficiency, and energy use. E-commerce can leverage centralized warehouses that use renewable energy and efficient logistics to reduce emissions, while traditional retail can reduce its footprint by improving store energy efficiency and encouraging sustainable consumer behaviour such as using public transportation. Both modes have unique environmental impacts, and their relative footprints can be influenced by choices made by retailers and consumers alike. Understanding these dynamics is essential for developing strategies to minimize carbon emissions in the retail sector.

Sources: Edwards et al. (2010); Earth.org (https://earth.org/online-shopping-and-its-environmental-impact); DHL (www.dhl.com/discover/en-global/e-commerce-advice/e-commerce-best-practice/companies-reduce-carbon-footprint)

10.5 PEOPLE: SUPPORTING INTERNATIONAL MARKET ACTIVITIES

The people behind a company play a crucial role when it comes to customer interaction. They handle customer enquiries, orders, and complaints through various channels such as telephone calls, online chats, social media and in person. Employees get in touch with the customer personally and become the 'face' of the firm for them. They explain how to use products and they assist in purchases. Employees who reflect the values of the company sharpen the consumer's perception of the brand. Thus, recruiting, training, and motivating employees is another key aspect of the international marketing strategy. Employees' understanding of the company's products and services and their approach to communicating information to customers needs to be improved on an ongoing basis. The ability to build long-term customer relationships is particularly important as it retains their custom instead of losing them to competitors.

In summary, finding, retaining, developing, and deploying the right employees are important parts of an MNC's human resource management (HRM) activity. International HRM is a crucial aspect of a firm's strategy (see Chapter 11).

10.6 PROCESS

The underlying processes describe how a firm does what it does. Every company tries to create customer-friendly and efficient journeys, which can only be achieved by having effective processes. Badly designed processes can lead to ineffective service delivery and sluggish administration, resulting in poor customer experiences. They also make it difficult for front-line employees to meet customers' expectations. When a customer makes an online enquiry, the processes determine how long they have to wait to receive a response, how long it takes between scheduling a meeting and the meeting taking place, how the shopper is treated once an order is made, and so on. The company is most likely to develop loyal customers if they have pleasant buying experiences (Lovelock & Wirtz, 2011; Helmold, 2022).

This part of a company's marketing strategy is closely related to the HRM of a multinational firm. We already know that many buying decisions are shaped by cultural factors that influence shopping behaviour. As a result, employees are responsible for knowing and providing a familiar shopping process to customers across countries. This includes consideration of specific cultural and religious values across countries, for example:

- In countries with a predominantly Muslim population, it is inappropriate to offer alcoholic beverages during shopping interactions. It might even be considered offensive. In contrast, in Western countries, it is common for high-end retailers to offer champagne or wine to the customer as part of the shopping experience.
- In some cultures, such as Japan, shaking hands is not part of a business or shopping interaction. Instead, a nod of the head is used as a sign of greeting and respect.
- In many Middle Eastern and Asian countries, haggling and negotiating the price is common and even expected. Most Western countries have a fixed price as standard and haggling is unusual.
- In some countries customers are expected to bring reusable shopping bags for the good of the environment protection; in others single-use plastic bags are still common.

A good example of an MNC that has managed to standardize many processes globally is McDonald's, whose goal is that each global consumer has almost the same experience when eating at a McDonald's outlet. McDonald's has homogenous processes with minor cultural and legal modifications where necessary (Helmold, 2022).

The process strongly determines customer satisfaction. Consequently, MNCs aim to provide, as far as possible, the same level of quality wherever their products are bought. However, in many cases processes must be adapted to local conditions because of different institutional environments.

10.7 PHYSICAL EVIDENCE

Considerations regarding the physical environment are essential if the physical presence of the customer is involved. The visual elements – signs, the interior, staff uniforms, and other artefacts – provide tangible evidence of the firm's quality of service and guide the customer through the service process. As with the 7Ps, the physical environment can either be standardized or adapted to local circumstances.

Apple's retail stores are a good example of strong standardization of physical presence and look very similar all over the world. The stores have a modern aesthetic with a glass frontage and minimalistic furniture. The stores are located in popular and central areas, mostly in larger towns and cities. When visiting an outlet, customers are greeted by an employee. All employees wear Apple outfits designed to connect well with the Apple brand. Products are displayed similarly no matter where in the world a shop is located. In these ways, Apple tries to transfer the 'Apple lifestyle' around the world. This is intended to increase customers' identification with the brand (Coget, 2017).

The physical evidence in the marketing mix is a crucial component when service is part of the shopping experience. Local adaptions in stores have to be made depending on the products and the firm's strategy.

10.8 MARKET POTENTIAL

The institutional environment (see Chapters 2–5) in combination with a detailed analysis of needs for adaptation across the 7Ps, discussed earlier in this chapter, is often connected with an assessment of market size and competition to evaluate the potential of an international market (Schlegelmilch, 2022). This assessment of market potential usually starts by screening the market, including an analysis of market size, growth, and competition.

Market sizing is the process of estimating the total potential market for a product, service, or business in a country. The two primary methodologies employed in market sizing are the top-down approach and the bottom-up approach, each offering distinct advantages and challenges.

The top-down approach begins with a broad estimate of the total market size, often derived from secondary data such as industry reports, government statistics, and macroeconomic indicators. From this comprehensive perspective, the analysis progressively narrows to the target market segment through segmentation and filtering processes. This method is particularly useful for generating quick, high-level estimates, especially in markets where detailed data is readily available.

For instance, a company seeking to estimate the market size for electric scooters in India might start with the total value of the country's two-wheeler market, which is approximately $25 billion annually. Industry reports might indicate that electric vehicles account for 10% of this market, translating to $2.5 billion. Further segmentation could reveal that electric scooters make up 60% of this electric vehicle category, equating to a target market size of $1.5 billion. Adjustments for market-specific factors, such as competition and growth trends, might project an annual increase of 20% in this segment.

While efficient and less resource-intensive than the bottom-up approach, the top-down approach can be imprecise if the filters applied are overly broad or if the secondary data is outdated or unreliable. This method also assumes the availability of comprehensive market data, which may not always be the case in nascent or niche markets.

In contrast, the bottom-up approach builds the market size estimate from granular data, starting with specific and localized inputs and aggregating them to estimate the total market. This method often relies on primary data collection, such as customer surveys, sales figures, or localized market analyses, making it particularly suited for detailed and accurate assessments of niche markets.

A start-up aiming to estimate the market potential for a fitness app targeted at working professionals in U.S. metropolitan areas provides an example of the bottom-up approach. By analysing user data, the company might determine that the average annual revenue per subscriber is $120, based on a $10 monthly subscription fee. Research could reveal that there are approximately 50 million working professionals in urban areas, with 10% expressing interest in adopting a fitness app. This translates to a potential user base of 5 million individuals. Multiplying the user base by the annual revenue per user, the company estimates a total market size of $600 million. Accounting for factors such as competition and early adoption rates, the company might realistically expect to capture only 5% of the market in its first year, equating to $30 million in revenue.

The bottom-up approach is more labour intensive and requires precise data collection, but it offers a highly tailored estimate, making it ideal for new or specific market segments. This method also allows for a more detailed understanding of market dynamics and customer behaviour, which can inform strategic decision-making.

This comprehensive assessment of market size should then be combined with an analysis of potential future market growth or decline. This is important as foreign market entry decisions are oriented to the longer term and therefore future market developments are at least as important as today's market size. Firms often rely on expert opinions in combination with past market developments to forecast future growth or decline.

As firms are hardly ever able to cater for 100% of a market, the level and structure of competition in the market, today and tomorrow, also need to be included in the analysis. Porter's five forces (see Chapter 8, Section 8.2.2) can be a good starting point to understand the competitive structure in the market but should be combined with a detailed analysis of competitors and their expected strategies.

To provide a holistic understanding of market potential, this economic assessment of a market is combined with an analysis of the formal and informal institutional environment, often alongside the 7 Ps analyses. This analysis is designed to create an understanding of the firm's ability to standardise marketing processes along the lines of the 7 Ps and to identify potential barriers to entry, both formal and informal.

10.9 RECENT DEVELOPMENTS IN INTERNATIONAL MARKETING

There is substantial recent research on the principles of international marketing, ranging from adaptation and standardization to forecasting.

In a study of marketing strategies of companies that operate in the international context, researchers investigated whether MNCs adopt or standardize elements (one or more of the 7 Ps) of their marketing mix across nations. This usually depends on the product and the nature of the market. Different companies have different strategies to address these issues. Nevertheless, it might be assumed that within the same industry, a similar international marketing strategy is pursued. However, Apple sells the same devices worldwide, while Samsung sells a variety of models with diverse characteristics to meet the needs of customers in various nations. This illustrates that even in the same industry, there are no uniform rules for a successful marketing concept (Venaik & Midgley, 2019). Different approaches can both result in a profitable business strategy, although their concept does not, in theory, fit their business environment (Agic et al., 2016). In this regard, researchers identified four typical approaches by MNCs of marketing mix standardization vs adaptation. One model, for instance, shows how multinational firms standardize all of the 7 Ps across markets except for price and place while another model shows a hybrid approach in which the product is standardized, promotion is adapted and there is no distinct rule for pricing. The results show that some MNC subsidiaries successfully use a similar marketing strategy, although the market conditions differ widely from one another. At first, these findings seem to be contradictory to the theory of successful international marketing approaches. However, there are some plausible reasons for these results, such as changing business environments, industry dynamics, customer preferences and regulatory conditions. It can also be a strategic decision not to alter the marketing strategy in order to gain first mover advantage in a specific market. What we can learn from the study is that several strategies can be effective and that marketers have a larger tool-kit than simply adapting every P of the MNC's marketing mix to the foreign market (Venaik & Midgley, 2019).

Theory on international marketing strategy implies that the choice of the right distribution channel is a key factor to a successful international marketing concept. Looking at a case study of Nigerian commercial banks, it was found that effective selection, application, and management of distribution channel strategies have a significant influence on the performance of the bank. The commercial banks in Nigeria apply different marketing strategies to increase competitiveness. In this regard, the study emphasizes the importance of electronic banking to increase the performance of banks and to minimize costs at the same time, but mostly in order to meet customer needs and preferences. The study by Uche et al. (2022) draws parallels between the challenges in international marketing for commercial banks in Nigeria and general challenges in the service sector. Thus, understanding the market, the customers and taking customer preferences into account are of great importance. What seems to be obvious in some countries may not be in others.

When China attempted to liberalize its centralized economy and transform its path to a decentralized and private sector structure, wholly foreign owned enterprises (WFOEs) played a major role in this process. WFOEs are firms that are mostly owned by foreigners but are located and operated in the Chinese market. When China opened its economy to international companies, it experienced great economic growth. WFOEs contributed significantly to China's economic transformation, and in the retail sector especially they play a crucial role in promoting economic growth (Alfayad, 2019).

In this context, countries such as Saudi Arabia have recognized that in order to operate sustainably, they need to shift their economic thinking from national to international sales strategies. Saudi Arabia did not have much market diversification and was mainly trading in oil, which made the country dependent on one source of income. The researchers are confident that Saudi Arabia and other countries can benefit from the experience and lessons learned from China's economic reforms to successfully implement their own diversification policies. Especially in the internationally traded retail sector and online trade, these countries are seen to have an extremely high potential for economic growth (Alfayad, 2019).

MNCs face the challenge of understanding economic developments in foreign markets accurately, especially inflation forecasts. A country's inflation rate influences the life of common people and their behaviour on the market directly. A study by Banerjee (2021) looks at a model for predicting price levels in India using time series data from the consumer price index (CPI). The model can be used by policymakers to design monetary and fiscal policies in order to regulate inflation, resulting in political stability and economic success. The researcher considers the CPI as representative of the inflation rate.

Monitoring and forecasting price levels can help international companies to make informed business decisions. They enable MNCs to adjust their marketing and business strategies accordingly. Knowing these economic aspects is essential for multinational businesses that operate in foreign marketplaces and have to respond in a marketing-related way. The rate of inflation can affect consumer buying behaviour, demand for products and services, and overall economic stability. The study by Banerjee emphasizes the importance of forecasting models in predicting inflation. Companies in international marketing can benefit from such forecasts to adjust their pricing strategies, offers, and marketing campaigns, and maintain their competitiveness in the market (Banerjee, 2021).

Spotlight: Anti-smoking in India

Both active and passive smokers experience health issues as a result of smoking. Consequently, smoking-related advertising is prohibited in many countries. A study from India (Ramasundaram et al., 2022) investigates whether anti-smoking messages in cinemas can influence the behaviour of the target audience. The study tries to understand how such advertising efforts can help influence smoking habits and promote good health. Governments use various measures to curb smoking habits, including public advertising campaigns. A study from India shows that using cinemas for promotional activities is an effective strategy to educate the public about the harmful effects of smoking. Looking at the results from an international marketing perspective, the findings of this study can help develop more effective advertising audience-targeted campaigns. Anti-smoking advertising campaigns could be launched internationally in cinemas to promote the health of active and passive smokers. The results of this study have far-reaching implications for the design of anti-smoking campaigns in international marketing. They show that targeted advertising in cinema halls can be an effective way to promote behaviour change in smoking habits and consequently have a positive influence on people's health.

Source: Ramasundaram et al. (2022)

SUMMARY

Entering the global market requires multinational companies (MNCs) to navigate a complex landscape of strategies and challenges. One significant framework, Raymond Vernon's product life cycle theory (1966), outlines the typical trajectory of a new product from introduction to market maturity. MNCs can use this theory to strategize against competitive threats by either extending the maturity phase through new market exploration or shortening the cycle with innovative product offerings.

Adapting to foreign markets involves addressing diverse factors such as legal frameworks, cultural norms, economic conditions, and political environments. Successful entry often demands adjustments in product features, advertising messages, and pricing strategies to align with local dynamics like currency fluctuations and governmental regulations. Moreover, selecting appropriate distribution channels – whether direct sales or intermediaries – is crucial, tailored to local shopping behaviours such as online preferences and in-store habits. In service marketing, additional considerations include the selection of personnel who represent the company, ensuring a positive customer experience across cultural contexts, and optimizing physical elements for locations where direct customer interaction occurs.

11

INTERNATIONAL HUMAN RESOURCE MANAGEMENT

CHAPTER INTRODUCTION

In today's globalized business landscape, human resource management (HRM) has emerged as a relevant strategic element for multinational companies (MNCs) seeking a competitive edge. While products and brands can be imitated, the knowledge, capabilities, and processes that drive a company's success are often difficult to replicate. This is where effective HRM practices come into play. By carefully selecting, training, and compensating their personnel, MNCs can cultivate a pool of talent that sets them apart from their competitors and gives them a competitive edge (Schuler & Jackson, 1987).

A critical consideration for firms operating internationally is the careful formulation of staffing strategies and policies that align with their global expansion efforts. It becomes important for organizations to establish effective systems for training, performance appraisal, and compensation that cater specifically to employees engaged in international activities. Simultaneously, companies must be mindful of the need to address diversity and equity objectives throughout their operations, while also striving to attract, retain, and develop talent on a global scale.

This chapter explores the realm of international human resource management (IHRM) and explores how multinational companies prepare their workforce to tackle the unique challenges of operating on a global scale. It focuses on key areas such as personnel selection, training, managerial development, compensation, and labour relations. The aim of this chapter is to explore the intricacies of managing a global workforce and to offer valuable guidance, strategies, and practical solutions to successfully navigate and overcome the challenges associated with IHRM.

International human resource management refers to the management of human resources in a multinational setting, which involves staffing, hiring, training, coaching, and compensating personnel in cross-border positions. The importance of IHRM lies in its ability to facilitate effective management of a diverse and geographically dispersed workforce in order to achieve a firm's strategic objectives. By understanding and addressing the unique challenges presented by international operations, IHRM seeks to harness the potential of a geographically dispersed workforce and leverage it for competitive advantage. International human resource management presents unique challenges that distinguish it from domestic HRM practices. These challenges arise due to the complex nature of operating in a global business environment, specifically across varying formal and informal institutions (see Chapters 3 and 4). Addressing these challenges requires a comprehensive understanding of the unique dynamics of international operations and the implementation of strategic HR practices tailored to the global context.

LEARNING OUTCOMES

After reading this chapter you should be able to:

1. Describe ways in which human resource management and International Business are related
2. Demonstrate an understanding of the challenges faced by expatriates
3. Outline the basic principles of international hiring, training, and compensation
4. Explain how international coaching and HR development can contribute to successful international human resource management, including expatriation.

Case Study: International HRM in the Daimler-Chrysler Merger

The merger between Daimler-Benz AG and Chrysler Corporation in 1998 was initially hailed as a groundbreaking partnership that would create a global automotive powerhouse. However, the merger, valued at US$36 billion, ultimately failed due to deep-seated conflicts between employees driven by cultural differences. These cultural clashes permeated various aspects of the organization, leading to significant operational challenges and a lack of cohesion, which undermined the merger's success. Insights from international human resource management (IHRM) could have mitigated these issues and improved integration efforts.

One of the primary cultural conflicts stemmed from the differing corporate cultures of Daimler and Chrysler. Daimler-Benz, a German company, was characterized by a formal, hierarchical, and engineering-driven culture. The German approach emphasized meticulous planning, long-term strategic thinking, and a conservative management style. In contrast, Chrysler, an American company, had a more informal, entrepreneurial, and market-driven culture. Chrysler's management style was known for being aggressive, fast-paced, and flexible, focusing on short-term results and innovation. Effective international HRM strategies could have bridged these cultural gaps by fostering mutual understanding and respect.

These cultural differences manifested in various operational and managerial conflicts. For instance, Daimler's management style, which prioritized structure and precision, clashed with Chrysler's more dynamic and risk-taking approach. German managers often perceived their American counterparts as undisciplined and overly aggressive, while Chrysler employees viewed Daimler's approach as rigid and slow-moving. This led to significant friction in decision-making processes, with each side struggling to understand and respect the other's way of operating. International HRM could have facilitated cross-cultural training programmes to help employees adapt to and appreciate each other's working styles, thus reducing friction.

Communication barriers also played a role in the failure of the merger. Language differences and different communication styles exacerbated misunderstandings and misinterpretations. Daimler employees were accustomed to a formal communication style, often involving detailed documentation and rigorous approval processes. In contrast, Chrysler employees favoured a more direct and informal approach, leading to frustration and confusion on both sides, hindering effective collaboration and integration efforts. International HRM could have implemented bilingual communication platforms and regular intercultural workshops to improve mutual understanding and streamline communication.

The clash of corporate cultures also affected employee morale and trust. Many Chrysler employees felt marginalized and undervalued, perceiving that Daimler executives were imposing their culture and practices without considering the strengths and contributions of Chrysler's approach. This perception was reinforced by decisions such as the replacement of Chrysler executives with German managers and the imposition of Daimler's management practices. This led to a decline in morale and a sense of alienation among Chrysler employees, further impeding the integration process. International HRM strategies such as joint leadership development programmes and inclusive decision-making processes could have promoted a more balanced and integrated corporate culture, preserving employee morale and trust.

Financial performance suffered as a result of these cultural conflicts. The anticipated synergies and efficiencies from the merger failed to materialize, leading to disappointing financial results. Operational inefficiencies, coupled with declining employee morale, contributed to significant losses. By 2007, Daimler decided to divest its stake in Chrysler, selling it to the private equity firm Cerberus Capital Management for a fraction of the original merger's value.

Source: Mercedes-Benz Group (https://group.mercedes-benz.com/company/tradition/company-history/1995-2007.html)

(Continued)

Case Study Questions

1. What is the role of organizational culture in corporate success? When does it make sense to foster a strong organizational culture?
2. How does organizational culture relate to national culture?
3. Which processes can help align two partially conflicting organizational cultures?

11.1 KEY CONCEPTS IN IHRM

The ongoing globalization of business has resulted in a significant rise in the number of employees being assigned to foreign postings, so-called expatriates and inpatriates, and this trend is expected to continue in the future. However, it is concerning that a considerable percentage, estimated to be between 10% and 80% of expatriates sent on foreign assignments end up returning home prematurely (Mendenhall et al., 1987; Kim & Slocum, 2008; Okpara & Kabongo, 2011). To tackle the high failure rates and ensure the success of overseas operations for both assigned managers and the organization as a whole, IHRM must carefully consider several important concepts. These include appropriate staffing of overseas positions, comprehensive international training programmes, appropriate compensation strategies, and a well-designed offering of international coaching and HR development.

Spotlight: Business Travel after Covid-19

After Covid-19, companies significantly reduced business travel due to several factors that emerged during the pandemic. The widespread adoption of digital communication tools, such as Zoom, Microsoft Teams, and Google Meet, demonstrated that virtual meetings could replace many in-person interactions in an effective way. This shift highlighted the cost-saving potential of reducing travel expenses, including flights, accommodation, and other related costs.

Health and safety concerns were also important. The ongoing risks associated with Covid-19 variants and other health threats made companies more cautious about exposing their employees to potential infections. Additionally, many organizations adopted remote work policies during the pandemic, and these policies have continued, reducing the need for travel to central offices or client sites.

The reduction in business travel has made a significant contribution to corporate sustainability efforts. By cutting down on air travel, companies have been able to decrease their carbon footprints, aligning with global initiatives to combat climate change. Air travel is one of the largest sources of greenhouse gas emissions in the corporate sector, and reducing flights has a direct and positive impact on environmental sustainability. Additionally, fewer business trips mean less reliance on other high-emission activities such as car rentals and hotel stays, further contributing to lower overall carbon emissions. This shift supports companies' sustainability goals and corporate social responsibility (CSR) initiatives, enhancing their reputation among environmentally conscious stakeholders. Furthermore, the emphasis on virtual meetings reduces waste associated with business travel, such as paper usage and single-use plastics commonly found in conference settings. Overall, the move away from frequent business travel has become a cornerstone of broader corporate efforts to create a more sustainable and environmentally friendly business model.

Sources: World Economic Forum (www.weforum.org/agenda/2022/11/business-travel-energy-work-sustainable-pandemic) and Forbes (www.forbes.com/sites/suzannerowankelleher/2022/03/12/covid-changed-business-travel)

11.2 EXPATRIATION

Expatriation is a commonly employed term to describe the international relocation of managers. While the literal definition of 'expatriate' could encompass any employee working outside their home country, it is typically used to refer to parent-country nationals, who are assigned to work in foreign subsidiaries of multinational companies (MNCs) for a set time, typically ranging from two to five years. Another approach to such international transfers is known as inpatriation, which involves the movement of subsidiary managers to the headquarters of the MNC, or in a broader sense the movement of citizens of a foreign country working in the home country of their multinational employer.

Due to the expansion of global operations, increasing diversity in the workplace and the growing demand for specialized skills, the number of people employed on international assignments is steadily increasing. This trend can be attributed to a diverse array of factors, both organizational and individual. They generally fall into three categories (Harzing, 2001):

- *Filling positions*: International transfers of managers in order to transfer technical knowledge to developing countries where qualified local nationals are not available
- *Management development*: International transfers of managers, providing them with international experience and developing them for future important tasks in subsidiaries abroad or with the parent company
- *Organizational development*: International transfers of managers as a coordination and control strategy.

11.2.1 Expatriates' Journey in the Foreign Environment

To manage international operations and local employees effectively, expatriates are expected to navigate local work environments (see the analyses of the institutional environments in Chapters 2–5) and assume new role responsibilities, all while adapting to foreign cultural perspectives and values. The process of expatriate adjustment can be defined as 'the degree of psychological adjustment experienced by the individual within a new society or the degree of psychological comfort and familiarity perceived within a new environment' (Puck et al., 2008). It is important to recognize that expatriate adjustment is a multifaceted process involving adaptation to the overall environment, the work situation, and interactions with host nationals. This multifaceted perspective highlights that while some expatriates may thrive in one dimension of adjustment, they may face challenges in others. For example, an expatriate might adapt to their work environment effectively but encounter difficulties in socializing with individuals from the host country.

In fact, when embarking on an international assignment, expatriates often find themselves faced with a phenomenon referred to as a 'cultural shock'. A cultural shock describes the disorientation and adjustment difficulties experienced when encountering a foreign environment. The process of acculturation becomes important during this period, as expatriates navigate the stages of adapting to their new environment (see Figure 11.1). More specifically, this acculturation process can be split into four different stages (Lysgaard, 1955; Winkelman, 1994):

- *Honeymoon stage*: This initial phase is marked by excitement and fascination with the new culture, typically lasting for a couple of weeks or months. Similarities are identified, and the local people are viewed as welcoming. Even mundane aspects of daily life are seen as charming and amusing.
- *Culture shock*: Around three months into the experience, frustration and anxiety set in. Difficulties and uncomfortable situations arise, leading to a sense of disconnect. Simple tasks like navigating or ordering food become challenging. Homesickness and idealizing the life left behind become prominent. Feelings of confusion, discontent, and even anger may emerge.
- *Adjustment stage*: This phase sees a gradual improvement and the establishment of routine. Familiarity with the local customs, language, and way of life increases. The expatriate may form friendships and gain a deeper understanding of the culture. Although challenges may persist, they are handled more effectively.
- *Adaptation stage*: This final phase signifies a high level of comfort and integration into the new country. Feelings of isolation and loneliness diminish, and the individual becomes accustomed to daily activities and social circles. While the initial euphoria may not return, a sense of belonging and a feeling of being at home in the new environment are established. The expatriate has successfully mastered the acculturation process.

To address the challenges of cultural shock faced by expatriates effectively, proactive cognitive orientation is important. This involves taking an analytical approach in order to anticipate potential conflicts, identify their underlying causes, and implement effective problem-resolution processes. A deep understanding of cultural shock and its resolution, as well as knowledge about cultural values and social dynamics, is essential. By learning and adopting culturally appropriate behaviours and implementing successful problem-solving strategies, expatriates can lay the foundation for a smooth adaptation process. Organizations can play a pivotal role in supporting expatriates by providing international training and coaching, while also carefully selecting candidates for international assignments who demonstrate the highest potential to navigate the challenges encountered abroad. For further insights, see Sections 11.4, 11.5, and 11.7.

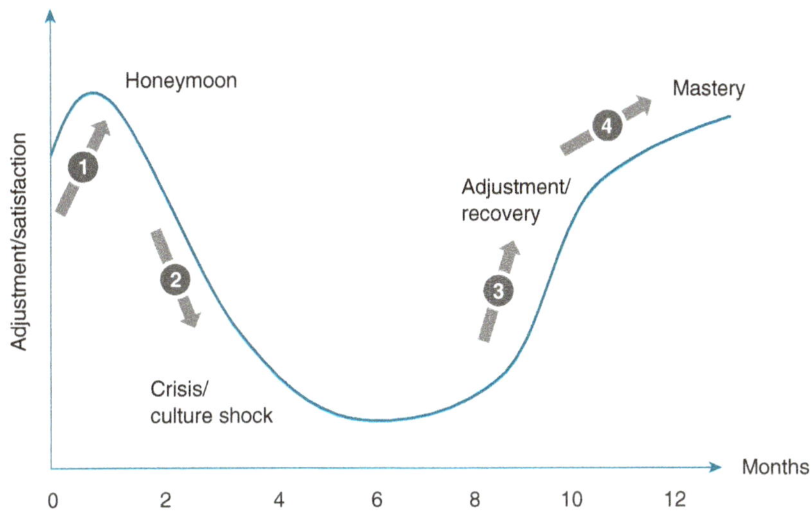

Figure 11.1 The adjustment process of expatriates

11.2.2 Expatriate Failure

Despite its usefulness in managing and overseeing multinational companies (Harzing, 2001), the relocation of expatriates comes with considerable financial, professional, and personal challenges. In fact, expatriate failure, which refers to the premature termination or unsuccessful completion of overseas assignments, presents significant challenges for multinational companies (MNCs). Premature repatriation rates, which can range from 10% to 80% according to Okpara and Kabongo (2011), impose significant costs on both organizations and individuals. Expatriate assignments involve substantial costs, in the first year alone estimated to be at least three times the salary of a domestic counterpart (Shaffer et al., 1999). However, they go beyond direct expenses for salary, travel, relocation, allowances, training, and coaching. These indirect costs can include missed opportunities in new markets, loss of valuable time, potential damage to networks with host-country institutions, and reputational harm. A failed expatriation experience also comes at a substantial personal cost to the individual, such as emotional turmoil, diminished self-esteem and self-confidence, lack of job satisfaction, and reduced motivation.

Expatriate failure can stem from various factors, which might be personal, cultural, or organizational. Personal reasons, such as struggles with adapting to a new environment, feelings of homesickness, or family issues, can contribute to the failure. Cultural challenges, including communication barriers and unfamiliar work practices, also play a significant role. Moreover, organizational factors like inadequate support, insufficient training, or a mismatch between the individual and the assignment can lead to expatriate failure. Researchers have highlighted the importance of the selection process as a key determinant of success or failure (Adler, 1981; Tung, 1982), for example, placing excessive emphasis on technical proficiency while neglecting critical factors such as adaptability, personal and relational abilities, and family circumstances. Additionally, inadequate training and preparation of assigned managers can contribute to underperformance in overseas assignments. Tung (1982) analysed the reasons for expatriate failure in European, US, and Japanese multinationals. Some of the reasons are presented in Table 11.1 (in rank order). As becomes evident in Tung's study, the reasons why expatriates fail vary significantly. Nationality and culture emerge as pivotal determinants of expatriates' performance and the difficulties they tend to encounter. Another noteworthy finding is that, especially for European and US-based firms, it is not solely the expatriate themselves who may encounter challenges leading to expatriate failure. Instead, it is primarily the spouse or family who face difficulties. In contrast, Japanese expatriates tend to struggle more with the increased responsibilities associated with overseas assignments.

Table 11.1 Reasons for failure in expatriation

European MNCs	US MNCs	Japanese MNCs
Spouse having difficulties/being unable to adjust	Spouse having difficulties/being unable to adjust	Difficulty dealing with increased overseas responsibilities
	Manager having difficulties adapting	Struggles with the new environment
	Other family problems	Personal and emotional troubles
	Manager being personally or emotionally immature	Insufficient technical competence
	Difficulty dealing with increased overseas responsibilities	Spouse having difficulties/being unable to adjust

Source: Based on Tung (1982)

To mitigate expatriate failure, organizations should carefully refine their selection criteria and assessment instruments to ensure the selection of candidates possessing the necessary technical, intercultural, and personal competencies. Furthermore, comprehensive pre-departure training and ongoing support during the assignment, for both the expatriate and their family, are vital. Successful management of expatriate assignments necessitates a proactive approach that addresses the personal and organizational dimensions, aiming to enhance cross-cultural adjustment and increase the likelihood of success.

Spotlight: Digital Nomads

The Covid-19 pandemic accelerated the prevalence of digital nomads - individuals who leverage technology to work remotely while travelling. Digital nomads are typically not considered expatriates, however. The global health crisis prompted widespread lockdowns and travel restrictions, forcing companies to adopt remote working models. As traditional office settings became untenable, employees and freelancers embraced the digital nomad lifestyle, combining work and travel in unprecedented ways.

Several factors contributed to an increase in the number of digital nomads during the pandemic. Firstly, advances in digital technology and connectivity made it possible for professionals to perform their tasks from virtually anywhere. Tools such as video conferencing, cloud computing, and collaboration platforms ensured that work could continue seamlessly outside traditional office environments. Secondly, the pandemic-induced shift in corporate culture normalized remote work, making employers more open to flexible work arrangements. Companies recognized that productivity could be maintained or even improved without physical office spaces, leading to a more widespread acceptance of remote work.

Digital nomads make a significant contribution to multinational companies in several ways. They provide access to a diverse talent pool, allowing companies to hire the best professionals regardless of geographic location. This geographic flexibility enables multinational companies to tap into global talent markets, filling skills gaps and bringing diverse perspectives to their teams. Additionally, digital nomads often bring a high degree of adaptability and self-motivation, traits that are invaluable in dynamic and rapidly changing business environments.

The presence of digital nomads can also lead to cost savings for multinational companies. Without the need for physical office space and related overheads, companies can reduce operational costs. Furthermore, digital nomads often work as freelancers or contractors, which can provide financial flexibility and reduce the long-term commitments associated with traditional employment models.

Digital nomads also contribute to innovation in multinational companies. By experiencing different cultures and working environments, they bring fresh ideas and perspectives that can inspire creative solutions and drive innovation. Their unique insights can help companies adapt products and services to different markets, enhancing global competitiveness. Moreover, digital nomads' familiarity with a variety of digital tools and platforms can lead to more efficient workflows and the adoption of cutting-edge technologies.

However, an increase in the number of digital nomads also presents challenges. Ensuring data security and maintaining effective communication across time zones can

(Continued)

be complex. Multinational companies must implement robust cybersecurity measures and develop strategies to foster collaboration and team cohesion among geographically dispersed employees. Additionally, different labour laws and tax regulations across countries can complicate employment arrangements for digital nomads.

Sources: McKinsey (www.mckinsey.com/featured-insights/future-of-work/whats-next-for-remote-work-an-analysis-of-2000-tasks-800-jobs-and-nine-countries)

11.3 INTERNATIONAL STAFFING

There are three distinct staffing policies that organizations can adopt when selecting employees (see Table 11.2). The first policy involves choosing staff from among parent-country nationals (an ethnocentric approach). These individuals are citizens of the multinational company's home country but reside abroad. For instance, a German manager assigned to lead a sales department for Volkswagen in China would fall under this category. The second policy revolves around host-country nationals (a *polycentric* approach), who are local individuals hired by the multinational company. For example, if the sales department in China was led by a Chinese manager, this approach would represent a host-country national staffing policy. The third policy entails recruiting third-country nationals (a geocentric approach), who are citizens of countries other than the multinational's home country or the country where they are assigned to work. An illustration of this policy is a French manager employed by Volkswagen in China.

Table 11.2 International staffing orientations

Ethnocentric	Polycentric	Geocentric
Hire and develop employees of the HQ's home country	Hire and develop employees of the subsidiaries' countries	Hire and develop the best people from around the world

Source: Adapted from Harzing (2004)

When it comes to determining the right staffing policy, different perspectives can guide the decision-making process (see Table 11.3). The ethnocentric perspective entails a focus on the home country, where parent-country nationals are considered more suitable for top management positions, both at the headquarters and in subsidiaries. The polycentric viewpoint, on the other hand, acknowledges the differences between countries and places importance on employing local nationals who possess a better understanding of country-specific factors. Hence, this approach focuses on utilizing local talent for managerial positions. Lastly, geocentrism embodies a globally oriented mindset, emphasizing a broad outlook that transcends national boundaries. Geocentric companies draw talent from a diverse pool of managers worldwide and assign them to positions at the headquarters or subsidiaries irrespective of their nationality.

Table 11.3 Staffing strategies

Staffing strategy	Employees	Advantages	Disadvantages
Ethnocentric	Parent-country nationals	• Managers familiar with company culture: Parent-country nationals are already familiar with the firm's culture, values, and practices, which can result in better and smoother integration into key managerial positions. • Coordination and communication: Communication between HQ and subsidiaries can be easier when placing parent-country nationals in top management positions across subsidiaries. It can also facilitate coordination of operations according to the HQ's vision and objectives. • Knowledge transfer: Parent-country nationals can transfer their knowledge, technical expertise, and best practices from the HQ country to subsidiaries. This helps to replicate proven and standardized policies and processes in other countries.	• Lack of local knowledge: Parent-country nationals may have insufficient knowledge of the local culture, market dynamics, business practices and governmental regulations, which may hinder effective decision-making in foreign markets. • Cultural clashes: Differences in values and ethical norms, communication styles, working practices between local employees and parent-country nationals can lead to cultural conflicts, thereby impeding collaboration, motivation, team cohesion and overall performance. • Limited talent pool: If the firm primarily relies on parent-country nationals, it won't be able to benefit from the diverse perspectives, talents, and skills available in the global labour market. Additionally, the ethnocentric approach offers limited career prospects for host-country nationals (Moore & Enderwick, 2022), which may lead to retention problems of highly qualified talent from inside the subsidiary country. • High costs: Relocating and compensating parent-country nationals can be expensive, as it can involve language training, relocation packages and higher salaries compared to local employees.
Polycentric	Host country nationals	• Local expertise: Hiring host-country nationals allows the firm to benefit from these employees' knowledge of the local culture, market dynamics and business practices, which facilitates decision-making in foreign markets. • Adaptability and acceptance: Host-country nationals are more likely to be accepted and trusted by local employees, customers, and stakeholders, as they share the same nationality. This can allow for smoother operations and potentially lower liabilities of outsidership.	• Limited global perspective: Host-country nationals may have limited exposure to International Business practices and global strategies. Thus, the transfer of knowledge and best practices across subsidiaries might be harder for these employees. • Lack of coordination: Coordination and alignment with the HQ strategies may become more challenging when subsidiaries are managed by host-country nationals, potentially leading to inconsistencies in decision-making and implementation. • Reduced control: As decision-making power is decentralized to local host-country nationals, the HQs may have less direct control over operations in different subsidiaries.
Geocentric	Third country nationals	• Global perspective and synergy: Leveraging the diverse knowledge, expertise, and cultural insights of managers from different countries can foster a global mindset and facilitate the sharing of best practices across the organization. • Flexibility and adaptability: Placing the most qualified individuals in key managerial positions regardless of their nationality, allows the organization to adapt to local market conditions while maintaining a global outlook.	• Visa and work permit challenges: A geocentric approach may be difficult to implement due to employment regulations for foreign nationals. Complex visa requirements, immigration processes and rules for work permits can lead to legal and administrative challenges. • High costs: Relocating managers from different countries can be costly due to training, relocation expenses and compensation packages.

It is important to note that the advantages and disadvantages may vary based on the specific context and industry of the multinational company. Furthermore, staffing patterns are not fixed and can evolve over time, particularly based on the MNC's operational experience. Initially, many MNCs rely on home-country managers to staff their overseas units. However, as the organization gains experience and expands its global presence, there is often a gradual transition towards incorporating more host-country nationals into management positions. This shift allows for a better understanding of local markets, culture, and consumer preferences. Another approach, observed among US and European MNCs, involves deploying home-country nationals in less developed countries and employing host-country nationals in more advanced regions. This strategy leverages the expertise of home-country managers in introducing and implementing established business practices in emerging markets, while benefiting from the local knowledge and networks of host-country managers in more developed regions. A third staffing pattern involves initially assigning a new operation to a home-country manager for supervision and control. However, once the operation is fully established and has adapted to the local environment, there is a transition to a host-country manager who possesses a deeper understanding of the local market dynamics and can manage the operation effectively.

11.4 INTERNATIONAL HIRING

One of the major tasks of IHRM is to select qualified individuals for cross-border assignments. In an era of increasing globalization and multinational operations, organizations are expanding their activities across international borders to tap into new markets, leverage competitive advantages, and foster innovation. As a result, the need for talented professionals who can navigate the complexities of operating in diverse cultural, economic, and regulatory environments has become increasingly important. The recruitment process in international hiring goes beyond traditional recruitment practices, as it requires a careful evaluation of candidates' capabilities, adaptability, and potential to navigate the complexities of global business environments.

IHRM needs to determine the criteria it wants to apply in its international hiring endeavours. They are the foundation for assessing individuals' suitability for overseas assignments and help organizations identify the most qualified candidates who possess the essential attributes to thrive in cross-border roles.

11.4.1 Approaches to International Hiring

The field of international recruitment was initially explored through a seminal study conducted by Tung (1982). By analysing existing literature on the topic, Tung identified four distinct categories of variable that have a significant impact on the success or failure of overseas assignments. These variables, he argued, still serve as valuable guidelines in the recruitment process.

1 *Technical proficiency*: In recruitment to domestic operations, the technical competence of individuals is fundamental in determining their success. This is even more important when appointing to international assignments. Individuals often find themselves physically distant from headquarters, where technical expertise is centralized. As a result, the ability to perform the job effectively without immediate access to peers and superiors can be critical.
2 *Adaptability to environmental factors*: In domestic operations, the ability to identify and work with aspects of the environment, such as governmental regulations, labour unions, competitors, and customers, is important for achieving effectiveness. Similarly, in the international context, candidates must demonstrate their ability to cope with diverse and unfamiliar environmental variables. This includes navigating political landscapes, understanding local market conditions, and adapting to unique cultural, social, and economic circumstances (see Section 11.2 below).
3 *Personal qualities and relational abilities*: The capacity to engage effectively with superiors, peers, subordinates, business partners, and clients is an essential consideration. In international assignments, this variable greatly influences the likelihood of performing successfully. It entails more than knowledge of different cultures; the key lies in the ability to coexist and collaborate with individuals whose value systems, beliefs, customs, etiquette, and business practices may differ significantly from one's own.
4 *Family and individual characteristics*: Recognizing the influence of personal and family factors is vital in the recruitment process. The support and adjustment of family members to the new location can significantly impact an individual's ability to perform optimally in an overseas assignment. Factors such as marital status, dependents, and the spouse's willingness to relocate and adapt to a new environment can have significant implications for success in international roles.

While Tung's findings continue to provide a solid foundation for IHRM in defining recruitment criteria for international managers, many companies today have extended and adapted this list to meet the evolving demands of the global business environment. Drawing from a comprehensive understanding of the complexities involved in international assignments, modern IHRM practices have extended the range of criteria to include:

1 Self-reliance, an entrepreneurial and proactive mindset, and strong sense of the importance of innovation
2 Physical and emotional health
3 Leadership ability (i.e., skill in managing threats and opportunities, working collaboratively, and seeking consensus).

The failure of overseas assignments can attributed in part to deficiencies in the recruitment process. One of the key reasons is the disproportionate focus on a candidate's technical proficiency, neglecting important factors such as adaptability, personal and relational abilities as well as private and family characteristics (see Section 11.2.2). It is equally important to consider the perspective of managers and examine the factors that influence their willingness to embrace overseas assignments. While organizations focus on identifying the right candidates based on various criteria, it is important to recognize that managers may have their own considerations and preferences when it comes to taking on international roles. By aligning organizational criteria with candidates' perspectives, IHRM can create an environment that encourages managers to seize the chance of working abroad and contribute to the success of international operations. Recent research has identified several factors that influence employees' willingness to work abroad:

Marital status: Unmarried employees display a higher level of willingness compared to other groups when it comes to accepting expatriate assignments. Among married employees, those without children at home or with non-teenage children tend to be more open to relocation.

Previous international experience: Employees with prior exposure to international environments and cultures demonstrate a greater inclination to work as expatriates. Their familiarity with different work settings contributes to their readiness to take on overseas assignments.

Career commitment: Individuals who are clearly dedicated to their professional development and have a high level of commitment to their employing organizations are more likely to embrace expatriate roles. The career aspirations and attitudes of an employee's spouse also influence their willingness to relocate overseas.

Organizational support: Employee and spouse perceptions of the organization's support for expatriates have a profound impact on their willingness to work overseas. Comprehensive support systems and resources provided by the organization foster employees' confidence and readiness to undertake international assignments.

Spotlight: Immigration and the US Labour Market

Immigrants play a central role in supporting and enriching the labour market in the United States, impacting economic growth, innovation, and workforce dynamism across various sectors and skill levels. Immigrants fill essential roles in both high-skill and low-skill sectors, addressing labour shortages. In high-skill sectors, immigrants are prominent in science, technology, engineering, and mathematics (STEM) fields, bringing specialized knowledge and driving innovation. They contribute significantly to technology, research, healthcare, and academia. In low-skill sectors, immigrants often take on jobs that are less attractive to native-born workers, such as in agriculture, construction, hospitality, and caregiving. This workforce is important for the smooth functioning and price stability of these industries.

Immigrants also help address demographic challenges. As the native-born population ages, immigrants, who are typically younger, increase the size of the labour force and support the sustainability of social security systems. Their presence helps the workforce be more balanced in terms of age. Entrepreneurship is another area where immigrants have an important role. They are more likely to start businesses, which contributes to job creation and economic dynamism. Immigrant entrepreneurs establish small businesses that serve local communities and create employment opportunities, as well as high-growth companies that drive technological advances. Iconic American companies like Google, Tesla, and Pfizer were founded or co-founded by immigrants, highlighting their significant contributions.

The H1-B visa programme plays a critical role in this dynamic. The H1-B visa allows US companies to employ foreign workers in specialty occupations that require theoretical or technical expertise. However, the annual cap on H1-B visas leads to a lottery system, making it uncertain for both employers and potential employees. This system can limit the ability of US companies to secure the talent they need to remain competitive. The cap and the lottery process can also discourage skilled workers from pursuing opportunities in the US, pushing talent to other countries with more predictable immigration policies.

Despite their contributions, immigrants face challenges such as language barriers, recognition of foreign qualifications, and access to legal status. Policies that support language education, credential recognition, and pathways to citizenship can enhance their ability to contribute fully to the labour market.

Sources: US Citizenship and Immigration Services (www.uscis.gov/working-in-the-united-states/h-1b-specialty-occupations); American Immigration Council (www.americanimmigrationcouncil.org/research/foreign-born-stem-workers-united-states#)

11.5 INTERNATIONAL TRAINING

Retention of expatriates in global operations poses a significant challenge for multinational companies (MNCs). A major contributing factor to expatriate failure is the inability of managers and their spouses to adjust to the new host country environment. Expatriate adjustment can be described as 'the degree of psychological adjustment experienced by the individual within a new society or the degree of psychological comfort and familiarity perceived within a new environment' (Puck et al., 2008: 2183). Recent studies consider adjustment to be multifaceted, consisting of three major dimensions: adjustment to the general environment, adjustment to the work situation and adjustment to interacting with host nationals (Puck et al., 2017). This multifaceted perspective of adjustment makes it evident that some expatriates may be well adjusted in one dimension, while facing difficulties in another. For instance, an expatriate might successfully adapt to their work environment but struggle to engage socially with individuals from the host country (see Section 11.2).

Recognizing the value of preparing expatriates for their future host country environments (see Chapters 2–5), many MNCs now provide pre-departure international training that takes into account the different aspects of adjustment for the expatriate and their family. By offering international training, organizations try to ensure that expatriates are well equipped to navigate the many challenges they may encounter during their assignments and adapt effectively to their new environments. In recent decades, it has been recognized that international training is a valuable strategy in promoting effective adjustment in cross-cultural contexts (Okpara & Kabongo, 2011).

International training programmes can either be standardized or tailor-made.

11.5.1 Standardized Training Programmes

Standardized training programmes are general programmes that managers anywhere in the world can use and benefit from. These programmes encompass various areas such as enhancing quantitative analysis skills or technical competencies that are universally applicable. Moreover, research indicates that certain behaviour-oriented concepts can also be effectively addressed through standardized training programmes, although follow-up initiatives may need to be customized to meet specific country requirements. For instance, programmes focusing on fundamental aspects of communication, motivation, or leadership can be standardized to a certain extent. Another form of standardized training currently provided by large multinational companies (MNCs) addresses cultural differences on a global scale. A notable example is Colgate-Palmolive, which operates in 200 countries, exposing its managers to multiple foreign cultures. For all these foreign markets, however, Colgate-Palmolive offers standardized intercultural awareness training.

11.5.2 Tailor-Made Training Programmes

Tailor-made training programmes are designed to address the specific requirements of participants. For the target audience we are discussing here they would include a substantial amount of culturally oriented material. These programmes are frequently developed by large multinational companies (MNCs) and other organizations with a global presence, and would reflect a sound understanding of the host country's beliefs, norms, attitudes, and values, including those relating to work. These programmes often include valuable insights from managers working in the country or from other individuals with recent firsthand experience.

To ensure the effectiveness of such training, careful attention must be given to the content and sequencing of training materials. In this regard, Yoshida and Brislin (1995) offer guidelines that IHRM professionals can follow when developing tailor-made training programmes. IHRM should guide expatriates through a series of essential steps during their international training. Firstly, expatriates should be able to identify the specific skills required to navigate and thrive in the culture of the host country. Secondly, it is important for them to understand why, where, when, to whom, and how certain behaviours are considered appropriate. Thirdly, they should learn about the culture from colleagues who have lived and worked in the country. By observing and consulting individuals from the target culture, trainees can ensure they behave appropriately. Fourthly, practice is essential as it is through ongoing training that proficiency in new skills is achieved. Finally, dealing with emotional aspects should not be overlooked, as trainees should be prepared for intense emotional reactions to cultural differences and the adoption of new behaviours. Tailor-made training programmes can include the components seen in Table 11.4.

Table 11.4 Components of training

Tailor-made training component	Description
Environmental briefings	Information about the geographical features, climate, housing options, and educational facilities of the host country
Cultural orientation	Acquainting participants with the cultural institutions and value systems prevalent in the host country
Cultural simulations	Programmed learning approaches to expose participants to intercultural encounters and facilitate their cultural adaptation
Language programmes	Develop participants' proficiency in the local language
Sensitivity training	Geared towards cultivating attitudinal flexibility and fostering cultural sensitivity.

Source: Adapted from Puck et al. (2008)

There are two distinct methods that can be used to deliver international training (Gertsen, 1990). The first method is conventional training, characterized by the transmission of information through unidirectional communication. This approach resembles the teaching methods employed in educational institutions such as colleges, universities, and management development centres. In conventional training, instructors primarily impart knowledge to trainees in a lecture-style format. These can include short briefings of the foreign country, lectures held in-person or online or the provision of training material for self-paced learning (e.g., books, online material). In contrast, the second method, known as experimental training, takes a more interactive approach. It involves conducting role plays, creating (simulated) real-life scenarios and hands-on situations that actively engage trainees. This method might also include hands-on training in the country an employee would be locating to. Overall, the implementation and design of an effective expatriate training programme should match the degree of participant involvement with the rigour of the training as presented in Figure 11.2.

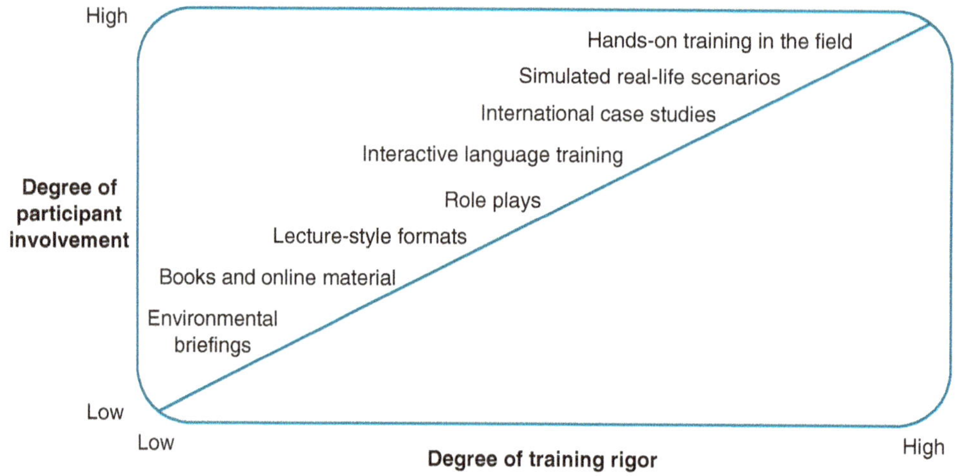

Figure 11.2 Training rigour

Usually, these training programmes are provided to employees before going abroad, although on-site training post-departure is also provided in some cases. Recent research calls for more post-departure training as pre-departure training is not always effective (Puck et al., 2008). Frequent points of criticism are that participants in pre-departure training are prepared for challenges that they may not face (while they may face challenges they are not prepared for), that trainers for pre-departure training are often evaluated based on feedback collected directly after training but before the international assignment (making it impossible for participants to reflect on the usefulness of the content delivered), and that trainers living in a foreign culture will be better able to provide meaning and support than trainers living in the home country of the trainee.

11.6 INTERNATIONAL COMPENSATION

Although international assignments are widely recognized as an effective means of managing multinational companies and overseeing foreign subsidiaries, it is important to acknowledge that their implementation is not without associated costs. Research indicates that the cost of redeploying employees on foreign assignments can, in the first year alone, be more than three times the base salaries of their domestic counterparts (Shaffer et al., 1999; Puck, et al., 2008). The high costs associated with international assignments on the one hand, and the need to maintain executive talent on the other have forced MNCs to evaluate their compensation strategies more carefully.

Putting together suitable compensation packages for expatriate personnel poses a formidable challenge for multinational companies. Such packages have to achieve several objectives: attract suitable talent, facilitate seamless mobility across subsidiaries and offices, while also preserving equity and fairness among diverse staff groups (i.e., parent-country nationals, host-country nationals, and third-country nationals). A suitable compensation package should not only help reduce costs but also foster a strong sense of commitment to the employer, enhance job satisfaction, and cultivate a willingness to undertake international relocations.

Most multinational companies (MNCs) structure their expatriate compensation packages around four core elements: a base salary, incentives, tax considerations, and allowances:

- *Base salary*: The base salary describes the fixed amount of compensation that employees receive for their work.
- *Incentives*: Organizations often provide incentive schemes that complement the compensation package – for example, profit sharing or bonus plans, which are typically based on performance evaluations or competency-based assessments. The rewards can be disbursed in the form of immediate cash payments or deferred payments, depending on the specific arrangements. These incentive plans can be based on home-country practices, host-country practices, or a combination of both, allowing for flexibility and alignment with organizational goals and local market conditions.
- *Tax equalization*: Tax equalization ensures that expatriates are not in a better or worse tax position than if they were working in their home country. Employers calculate the hypothetical tax liability based on the home country's rates and cover any difference between that and the actual tax liability in the host country.
- Allowances: Allowances are additional financial benefits provided to compensate for specific expenses or challenges. There are two main types of allowance commonly included in compensation packages: cost-of-living and hardship allowances. Each serves a specific purpose and contributes to the overall support and well-being of expatriate employees.
- *Cost-of-living allowance*: This allowance (see Table 11.5) is provided to bridge the gap between a higher cost of living in the host country compared to the employee's home location. It covers various expenses, such as housing, education, home-country visits, and relocation costs.

For more detailed descriptions of these allowances, refer to Black et al. (1999). A survey conducted by Suutari and Tornikoski (2001) revealed that the housing allowance was the most commonly provided allowance in expatriate compensation packages, followed by education for dependants and car/transportation. Hardship allowances were found to be included in less than 10% of cases. Despite their relatively lower prevalence, hardship allowances should not be overlooked, especially in light of the current geopolitical landscape. It is a payment made to expatriates who are sent to assignments in areas considered as less desirable. This allowance acknowledges the difficulties and risks associated with working in demanding or challenging environments. Employees stationed in such locations may face isolation, political instability, high crime rates, or natural hazards. Parts of

Europe, the Middle East and China are often considered to be challenging locations. The hardship allowance is paid in the form of a lump sum or as a percentage of the expatriate's base salary and is intended to compensate them for these additional difficulties, representing the employer's commitment to their well-being.

Table 11.5 Components of the cost of living

Component	Function
Housing allowances	Covering costs of housing for expatriates to ensure that their standard of living in the host country remains at a similar level to that in their home country
Transportation allowance	Assisting with transportation-related expenses, such as vehicle maintenance, public transportation fares, or even vehicle leasing with coverage for fuel, insurance and/or a local driver, depending on the circumstances of the assignment location
Travel allowance	Reimbursing travel costs to the home country
Education allowance	Covering costs of private schooling for children
Healthcare allowance	Covering costs of healthcare, medical insurance, and related expenses in the host country. It ensures that employees have access to necessary medical services and can maintain their well-being
Other	Expatriates may also receive financial support with language courses, leisure activities (sports memberships) and more

In summary, a cost-of-living allowance is provided to compensate for the higher expenses associated with living in an expensive area, while a hardship allowance is given to employees working in challenging or adverse environments to compensate for the additional risks and difficulties they encounter. Both allowances serve different purposes and are designed to provide fair compensation to employees based on the circumstances they face in their work locations.

Table 11.6 provides a list of major cities worldwide based on their cost of living. Two of the ten most expensive cities are Asian cities: Hong Kong and Singapore. These two cities are at the top of the ranking and were the most expensive cities for international employees in 2023. Furthermore, the global top ten list includes five European cities, four of them in Switzerland.

11.7 INTERNATIONAL COACHING AND HR DEVELOPMENT

As organizations expand their operations globally, the effective development and management of their expatriate workforce becomes increasingly important. International coaching and HR development strategies play a pivotal role in expatriate management and in facilitating the success and effectiveness of expatriate assignments. In addition to the traditional approaches of training and mentoring, one-to-one professional coaching is a powerful supplement. The interactive nature of coaching aligns well with the multi-faceted expatriate experience. By working closely with expatriate managers, coaches can address their unique contexts, considering the complexity of the circumstances. Moreover, coaching can enhance the effectiveness of training and mentoring programmes, enabling managers to fully leverage the benefits of these interventions.

Table 11.6 The cities with the highest cost of living according to Mercer (2024)

Rank	City	Location
1	Hong Kong	Hong Kong (SAR)
2	Singapore	Singapore
3	Zurich	Switzerland
4	Geneva	Switzerland
5	Basel	Switzerland
6	New York City, NY	United States
7	Bern	Switzerland
8	Tel Aviv	Israel
9	Copenhagen	Denmark
10	Nassau	Bahamas

11.7.1 Definition of International Coaching

Coaching in this context is a means of supporting individuals working on international assignments on a one-to-one basis. It involves structured and focused interactions between a coach and expatriate. The goal is to facilitate positive and lasting changes for the benefit of the person being coached and potentially for other individuals or groups involved in the assignment, such as the expatriate's family.

Coaching and training, despite often being compared, have distinct characteristics (Abbott et al., 2006). Training is designed for a broader audience and follows a predetermined agenda, whereas coaching is a personalized development process that centres on the expatriate's unique circumstances. Coaching takes a holistic approach, addressing not only professional growth but also personal challenges. For instance, if an expatriate experiences a personal crisis, such as a family issue, they can discuss it within a trusting environment with their coach. In an international setting, coaching also plays a crucial role in facilitating meaning-making processes, allowing the expatriate to explore and address deeply ingrained beliefs and behaviours shaped by cultural and cognitive frameworks. Consider a situation in which an expatriate encounters intercultural challenges or misunderstandings while interacting with local employees. In the safe space of the coaching relationship, the expatriate can openly explore and reflect on these issues. The coach can help the expatriate learn about the cultural schemas and identity construction that underlie beliefs and behaviours and that potentially hinder the expatriate's performance. While training is typically conducted at the beginning of an assignment, acculturation is an ongoing process that extends beyond the initial months. It is during this acculturation phase that coaching emerges as a powerful tool, showcasing its effectiveness and value. Rather than viewing coaching as a replacement for training, it is proposed as a complementary intervention (Abbott et al., 2006). By combining coaching with training, organizations can provide comprehensive support that addresses both general knowledge and skill development gained through training and the personalized guidance offered by coaching.

11.7.2 International Coaching and HR

Coaching should be implemented systematically by HR for optimal effectiveness. Although many organisations use it, often it is not as effective as it could be because of unclear and inconsistent use, a dearth of organizational learning on how to manage it effectively, varying coaching quality, and a lack of structured goal setting and evaluation. Those that address these matters and articulate clearly why coaching is necessary are more likely to perceive it as successful and achieve better results – for example, in relation to leadership development and retention of talent.

11.7.3 Finding the Right Coach: Internal vs External

An international executive coach can be either an internal or external professional; each has its advantages. An internal coach is someone within the organization who possesses coaching expertise and is designated to provide coaching support. Internal coaches have a thorough understanding of the organization's objectives, culture, and processes, enabling them to align the coaching with organizational goals. An external coach is often hired specifically for their coaching proficiency, their cross-cultural expertise and impartiality. The independence of external coaches can help create an environment of trust and confidentiality. This allows executives to explore their challenges and areas for growth safely, particularly when discussing sensitive issues that involve critiquing the organization (Abbott et al., 2006). Both internal and external coaches can play a crucial role in guiding expatriates through their personal and professional development journeys, and the choice between them depends on the organization's resources, preferences, and specific coaching needs.

11.7.4 International Coaching Content

Executive coaching is a versatile practice that addresses various topics, including leadership development, performance enhancement, and career transitions. However, international coaching distinguishes itself from general executive coaching through its unique focus on cross-cultural dynamics and the challenges faced by executives working on overseas assignments. International coaching recognizes the importance of navigating cultural differences, adapting to diverse work environments, and developing intercultural competence to achieve success in global business settings.

Working in a foreign environment, expatriates often face challenges in comprehending and adapting to the subtle nuances of a foreign culture. In these situations, international coaching emerges as a valuable resource, serving as a complementary element to broader international training initiatives. Through personalized one-to-one coaching sessions, expatriates can engage in open discussions and reflect on their personal experiences, successes, and failures with their coach. International coaching provides a supportive space for expatriates to seek external perspectives, guidance, and advice, and learn to uncover and deal with the underlying cultural values, norms, and basic cultural assumptions of the foreign culture.

11.8 RECENT DEVELOPMENTS IN INTERNATIONAL HUMAN RESOURCE MANAGEMENT

Recent developments in IHRM reflect changes in the international environment as well as new capabilities and resources available for MNCs. We specifically highlight virtual delegation, diversity, equity, and inclusion, and digital learning opportunities.

Virtual delegation (Holtbrügge & Schillo, 2011) refers to the practice of assigning tasks, responsibilities, or decision-making authority to individuals or teams who are not physically present in the same location as their managers or colleagues. The topic became especially relevant during the Covid-19 pandemic. To some extent, virtual delegates can replace classical expatriates in International Business. Virtual delegations are possible due to the development of new technologies, such as video conferencing, collaboration tools, and project management software to facilitate communication, coordination, and oversight across distances. Research indicates that virtual delegation can enhance organizational flexibility, efficiency, and responsiveness by enabling access to diverse talent pools and reducing operational costs associated with traditional office systems. However, challenges such as maintaining team cohesion, ensuring effective communication, and managing cultural differences across geographically dispersed teams require careful consideration and strategic implementation to maximize their effectiveness.

Another important development in international human resource management is a stronger focus on diversity, equality and inclusion (DEI) (Shen et al., 2009). Beyond compliance with local regulations, multinational companies are increasingly focusing on diversity, equity, and inclusion on a global scale. These initiatives aim not only to address representation across diverse cultures, genders, and backgrounds but also foster a workplace culture that values and respects difference. Companies are developing comprehensive

DEI strategies that include recruitment practices, leadership development programmes, and policies promoting equal opportunities for career development.

As a last recent development, we see that MNCs are increasingly investing in online platforms and virtual classrooms to provide more flexible and personalized training experiences (Škudienė et al., 2020). One objective is to empower employees to enhance their skills at their own pace and from any location. These digital tools can support cross-cultural training by facilitating collaboration among diverse teams and preparing employees for effective engagement across international markets. By leveraging digital learning, companies can track learning outcomes, tailor training initiatives, and cultivate a resilient workforce capable of navigating the complexities of global business environments more effectively.

SUMMARY

International human resource management (IHRM) involves managing personnel deployed across borders, focusing on expatriates, inpatriates, and various staffing policies. Expatriation involves the international relocation of managers, typically parent-country nationals assigned to foreign subsidiaries of multinational companies for a defined period, often two to five years. This trend is fuelled by global business expansion, diversity in workplaces, and the need for specialized skills. Expatriates face challenges like cultural adjustment, which progresses through stages from initial fascination to potential cultural shock, followed by adaptation and integration into the new environment. Expatriate failure, a premature end to assignments, stems from personal, cultural, and organizational factors, highlighting the importance of careful selection, adequate training, and ongoing support to enhance assignment success and mitigate associated costs and risks.

Three staffing approaches – ethnocentric, polycentric, and geocentric – offer different perspectives on selecting employees for international roles. Selection criteria for international managers emphasize adaptability, cultural awareness, and personal characteristics beyond technical skills to enhance assignment success. Comprehensive international training programmes, both standardized and tailor-made, prepare expatriates for the diverse cultural and operational challenges they may encounter. Compensation packages for expatriates include base salaries, incentives, tax equalization, and allowances such as cost-of-living and hardship allowances, ensuring fairness and support. International coaching complements training by providing personalized support to expatriates in navigating cultural differences and professional challenges.

12

GLOBAL SUPPLY CHAIN MANAGEMENT

CHAPTER INTRODUCTION

Navigating the global business environment is a substantial challenge for firms active across nations – particularly in relation to supply chain management (SCM). In this chapter, we introduce some of the basic challenges firms face in this context and present foundational concepts that help businesses make sense of SCM in a global context.

Decades of intense globalization have created international networks of firms operating and distributing products around the world. SCM has emerged as a crucial function that orchestrates the movement of goods, services, and information across national borders. In recent years, multinational companies (MNCs) have witnessed changes and challenges as well as great opportunities. Communication and information technologies have enabled firms to interact and cooperate with each other in new ways. The development of trade agreements has diminished the importance of national borders and made global networks even more important. At the same time, recent developments in geopolitics, health-crises like the Covid-19 pandemic, and changes in national political policies led to a reemergence of some of these borders.

In this chapter, we shed light on the function of global SCM and its importance. We start by reviewing the history of global SCM (12.1) before looking into the activities involved in global SCM (12.2) and the problems that may occur (12.3). We go on to analyse the methods used by firms to design and manage global supply chains (12.4– 12.6) and trends (12.7) in global SCM, which, after years of global trade disruptions, are more relevant than ever before.

LEARNING OUTCOMES

1. Learn about the main theories and activities involved in international supply chain management.
2. Understand how companies plan and execute supply chain management in a dynamic global context.

3. Build resilience into global supply chains and understand why resilience is central in preventing supply chains from breaking down.
4. Relate learning to trends in modern supply chain management, including digitalization, sustainability and practices surrounding re-shoring.

Case Study: The Covid-Shock to Bosch's Global Supply Chain

Bosch, a multinational engineering and technology company, faced substantial disruption in its global supply chain due to the Covid-19 pandemic. The outbreak, which originated in late 2019 and escalated into a global crisis in 2020, had widespread ramifications in various industries, including manufacturing. Bosch, a key player in the automotive, industrial technology, and consumer goods sectors, encountered significant challenges that reverberated across its supply chain.

One of the main effects of the pandemic on Bosch's supply chain was disruption in the flow of materials and components. The virus-induced lockdowns and restrictions imposed by many countries led to the closure of factories and transportation hubs, disrupting the smooth movement of goods. This caused shortages in the supply of critical components, affecting Bosch's ability to manufacture products and fulfil customer orders. The company had to grapple with delays and uncertainties in sourcing raw materials, exacerbating existing challenges in maintaining a just-in-time production model.

Furthermore, the pandemic brought about a shift in consumer behaviour and demand patterns, influencing Bosch's product portfolio. As lockdowns were implemented globally, there was a decrease in consumer spending on non-essential items, impacting the demand for certain Bosch products, such as automotive components and consumer electronics. Conversely, there was a surge in demand for products related to healthcare and home improvement, creating a mismatch in Bosch's production capabilities and market requirements. Adapting to these changing dynamics required the company to reassess its production plans and adjust its supply chain strategies accordingly.

The workforce-related challenges posed another layer of complexity for Bosch during the pandemic. Social distancing measures and lockdowns compelled the company to implement safety protocols within its manufacturing facilities, leading to reduced workforce capacity. This hindered production efficiency and contributed to labour shortages, further impeding Bosch's ability to meet demand. The need to prioritize employee safety also resulted in temporary closures of some production facilities, adding to the overall disruption.

Transportation bottlenecks emerged as a critical concern for Bosch as well. Restrictions on international travel and logistics posed obstacles to the movement of finished goods across borders. This not only led to delays in delivering products to customers but also increased transportation costs due to limited availability and increased demand for freight services. Bosch had to recalibrate its logistics and distribution strategies to navigate these challenges, exploring alternative routes and transportation modes to ensure a more resilient supply chain.

In response to the unprecedented disruptions, Bosch undertook various measures to mitigate the impact and enhance the resilience of its supply chain. The company diversified its supplier base, reducing reliance on specific regions and sources for crucial components. This strategic shift aimed to minimize the risk of supply chain disruptions in the future. Additionally, Bosch embraced digitalization and advanced analytics to enhance visibility into its supply chain, enabling real-time monitoring and quicker response to emerging challenges.

As the global situation evolved, Bosch also demonstrated agility in adapting its production capacity to align with the changing demand landscape. The company engaged in collaborative efforts with suppliers, leveraging communication and coordination to navigate the uncertainties posed by the pandemic. Proactive risk management and scenario planning became integral parts of Bosch's supply chain strategy, allowing the company to anticipate and respond effectively to potential disruption.

Sources: McKinsey (www.mckinsey.com/capabilities/operations/our-insights/how-covid-19-is-reshaping-supply-chains); Bain (www.bain.com/insights/supply-chain-lessons-from-covid-19); Bosch (www.boschaftermarket.com/fr/fr/actualites/dernieres-actualites/supply-chain)

Case Study Questions

1. How has Covid-19 changed the overall optimization in supply chains? How can you trade off resilience and efficiency in supply chains?
2. Which types of risks does nearshoring reduce; which does it possibly increase?
3. How have working environments changed more generally in the aftermath of the Covid-19 pandemic?

12.1 WHAT IS GLOBAL SUPPLY CHAIN MANAGEMENT?

Supply chain management refers to firms' actions to seamlessly integrate the different processes in a product life cycle – from sourcing raw materials, to manufacturing, storing, distributing, and returning the final product. Rapid globalization during the twentieth century brought global SCM into the core of business strategies. Free trade agreements and technological innovations created opportunities for firms to internationalize their supply chains and create a global network of partners and customers. Yet it was not only accessibility to global supply chains that contributed to the importance of the function. The main strategic considerations that contributed to its growing importance were opportunities for market expansion, cost benefits abroad, new customer expectations, the benefits of collaboration, and the need for improved risk management.

- *Market expansion*: The opening of new markets due to free trade agreements and economic liberalization enabled companies to access diverse customer bases and expand their global footprint. Growth is among the most prominent business objectives, to which global SCM can make a significant contribution.
- *Cost benefits*: Cost optimization has impacted the importance of global supply chain management. Offshoring production to countries with lower labour costs and accessing more cost-effective resources became imperative for companies seeking to remain competitive in a globalized economy.
- *Customer satisfaction*: Global SCM is highly relevant to the customer experience. Expectations of timely and reliable deliveries heightened the need for streamlined global supply chains.
- *Collaboration benefits*: Interest in SCM has steadily increased since the 1980s when firms saw the benefits of collaborative relationships within and beyond their own organization.
- *Risk management*: Global SCM has become an important function in managing a firm's risk and resilience performance. With internationalization came increased vulnerability to geopolitical, economic, and natural disruptions. Effective SCM became essential for building resilience and reducing risks.

Some of the central theories we introduced earlier in this book have substantial bearing on global supply chain management. In particular, the resource-based view, transaction cost economics (also referred to as 'transaction cost theory') and institutional theory help us understand global supply chain management (see Chapter 7 – sections 7.1.3 and 7.4.2 – and Chapters 3–5). Here we repeat the most important aspects of those theories, with a focus on supply chain management.

- *Resource-based view (RBV)*: The RBV posits that a firm's competitive advantage lies in its unique resources and capabilities. Through the lens of RBV, firms that can accumulate resources and capabilities that are valuable, rare, inimitable and organizationally embedded will achieve a competitive advantage over competing firms. In the context of international supply chain management, this theory emphasizes the strategic importance of efficient resource allocation and leveraging core competencies to gain a competitive edge. Companies must identify and optimize resources, such as supplier relationships, logistics infrastructure, and information systems, to create a sustainable competitive advantage in global markets (Gligor & Holcomb, 2014).
- *Transaction cost economics (TCE)*: In SCM, TCE helps understand the make-or-buy decision, whereby companies must decide whether to produce components in-house or outsource them from external suppliers. TCE, in its essence, is a theory of governance of transactions related to competence, power, and efficiency (Ketokivi & Mahoney, 2020). In the global supply chain context, TCE helps managers assess the risks, coordination costs and benefits of global sourcing.

By understanding transaction costs, companies can make informed decisions on the most efficient and cost-effective methods of procurement and production.

- *Institutional theory*: Institutional theory explores how organizations' actions and structures are influenced by social norms, regulations, and cultural practices. In the realm of global supply chain management, understanding institutional contexts is crucial. Companies must adapt their supply chain strategies to comply with diverse regulations, cultural norms, and ethical considerations in various countries, which may differ significantly from their home market (Kauppi, 2013).

Case Study: International Supply Chains in Ancient Rome

The Roman Empire (27 BCE-396 CE) is known for its innovation and remarkable civilization in history. The enormous territory, diverse population, and advanced administrative structures all contributed to sophisticated supply chain networks which enabled not only military activities but also economic and societal advances. This case study describes aspects of international supply chain management activity in the Roman Empire which emphasize the innovative power and impact of this period in history for International Business.

- *Procurement*: The empire's vast expanse was used for regional specialization in various industries. Marble was quarried in specific provinces, while iron and other metals were mined elsewhere. Roman administrators implemented a system of taxation and resource allocation that ensured a steady supply of raw materials to urban centres, contributing to economic growth. The Roman military contracted with private suppliers for a variety of equipment and supplies. These contracts specified quality, quantity, and delivery timelines, reflecting a rudimentary form of procurement and supplier management.
- *Warehousing*: The Roman Empire utilized warehouses strategically positioned along trade routes and military routes. These warehouses served as hubs for storing and redistributing goods efficiently. Stored goods were labelled and inventoried, an early example of inventory management. With their advanced storage systems, the Romans were able to preserve food and resources around the year.
- *Logistics*: The Roman Empire was able to build a sophisticated and comprehensive network of roads, which facilitated efficient supply chains. These roads connected far-flung regions of the empire. The roads enabled the troops, goods, and information to be moved quicky, reducing transportation time and costs. This infrastructure laid the foundation for effective supply chain management.

Sources: SCM Globe (www.scmglobe.com/supply-chains-roman-empire) and Bryan Mawr (https://bmcr.brynmawr.edu/1999/1999.11.01)

12.2 ACTIVITIES IN GLOBAL SUPPLY CHAIN MANAGEMENT

Global SCM includes various activities that together ensure a smooth flow of goods, services, and information across international borders. In this section, we highlight the key activities that form the backbone of the physical supply chain including procurement, manufacturing, inventory management, logistics management, return management, and the various digital aspects of supply chain planning, such as sales and operations planning (S&OP) and demand forecasting (see Figure 12.1).

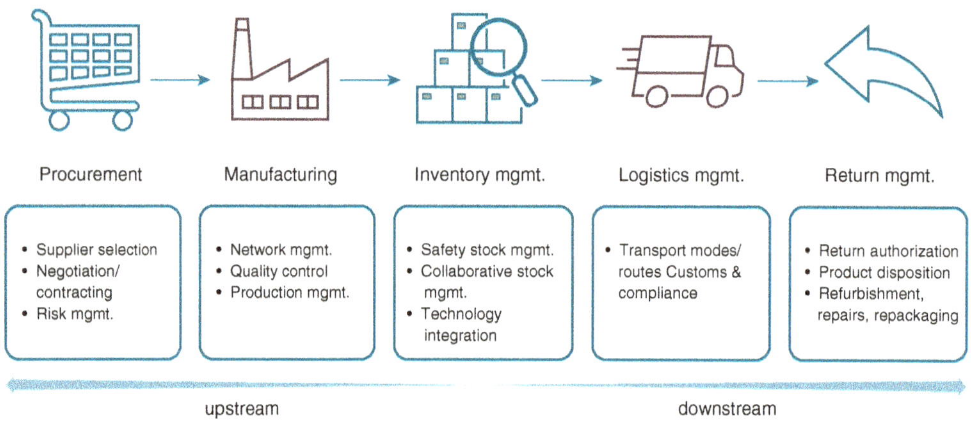

Figure 12.1 Activities in supply chain management

12.2.1 Procurement

Procurement is a fundamental activity in global SCM that involves the sourcing and acquisition of raw materials, components, and finished goods from suppliers located in different countries. Effective procurement is crucial for businesses seeking to optimize costs, ensure product quality, and reduce supply chain risks. In the context of international supply chains, procurement managers face unique challenges, such as navigating complex trade regulations, managing currency fluctuations, and building strong supplier relationships across borders.

The main activities involved in procurement are supplier selection and evaluation, negotiation and contracting, and risk management.

- *Supplier selection and evaluation*: Identifying reliable suppliers who can meet quality, cost, and delivery requirements is essential. This process involves conducting thorough evaluations, considering factors such as supplier capabilities, financial stability, and ethical practices.
- *Negotiation and contracting*: Negotiating favourable terms with international suppliers requires an understanding of cultural differences, international trade

laws, and contract management principles to ensure that both parties' interests are considered.
- *Risk management*: Supply chain disruptions can occur due to geopolitical tensions, natural disasters, or economic fluctuations. The procurement function must implement risk mitigation strategies, such as dual sourcing or buffer stock, to enhance supply chain resilience.

12.2.2 Manufacturing

Manufacturing, often considered the heart of the supply chain, involves transforming raw materials and components into finished products. In global SCM, manufacturing activities can be distributed across various countries to leverage cost advantages, access specialized skills, and reduce time-to-market. However, coordinating global manufacturing processes introduces complexities that require efficient communication and collaboration.

Among the key aspects of manufacturing in global SCM are setting up a global production network, providing quality control mechanisms and applying lean manufacturing principles.

- *Global production networks*: Companies strategically distribute production facilities across different countries, forming global production networks to optimize costs and enhance efficiency. This requires the international management of each production facility, either owned or outsourced.
- *Quality control and standards*: Ensuring consistent product quality across geographically dispersed manufacturing sites requires standardized quality control procedures and compliance with international quality standards.
- *Lean manufacturing and just-in-time (JIT) practices*: Lean principles and JIT practices are often employed to minimize waste, reduce inventory holding costs, and improve overall production efficiency.

12.2.3 Inventory Management

Inventory management aims to strike a delicate balance between maintaining adequate stock levels to meet customer demands while minimizing holding costs and risk of obsolescence. In global supply chain management, effective inventory management is particularly critical due to longer lead times and increased uncertainty associated with global transportation and customs procedures.

Important elements of inventory management are (safety) stock management, collaborative inventory management, and the integration of key technologies.

- *Safety stock and lead time management*: Maintaining safety stock levels becomes imperative in the face of unpredictable lead times, ensuring that supply disruptions do not impact customer satisfaction.

- *Collaborative inventory management*: Collaboration with suppliers and customers enables better demand forecasting and inventory planning, leading to reduced stockouts and increased supply chain responsiveness. It also entails the storage of inventories at the suppliers' or customers' facilities.
- *Technology integration*: Leveraging advanced technologies, such as Internet of Things (IoT) sensors and RFID tagging, facilitates real-time visibility into inventory levels, helping organizations make data-driven decisions.

12.2.4 Logistics Management

Logistics management is concerned with the physical movement and distribution of goods. Logistics management can be divided into inbound and outbound logistics. The former is concerned with the import of raw materials, whereas the latter describes the transport of (finished) goods.

In an international context, logistics management in global SCM includes, for example, the selection of transportation modes and routes, and customs clearance and compliance.

- *Transportation modes and routes*: Selecting appropriate transportation modes, whether by air, sea, rail, or road, depends on factors such as urgency, cost, and the nature of the goods being transported.
- *Customs and compliance*: Managing customs clearance and compliance with import and export regulations is crucial to avoid delays and penalties at international borders.

12.2.5 Returns Management

Reverse logistics, also known as returns management, deals with the handling of returned goods, repairs, or recycling of products. In international supply chain management, returns management takes on added complexities due to cross-border logistics and compliance with regulations relating to product returns.

Returns management in international supply chain management is primarily concerned with return authorization, product disposition and recycling, and product refurbishment and repairs.

- *Return authorization and return merchandise authorization processes*: Implementing efficient return authorization procedures ensures that customers and suppliers follow standardized processes for returns.
- *Product disposition and recycling*: Organizations must devise eco-friendly and cost-effective methods for recycling or disposing of returned products, considering environmental sustainability.
- *Product refurbishment and repairs*: Streamlining refurbishment and repair processes helps organizations recover value from returned products and minimize waste.

12.2.6 Planning

Planning is an integral part of global supply chain management, guiding decision-making and resource allocation to align supply with demand. Effective planning ensures that companies can meet customer expectations, optimize inventory, and respond to dynamic market conditions.

Key aspects of planning in international supply chain management include sales and operations planning (S&OP) and demand forecasting. Sales and operations planning (S&OP) is a collaborative process that aligns sales forecasts, production plans, and inventory management to maintain an optimal balance between demand and supply. Accurate demand forecasting is important for planning procurement, manufacturing, and inventory levels. Forecasting methods, such as statistical analysis and market intelligence, are applied to predict future customer demands.

Case Study: How SCM Can Save Lives: The Blood Supply Chain

The supply chain of blood is, due to the characteristics of blood, an interesting as well as challenging topic regarding various topics and themes within the field of supply chain management. The constant conflict between shortage and waste makes this supply chain exceptionally challenging.

The blood supply chain is made up of the following four components and actors: donors (as 'suppliers'), blood banks (as 'production'), and hospitals and patients (as 'customers'). Throughout this chain, constant testing, processing, cooling and storing of the transfusions is required. Due to its perishability, the variety of blood groups and Rhesus factors, as well as geographical dispersion, supply chain planning is a pivotal function in this chain.

The supply chain of blood shows a moderately high level of stability and forecasting ability in the long run but is determined by spontaneous fluctuations of demand as an extra level of planning difficulty. Resources are scarce, potentially lifesaving, and therefore of extreme importance for the efficiency of healthcare services and public health. Hospitals try to avoid shortage since the lack of available transfusions could have crucial effects on lives. However, over-planning and ordering may lead to wastage, which is unacceptable due to the value of the product. This context illustrates very well the balance between over- and under-supply which supply chain managers must try to achieve.

Sources: Alghamdi (2023) and Williamson & Devine (2013)

Case Study Questions

1 What are the motivations behind blood donations?
2 How can financial incentives support or possibly hinder blood donation?

12.3 PROBLEMS IN INTERNATIONAL SUPPLY CHAIN MANAGEMENT

Managing a global supply chain presents numerous challenges that can have a significant impact on the efficiency, stability, and profitability of MNCs. Navigating global markets requires a thorough understanding of the risks, challenges, and regulatory landscapes that affect international supply chain management. In this section, we therefore elaborate on various sources of disruption, regulation, trade-barriers, and the bullwhip effect in international supply chains.

12.3.1 Risk and Disruptions

Supply chain disruptions are various kinds of uncertain events that disrupt flows of goods and services. Disruptions can be classified by their impact, frequency, and sources. The scale of the impact of disruptions can be categorized in two typologies: (a) idiosyncratic disruptions that affect a single relationship and (b) broader disruptions of an entire region or industry (Grossman et al., 2023). By their uncertain occurrence and rare frequencies, Global value chain (GVC) disruptions are clearly distinguishable from recurring risks such as operational demand fluctuations. These types of risk do not entirely map onto the classifications of risk we introduced earlier (in Chapter 9, Section 9.1) but a comparison can serve as a basis for an instructive discussion.

Disruption can originate from a variety of sources. In an international context, political disruptions (e.g., the election of a protectionist party) can pose significant challenges to MNCs. Environmental disruptions cover geophysical, meteoritical, hydrological, climatological, and biological forces that trigger natural catastrophes which hit entire ecosystems (Oh & Oetzel, 2022). Environmental catastrophes, erratic and often powerful, can pose tremendous challenges to a firm's international supply chains. A defining external, global disruption in recent years has been the Covid-19 pandemic. As well as putting enormous pressure on the healthcare systems, the abrupt impact on global trade stress-tested many firms and institutions.

Other environmental catastrophes also provide severe threats to international supply chains. Wildfires in many parts of North America and Europe, flooding in Germany in the summer of 2021, and the earthquake in Japan in 2011 causing a tsunami that hit Fukushima's nuclear power plant are examples of environmental disruptions that severely impacted international supply chains. The latter particularly impacted GVCs of the automobile industry and the food supply chain, causing shortages, unsatisfied customer demand and other negative economic effects (Oh & Oetzel, 2022). As natural catastrophes become more prevalent as a result of climate change, MNCs will need to consider adaptations to their value chains to brace for future events.

12.3.2 Regulations and Trade Barriers

Global supply chains embed firms in national, regional, and transnational legal regimes, the complexity of which shapes the way MNCs *can* and *must* engage in international operations. Tax law (discussed in Chapter 9, Section 9.5.2), IP law and legal structures of MNCs cover aspects of legal entitlement relating to the creation and distribution of value within supply chains. When complying with new regulations, firms might respond by reconfiguring their supply chain structure.

Trade barriers are an important political instrument in addressing relations between two or more countries. They represent a restrictive trade policy that aims to motivate firms to relocate the international activities of their value chain to different countries or regions. Restrictive trade barriers might be reinforced by populist and nationalist sentiments in a country and can lead to more regionalized supply chains (Ciravegna & Michailova, 2022). Additionally, the shift towards regional and bilateral trade policies instead of multilateral agreements illustrate the move to regional rather than global value chains (Zhan, 2021).

However, as the US infant formula crisis in 2022 demonstrates (see the case study below), restrictive trade policies and protectionist measures do not always achieve the intended results. What are often referred to as 'de-globalized' supply chains often promise increased resilience, yet they can create rigidity and limit flexibility through a lack of global alternatives.

Case Study: The US Infant Formula Crisis in 2022

It goes without saying that food and nutrition play an essential role in sustaining human life and therefore command a high priority in policymakers' decision making. However, in 2022, parents and caregivers in the United States who depended on infant formulas to meet health and nutritional needs were confronted with significant, at times dramatic, shortages. Over a short period of time national weekly out-of-stock rates of infant formula products skyrocketed from 28% at the end of February to more than 74% at the end of May.

The international infant formula trade relies heavily on China, where infant formula is in high demand and there is a willingness to pay for imported infant formula products. China is by far the world's largest export destination, accounting for 27% of international infant formula trade volume in 2021. It is followed by the UK with 5%. The United States, on the other hand, is a net infant formula exporter, with an average annual export volume until 2021 that sat at around seven times its import volume, mostly to Canada. Other net exporters are the Netherlands, France, New Zealand, and Ireland. Although there is, as just described, some international trade in infant formula, it is limited by a range of regulatory

(Continued)

requirements, certifications, and specifications on top of extensive tariff regimes. Consequently, about 80% of global infant formula production is consumed domestically. The regulatory environment not only limits the volume traded but also hampers trade flexibility and complicates adjustments. Looking at the state of the US market immediately prior to the 2022 crisis, domestic suppliers of baby formula in the US were highly concentrated. Three domestic producers - Abbott, Mead-Johnson, and Nestlé - supplied about 98% of all infant formula domestically. We can subsequently conclude that US infant formula production is highly protected and 'near shored'.

In 2022, whilst the world was already facing unprecedented disruptions, the US was hit by a shock as stocks of infant formula began to run dangerously low. By the beginning of May 2022, the out-of-stock rates of infant formula in retail stores nationwide had reached 43% (Weixel, 2022), and out-of-stock rates grew further until end of May. Over the course of an FDA investigation at one of the largest production sites, Abbott Nutrition's Sturgis plant, unsanitary conditions were found. The investigation was prompted by reports of illness and even deaths caused by Cronobacter bacterial infections in infants who had previously consumed infant formula produced at the Sturgis plant. Following the investigation, the FDA swiftly moved to effect the immediate closure of the Sturgis plant. At the time, the Sturgis plant accounted for around 20% of infant formula production in the US and thus subsequently severely impacted the availability of infant formula products in the US. The situation was aggravated by the US's inability to easily mitigate the shortage by way of imports due to the trade barrier regime. The shortage started to improve slightly by mid-August due to a variety of factors, including the eventual reopening of the Sturgis plant, efforts from other industry players to increase availability, and a decrease in consumer stockpiling behaviour. Although the Sturgis plant resumed production in June 2022, it faced further setbacks due to flooding, resulting in temporary closures, and a gradual resumption of production started from 1 July 2022.

Overall, the US's trade regime of infant formula severely limited its ability to offset domestic production shortfalls with imports. While the hasty temporary revision of the rigid US import regime helped ease supply shortages, it could not, in the short run, entirely compensate for the massive disruption caused by the Sturgis plant closure. The fact that infant formula was almost entirely produced in the US did not increase its resilience. On the contrary, the lack of competition and potential substitutes due to a protectionist trade policy which came in the form of a complex mix of tariff-rate quotas and non-tariff barriers has led to unusually high levels of concentration. All in all, this case illustrates the downside of 'de-globalized' supply chains. Whilst they often promise increased resilience, they can create rigidity and limited flexibility due to the lack of global alternatives.

Sources: Federal Trade Commission (www.ftc.gov/system/files/ftc_gov/pdf/infant_formula_report_final.pdf#:~:text=URL%3A%20https%3A%2F%2Fwww.ftc.gov%2Fsystem%2Ffiles%2Fftc_gov%2Fpdf%2Finfant_formula_report_final.pdf%0AVisible%3A%200%25%20) and White House (www.whitehouse.gov/briefing-room/statements-releases/2022/05/12/fact-sheet-president-biden-announces-additional-steps-to-address-infant-formula-shortage)

12.3.3 The Bullwhip Effect

In the complex web of global supply chains, the bullwhip effect represents a phenomenon that echoes through the system, creating ripples of inefficiency, excess inventory, and increased costs. Also known as the Forrester effect, it refers to the amplified fluctuations in orders and inventory levels as they move upstream from consumers to suppliers. While the bullwhip effect is observed in many supply chains, its impact is particularly present in the context of international supply chain management, where extended lead times, diverse markets, and tangled logistics add complexity.

At its core, the bullwhip effect arises from information distortion and communication gaps among supply chain partners. It begins innocuously with slight variations in consumer demand at the downstream end of the supply chain. These fluctuations are magnified as they travel upstream, creating a demand signal that ripples with increasing intensity (see Figure 12.2).

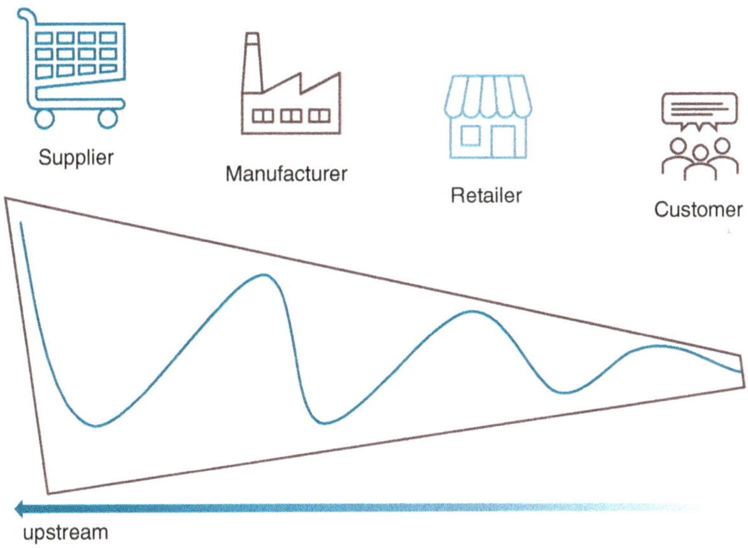

Figure 12.2 The bullwhip effect

12.4 METHODS IN INTERNATIONAL SUPPLY CHAIN MANAGEMENT

Successful management of global supply chains requires the implementation of methods and strategies that help MNCs to ensure smooth operations and a competitive advantage. The disruptions that affect international flows of goods and services (see Section 12.3) have increased the focus on building resilient supply chains.

Resilience is defined as the ability of a firm to rapidly adapt to shocks, ensuring it can continue to operate and avoid prolonged disruptions. A resilient supply chain can mitigate disruptions, reduce vulnerability, and facilitate swift recovery by adapting its operational strategy. Resilience is often characterized by a high level of visibility across the supply chain, sophisticated risk management strategies, flexibility in response to internal and external changes, and strong collaborative relationships among the members of the supply chain.

In general, we can distinguish between two categories of resilience strategy. On the one hand are preventive strategies to improve supply chain resilience before disruption takes place. They include not only forecasting, simulations, and evaluation of potential future events and their effects, but also flexible and robust improvements to the different supply chain sections. On the other hand are recovery strategies during disruption and afterwards when a company needs to swiftly understand the damage, find appropriate solutions and implement them.

12.4.1 Preventive Resilience Strategies: Designing the International Supply Chain

The design of a global supply chain design which is developed and set up before any disruptive event usually includes different structural choices, such as various distribution systems and decisions about integration vs outsourcing. In global SCM, factors such as geographical distance, trade regulations, competitive advantage, and market demand influence the design of distribution networks. In the face of potential disruption, such as geopolitical tensions or natural disasters, a sophisticated network provides the flexibility to re-route supply flows efficiently.

12.4.1.1 Insourcing vs Outsourcing

When designing an international supply chain, MNCs need to consider levels of integration – decisions about who carries out a particular supply chain activity and where. This is often referred to as the 'make or buy decision'. In an integrated supply chain, the lead firm carries out most parts of the value chain itself (i.e. it is internalized). This minimizes the number of intermediaries, and the lead firm has more control over the process and is more visible. This does not necessarily mean that the supply chain is localized. The lead firm might decide to offshore certain activities, to low-cost countries for example, to benefit from cost advantages. This is called captive offshoring (Tallman, 2011). Yet, due to quality, cost, and time advantages, firms might decide to outsource certain parts of their supply chain, either domestically (onshore) or abroad (offshore) (see Figure 12.3).

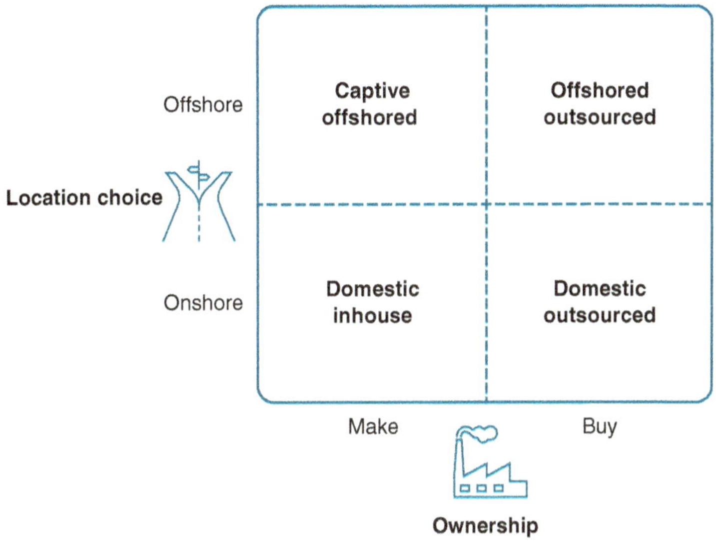

Figure 12.3 Outsourcing and offshoring

12.4.1.2 International Distribution Systems

Optimizing the network of distribution systems is critical in enhancing supply chain efficiency, reducing lead times, and managing costs (see Figure 12.4). In global supply chain management, factors such as geographical distance, trade regulations, and market demands influence the design of distribution networks. Methods such as multi-echelon distribution, cross-docking, and intermodal transport can improve a firm's performance and resilience. Employing multi-echelon distribution networks involves placing regional distribution centres or warehouses strategically in various countries to minimize transportation costs, improve response times, and enhance customer service levels. Cross-docking is a practice that streamlines distribution by eliminating the need for storage. Goods are unloaded from inbound shipments and immediately reloaded onto outbound shipments, reducing inventory holding costs, and expediting order fulfilment. In an international context, intermodal transport is often a prerequisite. Utilizing multiple transportation modes (e.g., sea, air, rail, road) in an integrated manner optimizes global transportation routes and can lead to cost savings and reduced lead times.

The internationalization process of a firm raises questions about how to manufacture, store, and sell a product in a new market. Depending on the choice of distribution channel, the system might consist of retailers, wholesalers, and other 'middlemen'. Whilst these can support a firm – with local knowledge or market access for example – they can also make international distribution systems more complex, less transparent, and inefficient.

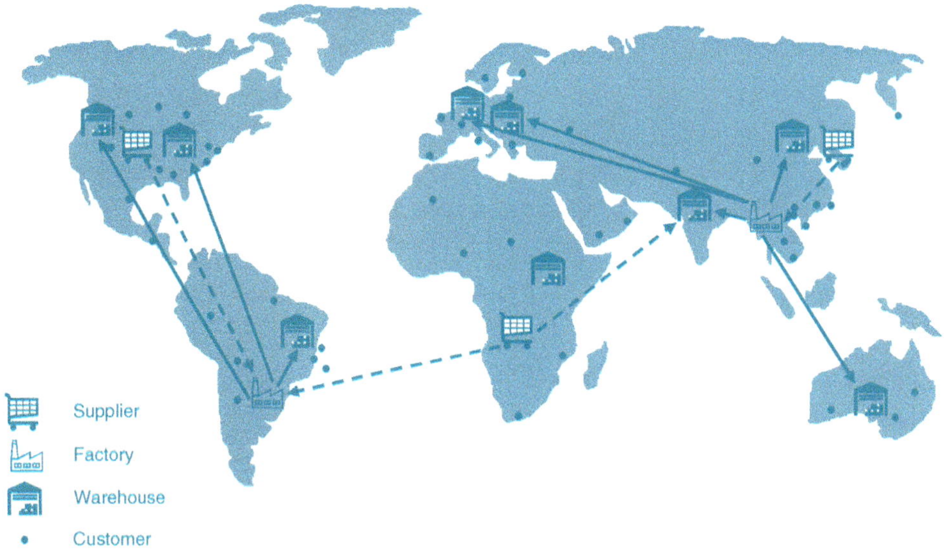

Figure 12.4 An example of an international distribution system

12.4.2 Recovery Resilience Strategies: Managing the International Supply Chain

Recovery resilience strategies come into play when disruptions occur despite preventive measures. These strategies are geared towards minimizing downtime, restoring operations quickly, and learning from the experience to improve future preparedness. Effective inventory management is crucial in international supply chain management, where longer lead times, uncertain transportation, and customs procedures can impact stock levels. Adopting inventory control techniques, such as just-in-time (JIT), 5S methodology, and demand forecasting techniques ensures that companies maintain the right amount of inventory to meet customer demands while minimizing holding costs and obsolescence risks.

- *JIT (just-in-time)*: JIT is a lean production method aimed at minimizing waste and reducing inventory levels. In an international context, it relies on efficient logistics, accurate demand forecasting, and close collaboration with suppliers to ensure materials arrive precisely when needed in the production process.
- *5S methodology*: Originating from Japanese lean manufacturing principles, the 5S methodology focuses on organizing and optimizing workspaces to improve efficiency and productivity. The five steps – sort, set in order, shine, standardize, and sustain – can be applied in international supply chain operations to create clean, organized, and standardized work environments, reducing errors and enhancing overall effectiveness.

- *Demand forecasting techniques (DFT)*: Accurate demand forecasting is essential for managing international supply chains. Leveraging statistical methods, historical data, market intelligence, and technological advances like machine learning and demand forecasting enable organizations to anticipate customer demands more accurately, reducing the risk of stockouts or excess inventory. For firms that operate internationally, demand forecasting for each market is important as products and inventories are often allocated to specific countries/regions, for labelling or regulatory reasons for example. The point where inventory is not interchangeable across markets is called the 'point of differentiation' – for example, once the label in a certain language is affixed. Pooling the demand (and inventory) of multiple regions or sales channels (online sales and physical sales), for example, reduces uncertainties (Bimpikis & Markakis, 2016). This is often referred to as a 'postponement' strategy as the point of differentiation is postponed.

Spotlight: The Suez Canal and Its Missing International Alternatives

The Suez Canal represents one of the most important transportation routes worldwide, connecting Europe and Asia. As shipping transport has increased in popularity the Suez Canal's importance has also risen. Additionally - due to many adaptions and expansions - the canal can harbour all container ships, nearly all bulk carriers and more than half of the fleet of international tankers. Overall, the past, present and future importance of the Suez Canal in connection with supply chains is clear. Therefore, the six-day blockage starting on 23 March 2021 had a significant impact on global supply chains by stopping more than 400 vessels and generating tremendous costs for the affected companies (Lee & Wong, 2021). These costs included not only those relating to delayed deliveries and the goods themselves, but also additional expenditure on solving the supply chain disruption. The blockage caused both short- and long-term effects. In the short term, increased shipping costs and oil prices had an impact on global markets. Short-term measures for recovery during the blockage included finding alternative routes for transportation (Lee & Wong, 2021). In the long term, there has been research into improving supply chain resilience and preventive strategies in case of future disruptions. Many companies have an interest in these preventive and recovery measures, which include diversification of transport options such as the search for alternative routes and use of railways. The Northern Sea Route might be an alternative in the future if weather conditions continue to change due to global warming. However, currently there is no comparable alternative to the Suez Canal as far as time, distance, and efficiency are concerned (Imamkulieva & Kondakova, 2022).

Sources: Imamkulieva & Kondakova (2022); Lee & Wong (2021)

12.5 SUSTAINABILITY IN GLOBAL SUPPLY CHAINS

Sustainable supply chain management integrates environmental and social considerations into the various activities of international supply chains. Sustainable supply chain management can have various triggers – for example, incentives or regulation by governments, and pressure from customers and stakeholders. In an international context, developed countries have gained an increased awareness of business practices abroad (Seuring & Müller, 2008).

Yet there are hindering factors that deter the implementation of more sustainable supply chain practices. Amongst these are costs, complexity in coordination, too little effort to communicate with supply chain partners, and a lack of management commitment (Seuring & Müller, 2008; Tay et al., 2015). However, improving collaboration and communication across supply chain partners have the potential to play a positive role in making supply chains more sustainable, as can the commitment of senior management and supportive cultures.

Sustainable supply chain management involves responsible sourcing of materials, reducing carbon footprints through efficient logistics and transportation networks, adopting eco-friendly packaging, and promoting ethical labour practices. Whilst there are many more mechanisms that foster sustainability, we now want to focus on circularity, de-globalization/nearshoring and packaging.

12.5.1 Circular and Closed Loop Supply Chains

Embracing circular supply chain principles involves designing products for durability, repairability, and recycling. Companies are moving towards creating closed-loop systems in which products and materials are continuously reused and repurposed, minimizing waste and resource consumption. Besides the positive environmental impact, firms can potentially achieve cost-savings and resource security by re-using waste as input materials. Closed loop and circular supply chains are, however, hard to implement, as the existing, linear infrastructure often remains more efficient.

12.5.2 Nearshoring

In response to environmental and social concerns, geopolitical uncertainties, and disruptions caused by the Covid-19 pandemic, organizations are reevaluating their global supply chain strategies. This involves reducing dependency on distant suppliers and considering nearshoring options to bring production closer to end markets. Nearshoring is aimed at improving supply chain flexibility, reducing lead times, and mitigating risks associated with extended supply chains. However, as the underlying rationale of globalization has not significantly changed and trade-offs need to be considered (see the case study on the US infant formula crisis in 2022 earlier in this chapter) it remains unclear whether this 'trend' will continue and disrupt the international supply chain system.

12.5.3 Sustainable Packaging

Sustainable packaging solutions, such as biodegradable materials and reusable packaging, are gaining popularity in international SCM. Eco-friendly packaging not only reduces environmental impact but also aligns with consumer demand for environmentally responsible products. Firms have two main mechanisms for sustainable packaging: using sustainable materials or less material. From a supply chain perspective, it is important to take all factors into consideration that affect the environmental impact of a certain packaging decision. Reusable glass bottles, for example, might require less glass, yet the bottles need to be heavier to be refillable and not to break on the filling line. This in turn has consequences for logistics capacity – as the reusable bottles are heavier, fewer bottles will be transportable on a truck. In an international context, the process of making packaging more sustainable might be hindered by local regulations and infrastructure as well as market preferences.

Spotlight: The EU's Supply Chain Directive

The European Union's Supply Chain Directive, introduced to address environmental and social concerns, is poised to have substantial effects on global supply chain management. The directive, which focuses on corporate responsibility and sustainability, is likely to influence how businesses operate worldwide, impacting both EU and non-EU companies engaged in international trade.

One major effect of the EU Supply Chain Directive is increased scrutiny on environmental and social aspects throughout the entire supply chain. Companies operating in or trading with the EU will need to ensure compliance with the directive's stringent requirements regarding human rights, labour conditions, and environmental sustainability. This not only affects EU-based businesses but also has ripple effects on global suppliers and partners who will be compelled to adhere to these standards to maintain their relationships with EU entities.

The directive's emphasis on due diligence is another critical aspect that will reshape global SCM. Businesses will be required to conduct thorough assessments of their supply chains to identify and mitigate any adverse environmental or social impacts. This may necessitate greater transparency and collaboration with suppliers, pushing for more sustainable and ethical practices throughout the supply chain. This shift towards comprehensive due diligence could become a benchmark for responsible business conduct globally, influencing supply chain practices beyond EU borders.

(Continued)

Furthermore, the directive may lead to increased demand for sustainable sourcing and production practices. Companies that wish to remain competitive within the EU market will have to adapt their supply chains to meet the directive's requirements, which could stimulate the development of new standards and certification, fostering a global push towards environmentally friendly and socially responsible business operations.

The Supply Chain Directive is likely to prompt a reassessment of risk management strategies in global SCM. Companies will need to consider not only traditional risks such as market fluctuations and geopolitical tensions but also the risks associated with non-compliance with the directive's sustainability requirements. This shift in risk perception may encourage a more holistic and long-term approach to supply chain planning and management.

Sources: European Commission (https://commission.europa.eu/business-economy-euro/doing-business-eu/corporate-sustainability-due-diligence_en); The Guardian (www.theguardian.com/world/2024/mar/15/eu-approves-watered-down-human-rights-and-supply-chain-law) and World Economic Forum (www.weforum.org/agenda/2024/03/eu-human-rights-environment-due-diligence-supply-chains)

12.6 AGILITY IN GLOBAL SUPPLY CHAINS

The term 'agility' can be defined as the ability of an organization to succeed under changing circumstances. In more detail, it is understood to be: 'the ability to thrive and prosper in an environment of constant and unpredictable change' (Maskell, 2001: 5); 'all about customer responsiveness and mastering market turbulence' (Van Hoek et al., 2001: 127); 'a business-wide capability that embraces organizational structures, information systems, logistics processes and, in particular, mindsets' (Christopher and Towill, 2000: 236). In other words, an agile firm successfully designs and manages its products, processes, and organization in a way that enables it to respond quickly to changes in its environment (Prater et al., 2001). With the increase in disruption, external shocks from various sources (see Section 12.3), and globalized and customized supply chains (Maskell, 2001), agility has become a key topic in international SCM.

Agility is often associated with flexibility and speed (Prater et al., 2001). Often, a firm's international supply chain is not able to adapt as quickly and reliably as the rest of the organization due to the complexity involved in supply chains after decades of intense globalization. For this reason, firms implement strategies which seek to improve agility in their supply chains. Customer prosperity, skills, knowledge within the company and tight cooperation with supply chain partners are important factors that positively influence agile manufacturing processes (Maskell, 2001). In today's Industry 4.0 era, new digital technologies have become important enablers of agile supply chains 'by enabling the acquisition of real-time information, supporting information-sharing, and coordinating responses between supply chain members' (Oliveira-Dias et al., 2022: 2).

12.7 RECENT DEVELOPMENTS IN GLOBAL SUPPLY CHAINS

As the global business landscape continues to evolve, so does the field of international supply chain management (SCM). Organizations must adapt to emerging trends and embrace innovative strategies to remain competitive and responsive in a global, interconnected world. One possible technological solution that could support international information flows is blockchain technology (BCT). BCT is a distributed ledger that consists of a database with a chain of 'blocks'. The 'blocks' are interconnected with each other and each consists of a set of records and data. The 'blocks' create a chain by being linked together through data that references data in other 'blocks'.

BCT has gained traction in international SCM due to its ability to create a secure, transparent, and traceable international supply chain network. BCT makes it possible to track products throughout the supply chain from the raw material to the retail store and records every point of transaction. It builds on a decentralized framework, a mechanism for distributed recording and storage, an agreed-upon algorithm, the possibility of smart contracts and asymmetric encryption (Dutta et al., 2020; Hastig & Sodhi, 2020; Tiwari et al., 2023). Even though BCT gives rise to high expectations, studies have critically questioned if it can create real business value. The immense amount of data collected in BCT creates scalability and efficiency concerns and requires the capacity to handle the transaction data. Managing the transaction data leads to higher energy consumption, which is detrimental to the environment. As BCT also relies heavily on the participation of the parties involved, they need to be incentivized and convinced to join regardless of the risk related to the sharing of sensitive information and its potential leakage. Lastly, as with all new developments, there is an increased risk posed by the investment of resources into BCT (Holmström et al., 2019; Klöckner et al., 2022).

The concept of digital twins involves creating a virtual, digital representation of a physical supply chain. This digital replica enables organizations to simulate scenarios, optimize processes, and identify potential bottlenecks before they occur. By using real-time data and analytics, digital twin technology helps organizations make data-driven decisions and improve overall supply chain performance. A digital twin can be used for proactive 'what-if' analysis and reactive decision-making support (e.g., after a disruption has occurred). The quality of a digital supply chain twin strongly depends on the completeness, fullness, validity, consistency, and timely availability of the data it is built on (Ivanov et al., 2019). Additionally, data needs to be added regularly to increase its effectiveness. This makes a digital twin a dynamic representation of reality, that can guide managers in international supply chains.

Spotlight: Prewave and Its Use of AI for Supply Chain Analytics

Prewave is a company leveraging artificial intelligence (AI) to enhance supply chain risk analysis by predicting, identifying, and mitigating potential disruptions. The core of Prewave's technology is its AI-driven platform, which monitors vast amounts of data from various sources, including news reports, social media, industry publications, and other online content, to detect and analyse risks that could impact supply chains.

Prewave's AI algorithms are designed to process this data in multiple languages, enabling the platform to provide a comprehensive and global overview of potential risks. The system uses natural language processing (NLP) and machine learning techniques to identify relevant information, filter out noise, and assess the significance of identified risks. This allows Prewave to detect issues such as political instability, natural disasters, labour strikes, and other events that could disrupt supply chains.

One of the key features of Prewave's platform is its predictive capability. By analysing historical data and current trends, it can forecast potential disruptions, giving companies valuable lead time to take preventive measures. For instance, if the platform detects early signs of a labour strike in a region critical to a company's supply chain, it can alert the company to take proactive steps, such as finding alternative suppliers or adjusting inventory levels.

Prewave also offers real-time monitoring and alerting services, providing up-to-date information on emerging risks. This continuous surveillance allows companies to respond quickly to unexpected events, minimizing the impact on their operations. The platform's user-friendly dashboard provides a clear overview of identified risks, their potential impact, and suggested mitigation strategies, making it easier for supply chain managers to make informed decisions.

By integrating AI into supply chain risk analysis, Prewave helps companies improve resilience, reduce vulnerability to disruptions, and maintain smoother operations. The platform's ability to provide early warnings and actionable insights empowers businesses to manage risks proactively, ensuring supply chain continuity and stability.

Sources: Prewave (www.prewave.com/blog/the-ai-revolution-in-supply-chain-mapping/) and IEEE Computer Society (www.computer.org/publications/tech-news/trends/ai-revolutionizing-supply-chain).

SUMMARY

International supply chain management (SCM) involves integrating processes across a product's life cycle, from sourcing raw materials to manufacturing, distributing, and returning final products. The importance of international SCM has grown with globalization, driven by market expansion opportunities, cost benefits, customer expectations, collaboration benefits, and risk management needs. Theories like the resource-based view (RBV), transaction cost economics (TCE), and institutional theory help us to understand SCM by emphasizing resource optimization, efficient procurement and production decisions, and compliance with diverse regulations and cultural norms.

Key activities in international SCM include procurement, manufacturing, inventory management, logistics, return management, and planning. Procurement involves sourcing from global suppliers, requiring effective supplier selection, negotiation, and risk management. Manufacturing includes setting up global production networks and maintaining quality standards. Inventory management focuses on balancing stock levels to meet demand while minimizing costs, using safety stock, collaborative inventory management, and technology integration. Logistics management ensures the efficient movement and distribution of goods, considering transportation modes and customs compliance.

International SCM also faces challenges such as disruption, regulation, and the bullwhip effect. Disruption from political, environmental, or economic sources can significantly impact supply chains. Regulations and trade barriers shape how MNCs engage in international operations, sometimes leading to regionalized supply chains. The bullwhip effect, characterized by amplified fluctuations in orders and inventory levels, creates inefficiencies and increased costs. Effective SCM requires strategies to build resilient supply chains, balancing preventive and recovery measures to mitigate risks and ensure smooth operations.

Emerging trends in international SCM include digitalization, sustainability, and agility. Blockchain technology and digital supply chain twins enhance transparency, traceability, and decision-making. Sustainable supply chain management focuses on responsible sourcing, reducing carbon footprints, and adopting eco-friendly practices. Agility, crucial for responding to disruption and market changes, involves flexible and responsive supply chains supported by digital technologies and strong collaboration among supply chain partners.

13

DIGITALIZATION IN INTERNATIONAL BUSINESS

CHAPTER INTRODUCTION

Digitalization, the integration of digital technologies into many areas of our lives, is reshaping the International Business landscape. Its influence transcends borders, affecting business practices and economic growth in both developed and developing countries (Brynjolfsson & McAfee, 2014). Scholars from diverse fields have explored digitalization, reflecting its interdisciplinary nature and wide-ranging impact. In International Business research, digitalization prompts a re-evaluation of traditional theories and models, revealing new avenues for enquiry and hypothesis generation. This extensive research landscape is enriched by its inherently global context, as digitalization impacts both developed and emerging economies, each with distinct implications and opportunities.

In developed countries, digitalization acts as a catalyst for business innovation, shaping competitive strategies and fostering new business models. Companies utilize digital platforms to reach a wider consumer base, exploit data analytics for predictive insights, and leverage automation for operational efficiency. Research in these contexts often examines the interplay between digitalization and organizational structure, strategy, and performance, providing insights into the transformative potential of digital technologies.

Despite infrastructural limitations and digital divides, emerging countries witness an emerging digital entrepreneurship ecosystem, leveraging mobile technology and localized digital solutions to address social and economic challenges. International Business research in these contexts often focuses on the role of digitalization in economic development, examining how local firms and multinational companies use digital technologies for inclusive growth.

Digitalization also has far-reaching methodological implications for International Business and management research. The surge of big data and data science methods enables researchers to adopt innovative methods for data collection, analysis, and interpretation. Consequently, the domain of International Business research is evolving to include these new methodological possibilities.

Digitalization is a broad domain that continues to expand. It is replete with buzzwords, often leading to the incorrect interchangeable use of different terms. Terms like data science, artificial intelligence, and machine learning have distinct identities but also intersect in practice. For clarity in discussion and research, it is vital to understand where one topic begins and another ends (see Figure 13.1). By distinguishing between these overlapping areas, International Business professionals and researchers can navigate the digital landscape more effectively.

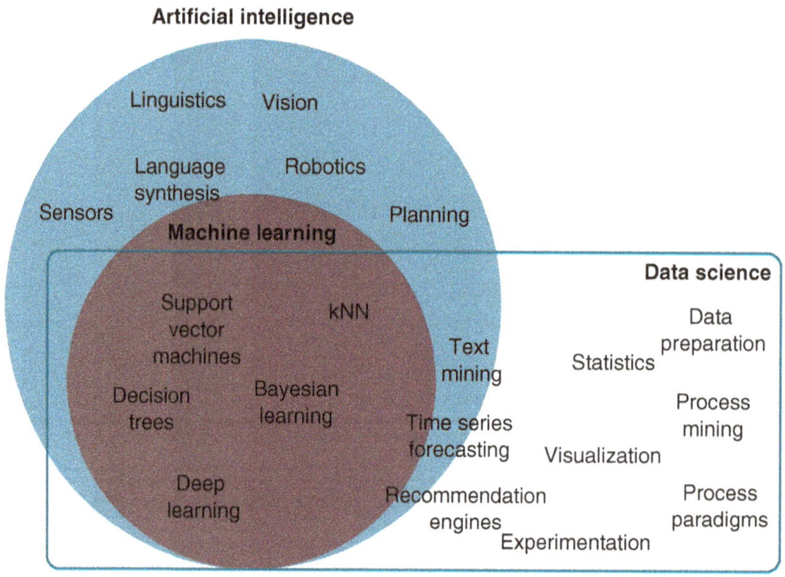

Figure 13.1 Artificial intelligence, machine learning, and data science

In this chapter, we explore the transformative impact of digitalization on International Business. Specifically, we analyse how this paradigm shift can represent a sustained competitive advantage to MNCs through the strategic utilization of big data and automation. Further, we look into the critical domain of data science, shedding light on its role in International Business and discussing key methods for data analysis, regressions, support-vector machines, tree-based models, train-test split and assembly methods. Furthermore, we explore the topic of artificial intelligence, introducing key terminology and examining its influence on human biases, as well as the trade-off between automation and augmentation.

LEARNING OUTCOMES

1 Understand how digitalization and artificial intelligence influence how companies operate in the global economy.

2 Explain the basic mechanisms in common methodologies that artificial intelligence, big data, and data science build on.
3 Know about the upsides and downsides of complementing human work with data-driven decision support.
4 Discuss the societal consequences of the adoption of digital technologies in International Business.

Case Study: Digitalization at Amazon

As Amazon's business rapidly expanded, the company faced various challenges in scaling its operations efficiently to meet growing customer demand. Some of the key challenges included optimizing warehouse operations, streamlining logistics, ensuring fast and reliable product delivery, and managing a vast network of sellers and suppliers worldwide. To address these challenges and maintain its position as an e-commerce leader, Amazon has invested heavily in automation and cutting-edge technology across its global operations.

1 *Automated warehouses*: Amazon deployed advanced robotic systems in its fulfilment centres to automate various tasks, such as product picking, packing, and sorting. These robots work alongside human workers, enhancing operational efficiency and speeding up order fulfilment.
2 *AI-driven supply chain*: Amazon utilizes AI algorithms to forecast customer demand, optimize inventory levels, and predict delivery times, allowing the company to manage its vast supply chain efficiently, reducing costs and improving delivery performance.
3 *Drone delivery*: Amazon has been testing drone delivery as an innovative solution to further expedite delivery, especially in remote or congested areas. Drones can autonomously transport small packages, reducing delivery times and enhancing the customer experience.

The strategic implementation of automation has provided Amazon with several remarkable benefits on an international scale:

1 *Scalable operations*: Automation has allowed Amazon to scale its operations efficiently to handle the increasing volume of orders and customer demands, ensuring a seamless shopping experience for customers worldwide.
2 *Faster order fulfilment*: Automated warehouses and AI-driven supply chain management have significantly reduced delivery times, enabling Amazon to offer faster shipping options to customers, including same-day and next-day delivery in various regions.
3 *Improved customer experience*: Automation has contributed to a more efficient shopping process, fewer errors, and enhanced overall customer satisfaction, making Amazon a preferred choice for online shopping globally.

(Continued)

4 *Innovation leadership*: Amazon's innovative use of automation, drones, and AI technologies has positioned the company as a global technology leader and trendsetter in the e-commerce industry.

Amazon has leveraged automation to transform global e-commerce and revolutionize the way people shop online. By embracing cutting-edge technology and automation solutions, Amazon has overcome various operational challenges, enhanced its customer experience, and solidified its position as a dominant force in International Business and e-commerce. Amazon serves as a prime example of how automation can drive growth and success for even the most famous and widely recognized MNCs.

Sources: Harvard Business School (https://d3.harvard.edu/platform-rctom/submission/automated-warehousing-systems-at-amazon); ThomasNet (www.thomasnet.com/insights/behind-the-scenes-exploring-amazon-s-logistics-and-supply-chains); Business Insider (www.businessinsider.com/amazons-just-walk-out-actually-1-000-people-in-india-2024-4); Amazon (www.amazon.com/b?ie=UTF8&node=16008589011)

Case Study Questions

1 How has Amazon managed to create positive cash flows in businesses such as bookselling, which tend to have low margins?
2 What is a platform business model? How has Amazon managed to monetize its platform role?
3 How has Amazon fared in its attempts to automate offline services, such as checkouts at retail stores?

13.1 DIGITALIZATION IN INTERNATIONAL BUSINESS

The transformative power of digitalization on the International Business landscape is profound and pervasive, shaping multinational companies' operations and strategies in unprecedented ways. The digital revolution, marked by advances in information technology and data processing, has ushered in a new era where digital capabilities serve as a potent source of competitive advantage. Notably, applications of big data and automation exemplify the influence of digitalization in International Business contexts, prompting a renewed focus on their role within the resource-based view (RBV) framework (see Chapter 7, Section 7.1.3).

Central to this discussion is the RBV, which asserts that a firm's internal resources, when unique and inimitable, can provide a sustainable competitive advantage. In the context of digitalization, the RBV offers a unique lens through which to examine how big data, automation, and other digital tools, when perceived as strategic resources, can foster a distinctive competitive advantage for MNCs operating in the international arena.

Big data, characterized by its high volume, velocity, and variety, offers insights into consumer behaviour, market trends, and operational efficiencies. The ability to collect, analyse, and utilize these vast datasets has been recognized as a strategic resource that, when harnessed effectively, can drive superior decision-making and strategic planning, thereby improving performance and creating value for MNCs.

Automation, meanwhile, is a driving force for process innovation within MNCs. Automated systems and processes not only improve operational efficiencies but also allow firms to scale their operations, enhancing their competitiveness in the global marketplace. Thus, the extent to which an MNC integrates automation into its business processes can be viewed as a unique, inimitable resource that contributes to its competitive advantage (Brynjolfsson & Mcafee, 2014).

However, gaining competitive advantage from digitalization in International Business depends on more than just adopting these advanced technologies. It involves leveraging these tools to create unique value propositions and aligning them with the company's strategic objectives. The RBV, which emphasizes a firm's internal resources as the primary source of competitive advantage, offers an insightful perspective in this regard. Digital resources, when effectively managed, can fulfil the criteria of valuable, rare, inimitable, and organizationally embedded (VRIO) resources, thus providing a sustainable competitive advantage.

This chapter will explore the interplay between digitalization, big data, and automation within the theoretical confines of competitive advantage. Drawing from empirical studies and theoretical frameworks, it will demonstrate how these digital resources can be leveraged within the International Business context to gain a competitive advantage, thereby shedding new light on the digital transformation of MNCs from a resource-based perspective.

Spotlight: Standardization and Digitalization of Consumer Banking

Online banking has fundamentally transformed consumer banking, offering convenience, efficiency, and enhanced accessibility. Consumers can now perform a wide range of banking activities from the comfort of their homes or on the go. Services such as checking account balances, transferring funds, paying bills, and applying for loans can now be completed online, eliminating the need to visit physical bank branches. This form of accessibility is particularly beneficial for individuals in remote areas or those with mobility issues, ensuring that banking services are available to a broader audience. The convenience of online banking is unmatched, allowing customers to manage their finances without the constraints of time or location.

One of the most significant advantages of online banking is its round-the-clock availability. Unlike traditional bank branches that operate within fixed hours, online platforms

(Continued)

are available 24/7. This means consumers can manage their finances at any time, accommodating different schedules and time zones. The digitization of banking services has significantly increased the efficiency and speed of transactions. Processes that once required manual intervention and lengthy wait times can now be completed in seconds. Fund transfers, bill payments, and account management tasks are processed almost instantaneously, reducing operational costs for banks and providing customers with a seamless banking experience.

Online banking has also spurred innovations in security measures. Banks invest heavily in advanced security technologies, such as encryption, multi-factor authentication, and biometric verification, to protect consumer data and prevent fraud. These security enhancements ensure that online banking is safe and trustworthy, encouraging more consumers to adopt digital banking solutions. The move to online banking has necessitated the standardization of many banking services, ensuring that customers receive consistent and reliable service regardless of the platform or device they use. Online banking interfaces often follow similar designs and functionalities, making it easier for users to navigate and perform transactions across different banks, enhancing the user experience and reducing the learning curve for consumers transitioning from one bank to another.

The rise of online banking has led to a decline in the reliance on physical branches, with many banks reducing their branch networks and focusing on enhancing their digital platforms. This shift allows banks to allocate resources more efficiently, investing in technology and customer service rather than maintaining costly physical infrastructure. Standardization benefits banks by streamlining operations; by adopting common protocols and procedures, banks can automate many processes, reducing the potential for human error and increasing operational efficiency. This consistency also simplifies compliance with regulatory requirements, as standardized processes are easier to monitor and audit. Overall, online banking has revolutionized consumer banking by providing unmatched convenience and efficiency, driving standardization, and prompting a strategic shift away from physical branches to digital solutions.

Sources: The Guardian (www.theguardian.com/money/2019/nov/30/should-we-really-care-about-bank-branch-closures) and KPMG (https://assets.kpmg.com/content/dam/kpmg/ua/pdf/2019/09/future-of-digital-banking-in-2030-cba.pd.pdf)

13.1.1 Big Data

Big data, characterized by its extensive volume, rapid velocity, and diverse variety, has emerged as a significant factor in transforming International Business and MNCs. This chapter will explore the role of big data within the theoretical frameworks of the RBV, focusing on its implications across multiple industries. Big data can capture, store, and analyse vast amounts of structured and unstructured data in real-time, providing opportunities to extract valuable insights that inform strategic decision-making. This capability can lead to improved market forecasting, customer segmentation, operational efficiency, and innovation – all factors contributing to an MNC's competitive advantage (Erevelles et al., 2016).

The retail industry, for instance, has been profoundly shaped by the advent of big data. Through big data analytics, retail businesses can customize consumer experiences, anticipate demand trends, manage inventories, and enhance customer service. The effective use of big data in retail is a critical factor contributing to their global competitiveness (Seetharaman et al., 2016). In the manufacturing industry, the influence of big data is likewise considerable. It has been used to enhance product quality, optimize production processes, and implement predictive maintenance. These advances have led to improvements in operational efficiency and cost reduction, providing a competitive edge (Alexopoulos et al., 2022).

The finance sector is another industry where big data has made significant strides. Financial institutions employ data analytics to analyse various factors that may impact customer credit risk, including credit history, income levels, and existing debt obligations. These risk assessments are pivotal to determining creditworthiness and influence decisions regarding loan approval and credit limit determination (Al-Lozi et al., 2022). Furthermore, big data has aided in providing financial services to underbanked regions. By leveraging mobile technology and data analytics, financial service providers can extend services like microcredit, savings, and insurance to these areas, fostering financial inclusion and economic growth. Similarly, the healthcare industry has tapped into the potential of big data for personalized treatment, disease outbreak prediction, and improved healthcare delivery. These advances show how big data analytics can be harnessed to improve disease diagnosis and treatment outcomes (Dash et al., 2019).

However, merely possessing large datasets does not automatically translate into a competitive advantage. Challenges lie in managing, analysing, and integrating this data into business strategies effectively. Ethical and regulatory considerations surrounding data privacy and security must also be addressed, ensuring compliance with international data protection standards, and maintaining consumer trust (Mittelstadt et al., 2016).

Case Study: Big Data at Tesla

When Tesla, a then-unknown American electric vehicle startup, emerged onto the scene in 2003, the global auto industry could hardly have anticipated the transformative wave it was about to trigger. Established with the goal of challenging the domination of gasoline vehicles, Tesla has not only established itself as a trailblazer in the electric mobility sector but has also led significant disruptions in the realms of self-driving technology and big data.

(Continued)

Tesla's self-driving car technology, known as Autopilot, is a significant aspect of the company's portfolio. Autopilot is an advanced driver-assistance system featuring functionalities like lane centring, adaptive cruise control, self-parking, and the ability to automatically change lanes. However, the truly groundbreaking work lies in Tesla's ongoing development of a fully self-driving capability.

Tesla's fleet of over a million vehicles on the road serves as a massive, real-world data collection network. Every mile driven by a Tesla vehicle contributes to a massive pool of data, which is used to constantly train and refine the company's self-driving algorithms. This data-driven approach has proven to be a key differentiator in Tesla's strategy.

Dimension		Tesla Case Study
V	**Valuable** Is the resource valuable?	Tesla's self-driving capabilities add significant value to their vehicles, enhancing safety, convenience, and offering a unique selling point that appeals to consumers. The technology has also allowed Tesla to generate additional revenue streams through sales of their full self-driving software package. The data gathered from Tesla vehicles on the road contributes to continuous improvements in the self-driving system, thereby adding further value.
R	**Rare** How difficult is it for competitors to obtain the same resource?	The extent of Tesla's self-driving capabilities and the scale at which they are deployed are currently rare in the automotive industry. The combination of advanced hardware in their vehicles and sophisticated machine learning algorithms, refined by billions of real-world driving miles, is not commonly found among competitors.
I	**Inimitable** Will it be realistically possible for competitors to imitate?	The development of self-driving technology requires significant financial resources, technical expertise, and an extensive database of real-world driving data. Tesla's culture of innovation and risk-taking is deeply ingrained in the organization, making it challenging for competitors to emulate. With a fleet of over a million vehicles on the road, each collecting valuable data, Tesla's ever-improving dataset for machine learning is difficult for competitors to replicate.
O	**Organized** Is the organization set up to exploit the advantage?	Tesla has shown its ability to leverage its self-driving technology effectively. The organization has not only developed the technology but also successfully marketed it to consumers. Tesla's management is heavily invested in the continuous development and implementation of self-driving technology. Furthermore, the entire organization, from software developers to manufacturing workers, is aligned with the goal of advancing autonomous driving.

Figure 13.2 The VRIO model of big data at Tesla

In 2023, Tesla started to build a crucial component of its self-driving and machine learning ecosystem – Tesla Dojo. Dojo is a supercomputer specifically designed to process vast amounts of video data. Its primary function is to train Tesla's neural networks for its self-driving cars by processing and learning from the petabytes of real-world data collected by Tesla vehicles. This technology enhances the accuracy of Tesla's self-driving predictions and decision-making capabilities, marking a significant stride in autonomous driving.

The VRIO (valuable, rare, inimitable, and organized) framework is a strategic analysis tool that enables organizations to identify the competitive potential of their internal resources. Applying the VRIO analysis to Tesla's self-driving capabilities provides a clear understanding of its unique competitive advantage in the global auto market. Figure 13.2 provides an example of how to begin analysing big data at Tesla using the VRIO model.

In conclusion, Tesla's self-driving capabilities align well with the VRIO framework, indicating that these capabilities provide Tesla with a sustainable competitive advantage. Tesla's continuous efforts to improve and leverage this technology could help maintain its leading position in the global electric vehicle market in the foreseeable future.

Sources: Tesla (www.tesla.com/autopilot) and Inside EVs (https://insideevs.com/news/717206/tesla-distributed-datacenter-on-wheels)

13.1.2 Automation

Automation technologies encompass a wide array of advances, such as industrial robots, service and social robots, artificial intelligence, vending machines, ATMs, kiosks, chatbots, automated trading algorithms, and various other innovations enabling the production and sale of goods and services with minimal human intervention. Technological progress over the past decades has significantly enhanced the capabilities of these automation technologies while reducing their costs, making them more accessible for implementation in diverse industries, including agriculture and services. These technologies are applied in autonomous vehicles for transportation, warehousing and supply chain management, customer interactions through chatbots, automated pricing decisions, facial recognition and automated border control, provision of legal services, trading on financial markets, and numerous other applications (Ivanov et al., 2020).

In terms of supply chain transformation, the highly competitive global environment offers manufacturers the opportunity to build highly efficient and flexible plants capable of meeting fluctuating market demands and supporting innovative production models. The integration of technologies such as the Internet of Things (IoT), cyber-physical systems, artificial intelligence (AI), robotics, data analytics, blockchain, and cloud technology has led to Logistics 4.0, an initiative with great potential to create more efficient production and distribution systems in supply chain management (Paksoy et al., 2020).

Companies are investing heavily in automation technologies and replacing some employees to achieve greater productivity, competitiveness, profitability, and reduced dependence on limited human resources (Ivanov et al., 2020). This trend suggests that automation impacts the labour market. Although automation may lead to a decline in employment in the short run, this effect might be mitigated in the long run by increased productivity and demand, which creates new needs for hiring.

On the one hand, automation supposedly leads to higher efficiency and lower costs for firms, resulting in lower prices for customers. On the other hand, automation is not always efficient in every case, as greater use of automation does not always result in higher service quality: the effectiveness of automation in providing service depends on the level of technological advances.

Additionally, International Business managers must support their employees when rationalizing jobs. Companies should prioritize the welfare of employees at higher risk of being replaced by automation by offering complimentary re-qualification programmes. They can also implement work sharing and reduced working hours to retain some of the displaced workforce. Transparent communication is essential: managers should keep workers informed about strategic decisions and plans regarding investment in robots, artificial intelligence, and automation technologies. Involving employees in the decision-making process enables them to prepare for their professional future within the company. Employees' support for adopting automation technologies is vital to ensure smooth and effective implementation, as opposition may hinder their efficient and productive usage (Ivanov et al., 2020).

13.2 DATA SCIENCE IN INTERNATIONAL BUSINESS

Spotlight: The Environmental Impact Of Cloud Services

Cloud services, especially those involved in training large machine learning (ML) models, have significantly reshaped the technological landscape. However, this transformation comes with considerable energy and resource demands, posing substantial challenges to sustainability efforts. Understanding the impact is crucial for developing strategies to mitigate the environmental footprint of cloud computing and AI development.

The training of large ML models, such as deep learning networks, is computationally intensive. These models require massive amounts of processing power, often provided by data centres equipped with thousands of servers. These data centres operate continuously, consuming vast amounts of electricity to power the servers and maintain optimal operating conditions, including cooling systems to prevent overheating. The energy consumption of these facilities is substantial, contributing to increased greenhouse gas emissions. For instance, training a single large ML model can emit as much carbon dioxide as several cars over their entire lifetimes, highlighting the significant environmental impact of these operations.

In addition to energy consumption, the production and maintenance of the hardware required for cloud services also demand considerable natural resources. Data centres rely on servers made from metals and rare earth elements, the extraction and processing of which can lead to environmental degradation, including habitat destruction, soil and water pollution, and increased carbon emissions. The lifecycle of these hardware components - from extraction to manufacturing, deployment, and disposal - adds another layer of environmental impact, emphasizing the need for sustainable practices in hardware production and recycling.

The high energy and resource demands of cloud services have substantial consequences for sustainability efforts. The rapid expansion of data centres, driven by the growing demand for cloud computing and AI services, intensifies these challenges. As the need for advanced ML models increases, so does the environmental footprint associated with their training and deployment. This trend underscores the importance of developing more energy-efficient algorithms and hardware, as well as adopting renewable energy sources to power data centres.

Efforts to mitigate the environmental impact of cloud services include the adoption of green data centres, which use energy-efficient technologies and renewable energy sources. Tech giants like Google, Microsoft, and Amazon have committed to powering their data centres with renewable energy and improving energy efficiency through innovative cooling techniques and hardware optimization. Additionally, the development of more efficient ML algorithms that require less computational power can help reduce energy consumption.

Sources: University of Pennsylvania (https://environment.upenn.edu/events-insights/news/hidden-costs-ai-impending-energy-and-resource-strain); Goldman Sachs (www.goldmansachs.com/intelligence/pages/AI-poised-to-drive-160-increase-in-power-demand.html); Office of Energy Efficiency and Renewable Energy (www.energy.gov/eere/buildings/data-centers-and-servers).

Unlike traditional information processing, data now occurs in various forms such as text, photos, and videos. Data analytics, however, refers to the interpretation of this structured or unstructured data into actionable insights (Vidgen et al., 2017). To harness actionable insights, there has been a significant surge in investment aimed at enhancing business infrastructure to utilize data over the past 55 years. This has greatly improved the capacity to gather data across entire enterprises. Today, almost every aspect of business operations is not only open to data collection but often equipped with instruments to facilitate data gathering. This includes areas such as operations, manufacturing, supply chain management, customer behaviour, marketing campaign performance, and workflow procedures, among others. Additionally, information regarding external events like market trends, industry news, and competitors' activities has become readily accessible. With this vast availability of data, there has been a growing interest in data science, specifically in developing methods to extract valuable information and knowledge from this data (Vidgen et al., 2017).

Big data and statistics can enhance the decision-making process. However, the effectiveness of any data mining tools is greatly influenced by the appropriate selection of variables and the creation of a robust model. Data science involves cleaning and structuring raw data to derive valuable insights.

For managers working internationally, a fundamental understanding of data science is becoming essential. This is not only because decision-making in any organization is increasingly data driven but also because data are the link between business operations and engineering. The following sections provide more detail of some of the most common techniques to use data in a target-oriented way, including regressions, support vector machines, tree-based models, neural networks, train–test split, and assembly methods.

13.2.1 Regressions

Regression analysis is a statistical approach to predictive modelling and is among the most widely used methods in various scientific disciplines, including engineering, physical and chemical sciences, economics, management, life sciences, and social sciences.

In general, regressions are used to understand and predict the relationship between variables. If you want to find a connection between years of education and income, for example, regressions help you to determine and quantify a potential relationship. There are four main objectives for regression analysis. Most commonly, regression is used for quantifying the influence of one variable on another. Secondly, regressions aim to predict an outcome – for example, an international organization might want to investigate a new market for their business and want to know the likelihood of it being profitable within a given range. The third objective of regression concerns the predictors of some factors. For instance, if a company strives for internationalization, they may want to determine which factors are crucial for long-term profitability. Last, regressions are applied when adjusting a result for various factors. In other words, if an organization within the health industry wants to evaluate their manager's performance in 2020, they may want to factor out the influence of Covid-19 on the industry.

13.2.2 Support Vector Machines

Since the 1990s, support vector machines (SVM) have gained increasing popularity and have been used for various issues. SVMs are among the best 'out-of-the-box' classifiers (James et al., 2013). In the field of data science, SVMs find significant utility in various domains, including function regression estimation, time sequence prediction, analysis of stock trends, and the classification and recognition of patterns.

Essentially, a support vector machine is an algorithm designed to label objects by maximizing mathematical functions as it processes a given collection of data (Noble, 2006). A prominent example of using SVM is in determining fraudulent credit card activity. After feeding SVM with data on both fraudulent and non-fraudulent transactions, it can distinguish between the two types of transactions and flag them accordingly.

Use of SVM is essentially limited to scenarios where the classes or groups are separable. In other words, SVMs work effectively in environments where both the given data and the related outcomes (or labels) are known. This requires a continuous line (the classifier or hyperplane) between two domains (see Figure 13.3). To create the hyperplane, one must find the data points with the biggest margin between the two domains; these are called support vectors. By using support vectors (including a line between the data points), one can determine the hyperplane and implement a machine learning algorithm to select the best line to separate the domains (Suthaharan, 2016b).

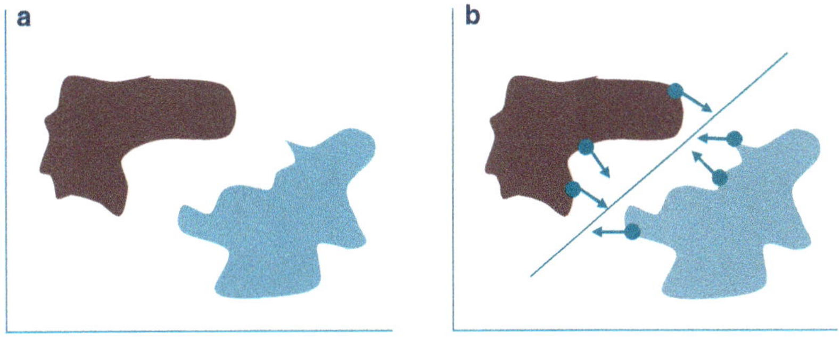

Figure 13.3 The boundaries in support vector machines

13.2.3 Tree-Based Models

In general, the main purpose of tree-based models is to understand and summarize the main insights of datasets. Two commonly used cases for tree-based methods are regression and classification. A key feature of tree-based methods is the stratification or segmentation of the prediction space into several simple regions. To predict an outcome based on a given observation, a typical approach is to use the mean or the mode of the training observations in the region where it belongs. These methods are referred to as decision tree methods because the set of splitting rules employed to divide the predictor space can be succinctly represented in a tree structure (James et al., 2013).

To further explain, let us look at the two domains mentioned earlier (Figure 13.3). The next step involves including horizontal and vertical lines (see Figure 13.4). The best way to perform this is to add decision trees (DTs) (Suthaharan, 2016b). When doing so, one must distinguish between regression trees and decision trees for classification. Whereas regression trees aim to predict an outcome, decision trees for classification are used to classify data into different categories. They are applied in classification problems where the goal is to assign a label or category to the input instances (James et al., 2013).

In the previous example, a decision tree for classification is applicable as the goal is to further segment the data. In this scenario, the parameters of the model include determining the appropriate vertical and horizontal intersection points (Suthaharan, 2016b).

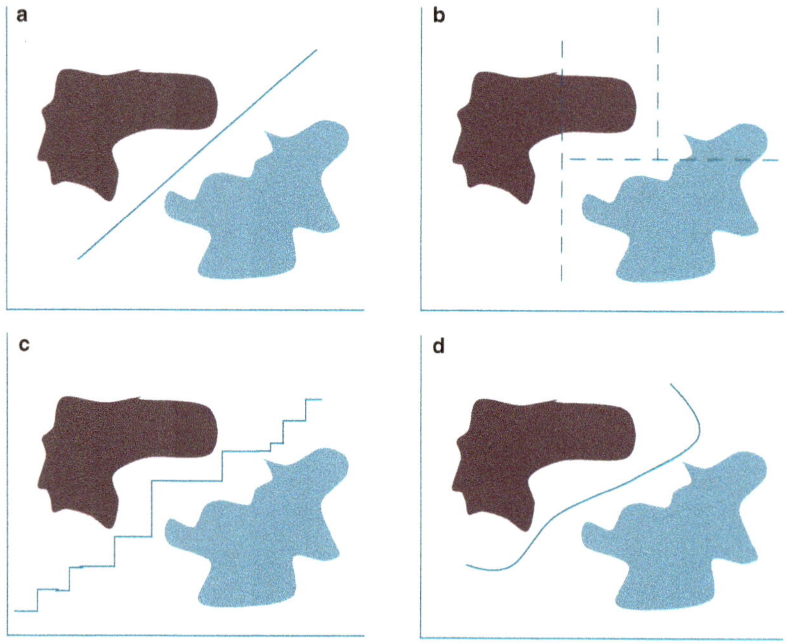

Figure 13.4 Determining the boundary based on a decision-tree based classification

13.2.4 Neural Networks

A neural network is a computational model inspired by the structure and function of the human brain. At its core, it consists of layers of interconnected neurons (or nodes), each representing a mathematical function. These neurons are grouped into three main types of layer: an input layer that receives data, one or more hidden layers that process information, and an output layer that produces predictions or classifications. Data passes through these layers, with each neuron performing a weighted sum of its inputs, applying a nonlinear activation function, and transmitting the result to subsequent neurons. This layered structure allows neural networks to learn and approximate complex patterns and relationships in data.

The learning process involves adjusting the weights of connections between neurons to minimize prediction errors. This is typically achieved using an algorithm known as backpropagation, which computes the gradient of a loss function with respect to each weight through a technique called gradient descent. As the network iterates through multiple training examples, it gradually refines its weights, improving its ability to predict or classify new data. Neural networks have become particularly effective with the rise of deep learning, a subset of machine learning that leverages deep architectures – networks with many hidden layers – to tackle complex tasks such as image recognition, natural language processing, and game playing.

Neural networks build upon basic statistical concepts like linear regression but go beyond these by introducing non-linear transformations and hierarchical feature learning.

While linear regression finds simple relationships between input and output variables, neural networks can capture intricate, non-linear patterns by combining features across multiple layers. Despite their power, neural networks require large amounts of data and computational resources, and they are often seen as 'black boxes' due to the difficulty in interpreting their internal decision-making processes. Nonetheless, their versatility and accuracy have made them indispensable tools in modern data science and artificial intelligence.

13.2.5 Train-Test Split

To work with manageable subsets of data while ensuring the robustness and generalizability of models, data scientists apply the technique of sampling. The use of sampling reduces the amount of data to be processed, which speeds up the modelling process. In many cases, it is sufficient to work with samples to gain insights, extract information, and build predictive models that accurately represent the larger dataset. While there is a theoretical risk that sampling will introduce errors, the benefits far outweigh any potential drawbacks. In the context of data science applications, it is essential to divide datasets into training and testing samples during model building. The training dataset is created by sampling from the original dataset, either through simple random sampling or by employing sampling methods specific to class labels.

Some machine learning (ML) models may perform well on a training dataset but may be less robust when applied to test data or when predicting unseen data. This issue is caused by overfitting (Srivastava et al., 2014). Overfitting is a common challenge in machine learning and can be influenced by several factors that impact a model's performance and generalization. These factors include the complexity of the model, the amount of training data available, and the presence of noise in the data.

First, the complexity of a model plays an important role in overfitting. A model with higher complexity and a large number of adjustable parameters may fit its predictions precisely to the training data, becoming too specialized to capture the subtleties of the training set, thus losing its ability to generalize well to unseen data (Suthaharan, 2016a). Second, an insufficient amount of data can lead to overfitting, as the model may not be able to understand the underlying patterns in the data. With a limited number of examples, the model may rely heavily on noise or certain outliers, impairing its ability to make accurate predictions on new, unseen data. Third, the presence of noise in the data can adversely affect the generalization of the model. If the training data contain noisy or irrelevant information, the model may inadvertently learn to account for these irregularities, exacerbating the problem of overfitting. By attempting to capture both true patterns and noise, the model's ability to generalize effectively may be compromised.

A common method to estimate the generalization performance of an ML model is to split data into training, test, and validation sets (Ripley, 1996) (see Figure 13.5). The goal is to provide high classification accuracy while avoiding overfitting. To this end, one must find the best possible values for the parameters of a model, using large amounts of data without overfitting the model (Suthaharan, 2016a). The extent to which a model can be generalized is dependent on its complexity, which is determined by its hyperparameters. Thus, finding optimal hyperparameters is crucial to balance model complexity with the available training data, reducing the risk of overfitting.

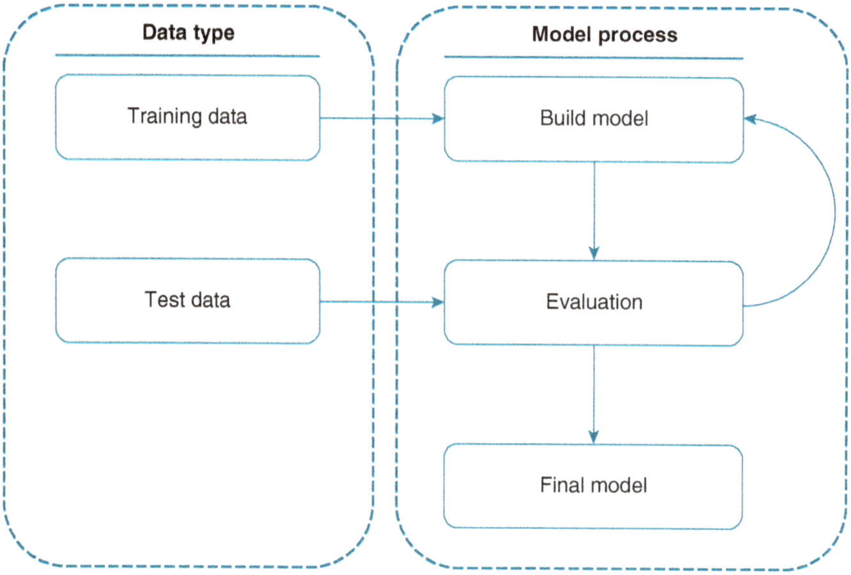

Figure 13.5 The train-test-split in machine learning

Splitting data into testing, training, and validation sets helps to find the optimal set of model parameters that balance the model's ability to generalize to new data and its complexity (Ripley, 1996; Suthaharan, 2016a). Techniques such as regularization and cross-validation can also help control overfitting and promote better generalization, ensuring that the model performs well on unseen data – an important goal in successful machine learning applications.

13.2.6 Cross-Validation

Ideally, to assess the generalization ability of a model, we would evaluate a machine learning model using new data that comes from the same population as the data used to build the model. However, in practice, it is often not possible to obtain new data from the same population (Berrar, 2018). For example, if we are developing a model to predict the success of a new International Business venture in South Africa, we may not be able to obtain new data from companies that have recently launched new ventures in the South African market.

In such cases, we can use a technique called cross-validation to estimate the model's performance. Cross-validation is a technique for estimating the true prediction error of machine learning models by repeatedly splitting the data into training and testing sets.

This helps to prevent the model from overfitting and increases generalization ability (Berrar, 2018). To build a model that can be used to predict real future cases, the learning function (or learning algorithm) is usually applied to the entire training set. This final model cannot be cross-validated, as it would not be a fair estimate of the model's performance on new data.

Feature selection is an essential part of the machine learning model-building process. It involves choosing the most important features from a dataset to improve the model's accuracy. It is crucial that predictive features are selected using only the training set, not the entire learning set. Otherwise, the estimate of the prediction error can be highly biased. For example, suppose you select predictive features based on the entire learning set first, then partition the learning set into validation sets and training sets. This means you are using information from the validation sets to select predictive features. However, the data in the validation sets should only be used to evaluate the model. Using this data for feature selection would introduce bias into the model.

Cross-validation is a technique that can be used to select features and tune model parameters. It works by dividing the data into multiple sets. The model is then trained on some of the sets and evaluated on the remaining sets. This process is repeated multiple times, and the results are averaged. For instance, for k-nearest neighbour classification, cross-validation can be used to select the optimal number of neighbours. Cross-validation is applied multiple times for different values of the number of neighbours. The value that minimizes the cross-validated error is then used to build the final model.

13.2.7 Assembly Methods

In general, assembly methods are a class of machine learning algorithms that combine the predictions of multiple base models to make a more accurate prediction. Assembly methods tend to be more complex than ensemble methods but can be more accurate for certain tasks. Typical examples of assembly methods are stacking and mixture models.

The main goal of using a stacking ensemble is to reduce generalization error and overfitting. The stacking ensemble can be used in both classification and regression tasks. This technique combines multiple base learning algorithms into a unified prediction function through a secondary learning process known as meta-learning, resulting in improved prediction accuracy and stability.

Essentially, the stacking ensemble in machine learning involves training a second-level 'meta-learner' to determine the optimal combination of base learning algorithms. By using different and well-chosen modelling algorithms, the stacking ensemble creates a robust model that benefits from the strengths of the individual models while compensating for their weaknesses or biases. The result is a more accurate forecast overall.

A mixture model is a probabilistic model that assumes the observed data were generated by a mixture of several underlying probability distributions. This means the data can be divided into different groups or clusters, each associated with a different distribution (Scrucca et al., 2016).

One of the most common mixture models is the Gaussian mixture model (GMM). A GMM assumes the data is generated by a mixture of Gaussian distributions. Gaussian distributions are a family of probability distributions commonly used to model continuous data.

Gaussian mixture models can be used to convert the output of a machine learning model into more interpretable probabilities. This is done by fitting the GMM to the training data and then using it to calculate the probability of a sample belonging to a class, given the output of the machine learning model. This procedure can improve the classification accuracy and precision of the machine learning model in some cases.

13.2.7.1 Note

You will find more information on the topics covered in section 13.2 in *An Introduction to Statistical Learning* (James et al.) Details at www.statlearning.com

13.3 ARTIFICIAL INTELLIGENCE

The emergence of artificial intelligence (AI) has transformed the landscape of International Business, becoming a driving force for competitive advantage. By automating tasks, predicting trends, and enhancing decision-making, AI is reshaping various aspects of multinational companies, from marketing and supply chain management to customer service and human resources. Its ability to process massive datasets has stimulated a shift towards data-driven strategies, enabling businesses to uncover valuable insights and predict market dynamics. However, its deployment also raises critical concerns about job displacement, privacy, and security, necessitating a balanced approach. Despite these challenges, the integration of AI in International Business holds vast potential for increased efficiency, innovation, and strategic development.

Artificial intelligence (AI), machine learning (ML), deep learning (DL), and neural networks (NN) represent a transformative wave in technology, significantly impacting various areas including multinational companies. Although these terms are sometimes used interchangeably, they define distinct but interconnected concepts, as illustrated in Figure 13.6.

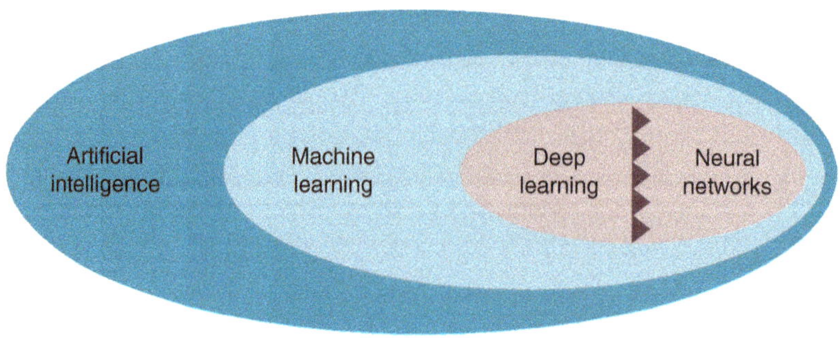

Figure 13.6 Distinguishing between artificial intelligence, machine learning, deep learning and neural networks

Artificial intelligence (AI) embarks on the ambitious quest of creating machines that simulate human intelligence. It extends beyond mere programming to give machines problem-solving, and learning capabilities, creating systems that can respond to changes and make informed decisions (Russell & Norvig, 2016). The scope of AI is broad, covering symbolic reasoning, expert systems, natural language processing, robotics, and more.

Machine learning (ML), a subset of AI, diverges from hard-coded rule-based systems, using statistical methods to enable machines to 'learn' from data. Rather than programming explicit rules, ML systems are fed with data and algorithms, upon which they deduce patterns and make predictions. It broadly consists of two types: supervised learning, where the system is trained on labelled data, and unsupervised learning, where the system identifies patterns in unlabelled data (Alpaydin, 2020).

Deep learning (DL), a further subset of ML, employs multi-layered artificial neural networks to carry out the process of machine learning. DL can automatically learn data representations, eliminating the need for manual feature extraction. The 'depth' in DL refers to the number of layers in the neural networks. Each layer extracts features and passes them onto the next, gradually forming a 'deep' understanding of the data. DL is particularly efficient for high-dimensional data such as images, speech, and text (Goodfellow et al., 2016).

Artificial neural networks (NN), central to DL, are algorithms modelled on the human brain, designed to replicate its ability to recognize patterns and learn from experience. A neural network consists of interconnected neurons (or nodes) arranged in layers: input, hidden, and output. The input layer ingests raw data, which the hidden layers process and pass onto the output layer that delivers the final result. The learning process involves the adjustment of the connections' strengths, also known as weights, among these neurons (Schmidhuber, 2015). NNs adapt to complex patterns in datasets over time, making them indispensable for tasks such as image and speech recognition, language translation, and even playing video games (LeCun et al., 2015).

Multinational companies increasingly harness these technologies to enhance operations, drive innovation, and sustain competitive advantage (Brynjolfsson & McAfee, 2014). ML allows these enterprises to process vast datasets for predictive analytics. For example, customer behaviour prediction is a key application, where ML models analyse customers' past actions to anticipate future behaviours. This has direct implications for personalizing customer service or marketing, which can increase customer loyalty and drive revenue.

In the realm of logistics, ML algorithms can process data from various sources (like GPS, traffic information, weather, etc.) to optimize routes and schedules, resulting in reduced costs and improved service (Vlahogianni et al., 2014). Furthermore, ML is employed to detect anomalies and potential fraud in financial transactions, making it crucial for corporations in maintaining financial security and integrity (Bhattacharyya et al., 2011).

DL complements these capabilities, excelling in tasks like natural language processing, image recognition, and complex decision-making. For instance, in healthcare, DL is used to analyse medical images to detect diseases, outperforming traditional methods in accuracy and speed (Litjens et al., 2017). In finance, DL is leveraged for credit scoring, algorithmic trading, and risk management, providing a more sophisticated analysis and prediction model than conventional methods (Sirignano & Cont, 2019). Retail businesses also benefit, as DL can recognize patterns in customer purchasing behaviour, improving inventory management and targeted marketing (Giri & Chen, 2022).

However, the adoption of AI and related technologies also brings challenges. Ethical implications, potential job displacement, security risks, and the 'black box' problem of unexplained AI decisions – referring to the lack of transparency and interpretability in the decision-making processes of these models – are pressing concerns that need to be addressed (Brynjolfsson & Mcafee, 2014).

In conclusion, the application of AI and related technologies in multinational companies offers significant advantages while posing challenges. As these technologies continue to advance, they will not only reshape International Business strategies but also demand a rethinking of societal norms and regulations.

Case Study: Shein

Founded in 2008, Shein, a Chinese online fashion company, has reshaped the global retail industry landscape within a short span of time. As of 2022, Shein's market valuation rose to US$100 billion, surpassing the combined worth of industry giants Inditex and H&M.

A significant component of Shein's success lies in its pioneering use of AI. Shein's AI algorithms analyse a vast amount of data, comprising social media trends, user engagement on its app, and historical sales data. This aids the company in forecasting trends and understanding customer preferences with a speed and precision unrivalled by conventional fashion houses. These AI-driven insights directly influence Shein's design process. Unlike traditional retailers, which rely on seasonal collections, Shein adopts a dynamic approach. Its product lineup is continuously updated, with thousands of new items added every week based on the latest data analysis. If a product performs well, it is immediately scaled up and if it underperforms, it is rapidly phased out. This approach minimizes forecasting errors and waste, marking a significant departure from traditional fashion cycles.

Despite its successes, Shein's rapid growth is not without controversy. Critics argue that the fast-fashion trend aggravates the fashion industry's sustainability crisis due to the short lifespan of the clothes and the resultant waste.

Sources: Glossy (www.glossy.co/fashion/fashion-briefing-the-shein-ification-of-fashion-and-the-rise-of-ai) and KrAsia (https://kr-asia.com/unveiling-sheins-secret-artificial-intelligence-and-the-complexities-behind-its-usd-66-billion-valuation)

Case Study Questions

1. How does Shein's business model influence working conditions in the workshops producing its fashion?
2. What are the challenges with Shein's AI focus, particularly when it comes to biases in the data?

13.3.1 Machine and Human Biases

Digital advances such as global interconnectedness, e-commerce activities, and advanced analytics have revolutionized International Business (IB) operations (Brynjolfsson & McAfee, 2014). Among these advances, AI and ML have had a significant influence on business processes, particularly by augmenting human decision-making. Incorporating AI into IB theory is crucial, as multinational companies adapt their behaviour based on AI-enhanced decision-making processes. This shift in decision-making patterns, influenced by 'augmented' decision-making using AI, will impact traditional biases and heuristics, consequently altering theoretical predictions of IB theories reliant on these factors (Raisch & Krakowski, 2021).

The cognitive limitations of human decision-makers, often termed 'bounded rationality', have shaped the strategy formulation of multinational companies. The complexities of International Business force human decision-makers to rely on heuristics due to limitations in processing power and time (Simon, 1956). The concept of bounded rationality, a key element of internalization theory, recognizes this phenomenon (Rugman & Verbeke, 2004). The introduction of AI in this process could significantly alter the prevailing heuristics and biases, prompting a re-evaluation of existing theoretical models. Furthermore, the interactions between AI and human decision-makers could lead to substantial changes in the strategies of multinational companies and, consequently, the theories explaining these strategies.

The advent of augmented decision-making, a fusion of human decision-making and AI, creates a complex interaction of human and machine biases, necessitating a better understanding of this interplay. While human biases often result from incomplete information, machine biases stem from skewed training data or algorithmic issues. Research suggests that the combination of AI and human decision-making could reduce these biases and lead to more informed decisions (Brynjolfsson & McAfee, 2014).

Artificial intelligence and human biases are intertwined in their influence on five dominant areas of International Business:

1 *Internationalization and growth processes (see Chapter 7, Section 7.4.6)*: Current literature reveals an intertwining of biases and heuristics in internationalization and growth. For example, managerial behaviours can introduce biases such as status quo bias, confirmation bias, and the familiarity effect significantly influencing internationalization decisions. The status quo bias favours the current state of affairs, meaning that individuals prefer to maintain their current decisions, beliefs, or behaviours instead of changing them. Confirmation bias is the tendency to search for, interpret, favour, and recall information in a way that confirms one's pre-existing beliefs or hypotheses, while giving disproportionately less consideration to alternative possibilities. The familiarity effect leads people to develop preferences for things merely because they are familiar, often favouring

the familiar over the unfamiliar. 'Fast and frugal' heuristics guided by context-specific experiences can also influence firm internationalization decisions (Niittymies, 2020). Cognitive mechanisms such as heuristics and biases are integrated into traditional models explaining internationalization behaviour and knowledge development.

2. *Foreign market entry (see Chapter 7, Sections 7.1–7.3)*: This diverse cluster of subtopics includes status quo bias affecting exporters and anchoring bias influencing international acquisitions. Anchoring bias is a cognitive bias whereby an individual depends too heavily on an initial piece of information when making decisions, which can lead to inaccurate estimates, predictions, and conclusions. Overconfidence can influence ownership decisions, while heuristics can serve as effective decision-making tools in uncertain environments (Maitland & Sammartino, 2015). Biases such as overconfidence, anchoring bias, and confirmation bias can increase the likelihood of entering a foreign market while reducing the likelihood of survival.
3. *Post-entry growth*: In the post-entry growth phase, overconfidence can influence strategic decisions, particularly in collective cultures like China. Other research posits that culture can distort perceptions of country distance (Nebus & Celo, 2020). Institutions in emerging economies can cultivate heuristics, skills, and routines that can be transferred to other proximate emerging countries.
4. *International finance (see Chapter 9)*: Research in international finance introduced the concept of the home bias, deeply rooted in the familiarity effect. Home bias is a tendency for investors to invest in a large number of domestic equities, disregarding the benefits of diversifying into foreign equities, primarily because they are more familiar and comfortable with companies from their own country. This bias creates barriers for multinational companies (MNCs) attempting to access capital in foreign markets (Bell et al., 2012).
5. *Knowledge management*: Biases and heuristics have a significant impact on knowledge transfer, absorption, and sourcing in organizations. Heuristics can facilitate the cross-border transfer of organizational learning systems, while biases, specifically those of functional and cultural similarity, can pose significant barriers to knowledge flow within an organization (Mäkelä et al., 2012).

AI might represent an evolution in the field of International Business (IB) not only due to its data analytics capabilities but also for its potential to transform decision-making processes traditionally undertaken by humans. This potential shift challenges the long-held focus on human biases and heuristics in decision-making processes, which are deeply embedded in central IB theories grounded on the assumption of bounded rationality (Simon, 1956). Models developed from the behavioural theory of the firm consider that decision-makers' cognitive abilities are influenced by biases and make use of heuristics.

AI is already making strides in domains like production robotics and high-frequency trading, but its greatest potential could be in 'augmented' decision-making – a hybrid model combining human and AI decision-making (Raisch & Krakowski, 2021). This symbiosis allows for tackling complex tasks while mitigating the biases inherent in human decision-making. Evidence suggests that AI-augmented decision-making can reduce human biases and change heuristics that influence organizational decisions (Cowgill, 2019).

It is crucial to understand how human biases and heuristics, foundational to many IB theories, will be impacted by AI integration. Four central IB theories that provide insights into these biases are the internationalization theory, knowledge-based view (KBV), transaction cost theory and agency theory. These theories consider biases such as representativeness and availability heuristics, recency bias, anchoring effect, confirmation bias, familiarity effect, loss aversion, status quo bias, and the endowment effect (Tversky & Kahneman, 1974; Samuelson & Zeckhauser, 1988; Klayman, 1995) (see Figure 13.7).

Biases and heuristics grounded in central IB theories		
• Recency bias	• Familiarity effect	• Loss aversion bias
• Anchoring effect	• Status quo bias	• Availability heuristics
• Confirmation bias	• Endowment effect	• Representativeness heuristics

Figure 13.7 Biases and heuristics in International Business

Representativeness heuristics, which equate similarity with probability, can skew judgements and often lead to bias in organizational decision-making. The emergence of AI promises an approach to curtail these biases, using measures like lift, support, and natural frequencies to condense complex data and predict outcomes.

Availability heuristics, where probability is judged by the ease of recalling examples, can also introduce bias (Tversky & Kahneman, 1974). Empirical research suggests that AI, when paired with human expertise, can alleviate this by mitigating the effects of data incompleteness that might lead to availability bias (Choudhury, Starr, & Agarwal, 2020).

The anchoring effect, which involves estimating outcomes based on initial values, can result in skewed decision-making (Tversky & Kahneman, 1974). AI can help by exploring a range of alternative outcomes, potentially neutralizing the anchoring bias.

Furthermore, AI's potential role in managing biases that affirm the present state is noteworthy. Confirmation bias, which favours information that corroborates one's view, can be mitigated through ML techniques that feature attributes of outcomes first. Familiarity bias, an inclination to opt for known contexts (Heath & Tversky, 1991), can be reduced as ML broadens the scope of familiarity by processing large datasets. Lastly, loss aversion, the tendency to weigh losses more heavily than gains (Tversky & Kahneman, 1974), could potentially be modulated by AI's capacity to model human decision-making processes under uncertainty.

In essence, while still in its nascent stage, research indicates that AI has significant potential to recognize and counter human biases in decision-making processes. By reframing these biases, AI can fundamentally reshape the landscape of organizational decision-making, paving the way for more balanced and informed choices. At the same time, it remains to be seen which new biases artificial intelligence will introduce into IB decision-making.

13.3.2 Automation-Augmentation Trade-Offs

Automation and augmentation represent two strategies in the use of technology such as AI in business processes. At the heart of their application lies a pivotal trade-off concerning the extent to which human labour is replaced by automation and enhanced by technological augmentation.

Automation involves the use of technology, often in the form of AI and robotics, to perform tasks traditionally performed by humans. Automation can increase productivity, efficiency, and accuracy while reducing labour costs and human error. However, it also raises concerns about job displacement and the de-skilling of workers (Frey & Osborne, 2017).

On the other hand, augmentation strategies employ technology to assist rather than replace human workers. Augmentation typically leverages AI to provide insights, enhance decision-making, and streamline tasks, thereby enabling humans to work more effectively and creatively. This approach acknowledges and capitalizes on the unique abilities of humans, such as problem-solving, creativity, and emotional intelligence, which are currently beyond the reach of AI (Brynjolfsson & McAfee, 2014).

The choice between automation and augmentation is not binary but rather a continuum, with varying degrees of both being present in most organizations. Rather than being seen as alternatives they should be regarded as interdependent and mutually enabling technologies. The optimal balance depends on various factors, including the nature of the task, the available technology, and the broader societal and regulatory context. A commonly suggested strategy is use of automation for low-level, time-consuming, unfulfilling tasks and augmentation for higher-level tasks to enable better decision-making.

The trade-off between automation and augmentation is not just a technical decision but also a strategic and ethical one. It involves careful consideration of the potential impact on jobs, skills, and worker well-being, alongside business performance. As technologies continue to advance, navigating trade-offs will remain a critical challenge for organizations and society at large.

Spotlight: Quantum Computing

Quantum computing represents a paradigm shift in computing technology, leveraging the principles of quantum mechanics to process information in fundamentally different ways compared to classical computers. At its core, quantum computing utilizes quantum bits, or qubits, which, unlike classical bits that are either 0 or 1, can exist in multiple states simultaneously due to superposition. This property enables quantum computers to perform many calculations at once, vastly increasing their potential computing power.

Entanglement is central to quantum computing. Entanglement is a phenomenon whereby qubits become interconnected so that the state of one qubit directly influences the state of another, regardless of the distance between them. This interconnectedness allows quantum computers to process complex correlations between data points more efficiently than classical computers. Additionally, quantum computers use quantum gates to manipulate qubits in ways that enable complex computations, taking advantage of interference to arrive at solutions to specific problems.

Quantum computing is still in its early stages, with significant ongoing research aimed at overcoming practical challenges such as qubit stability, error rates, and the development of scalable systems. Quantum bits are extremely sensitive to their environment and maintaining coherence - where qubits retain their quantum states long enough to perform meaningful computations - is a major hurdle. Researchers are exploring various approaches, including superconducting qubits, trapped ions, and topological qubits, each with their own advantages and challenges.

Multinational companies are actively investing in quantum computing research and development, recognizing its transformative potential across various industries. Technology giants such as IBM, Google, and Microsoft are at the forefront, developing quantum hardware and software platforms. IBM's Q System One, Google's Sycamore processor, and Microsoft's Azure Quantum are examples of platforms that are pushing the boundaries of what quantum computers can achieve. These companies offer cloud-based quantum computing services, allowing researchers and businesses to experiment with quantum algorithms and applications.

Quantum computing has the potential to revolutionize numerous fields. In finance, quantum algorithms could optimize complex portfolio management tasks and risk assessment models more efficiently than current methods. In healthcare, quantum computing could accelerate drug discovery and genomics by simulating molecular structures and interactions at unprecedented speed. The logistics and supply chain sectors could benefit from quantum computing's ability to solve optimization problems involving vast amounts of data and variables, leading to more efficient routing and resource management.

(Continued)

Moreover, advances in quantum cryptography promise to enhance data security by creating theoretically unbreakable encryption methods, safeguarding sensitive information against future cyber threats. The potential for quantum computing to address currently intractable problems is immense, driving multinational companies to invest in research and development despite the existing technical challenges.

Sources: Scientific American (www.scientificamerican.com/article/quantum-entanglement-isnt-all-that-spooky-after-all1) and McKinsey (www.mckinsey.com/featured-insights/mckinsey-explainers/what-is-quantum-computing)

SUMMARY

Digitalization has profoundly transformed International Business by erasing traditional boundaries and revolutionizing operational strategies worldwide. Leveraging digital platforms, data analytics, and automation, companies can now reach broader consumer bases with unprecedented efficiency. The integration of big data provides critical insights that enhance decision-making and strategic planning across various industries. However, the adoption of automation technologies necessitates careful consideration of their impact on the labour market and organizational dynamics. For sustained competitive advantage, businesses must strategically harness these digital resources, using frameworks like the resource-based view to optimize their capabilities effectively.

Data science plays a pivotal role in modern International Business by equipping organizations with powerful analytical tools to predict trends and optimize operations. Techniques such as regression analysis and machine learning algorithms (e.g., support vector machines and tree-based models) enable businesses to quantify relationships, classify data accurately, and make informed predictions. Overcoming challenges like overfitting through rigorous methodologies such as train-test splitting and cross-validation ensures that predictive models remain robust and reliable. By embracing assembly methods like stacking and neural networks, companies can further enhance the accuracy and reliability of their forecasting capabilities.

Artificial intelligence (AI) represents a significant advance in International Business, enabling automation, predictive analytics, and data-driven decision-making on an unprecedented scale. Through machine learning, deep learning, and neural networks, AI facilitates tasks ranging from customer behaviour prediction to logistics optimization and fraud detection. Despite its transformative potential, AI also challenges traditional decision-making processes by offering opportunities to mitigate biases and enhance the accuracy of strategic choices. Achieving a balanced approach between automation and augmentation strategies is crucial for organizations navigating the complexities of the global marketplace and harnessing AI's full potential.

In conclusion, the convergence of digitalization, data science, and artificial intelligence is reshaping International Business landscapes fundamentally. Companies that effectively integrate these technologies can gain a competitive edge by making informed decisions, optimizing operations, and anticipating market trends with precision. Understanding the strategic implications of these advances is essential for multinational enterprises aiming to thrive in an increasingly dynamic global economy.

14

SUSTAINABILITY IN INTERNATIONAL BUSINESS

CHAPTER INTRODUCTION

In this chapter, we discuss important topics related to ethics, social responsibility, and sustainability that permeate many different aspects of doing business. We begin by asking a question that should remain in your mind as you go through this chapter: What is the role of businesses in our society? We will explore how this question relates to the important topics of corporate social responsibility (CSR) and sustainability. Later, we will link these concepts to the international operations of a firm and relate them to important theories popular in International Business that we have already covered in previous chapters.

LEARNING OUTCOMES

1 Understand the roles diverse stakeholders play in companies, and how these stakeholders contribute to social responsibility.
2 Learn about the differences between sustainability and corporate social responsibility.
3 Understand the role the UN SDGs play for corporate sustainability.
4 Understand how MNCs contribute to climate change and how MNCs could help the transition towards climate neutrality.
5 Discuss and identify greenwashing.

Case Study: Responsibility at Patagonia

Patagonia, an outdoor apparel company founded in 1973, has long been recognized as a leader in corporate sustainability, embedding environmental and social responsibility into its mission and business practices. The company's commitment to sustainability extends beyond marketing rhetoric, permeating its entire business model, supply chain, and corporate ethos. This holistic approach to sustainability is encapsulated in its mission statement: 'We're in business to save our home planet.' Patagonia's sustainability strategy is structured around three core pillars: ethical sourcing, environmental stewardship, and activism.

Ethical sourcing is integral to Patagonia's business model. The company prioritizes organic and regenerative agricultural practices, sourcing organic cotton since the 1990s to minimize pesticide use and soil degradation. In addition, it incorporates recycled materials - such as polyester from plastic bottles, wool, and down - into its products to reduce waste. Patagonia also emphasizes transparency in its supply chain, working closely with factories certified by Fair Trade and adhering to strict labour standards. This commitment ensures not only the well-being of workers but also encourages fair wages and safe working conditions globally.

Environmental stewardship is another cornerstone of Patagonia's mission. The company has pledged 1% of its sales to environmental causes since 1985, co-founding the '1% for the Planet' initiative to encourage other companies to follow suit. In 2013, Patagonia launched the 'Worn Wear' programme, encouraging customers to repair and recycle their garments to reduce consumption and waste. Moreover, Patagonia is deeply committed to reducing its carbon footprint and has set ambitious targets to become carbon neutral across its supply chain by 2025. Its investments in renewable energy and the promotion of regenerative agriculture are pivotal components of this effort.

Patagonia's activism sets it apart in the corporate world. The company uses its brand platform to advocate for policy changes on climate action, public land protection, and sustainable resource management. It has filed lawsuits against government policies that threaten the environment and regularly donates to grassroots organizations dedicated to conservation and environmental justice. Patagonia's commitment to activism is also evident in its employee engagement programmes, offering paid time off for employees to volunteer with environmental organizations.

In a way, Patagonia exemplifies how sustainability can be seamlessly integrated into a corporate mission. By prioritizing ethical sourcing, environmental stewardship, and activism, the company has set a new standard for responsible business practices. This approach has not only enhanced its brand reputation but has also demonstrated that profitability and purpose can go hand in hand, inspiring other companies to follow suit in addressing the environmental challenges of the twenty-first century.

Sources: Patagonia (www.patagonia.com/our-footprint) and McKinsey (www.mckinsey.com/industries/agriculture/our-insights/patagonia-shows-how-turning-a-profit-doesnt-have-to-cost-the-earth)

Case Study Questions

1 What alternative explanations exist for Patagonia's focus on sustainability? Where can you identify clear business cases supporting sustainability initiatives at Patagonia?
2 How has Patagonia avoided controversies about greenwashing?
3 If you were an investor, would you be ready to give up on some of your expected returns from investment for a positive societal impact?

14.1 ETHICS

The field of ethics, also known as moral philosophy, is primarily concerned with determining what is right, what is wrong, and how to behave. Business ethics examines these questions in relation to businesses in society. There are many approaches to ethics, and there is no universally accepted ethical standard that managers can apply to all situations. As you might expect, what is considered right and what is considered wrong can vary widely depending on many factors. Thus, it is not uncommon for managers in organizations that cross national borders to face multiple ethical standards. Moreover, they are bound to encounter ethical dilemmas – situations in which none of the choices seem to be without ethical complications.

While MNCs are often praised for bringing much-needed economic development to regions in need of it, along with jobs, technologies, and economic progress that might not have been there for years, not all MNCs' contributions are as ethical as they could be. Managing through ethical behaviour is difficult enough for a firm operating in one context; it becomes exponentially more complicated when the operations of the firm expand globally.

How should managers behave? Should they adopt local practices considered ethical in the host country, or should they abide by the ethics of their home country? Ikea found out firsthand how difficult navigating this type of situation can be. In 2012, the Swedish company faced a backlash in the West and eventually apologized for modifying their catalogue to better fit Saudi Arabia's marketing standards. Ikea digitally removed women from their standard catalogue to use it in Saudi Arabia. Women are not often portrayed in Saudi advertisements, and if they are, they usually wear traditional hair and skin covers. Moreover, censors routinely blacked out women's body parts in magazines for import. Thus, in trying to adapt to one part of the world, Ikea sparked controversy in another (Quinn, 2012). The truth is that there is no easy answer to ethical dilemmas, and some flexibility will be required.

Some of the most common ethical dilemmas multinationals face revolve around corruption, workplace standards, and human rights. Managers of MNCs are bound to eventually deal with such problems. This is why it is important to have a solid code of conduct to help managers navigate these difficult positions. Most companies have elaborate codes of conduct that are specific to their situations. For example, an oil and gas company will need a code different from a software developer.

Spotlight: The Trolley Problem

The trolley problem is a thought experiment in ethics that explores the implications of consequentialist and deontological ethical theories. It was first introduced by British philosopher Philippa Foot in 1967 and has since become a fundamental scenario in discussions of moral dilemmas.

In its most basic form, the trolley problem presents a situation where a trolley (a train or tram) is headed towards five people tied to a track. You are standing next to a lever that can divert the trolley onto another track, where it would kill only one person instead. The moral question is whether you should pull the lever, sacrificing one person to save five others. This scenario raises significant philosophical challenges and prompts questions about the nature of morality and ethical decision-making.

One major philosophical challenge associated with the trolley problem is the conflict between consequentialism and deontology. Consequentialism, particularly utilitarianism, argues that the morally correct action is the one that maximizes overall happiness or minimizes suffering. From this perspective, pulling the lever to save five lives at the cost of one is the right choice because it results in a better overall outcome.

In contrast, deontological ethics, as championed by Immanuel Kant, focuses on the adherence to moral rules and duties regardless of the consequences. A deontologist might argue that pulling the lever is morally wrong because it involves actively causing harm to an innocent person, violating their inherent rights and dignity. This perspective emphasizes the importance of intention and the moral integrity of actions over their outcomes.

Another challenge is the question of moral responsibility and agency. By pulling the lever, you become directly responsible for the death of the one person, even though your intention is to save five others. This raises questions about the moral weight of action vs inaction. Is it worse to actively cause harm or to passively allow harm to occur? The trolley problem forces us to consider the extent of our moral responsibility and the ethical implications of our choices.

The problem also highlights the issue of moral intuitions and their reliability. People's intuitions often vary in response to different versions of the trolley problem, suggesting that our moral judgements may be influenced by emotional and contextual factors rather than consistent ethical principles. This variability challenges the notion of objective moral truths and suggests that moral reasoning might be more complex and dependent on context than previously thought.

The trolley problem has implications for real-world ethical dilemmas, such as autonomous vehicle programming and medical decision-making. For example, how should an autonomous car be programmed to react in scenarios where harm is unavoidable? These applications of the trolley problem illustrate the practical importance of resolving its ethical challenges.

Sources: Iowa State University (www2.econ.iastate.edu/classes/econ362/hallam/CaseStudies/Trolleys.pdf); Andrade (2019)

14.1.1 Corruption and Bribery

Transparency International, an NGO that works to end corruption, defines corruption as 'the abuse of entrusted power for private gain' (Transparency International, 2024). Corruption has been around for thousands of years, and there is no shortage of such cases in modern times. One of the most common forms of corruption involves bribery. Bribery occurs when one party pays (in money or gifts) in exchange for influence. However, corruption can also come in other forms, such as nepotism or kickbacks.

Corruption exists everywhere. There are important differences, however, in how common corrupt practices are and how tolerated they are by different societies. Bribery is illegal in all countries, but it is much more prevalent in some. Bribery and corruption are interpreted, manifested and punished in different ways from one country to another, even within the EU, and can be difficult to curb.

One of the largest corruption cases in the world involved the Brazilian firm Odebrecht. Odebrecht was one of many firms caught in an anti-corruption probe into Brazilian fossil fuel giant Petrobras. Stemming from this probe, a more in-depth review of Odebrecht's actions revealed massive long-term bribery of officials in multiple countries, ultimately resulting in political crises, several ongoing criminal investigations, and multiple people receiving prison sentences. In addition to the billions of US dollars in fines and a completely destroyed reputation, Odebrecht ultimately filed for bankruptcy in 2019 (Reuters, 2019).

Odebrecht was one of Latin America's largest construction groups, focusing on large infrastructure projects such as building the metro in Caracas. At their peak, it had more than 180,000 employees in 21 countries. After filing for bankruptcy and changing its name to Novonor, it is one-seventh of its former size. Novonor will have to make significant strides to rehabilitate its image after one of the most infamous bribery scandals in the world (DW, 2020).

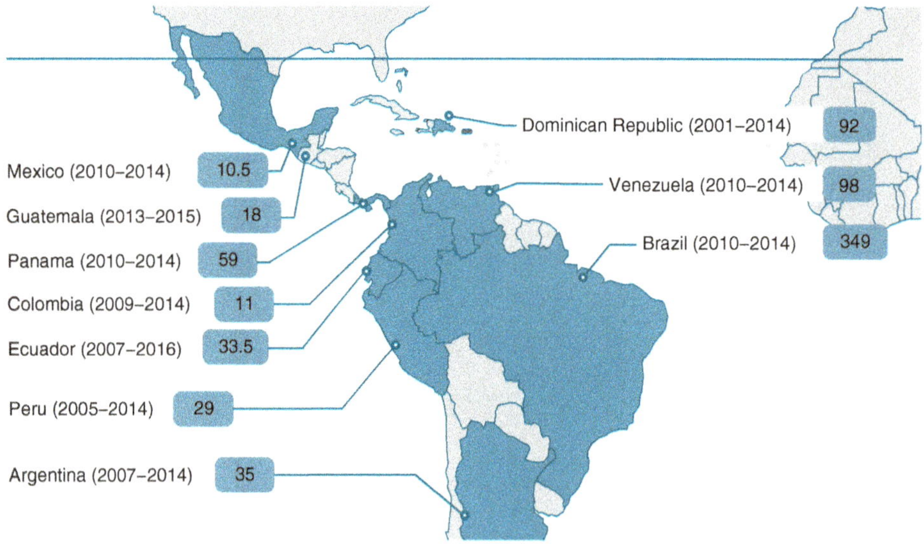

Figure 14.1 Odebrecht's bribery payments across Latin America in million USD

Source: DW (2020)

14.1.2 Human Rights and Workplace Standards

Workplace standards are another important aspect that can vary widely depending on the institutional setting. The United Nations International Labor Organization (ILO) provides useful guidelines to help firms avoid some of the most severe violations. For instance, minimum working ages can differ between countries, as can the length of the work day or week and employment safety regulations (e.g., protective equipment for those working around chemicals). Cultural differences play a significant role in the perception of many of these practices. For example, countries have different attitudes towards children working in the family business. Questions arise such as how young should they start working, for how long, and doing what tasks? A 2021 ILO report estimates that around 160 million children are involved in child labour. Not all work done by children is considered inherently negative. The ILO explains that the term 'child labour' is often defined as work that deprives children of their childhood, their potential and their dignity, and that is harmful to physical and mental development. It refers to work that is mentally, physically, socially, or morally dangerous and harmful to children and/or interferes with their schooling by depriving them of the opportunity to attend school, obliging them to leave school prematurely or requiring them to attempt to combine school attendance with excessively long and heavy work.

Some of these problems can be minimized by strong internal governance. For example, firms might set a minimum working age higher than the legal limit in the countries where they operate.

Similarly, there is no universally accepted definition for human rights. However, the most globally accepted version is the United Nations Universal Declaration of Human Rights (UDHR). The UDHR and its 30 articles are considered the foundation of all international human rights law. These rights are considered universal and inalienable, meaning that everyone has them and they cannot be lost. Based on the UDHR, the UN has established nine core human rights treaties. All UN members have ratified at least one of these treaties, and 80% have ratified four or more. For firms, this means that nations adopting the UDHR have the obligation to respect, protect, and fulfil human rights (OHCHR, n.d.). Since all member states have ratified at least one of the treaties based on the principles of the UDHR, firms need to take human rights seriously.

The chocolate industry is an example of an international industry facing severe human rights and workplace standards concerns. As a consumer of the finished product – a delicious chocolate bar – you have likely heard about these concerns. Although not new, they still persist. While chocolate makers are often thought to come from the USA, Switzerland, or Belgium, the vast majority of the world's cocoa, the key ingredient for chocolate, is sourced from West Africa. These cocoa farms are infamous for modern slavery and the use of illegal child labour. Despite the countries in this region having laws to protect against such practices, the laws are rarely enforced. The complexity of the chocolatiers' supply chain means that MNCs cannot trace where their cocoa is actually coming from. As the *Washington Post* reported in 2019:

> nearly 20 years after pledging to eradicate child labour, chocolate companies still cannot identify the farms where all their cocoa comes from, let alone whether child labour was used in producing it. Mars, maker of M&M's and Milky Way, can trace only 24 percent of its cocoa back to farms; Hershey, the maker of Kisses and Reese's, less than half; Nestlé can trace 49 percent of its global cocoa supply to farms. (Whoriskey & Siegel, 2019)

14.2 STAKEHOLDERS AND STAKEHOLDER THEORY

Academics and politicians have long argued over the role of business in society. Throughout history, there have been different trends. However, towards the end of the twentieth century, the rise in popularity of neo-classical economics, particularly in capitalist, market-driven economies, led to the notion of shareholder primacy taking over. Shareholder primacy focuses on maximizing shareholder profit, attributing a primarily economic role to business in society. This was illustrated in Milton Friedman's (in)famous quote: 'There is one and only one social responsibility of business – to use its resources and engage in activities designed to increase its profits so long as it stays within the rules of the game, which is to say, engages in open and free competition without deception or fraud' (Friedman, 1970). This doctrine was extremely influential and still shapes the opinions of many important business leaders and the public. As the name suggests, it prioritizes the role of one party, the shareholder.

However, a new paradigm focusing on stakeholders rose to prominence after Freeman's landmark 1984 book. Society now seems to be moving towards upholding an expanded role of business in society that goes beyond the purely economic realm and includes other important stakeholders such as employees, communities, and the natural environment:

> From a stakeholder perspective, business can be understood as a set of relationships among groups that have a stake in the activities that make up the business (Freeman, 1984; Jones, 1995; Walsh, 2005). It is about how customers, suppliers, employees, financiers (stockholders, bondholders, banks, etc.), communities and managers interact to jointly create and trade value. To understand a business is to know how these relationships work and change over time. (Parmar et al., 2010).

Stakeholder theory is important because it has shaped the way we view firms and their role in society. Thus, it often frames the conversation around social responsibility and sustainability.

These ideas are not new; stakeholder capitalism was already a popular management theory in the 1950s and 1960s, but has regained popularity recently. For example, it featured prominently in the World Economic Forum 2020. Stakeholder capitalism 'is a form of capitalism in which companies do not only optimize short-term profits for shareholders, but seek long-term value creation, by taking into account the needs of all their stakeholders, and society at large' (World Economic Forum, 2021).

So, who are these stakeholders? Very broadly, they can be categorized as internal stakeholders and external stakeholders. Internal stakeholders are the managers, shareholders, and employees. External stakeholders are the customers, suppliers, partners, the media, host-country and home-country governments, communities in which the firm operates, the natural environment, and more. It is important to consider that stakeholders are not passive victims of the MNCs' whims; they can exert pressure that ultimately shapes a firm's behaviour. Employees can form unions to get firms to address their demands. Governments can grant contracts or change laws that will affect MNC operations. Furthermore, sometimes actions that benefit one stakeholder might directly harm another. For example, implementing new cost-cutting measures might make the shareholders of a company happy but result in job losses for the employees. Stakeholder management is complex but crucial to the firm's operations.

As discussed in earlier chapters, MNCs must deal with additional complexity stemming from their international operations. This also applies to the number and diversity of stakeholders that they have to interact with on a daily basis. For example, MNCs need to interact with multiple governments and cater to the tastes of vastly different consumers. The interests of these stakeholders are often not aligned and are sometimes in direct conflict. Imagine a multinational firm that needs to open a new global factory; their home-country government has a clear interest in attempting to keep the potential new jobs in the domestic market. However, the governments of potential host countries might attempt to persuade the firm to attract new investment and improve their own countries' employment opportunities.

14.3 CORPORATE SOCIAL RESPONSIBILITY

Corporate social responsibility (CSR) is a concept with many definitions and one that has evolved over time to mean different things. The origins of the term are deeply rooted in the fields of ethics and welfare economics (Bansal & Song, 2017).

The European Commission has defined corporate social responsibility (CSR) as 'a concept whereby companies integrate social and environmental concerns in their business operations and in their interaction with their stakeholders on a voluntary basis' (European Commission, 2011). Corporate social responsibility relates to actions by companies over and above their legal obligations towards society and the environment. Certain regulatory measures create an environment more conducive to enterprises voluntarily meeting their social responsibility. These are, according to McWilliams and Siegel (2001), '[a]ctions that appear to further some social good, beyond the interests of the firm and that which is required by law.' Thus, obeying all the laws and regulations does not automatically mean that a firm is socially responsible. After all, not everything that is legal is ethical (e.g., most forms of lying) and there are no laws about everything (e.g., rapidly changing environments such as AI, or biotech in the past). How do firms use their economic power? Having economic power is neither necessarily good nor necessarily bad.

14.3.1 The Case Against CSR: Agency Theory

The case against CSR often hinges on the claim that CSR is a symptom of an agency problem. As you may recall (see Chapter 8, Section 8.7.1), an agency problem occurs when there is a conflict between the interests of the managers (agents) and those of the shareholders (principals). This perspective contends that managers pursue CSR in an attempt to further their own agendas and that this comes at the cost of profits, that society is better off when firms increase efficiency rather than use their resources on CSR initiatives. For example, managers might spend on CSR to improve their reputation. However, the majority of recent studies have a more positive perspective on CSR. At the same time, the recent past has seen a backlash against CSR, driven in part by the resurgence of populist politics in Europe and North America.

14.3.2 The Ethical Case for CSR

The normative, or ethical, case for CSR argues that firms should pursue CSR because it is the right thing to do. The firm is responsible to a wide range of stakeholders that demand different things (Bansal & Song, 2017). There are different ethical perspectives in support of CSR, but they often focus on the moral duty to contribute positively to society. As mentioned above, stakeholder theory has been influential in crafting the conversation around CSR. Stakeholder theory argues that:

(a) Stakeholders are persons or groups with legitimate interests in procedural and/or substantive aspects of corporate activity. Stakeholders are identified by their interests in the corporation, whether or not the corporation has any corresponding functional interest in them.

(b) The interests of all stakeholders are of intrinsic value. That is, each group of stakeholders merits consideration for its own sake and not merely because of its ability to further the interests of some other group, such as the shareowners (Donaldson & Preston, 1995).

14.3.3 The Business Case for CSR

The business case for CSR, often called instrumental CSR, rests on the idea that there are several advantages to being socially responsible, which ultimately make it good for business. This perspective argues that in the long run, firms will benefit from having strong CSR practices. For example, international firms might be able to reduce the liabilities of foreignness by being perceived as good firms. So far, scholars have linked a variety of positive effects to strong CSR, including positive financial performance, better reputation, encouragement of innovation, and employee attraction (Bansal & Song, 2017).

Research in responsibility focuses on the impacts of markets on society. Initially, these impacts were argued primarily from an ethical perspective. However, once the business case became popular, there was a significant increase in interest (Bansal & Song, 2017). While this has been very effective at persuading some people, it is not a risk-free proposition. The focus on the business case definition might lead to a self-fulfilling prophecy where managers only pursue CSR when it is beneficial for the firm. Similarly, there is concern that a disproportionate amount of attention will go to the more powerful stakeholders (those who can affect performance) at the expense of less powerful, quieter voices that are still important (Parmar et al., 2010). Finally, this sort of economic incentive for responsibility can lead to impression management.

Case Study: Dove

Dove, a personal care brand owned by Unilever, has successfully built an image of inclusivity that has significantly boosted its sales. This transformation began in 2004 with the launch of the Campaign for Real Beauty, which aimed to challenge the narrow and unrealistic beauty standards perpetuated by the beauty industry. The campaign's ethos was grounded in portraying beauty in all forms and sizes, featuring women of diverse ages, ethnicities, body shapes, and abilities. By positioning itself as a champion of inclusivity and self-esteem, Dove struck a chord with a global audience, translating this emotional connection into commercial success.

The Campaign for Real Beauty was revolutionary in its approach, as it shifted the conversation from promoting an idealized image of beauty to celebrating authenticity and individuality. Dove's advertisements featured real women rather than professional models, allowing consumers to see themselves represented. This inclusive messaging resonated deeply with women who felt marginalized by conventional beauty standards, fostering brand loyalty and trust. The campaign went viral, gaining widespread media attention and praise for challenging stereotypes, which contributed to a 20% increase in sales within the first year.

In subsequent years, Dove continued to refine its image of inclusivity with initiatives such as the Dove Self-Esteem Project and the #ShowUs campaign. The Dove Self-Esteem Project aimed to boost the confidence of young girls worldwide by providing educational resources on body positivity. This initiative solidified Dove's reputation as a brand that genuinely cared about the well-being of its consumers. The #ShowUs campaign, created in partnership with Getty Images and Girlgaze, amassed over 5,000 images showcasing women and non-binary individuals of all shapes, sizes, and backgrounds. These campaigns extended Dove's reach and reinforced its inclusive brand identity.

Furthermore, Dove's commitment to inclusivity and authenticity distinguished it from competitors and helped it capture new market segments. As the beauty industry evolved towards more diverse and inclusive marketing, Dove remained at the forefront, maintaining its market share and attracting a younger, more socially conscious demographic. This success is evident in Unilever's annual reports, which attribute Dove's consistent revenue growth to its inclusive branding strategy.

Dove's inclusive image has been instrumental in boosting its sales and in transforming the brand into a global leader in personal care. By challenging traditional beauty standards and celebrating diversity, Dove has created a strong emotional connection with consumers. This approach has not only enhanced its brand reputation but also underscored the potential of purpose-driven marketing to drive business success in an increasingly diverse and socially conscious marketplace. Nevertheless, Dove has also had to face controversy about its advertisements, particularly in 2017 when they ran a Facebook campaign where a woman of colour turned into a white woman.

Sources: Dove (www.dove.com/uk/stories/campaigns/real-beauty-pledge.html); Unilever (www.unilever.com/news/news-search/2024/20-years-on-dove-and-the-future-of-real-beauty); LinkedIn (www.linkedin.com/pulse/doves-real-beauty-campaign-marketing-case-study-abhishek-bajpai-8iwyc); The Guardian (www.theguardian.com/world/2017/oct/08/dove-apologises-for-ad-showing-black-woman-turning-into-white-one)

14.4 SUSTAINABILITY

In addition to conversations around social responsibility, you might also come across those about sustainability. As it became clear that the economic engines driven by globalization and capitalism were putting a strain on the earth's natural resources and breaching natural limits, society turned its focus towards sustainability. The term 'sustainable' originally referred primarily to the economic profits of a firm, indicating a strategy that could be maintained profitably over time. However, its meaning has expanded to encompass more than just the economic dimension. This broader focus on economic development within the natural planetary boundaries is known as sustainable development.

The UN defines sustainable development as meeting the needs of the present without compromising the ability of future generations to meet theirs. It recognizes that to achieve sustainable development, it is vital to address three interconnected dimensions: economic growth, social inclusion, and environmental protection. Similar to the business case for CSR, sustainability has been linked to a wide range of financial and non-financial performance benefits.

As we saw in the case study about Patagonia earlier in this chapter, the company is often praised for its focus on sustainability. Since its founding, Patagonia has maintained a strong connection to the natural environment, which is reflected in its business practices. Patagonia strives to use materials that are both environmentally sustainable and socially fair. Currently, more than 70% of its products are made from recycled materials, with a goal of reaching 100%. Additionally, Patagonia contributes 1% of annual sales to environmental causes. The company continues to be profitable and enjoys a strong reputation among customers, probably because its focus on sustainability is perceived as genuine. Notably, in one of its adverts, Patagonia famously encourages people not to buy its products and does not rely heavily on sustainability in its marketing communications. Many sceptics were convinced of the company's sincerity when the founder Yvon Chouinard and his family donated the entire company to further environmental causes, transferring 100% of the company's stock into a trust and a non-profit organisation (see https://eu.patagonia.com/gb/en/ownership).

14.4.1.1 Sustainable Development Goals (SDGs)

The United Nations Sustainable Development Goals (SDGs) are the core of the Agenda 2030 for Sustainable Development adopted by all United Nations Members in 2015. Agreeing on the 2030 Agenda was hailed as a great achievement of international cooperation. The formulation of the 17 goals (see Figure 14.2) and targets was a multiparty effort that included members from government, the private sector, academia, NGOs, and society at large. The UN commented: 'They recognize that ending poverty and other deprivations must go hand-in-hand with strategies that improve health and education, reduce inequality, and spur economic growth – all while tackling climate change and working to preserve our oceans and forests' (United Nations, n.d.).

The 17 SDGs might seem quite general at first glance, but the inclusion of 169 targets make them much more specific and mean progress is measurable. Take, for example, the first goal (1. No Poverty) and its targets (see below). With these targets, the efforts towards the SDGs are measurable across countries. The UN releases progress reports annually that analyse collective progress towards the SDGs, which are accessible online (https://unstats.un.org/sdgs).

Figure 14.2 The United Nations Sustainable Development Goals

The following are exemplary sub-goals for the UN SDGs (United Nations, n.d.):

1.1 By 2030, eradicate extreme poverty for all people everywhere, currently measured as people living on less than US$1.25 a day.

1.2 By 2030, reduce at least by half the proportion of men, women and children of all ages living in poverty in all its dimensions according to national definitions.

1.3 Implement nationally appropriate social protection systems and measures for all, including floors, and by 2030 achieve substantial coverage of the poor and the vulnerable.

1.4 By 2030, ensure that all men and women, in particular the poor and the vulnerable, have equal rights to economic resources, as well as access to basic services, ownership and control over land and other forms of property, inheritance, natural resources, appropriate new technology and financial services, including microfinance.

1.5 By 2030, build the resilience of the poor and those in vulnerable situations and reduce their exposure and vulnerability to climate-related extreme events and other economic, social and environmental shocks and disasters.

1.A Ensure significant mobilization of resources from a variety of sources, including through enhanced development cooperation, in order to provide adequate and predictable means for developing countries, in particular least developed countries, to implement programmes and policies to end poverty in all its dimensions.

1.B Create sound policy frameworks at the national, regional and international levels, based on pro-poor and gender-sensitive development strategies, to support accelerated investment in poverty eradication actions.

The Sustainable Development Goals (SDGs) are the most comprehensive global framework for sustainable development to date. Furthermore, they are interconnected, highlighting that collaboration is key to achieving them. These goals will not be met exclusively by public sector actors. The UN explicitly acknowledges and encourages private sector involvement and contribution to the SDGs. Multinational companies (MNCs) often wield significant economic power that can be directed towards supporting global efforts:

> The private sector is critical to achieving the Sustainable Development Goals (SDGs) – by creating employment, building skills, spurring innovation, providing essential infrastructure, and supplying affordable goods and services. The private sector is also crucial to SDG achievement as an investor of much-needed capital. Through its partnerships with private-sector actors, UNDP can influence the adoption of inclusive and sustainable business practices. (UNDP, 2024)

It is not uncommon for companies to issue SDG reports. Stakeholder pressure is mounting for firms to provide such disclosures. For example, important financial stakeholders, such as large institutional investors, who wish to align their investment strategy with the SDGs may demand such reporting from their portfolio companies. The UN Global Reporting Initiative (GRI) offers a tool called the SDG Compass that can assist businesses in reporting their SDG progress.

14.5 MNCS AND CLIMATE CHANGE

As discussed, MNCs have an impact on the natural environment. In the pursuit of economic prosperity, MNC activity is clearly affecting climate change. However, simultaneously, the effects of climate change are affecting MNC activity, and MNCs must be prepared to manage them.

Managers need to address the increasing possibility of more severe natural disasters. MNCs have always faced the risk of natural disasters, but with the growing effects of climate change, they are more probable, more severe, and likely to have cascading effects. The risk of natural disasters is different from political risk or currency risk in that it is often perceived as uncontrollable. Some countries are more prone to certain types of natural disasters. For example, there are no hurricanes in Austria, but there is a risk of wildfires in Australia. Moreover, some countries are better prepared to deal with the consequences of natural disasters than others. Disasters often cross national borders and require international cooperation. Multinationals invest in many countries with varying levels of risk, and the portfolio of their operations means that they carry different levels of exposure to extreme climate events. All of these factors make dealing with the risk of natural disasters especially challenging for managers of multinationals.

Considering the effects of potential disasters is particularly important when constructing global supply chains. Each firm must take responsibility for its own preparedness. There is a vast amount of information available – firms cannot fully insure against all risks, and often governments do not intervene successfully. As the risks increase, resilience becomes important, and firms need to plan accordingly Oh and Oetzel (2023: 4) put it this way: 'Resilience is an organizational capacity to absorb the impact of a shock and recover from the occurrence of an extreme event'. Different types of resilience capability – such as adaptability, agility, flexibility, and collaboration – are required, depending on the scope and duration of natural disasters. Figure 14.3 presents a framework elaborated by Oh and Oetzel (2023) that displays which types of natural hazards are likely to require which types of organizational response based on their duration and geographic scope.

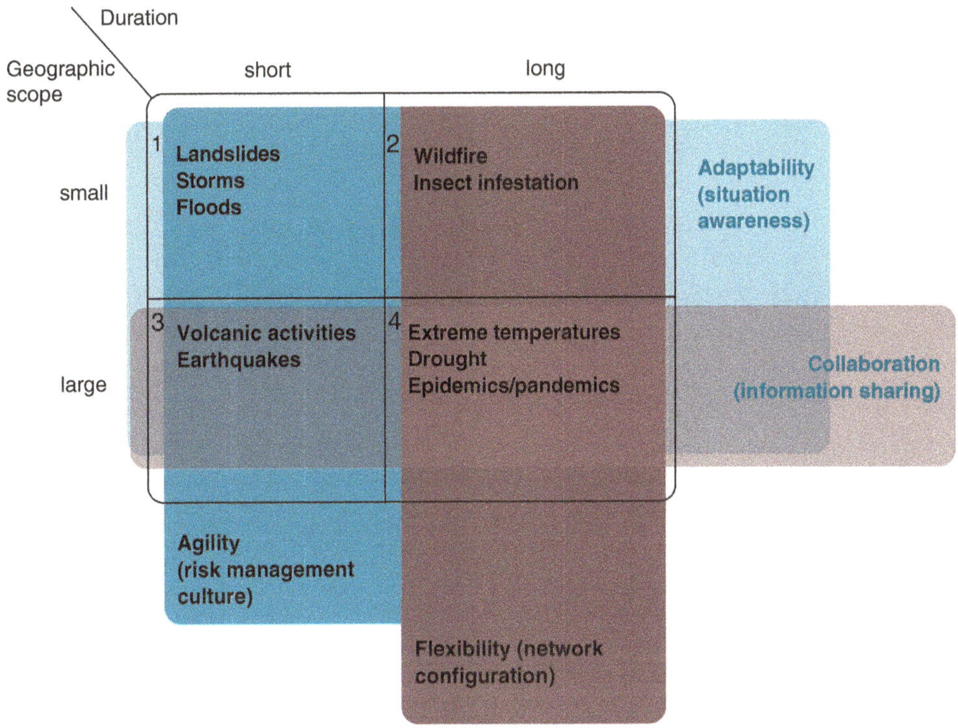

Figure 14.3 Organizational responses to natural disasters (adapted from Oh & Oetzel 2023)

As the world attempts to fight the effects of climate change, the business climate is rapidly changing. This might mean facing changing and more stringent regulations that affect a company's operations and bottom line. For example, over the last decade, China has introduced several policies that encourage the use of renewable energy. Technological innovation also provides opportunities and risks to different businesses. For example, Tesla has managed to capitalize on the automotive trend towards electric vehicles. Firms also face growing pressure to become more sustainable, which can affect previous globalized behaviour if firms decide to bring operations back to a local level. Firms need to recognize and act on the opportunities while minimizing the risks.

As policies surrounding climate change are shifting, MNCs' strategic decisions will be affected. The location of MNC subsidiaries and their partner operations is an important example. Location choice is a particularly important topic in IB. As we have already seen in Chapter 7, there are many considerations that affect the location chosen by a firm. Firms can leverage cross-country institutional differences to their advantage. MNCs might locate their HQs in countries where they pay less in corporate taxes. Similarly, firms might want to take advantage of differences in institutional quality by placing their operations where regulations are less stringent or where penalties for environmental violations are less severe (Berry et al., 2021). This is often called the 'pollution haven' effect. Since countries have different climate policies, firms might shop around for the country with the least restrictive regulations. There is extensive research supporting the existence of this effect in the context of firms' foreign direct investment (FDI), and this has been extended to global sourcing. This means that not only is there evidence of firms choosing to open subsidiaries in countries with lax environmental standards, but sourcing more from third parties located in such countries. This sourcing effect is stronger for industries with high toxic emissions and for industries with low technical intensity (Berry et al., 2021).

Investing in pollution havens is not, however, always beneficial for firms. There are some benefits in setting up shop in places with stringent regulations. The 'induced-innovation' effect suggests that countries with high environmental stringency will attract firms with higher environmental capabilities. This is because firms that possess those capabilities can compete at an advantage in those countries. Since firms with poor environmental capabilities have to invest to get themselves up to standard, those with strong environmental capabilities are already in an advantageous position. This is likely to mean that such countries attract firms with environmental capabilities and ultimately lead to the transfer of environmental capabilities to the host country. Thus, certain firms will benefit from countries with higher stringency, while others will benefit from taking advantage of pollution havens. This depends on their environmental capabilities and other characteristics.

In addition to attempting to maximize profits, firms must also deal with growing pressures to become more sustainable from multiple angles. This has prompted many firms to engage in re-shoring – voluntarily relocating totally or partially some of the previously globalized activities back to the home country. Studies show that firms consider economic, social, and environmental dimensions when deciding to re-shore (Gillani et al., 2023). The economic dimensions of re-shoring include wages, tariffs, efficient resource allocation, etc., while the social and environmental dimensions include the well-being of stakeholders (e.g., employees and communities), use of renewables, carbon footprints, etc. Furthermore, there is some evidence that consumers might reward firms that engage in such activities (Grappi et al., 2020).

Spotlight: Machine Learning for Climate Science

Machine learning (ML) has significantly enhanced climate modelling, enabling more specific and accurate predictions. Traditional climate models, while robust, often struggle with the complexity and variability of climate systems. ML addresses these challenges by processing vast amounts of data and identifying intricate patterns that might be overlooked by conventional methods.

One key advantage of ML in climate modelling is its ability to handle large datasets efficiently. Climate data, which includes variables such as temperature, precipitation, wind patterns, and ocean currents, is vast and complex. ML algorithms can analyse these datasets to identify trends and relationships that inform more accurate climate predictions. By learning from historical data, ML models can improve their predictive accuracy over time, refining their output as new data becomes available.

ML techniques, such as deep learning, are particularly effective in enhancing the resolution of climate models. High-resolution models provide more detailed regional and local climate projections, which are essential for understanding the impact of climate change on specific areas. For example, ML has been used to develop the WeatherBench benchmark dataset, which enhances weather prediction by improving the spatial and temporal resolution of forecasts. This model uses convolutional neural networks (CNNs) to process historical weather data and generate high-resolution climate predictions.

Moreover, ML algorithms can integrate diverse data sources, including satellite imagery, sensor networks, and historical climate records. This integration allows for a comprehensive understanding of climate dynamics, leading to better-informed predictions. The ClimateNet project, for instance, utilizes ML to classify and analyse cloud patterns and other atmospheric phenomena from satellite images, enhancing the accuracy of climate simulations. Similarly, the Climate Machine, developed by researchers at MIT, employs ML to improve the simulation of complex interactions within the climate system, such as feedback loops between the atmosphere, oceans, and biosphere.

Another significant contribution of ML is in reducing computational costs. Traditional climate models are computationally intensive, requiring significant time and resources. ML can streamline these processes, making climate modelling more efficient and accessible. For example, the IBM Green Horizon project uses ML to optimize climate models and reduce computational demands, enabling more frequent updates and real-time climate monitoring. This efficiency provides timely information for policy-making and environmental management.

Sources: Nature www.nature.com/articles/d41586-024-00780-8); IBM (https://uk.newsroom.ibm.com/2015-Dec-09-IBM-Expands-Green-Horizons-Initiative-Globally-To-Address-Pressing-Environmental-and-Pollution-Challenges); O'Gorman & Dwyer (2018).

14.6 FINANCE AND ENVIRONMENTAL, SOCIAL, AND GOVERNANCE INFORMATION

One example of stakeholders making an impact on MNC behaviour is the increasing importance of environmental, social, and governance (ESG) information for investors. As mentioned earlier in this chapter, (see also Chapter 9), investors are important internal stakeholders and quite powerful ones. This means they can enact change in the way public firms operate. For example, one of the world's largest asset managers, BlackRock, reportedly had assets under management totalling over US$ 10 trillion in 2021. This amount is more than twice Germany's GDP for the same year. So, what is ESG, and why should investors care?

ESG is very closely related to corporate social responsibility (CSR), and many authors use the terms interchangeably. However, unlike CSR, the origin of ESG does not stem from a normative perspective; instead, it has a quantitative measurement focus. The concept is newer and a bit different. The ESG acronym is becoming increasingly popular in the finance and accounting fields. Gillan et al. (2021: 2) comment: 'ESG is an acronym developed in a 2004 report by 20 financial institutions in response to a call from Kofi Annan, Secretary-General of the United Nations. As it implies, ESG refers to how corporations and investors integrate environmental, social, and governance concerns into their business models'. The focus on governance is particularly important to investors and is a key difference when compared to CSR.

Why should investors care about ESG information? The primary idea is that this information is important in managing some of the non-financial company risks and can serve as an important instrument to identify opportunities. Additionally, some investors view ESG as a way to obtain more information about the company that would otherwise be unavailable to them. This way, they can reduce the information asymmetry between the firm and the owners. However, just because ESG factors are measured does not automatically mean that they are integrated into investment decisions. There is a wide range of investment approaches that use ESG information through different methods to allow investors to flexibly address their chosen preferences. The increased interest in ESG factors has led to new and diverse investment products and a variety of approaches. The terminology around these investment approaches is in a constant state of flux as it is rapidly developing. In Figure 14.4, you can see the classification used by the Responsible Investment Association Australasia with some examples that range from 'ESG integration' to 'impact investing'.

In addition, existing investors have other strategies they can use to align their investment portfolios with their ethical or environmental stances. They could choose to divest or engage (or both). These are often referred to as strategies of exit and voice. Divestment, or exit, is the opposite of investing; it means removing capital already invested. For example, Norway's Government Pension Fund Global, a prominent investor, adopted this strategy when it decided to divest from fossil fuel investments (Ambrose, 2019). On the other hand, engagement is a popular alternative to divestment and involves shareholders trying to have a dialogue with the firm to enact meaningful change in the company's behaviour. This often means forming groups with other important investors to vote together for proposals to move the firm in a specific direction. Both exit and voice can be effective under different circumstances (Broccardo et al., 2022).

There is not only one reason or way to determine why investors are pushing in the direction of ESG adoption and integration. Some investors believe that doing so is simply good business. They believe in the business case for ESG and its impact on long-term financial performance. This belief can relate to a wide range of arguments – for example, that strong ESG performance grants reputational advantages or helps to attract and retain better talent. Moreover, some investors might have strong social preferences and are willing to pay an additional price for social outcomes on top of their financial expectations. There is evidence that all of these types of investors exist (Riedl & Smeets, 2017). Thus, the demand for ESG measurement and integration is driven by diverse motives and heterogeneous actors. However, there is no doubt that this trend is on the rise.

14.7 GREENWASHING

As the importance of CSR and sustainability grows in the eyes of the public, some firms might attempt to capitalize on the potential benefits associated with being perceived as responsible corporate citizens. This is particularly salient in the environmental sustainability realm as the effects of climate change become more evident than ever before. This has resulted in concerns over greenwashing. The definition of the term greenwashing is not so clear and straightforward. Most agree that barefaced lying about environmental performance constitutes greenwashing. However, some definitions include behaviour that might mislead the public into perceiving the firm as greener than their behaviour suggests. This includes the impact of selective disclosure and other kinds of misleading communication that can lead to a misrepresentation of the firm's environmental efforts – for example, overemphasizing communication about green behaviour while minimizing discussion of brown behaviour (a company's poor environmental performance).

The term 'greenwashing' is usually reserved for claims of impact on the natural environment, but many related terms that designate perceived corporate hypocrisy have sprung up. For example, participating in the United Nations Global Compact while not living up to the standards is called 'bluewashing'. 'Pinkwashing' is a term reserved for firms that might associate themselves with donations to breast cancer research centres while simultaneously having products that have been shown to increase the risk of breast cancer (Marquis et al., 2016). Firms might want to communicate their green behaviour in the hope that this will enhance their reputation. Consumers might prefer to buy products from a brand that has a green reputation and might be willing to pay a premium price for products they perceive as environmentally friendly. This could allow some firms to charge a green premium, sometimes called a 'greenium' (Seele & Gatti, 2017).

Determining what is the right amount of honest environmental disclosure is, however, not easy. Firms might be perceived as greenwashing when they are, in fact, honestly disclosing their environmental behaviour. Additionally, not all stakeholders might find environmental sustainability a noble pursuit. Indeed, there is evidence that some investors might perceive environmental friendliness as wasteful and that it leaves firms with high associated costs (DesJardine et al., 2020). There is also potential reputational damage in being caught lying or disappointing customers by under-delivering on environmental

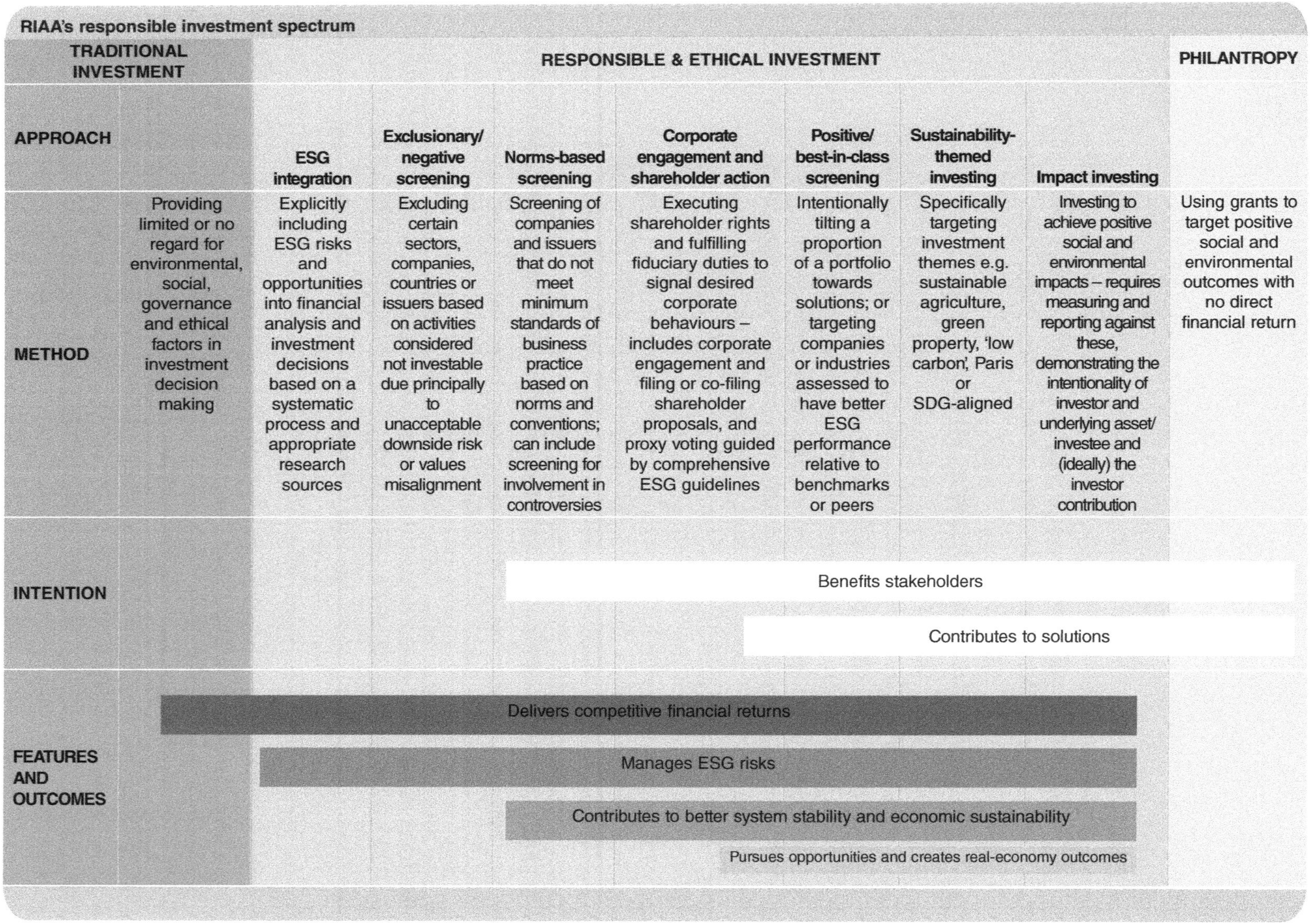

Figure 14.4 The spectrum of responsible financing

Source: This spectrum has been adapted from frameworks developed by Bridges Fund Management, Sonen Capital, and the Impact Management Project

promises. As attention to the environment increases, so does the scrutiny of firms. This makes greenwashing a risky proposition.

One of the most prominent recent examples of greenwashing is the Volkswagen (VW) emissions scandal, also known as 'Dieselgate'. In 2015, VW was charged by regulators in the USA with installing software to cheat emissions detection tests in their diesel-powered cars. This resulted in emissions levels being about 40 times more than the legal limits – all while the company marketed its vehicles as environmentally friendly. In an attempt to create the image of a more eco-friendly vehicle, Volkswagen lied to the public and to the regulators. The scandal resulted in fines amounting to billions of dollars and euros and many executives had to step down. Moreover, following the scandal, VW had to implement massive institutional changes in order to attempt to rehabilitate its image and regain the trust of stakeholders.

SUMMARY

MNCs often face dilemmas such as whether to conform to local customs or uphold ethical standards from their home countries, as illustrated by Ikea's cultural adaptation controversy in Saudi Arabia. Beyond cultural complexities, MNCs face significant ethical issues like corruption, exemplified by Odebrecht's bribery scandal, and a variety of workplace standards and human rights practices globally. Emphasizing corporate social responsibility (CSR), stakeholders advocate that firms should not only comply with legal requirements but also act ethically to benefit society and enhance their long-term sustainability.

Sustainability and corporate social responsibility (CSR) are intertwined yet distinct concepts. Sustainability evolved as a response to the environmental and societal impacts of economic growth driven by globalization and capitalism. Initially focused on maintaining profitable strategies over time, the concept expanded to encompass economic development within ecological limits, now known as sustainable development. The United Nations' Sustainable Development Goals (SDGs), adopted in 2015, highlight the interconnectedness of economic growth, social inclusion, and environmental protection as essential to meeting present needs without compromising future generations. Patagonia exemplifies a company praised for its sustainability efforts, from using recycled materials to supporting environmental causes financially.

In contrast, CSR broadly addresses corporate obligations beyond profit, including ethical practices, stakeholder well-being, and community involvement, reflecting a holistic approach to corporate citizenship. Both concepts, however, highlight the role of multinational companies (MNCs) in addressing climate change and natural disaster risks, alongside growing investor scrutiny regarding environmental, social, and governance (ESG) factors. Despite challenges such as greenwashing and a variety of regulatory landscapes, businesses are increasingly incentivized to integrate sustainability into their core strategies, reflecting broader societal expectations and the pursuit of long-term corporate resilience and legitimacy.

REFERENCES

CHAPTER 2

Ahlstrom, D., Arregle, J.-L., Hitt, M. A., Qian, G., Ma, X., & Faems, D. (2020). Managing technological, sociopolitical, and institutional change in the new normal. *Journal of Management Studies, 57*(3), 411–37.

Alcácer, J., Agrawal, A., & Vaish, H. (2013). *Walmart around the World*. Harvard Business Publishing.

Beugelsdijk, S. (2022). Capitalizing on the uniqueness of International Business: Towards a theory of place, space, and organization. *Journal of International Business Studies, 53*, 2050–67.

Caves, R. E. (1996). *Multinational Enterprise and Economic Analysis*. Cambridge University Press.

Chase-Dunn, C., Kawano, Y., & Brewer, B. D. (2000). Trade globalization since 1795: Waves of integration in the world-system. *American Sociological Review, 65*(1), 77.

Ciravegna, L., & Michailova, S. (2022). Why the world economy needs, but will not get, more globalization in the post-Covid-19 decade. *Journal of International Business Studies, 53*(1), 172–86.

Contractor, F. J. (2022). The world economy will need even more globalization in the post-pandemic 2021 decade. *Journal of International Business Studies, 53*, 156–71.

Cuervo-Cazurra, A., & Genc, M. (2008). Transforming disadvantages into advantages: Developing-country MNCs in the least developed countries. *Journal of International Business Studies, 39*(6), 957–79.

Cuervo-Cazurra, A., & Genc, M. (2011). Obligating, pressuring, and supporting dimensions of the environment and the non-market advantages of developing-country multinational companies. *Journal of Management Studies, 48*(2), 441–55.

Cui, V., Vertinsky, I., Wang, Y., & Zhou, D. (2023). Decoupling in International Business: The 'new' vulnerability of globalization and MNCs' response strategies. *Journal of International Business Studies, 54*, 1562–76.

Delios, A., Perchthold, G., & Capri, A. (2021). Cohesion, Covid-19 and contemporary challenges to globalization. *Journal of World Business, 56*(3), 101197.

Dunning, J. H. (1988). The eclectic paradigm of international production: A restatement and some possible extensions. *Journal of International Business Studies, 19*(1), 1–31.

Ghauri, P., Strange, R., & Cooke, F. L. (2021). Research on International Business: The new realities. *International Business Review, 30*(2), 101794.

Hartmann, S., Lindner, T., Müllner, J., & Puck, J. (2022). Beyond the nation-state: Anchoring supranational institutions in International Business research. *Journal of International Business Studies, 53*, 1282–1306.

Luo, Y., & Tung, R. L. (2007). International expansion of emerging market enterprises: A springboard perspective. *Journal of International Business Studies*, *38*(4), 481–98.

Luo, Y., & Tung, R. L. (2018). A general theory of springboard MNCs. *Journal of International Business Studies*, *49*(2), 129–52.

Luo, Y., & van Assche, A. (2023). The rise of techno-geopolitical uncertainty: Implications of the United States CHIPS and Science Act. *Journal of International Business Studies*, *19*(1), 119.

North, D. C. (1990). *Institutions, Institutional Change and Economic Performance*. Harvard University Press.

North, D. C. (1994). Economic performance through time. *The American Economic Review*, *84*(3), 359–68.

Scott, R. W. (1987). The adolescence of institutional theory. *Administrative Science Quarterly*, *32*(4), 493–522.

Scott, R. W. (ed.). (1995). *Institutions and Organizations: Ideas, Interests, and Identities* (4th edn). Sage Publications.

Witt, M. A. (2019). De-globalization: Theories, predictions, and opportunities for International Business research. *Journal of International Business Studies*, *50*(7), 1053–77.

Witt, M. A., Lewin, A. Y., Li, P. P., & Gaur, A. (2023). Decoupling in International Business: Evidence, drivers, impact, and implications for IB research. *Journal of World Business*, *58*(1), 101399.

CHAPTER 3

Bercuson, M. K. (1995). *Singapore: A Case Study in Rapid Development*. IMF eLibrary: www.elibrary.imf.org/display/book/9781557754639/9781557754639.xml

Boston Consulting Group. (2022). US Inflation Reduction Act: Global implications. Executive Perspectives.

Cambridge University Press. (n.d.). Ideology. Cambridge Dictionary. https://dictionarycambridge.org/dictionary/english/ideology

Chu, A., Roeder, O., & Irwin-Hunt, A. (2023). Inside the $220bn American cleantech project boom. Financial Times. www.ft.com/content/3b19c51d-462b-43fa-9e0e-3445640aabb5

Council of the EU and European Council. (2023). EU sanctions against Russia explained. www.consilium.europa.eu/en/policies/sanctions-against-russia/sanctions-against-russia-explained

Freeden, M. (2001). Ideology: Political Aspects. *International Encyclopedia of the Social & Behavioral Sciences*. Oxford University Press.

Gahvari, F. (1989). The nature of government expenditures and the shape of the Laffer Curve. *Journal of Public Economics*, *40*(2): 251–60.

Hall, P. A., & Soskice, D. (eds) (2001). An introduction to varieties of capitalism. In *Varieties of Capitalism: The Institutional Foundations of Comparative Advantage*, 1–68. Oxford University Press.

Heijman, W. J. M., & van Ophem, J. A. C. (2005). Willingness to pay tax: The Laffer Curve revisited for 12 OECD countries. *The Journal of Socio-Economics*, *34*(5), 714–23.

Henisz, W. J. (2000). The institutional environment for economic growth. *Economics and Politics*, *12*(1), 1–31.

Huang, Y. (2016). Understanding China's Belt & Road Initiative: Motivation, framework and assessment. *China Economic Review*, *40*, 314–21.

Leahy, J. (2023). US companies see China as 'uninvestable', warns Gina Raimondo. *Financial Times*. www.ft.com/content/8c1bbbf5-921e-4263-bf10-04b7e10b6b75

Mariotti, S., & Marzano, R. (2019). Varieties of capitalism and the internationalization of state-owned enterprises. *Journal of International Business Studies*, *50*, 669–91.

Müllner, J., & Dorobantu, S. (2022). Overcoming political risk in developing economies through non-local debt. *Journal of International Business Policy*, *6*(2), 159.

Müllner, J., & Puck, J. (2018). Towards a holistic framework of MNC–state bargaining: A formal model and case-based analysis. *Journal of World Business*, *53*(1), 15–26.

OECD & AIAS (2021). Institutional Characteristics of Trade Unions, Wage Setting, State Intervention and Social Pacts. OECD Publishing.

Schott, J. (2023). Which countries are in the CPTPP and RCEP trade agreements and which want in? PIIE: Peterson Institute for International Economics. United States of America. Retrieved from https://coilink.org/20.500.12592/nxqs72

Sevastopulo, D. (2023). US weighs tougher restrictions on AI chip exports to China. *Financial Times*. www.ft.com/content/a6c6b769-349e-440f-a55b-c92371d00dd9

Sheppard, D. (2022). Russia weaponisation of gas spurs clean energy push to secure supply. *Financial Times*. www.ft.com/content/50816240-9b68-43a8-8541-c3a728d63799

Smith, A. (1937/1776). *The Wealth of Nations* (edited by Edwin Cannan, 1904). Modern Library.

Speed, M. (2023). Carlsberg 'shocked' at seizure of Russian subsidiary. *Financial Times*. www.ft.com/content/ceb08a80-3b88-4f28-b8bb-7bce67743a84

The PRS Group. (n.d.). *International Country Risk Guide (ICRG)*. Retrieved from www.prsgroup.com/explore-our-products/icrg

United Nations. (1987). *Report of the World Commission on Environment and Development: Our Common Future*. www.un-documents.net/our-common-future.pdf

Yeo, P. (2016). Going beyond comparative advantage: How Singapore did it. In Breaking the Oil Spell: The Gulf Falcons' Path to Diversification, 65. IMF eLibrary: www.elibrary.imf.org/display/book/9781513537863/ch004.xml

CHAPTER 4

Appadurai, A. (1994). Disjuncture and difference in the global cultural economy. In M. Featherstone (ed.), *Global Culture*, pp. 295–310, accessed via Amherst College. www.amherst.edu/system/files/media/0440/Appadurai%2C%20Disjuncture%20and%20Difference.pdf

Berrone, P., Duran, P., Gómez-Mejía, L., Heugens, P. Kostova, T. & van Essen, M. (2022). Impact of informal institutions on the prevalence, strategy, and performance of family firms: A meta-analysis. *Journal of International Business Studies*, *53*, 1153–77.

Hall, E. T. (1959). *The Silent Language*. Doubleday & Co.

Hall, E. T. (1966). *The Hidden Dimension* (1st edn). Doubleday & Co.

Hall, E. T. (1976). *Beyond Culture*. Anchor.

Hall, E. T. (1983). *The Dance of Life: The Other Dimension of Time*. Anchor Press.

Hall, E. T. (1992). *An Anthropology of Everyday Life*. Doubleday & Co.

Hofstede, G. (1980). Culture and organizations. *International Studies of Management & Organization, 10*(4), 15–41.

Hofstede, G. (1996). Riding the waves of commerce: A test of trompenaars 'model' of national culture differences. *International Journal of Intercultural Relations, 20*(2), 189–198.

Hofstede, G. (2001). *Culture's Consequences: Comparing Values, Behaviors, Institutions and Organizations across Nations*. Sage Publications.

House, R. J., Hanges, P. J., Javidan, M., Dorfman, P., & Gupta, V. (2004). *Culture, Leadership, and Organizations: The GLOBE Study of 62 Societies*. Sage Publications.

Jiyoung Shin, J., Moon, J. J., & Kang, J. (2023). Where does ESG pay? The role of national culture in moderating the relationship between ESG performance and financial performance. *International Business Review, 32*(3),102071.

Kluckhohn, F. R., & Strodtbeck, F. L. (1961). *Variations in Value Orientations*. Peterson.

Osgood, C. (1951). Culture: Its empirical and non-empirical character. *Southwestern Journal of Anthropology*, *7*(2), 202–14.

Puck, J. F., Mohr, A. T., & Holtbrügge, D. (2006). Cultural convergence through web-based management techniques? The case of corporate web site recruiting. *Journal of International Management, 12*(2), 181–95.

Schein, E. H. (2010). *Organizational Culture and Leadership* (2nd edn). John Wiley & Sons.

Trompenaars, F., & Hampden-Turner, C. (2011). *Riding the Waves of Culture: Understanding Diversity in Global Business*. Nicholas Brealey International.

Tsai, K. S. (2006). Adaptive informal institutions and endogenous institutional change in China. *World Politics, 59*(1), 116–41.

Yiu, D. W., Wan, W. P., Chen, K. X., & Tian, X. (2022). Public sentiment is everything: Host-country public sentiment toward home country and acquisition ownership during institutional transition. *Journal of International Business Studies*, *53*, 1202–27.

CHAPTER 5

Balassa, B. (1961). Towards a theory of economic integration. *International Review for Social Science, 14*(1), 1–17.

Berry, H., Guillén, M. F., & Zhou, N. (2010). An institutional approach to cross-national distance. *Journal of International Business Studies, 41*, 1460–80.

Bhagwati, J. (1995). Trade liberalisation and 'fair trade' demands: Addressing the environmental and labour standards issues. *The World Economy, 18*(6), 745–59.

Bown, C. P. (2017). Mega-regional trade agreements and the future of the WTO. *Global Policy, 8*(1), 107–12.

Caribbean Community (CARICOM). (2023). Who we are. https://caricom.org/our-community/who-we-are

Chakravarthy, B., & Pallivathukkal, C. A. (2017). *Thai Union: The Making of a World-leading Seafood Company*. International Institute for Management Development (IMD).

Communidad Andina. (2021). The Andean Community. www.comunidadandina.org/quienes-somos

Crowley, P. M. (2006). Is there a logical integration sequence after EMU? *Journal of Economic Integration*, *21*(1), 1–20.

Disdier, A. C., & Fugazza, M. (2019). *A Practical Guide to the Economic Analysis of Non-Tariff Barriers*. www.wto.org/english/res_e/booksp_e/non_tariff_measures_e.pdf

European Commission (n.d.). *The common agricultural policy at a glance*. https://agriculture.ec.europa.eu/common-agricultural-policy/cap-overview/cap-glance_en

Gantz, D. A. (2018). The risks and rewards of renegotiating the North American Trade Relationship. *Maryland Journal of International Law*, *33*, 127.

Ghemawat, P. (2001). Distance still matters: The hard reality of global expansion. *Harvard Business Review*, *9*, 1–12.

Hartmann, S., Lindner, T., Müllner, J., & Puck, J. (2022). Beyond the nation-state: Anchoring supranational institutions in International Business research. *Journal of International Business Studies*, *53*(6), 1282–1306.

International Monetary Fund. (1992). *Regional trade arrangements*. www.elibrary.imf.org/display/book/9781557752277/9781557752277.xml

Lindner, T. & Puck, J. (2024). Information distance: Conceptual development and empirical tests of a novel measure of cross-national distance. *Journal of International Management*, *30*(2), 101087.

Molle, W. (1997). *The Economics of European Integration*. Routledge.

Robson, P. (1998). *The Economics of International Integration*. Routledge.

Schott, J. J. (2023) Which countries are in the CPTPP and RCEP trade agreements and which want in? Blog. https://coilink.org/20.500.12592/nxqs72

Staiger, R. W. (2012). Non-tariff measures and the WTO. www.wto.org/english/res_e/reser_e/ersd201201_e.pdf

UNCTAD. (2022). *Trade and Development Report 2022*. https://unctad.org/publication/trade-and-development-report-2022

Viner, J. (1950). *The Customs Union Issue*. Carnegie Endowment for International Peace.

Whitley, R. (1992) *European Business Systems; Firms and Markets in Their National Contexts*. Sage.

World Trade Organization. (2022). *Digital Trade: Opportunities and Challenges*. www.wto.org/english/tratop_e/devel_e/digital_trade2022_e.pdf

World Trade Organization. (2023a). Regional trade agreements database. https://rtais.wto.org/UI/PublicMaintainRTAHome.aspx

World Trade Organization. (2023b). Figures on regional trade agreements notified to the GATT/WTO and in force. https://rtais.wto.org/UI/publicsummarytable.aspx

World Trade Organization. (2023c). Understanding the WTO: settling disputes. www.wto.org/english/thewto_e/whatis_e/tif_e/disp1_e.htm

CHAPTER 6

Alexy, O., West, J., Klapper, H., & Reitzig, M. (2018). Surrendering control to gain advantage: Reconciling openness and the resource-based view of the firm. *Strategic Management Journal, 39*(6), 1704–27.

Arda, O. A., Montabon, F., Tatoglu, E., Golgeci, I., & Zaim, S. (2023). Toward a holistic understanding of sustainability in corporations: Resource-based view of sustainable supply chain management. *Supply Chain Management: An International Journal, 28*(2), 193–208.

Bellino, E., & Fratini, S. M. (2022). Absolute advantages and capital mobility in international trade theory. *The European Journal of the History of Economic Thought, 29*(2), 271–93.

Collinson, S., Narula, R., Qamar, A., & Rugman, A. M. (2020). *International Business.* Pearson UK.

Costinot, A. (2009). An elementary theory of comparative advantage. *Econometrica, 77*(4), 1165–92.

Heckscher, E. (1949). The effects of foreign trade on the distribution of income. Reprinted in H. Ellis and L. Metzler (eds), *Readings in the Theory of International Trade.* Irwin.

Krugman, P. (1979). Increasing returns, monopolistic competition, and international trade. *Journal of International Economics, 9*, 469–79.

Kunroo, M. H., & Ahmad, I. (2023). Heckscher-Ohlin theory or the modern trade theory: How the overall trade characterizes at the global level? *Journal of Quantitative Economics, 21*(1), 151–74.

Leamer, E. E. (1980). The Leontief paradox, reconsidered. *Journal of Political Economy, 88*(3), 495–503.

Leontief, W. (1953). Domestic production and foreign trade: The American capital position re-examined. *Proceedings of the American Philosophical Society, 97*(4), 332–49.

Linder, S. B. (1961). *An Essay on Trade and Transformation.* John Wiley and Sons.

Markusen, J. R., & Venables, A. J. (1998) Multinational firms and the new trade theory. *Journal of International Economics, 46*(2), 183–203.

Minabe, N. (1966). The Heckscher-Ohlin theorem, the Leontief paradox, and patterns of economic growth. *The American Economic Review, 56*(5), 1193–211.

Ohlin, B. (1933). *International and Interregional Trade* (revised edn). Harvard Economic Studies.

Ricardo, D. (1948). *On the Principles of Political Economy and Taxation.* Dutton.

Rink, D. R., & Swan, J. E. (1979). Product life cycle research: A literature review. *Journal of Business Research, 7*(3), 219–42.

Smith, A. (1937/1776). *The Wealth of Nations* (edited by Edwin Cannan, 1904). Modern Library.

Vernon, R. (1992). International investment and international trade in the product cycle. In J. M. Letiche (ed.), *International Economic Policies and Their Theoretical Foundations*, pp. 415–35. Academic Press.

CHAPTER 7

Alexy, O., West, J., Klapper, H., & Reitzig, M. (2018). Surrendering control to gain advantage: Reconciling openness and the resource-based view of the firm. *Strategic Management Journal, 39*(6), 1704–27.

Anderson, E., & Gatignon, H. (1986). Modes of foreign entry: A transaction cost analysis and propositions. *Journal of International Business Studies, 17*, 1–26.

Arda, O. A., Montabon, F., Tatoglu, E., Golgeci, I., & Zaim, S. (2023). Toward a holistic understanding of sustainability in corporations: Resource-based view of sustainable supply chain management. *Supply Chain Management, 28*(2): 193–208.

Barney, J. (1991). Firm resources and sustained competitive advantage. *Journal of Management, 17*(1), 99–120.

Beckerman, W. (1956). Distance and the pattern of intra-European trade. *The Review of Economics and Statistics, 38*(1), 31–40.

Carlson, S. (1974) International transmission of information and the business firm. *Annals of the American Academy of Political and Social Science, 412*, 1, 55–63.

Chatzoglou, P., Chatzoudes, D., Sarigiannidis, L., & Theriou, G. (2018). The role of firm-specific factors in the strategy–performance relationship: Revisiting the resource-based view of the firm and the VRIO framework. *Management Research Review, 41*(1), 46–73.

Chen, W., Botchie, D., Braganza, A., & Han, H. (2022). A transaction cost perspective on blockchain governance in global value chains. *Strategic Change, 31*(1), 75–87.

Cuervo-Cazurra, A., & Narula, R. (2015). A set of motives to unite them all? Revisiting the principles and typology of internationalization motives. *The Multinational Business Review, 23*(1), 2–14.

Cuypers, I. R., Hennart, J. F., Silverman, B. S., & Ertug, G. (2021). Transaction cost theory: Past progress, current challenges, and suggestions for the future. *Academy of Management Annals, 15*(1), 111–50.

Cyert, R. M., & March, J. G. (1963). *A Behavioral Theory of the Firm*. Prentice Hall/Pearson Education.

Dow, D., & Karunaratna, A. (2006). Developing a multidimensional instrument to measure psychic distance stimuli. *Journal of International Business Studies, 37*, 578–602.

Dunning, J. H. (1979). Explaining changing patterns of international production: In defense of the eclectic theory. *Oxford Bulletin of Economics & Statistics, 41*(4), 269–95.

Dunning, J. H. (2000). The eclectic paradigm as an envelope for economic and business theories of MNE activity. *International Business Review, 9*, 163–90.

Dunning, J. H., & Lundan, S. M. (2008). *Multinational Enterprises and the Global Economy*. Edward Elgar Publishing.

Foss, N. J. (1998). The resource-based perspective: An assessment and diagnosis of problems. *Scandinavian Journal of Management, 14*(3), 133–49.

Ghoshal, S., & Moran, P. (1996). Bad for practice: A critique of the transaction cost theory. *Academy of Management Review, 21*(1), 13–47.

Hennart, J. F. (1988). A transaction costs theory of equity joint ventures. *Strategic Management Journal, 9*(4), 361–74.

Johanson, J., & Vahlne, J. E. (1977). The internationalization process of the firm – a model of knowledge development and increasing foreign market commitments. *Journal of International Business Studies*, *8*, 23–32.

Kerin, R. A., Varadarajan, P. R., & Peterson, R. A. (1992). First-mover advantage: A synthesis, conceptual framework, and research propositions. *Journal of Marketing*, *56*(4), 33–52.

Kim, D. (2020). Internet and SMEs' internationalization: The role of platform and website. *Journal of International Management*, *26*(1), 100690.

Kim, D., & Cavusgil, E. (2020). Antecedents and outcomes of digital platform risk for international new ventures' internationalization. *Journal of World Business*, *55*(1), 101021.

Knight, G. A., & Cavusgil, S. T. (1996). The born global firm: A challenge to traditional internationalization theory. *Advances in International Marketing*, *8*(1), 11–26.

Konara, P., & Shirodkar, V. (2018). Regulatory institutional distance and MNC's subsidiary performance: Climbing up vs climbing down the institutional ladder. *Journal of International Management*, *24*(4), 333–47.

Kraaijenbrink, J., Spender, J. C., & Groen, A. J. (2010). The resource-based view: A review and assessment of its critiques. *Journal of Management*, *36*(1), 349–72.

Lindner, T., & Puck, J. (2024). Information distance: Conceptual development and empirical tests of a novel measure of cross-national distance. *Journal of International Management*, *30*(2), 101087.

Nagle, F., Seamans, R., & Tadelis, S. (2020). Transaction cost economics in the digital economy: A research agenda. *Harvard Business School Working Paper*, No. 21-009, July.

North, D. C. (1990). *Institutions, Institutional Change and Economic Performance*. Harvard University Press.

Pan, Y., & Tse, D. K. (2000). The hierarchical model of market entry modes. *Journal of International Business Studies*, *31*, 535–54.

Peng, M. W. (2002). Towards an institution-based view of business strategy. *Asia Pacific Journal of Management*, *19*, 251–67.

Penrose, E. T. (1959). *The Theory of the Growth of the Firm*. John Wiley.

Porter, M. E. (2001). The value chain and competitive advantage. *Understanding Business Processes*, *2*, 50–66.

Porter, M. E. (2011). *Competitive Advantage of Nations: Creating and Sustaining Superior Performance* (11th edn). Simon & Schuster.

Schmidt, C., & Wagner, S. (2019). Blockchain and supply chain relations: A transaction cost theory perspective. *Journal of Purchasing and Supply Management*, *25*, 100552.

Shaver, J. M. (2013). Do we really need more entry mode studies? *Journal of International Business Studies*, *44*, 23–7.

Stallkamp, M., & Schotter, A. P. (2021). Platforms without borders? The international strategies of digital platform firms. *Global Strategy Journal*, *11*(1), 58–80.

Ullah, S., Khan, F., & Ahmad, N. (2021). Promoting sustainability through green innovation adoption: A case of manufacturing industry. *Environmental Science and Pollution Research*, *29*, 21119–21139.

Williamson, O. E. (1985). *The Economic Institutions of Capitalism*. Free Press.
Williamson, O. E. (1991). Comparative economic organization: The analysis of discrete structural alternatives. *Administrative Science Quarterly, 36*, 269–96.
Zaheer, S. (1995). Overcoming the liability of foreignness. *Academy of Management Journal, 38*(2): 341–63.

CHAPTER 8

Ambos, T. C., Cesinger, B., Eggers, F., & Kraus, S. (2020). How does de-globalization affect location decisions? A study of managerial perceptions of risk and return. *Global Strategy Journal, 10*(1), 210–236.
Bals, L., Kirchoff, J. F., & Foerstl, K. (2016). Exploring the reshoring and insourcing decision making process: Toward an agenda for future research. *Operations Management Research, 9*(3–4), 102–16.
Bals, L., Ørberg Jensen, P. D., Larsen, M. M., & Pedersen, T. (2013). Exploring layers of complexity in offshoring research and practice. In T. Pedersen, L. Bals, P. D. Ørberg Jensen, & M. M. Larsen, (eds), *The Offshoring Challenge: Strategic Design and Innovation for Tomorrow's Organization*. Springer.
Bartlett, C., & Ghoshal, S. (1989). *Managing across Borders: The Transnational Solution*. Harvard Business School Press.
Berle, A., & Means, G. (1932). *The Modern Corporation and Private Property*. Macmillan.
Caldicott, S. M. (2014). Why Ford's Alan Mulally is an innovation CEO for the record books. *Forbes*, 25 June.
Chakravarthy, B. S., & Perlmutter, H.V. (1986). Strategic planning for a global business. *The International Executive, 28*(1): 1–91.
Chen, M.-J., Su, K.-H., & Tsai, W. (2007). Competitive tension: The awareness–motivation–capability perspective. *Academy of Management Journal, 50*, 101–18.
Daily, C. M., Dalton, D. R., & Rajagopalan, N. (2003). Governance through ownership: Centuries of practices, decades of research. *Academy of Management Journal, 46*(2), 151–8.
Eisenhardt, K. M. (1989). Agency theory: An assessment and review. *Academy of Management Review, 14*(1), 57–74.
Harris, M., & Raviv, A. (1978). Some results on incentive contracts with applications to education and employment, health insurance, and law enforcement. *The American Economic Review, 68*(1), 20–30.
Ingrassia, P. (2013). The weekend interview with Alan Mulally: Ford's renaissance man. *Wall Street Journal*, 27 February.
Jensen, M., & Meckling, W. (1976). Theory of the firm: Managerial behavior, agency costs, and ownership structure. *Journal of Financial Economics, 3*(4), 305–60.
Johanson, J., & Vahlne, J.-E. (1977). The internationalization process of the firm – a model of knowledge development and increasing foreign market commitments. *Journal of International Business Studies, 8*(1), 23–32.

Li, J., & Rugman, A. M. (2007). Real options and the theory of foreign direct investment. *International Business Review, 16*(6), 687–712.

Lieberman, M. B., & Montgomery, D. B. (1988). First-mover advantages. *Strategic Management Journal, 9*(1 S), 41–58.

Luo, Y., & Witt, M. A. (2022). Springboard MNEs under de-globalization. *Journal of International Business Studies, 53*(4), 767–780.

McGregor, J. (2014). How stock options lead CEOs to put their own interests first. *The Washington Post*. www.washingtonpost.com/news/on-leadership/wp/2014/02/11/how-stock-options-lead-ceos-to-put-their-own-interests-first

Mulally, A., & McArthur, S. (2022). A conversation with Alan Mulally about his 'working together' strategic, operational, and stakeholder-centered management system. *Leader to Leader*, 27 January.

Myers, S. C. (1977). Determinants of corporate borrowing. *Journal of Financial Economics, 5*(2), 147–75.

Perrow, C. (1986). *Complex Organizations*. Random House.

Porter, M. E. (2008). *Competitive Advantage: Creating and Sustaining Superior Performance*. Free Press.

Prahalad, C. K., & Doz, Y. L. (1987). *The Multinational Mission: Balancing Local Demands and Global Vision*. Free Press.

Prahalad, C. K., & Hamel, G. (2009). The core competence of the corporation. In *Knowledge and Strategy*, pp. 41–59. Routledge.

Puck, J., Lawton, T., & Mohr, A. (2018). The corporate political activity of MNCs: Taking stock and moving forward. *Management International Review, 58*, 663–673.

Ramaswamy, K., Li., M., & Veliyath, R. (2002). Variations in ownership behavior and propensity to diversify: A study of the Indian corporate context. *Strategic Management Journal, 23*(4), 345–58.

Roth, K., & Morrison, A. J. (1990). An empirical analysis of the integration-responsiveness framework in global industries. *Journal of International Business Studies, 21*, 541–64.

Shleifer, A., & Vishny, R. W. (1997). A survey of corporate governance. *Journal of Finance, 52*(2), 737–89.

Smith, A. (1937/1776). *The Wealth of Nations* (edited by Edwin Cannan, 1904). Modern Library.

Stallkamp, M., & Schotter, A. P. (2021). Platforms without borders? The international strategies of digital platform firms. *Global Strategy Journal, 11*(1), 58–80.

Thomsen, S., & Pedersen, T. (2000). Ownership structure and economic performance in the largest European companies. *Strategic Management Journal, 21*(6), 689–705.

CHAPTER 9

Bouchet, M. H., Clark, E., & Groslambert, B. (2003). *Country Risk Assessment: A Guide to Global Investment Strategy*. John Wiley & Sons.

Gatti, S. (2023). *Project Finance in Theory and Practice: Designing, Structuring and Financing Private and Public Projects*. Elsevier.

Homaifar, G. A. (2004). *Managing Global Financial and Foreign Exchange Rate Risk.* John Wiley & Sons.

International Monetary Fund. (2003, 31 December). Classification of exchange rate arrangements and monetary policy frameworks. www.imf.org/external/np/mfd/er/2003/eng/1203.htm

International Monetary Fund (2020). *Annual Report on Exchange Arrangements and Exchange Restrictions 2019.* IMF Publications.

Jüttner, D. J. (2000). Message to Basle: Risk reduction rather than management. In B. E. Gup (ed.), The New Financial Architecture, pp.207–35. Quorum Books. https://epdf.pub/the-new-financial-architecture-banking-regulation-in-the-21st-century.html

Lindner, T., Klein, F., & Schmidt, S. (2018). The effect of internationalization on firm capital structure: A meta-analysis and exploration of institutional contingencies. *International Business Review, 27*(6), 1238–49.

Meldrum, D. (2000). Country risk and foreign direct investment. *Business Economics, 35*(1), 33–40.

Mishkin, F. S., & Simon, J. (1995). An empirical examination of the Fisher effect in Australia. *Economic Record, 71*(3), 217–29.

Moffett, M. H., Stonehill, A. I., & Eiteman, D.K. (2021). *Fundamentals of Multinational Finance* (6th edn). Pearson.

OECD (1996). OECD Benchmark Definition of Foreign Direct Investment (3rd edn). www.oecd.org/content/dam/oecd/en/publications/reports/1996/11/oecd-benchmark-definition-of-foreign-direct-investment_g1gh5da0/9789264064805-en.pdf

Rossi, E., & Stepic, R. (2015). *Infrastructure Project Finance and Project Bonds in Europe.* Palgrave Macmillan.

Shenkar, O., Luo, Y., & Chi, T. (2021). *International Business.* Routledge.

Solnik, B., & McLeavey, D. (2004). *International Investments* (5th edn). Pearson Addison Wesley.

Takefman, B. (2022). What are greenfield investments? Research FDI. https://researchfdi.com/what-are-greenfield-investments

The World Bank. (2020). Global Investment Competitiveness Report 2019/2020. *Rebuilding Investor Confidence in Times of Uncertainty.* https://openknowledge.worldbank.org/server/api/core/bitstreams/736358db-40d6-5ad3-8571-45c89ee8a697/content

UNCTAD. (2023). World Investment Report 2023. *Investing in Susutainable Energy for All.* https://unctad.org/system/files/official-document/wir2023_en.pdf

Wall, S., Minocha, S., & Rees, B. (2015) *International Business* (4th edn). Pearson.

Yescombe, E. R. (2014). *Principles of Project Finance* (2nd edn). Elsevier.

CHAPTER 10

Agic, E., Cinjarevic, M., Kurtovic, E., & Cicic, M. (2016). Strategic marketing patterns and performance implications. *European Journal of Marketing, 50*(12), 2216–48.

Alfayad, F. S. (2019). Economic reform and wholly foreign-owned enterprises in China: Marketing lessons for Saudi Arabia in implementing its own economic reforms.

Academy of Marketing Studies Journal, 23(3). www.abacademies.org/articles/economic-reform-and-wholly-foreign-owned-enterprises-in-china-marketing-lessons-for-saudi-arabia-in-implementing-its-own-economic-8361.html

Banerjee, A. (2021). Forecasting price levels in India – an ARIMA framework. *Academy of Marketing Studies Journal, 25*(1), 1–15.

Betancourt, J. M., Hortaçsu, A., Oery, A., & Williams, K. R. (2022). Dynamic price competition: Theory and evidence from airline markets. National Bureau of Economic Research, Working Paper 30347. www.nber.org/papers/w30347

Booms, B. H., & Bittner, M. J. (1981). Marketing strategies and organization for service firms. In J. H. Donnelly, & W. R. George (eds), *Marketing of Services*, pp. 47–51. American Marketing Association.

Coget, J. (2017). The Apple Store effect: Does organizational identification trickle down to customers? *Academy of Management Perspectives, 25*(1). https://doi.org/10.5465/amp.25.1.94

Edwards, J., Mckinnon, A., & Cullinane, S. (2010). Comparative analysis of the carbon footprints of conventional and online retailing: A 'last mile' perspective. *International Journal of Physical Distribution & Logistics Management, 40*(1–2), 103–23.

Ercan, M., Malmodin, J., Bergmark, P., Kimfalk, E., & Nilsson, E. (2016). Life cycle assessment of a smartphone. *Proceedings of ICT for Sustainability 2016*, August, 124–33.

Fischer, J. (2016). Markets, religion, regulation: Kosher, halal and Hindu vegetarianism in global perspective. *Geoforum, 69*, 67–70.

Foscht, T., Sinha, I., Maloles, C., & Schloffer, J. (2011). The product and branding strategy of 'Muji'. In J. Zentes, B. Swoboda, & D. Morschett (eds), *Fallstudien zum Internationalen Management*, pp. 493–510. Gabler Verlag.

Helmold, M. (2022). *Performance Excellence in Marketing, Sales and Pricing. Leveraging Change, Lean and Innovation Management.* Springer.

Jamal, Z. B. (2014). Cross-cultural impact on marketing strategies: A study on automobile industry. International Conference on Business, Law and Corporate Social Responsibility, Phuket (Thailand). https://icehm.org/images/upload/1831ED1014004.pdf

Lovelock, C., & Wirtz, J. (2011). *Services Marketing. People, Technology, Strategy* (7th edn). Pearson.

McCarthy, J. (1960). *Basic Marketing: A Managerial Approach*. Richard D. Irwin.

Ramasundaram, G., Aishwarya, B., Ajit, B., & Vakayil, S. (2022). Effectiveness of advertisements by national tobacco control organisation of India: An experimental research. *Academy of Marketing Studies Journal, 26*(3), 1–11.

Schlegelmilch, B. B. (2022). *Global Marketing Strategy: An Executive Digest* (2nd edn). Springer.

Terry, A., & Forrest, H. (2007). Where's the beef? Why Burger King is Hungry Jack's in Australia and other complications in building a global franchise brand. *Northwestern Journal of International Law and Business, 28*, 171.

Uche, D. B., Anene, J. N., & Nnabugwu, E. L. (2022). Effect of distribution channel strategies on the performance of banks. *Journal of Humanities and Social Science Innovation, 2*(2). https://jurnal.ahmar.id/index.php/daengku/article/view/732

Venaik, S., & Midgley, D. F. (2019). Archetypes of marketing mix standardization-adaptation in MNC subsidiaries. Fit and equifinality as complementary explanation of performance. *European Journal of Marketing*, *53*(2), 366–99.

Vernon, R. (1966). International investment and international trade in product cycle. *The Quarterly Journal of Economics*, *80*(2), 190–207.

CHAPTER 11

Abbott, G., Stening, B., Atkins, P., & Grant, A. (2006). Coaching expatriate managers for success: Adding value beyond training and mentoring. *Asia Pacific Journal of Human Resources*, *44*(3), 295–317.

Adler, N. (1981). Re-entry: Managing cross-cultural transitions. *Group and Organizational Studies*, *6*(3), 341–56.

Bader, B. (2017). Motivations of global careers among expatriates in German companies: A comparison with the year 2002. In B. Bader, T. Schuster, & A. Bader (eds), *Expatriate Management*, pp. 1–26. Palgrave Macmillan.

Black, J., Gregersen, H., Mendenhall, M., & Stroh, L. (1999). *Globalizing People through International Assignment*. Addison-Wesley.

Gertsen, M. (1990). Intercultural competence and expatriates. *International Journal of Human Resource Management*, *1*(3), 341–62.

Harzing, A. (2001). Of bears, bumble-bees and spiders: The role of expatriates in controlling foreign subsidiaries. *Journal of World Business*, *36*(4), 366–79.

Harzing, A. W. (2004). Composing an international staff. In A. W.

Harzing, & J. Van Ruysseveldt (eds), *International Human Resource Management* (2nd edn), pp. 251–82. Sage.

Holtbrügge, D., & Schillo, K. (2011). Virtual delegation across borders: A knowledge-based perspective. *European Management Journal*, *29*(1), 1–10.

Kim, K., & Slocum, J. (2008). Individual differences and expatriate assignment effectiveness: The case of US based Korean expatriates. *Journal of World Business*, *43*, 109–26.

Lysgaard, S. (1955). Adjustment in a foreign society: Norwegian Fulbright grantees visiting the United States. *International Social Science Bulletin*, *7*, 45–51.

Mendenhall, M., Dunbar, E., & Oddou, G. (1987). Expatriate selection, training and career-pathing: A review and critique. *Human Resource Management*, *26*(3), 331–45.

Mercer (2024). Cost of living city ranking 2024. www.mercer.com/insights/total-rewards/talent-mobility-insights/cost-of-living

Okpara, J., & Kabongo, J. (2011). Cross-cultural training and expatriate adjustment: A study of western expatriates in Nigeria. *Journal of World Business*, *46*(1), 22–30.

Puck, J., Holtbrügge, D., & Raupp, J. (2017). Expatriate adjustment: A review of concepts, drivers, and consequences. In B. Bader, T. Schuster, & A. Bader (eds), *Expatriate Management*, pp. 297–336. Palgrave Macmillan.

Puck, J. F., Kittler, M. G., & Wright, C. (2008). Does it really work? Re-assessing the impact of pre-departure cross-cultural training on expatriate adjustment. *The International Journal of Human Resource Management*, *19*(12), 2182–97.

Schuler, R., & Jackson, S. (1987). Linking competitive strategies with human resource management practices. *The Academy of Management Executive*, *1*(3), 207–19.

Shaffer, M., Harrison, D., & Gilley, K. (1999). Dimension, determinants, and differences in the expatriate adjustment process. *Journal of International Business Studies*, *30*(3), 557–81.

Shen, J., Chanda, A., D'netto, B., & Monga, M. (2009). Managing diversity through human resource management: An international perspective and conceptual framework. *The International Journal of Human Resource Management*, *20*(2), 235–51.

Škudiene˙, V., Vezeliene, G., & Stangej, O. (2020). Transforming human resource management: Innovative e-HRM value creation for multinational companies. In V. Škudienė, J. Li-Ying, & F. Bernhard (eds), *Innovation Management*, pp. 140–66. Edward Elgar Publishing.

Suutari, V., & Tornikoski, C. (2001). The challenge of expatriate compensation: The sources of satisfaction and dissatisfaction among expatriates. *International Journal of Human Resource Management*, *12*(3), 389–404.

Tung, R. (1982). Selection and training procedures of US, European, and Japanese multinationals. *California Management Review*, *25*(1), 57–71.

Winkelman, M. (1994). Cultural shock and adaptation. *Journal of Counseling & Development*, *73*, 121–6.

Yoshida, T., & Brislin, R. (1995). Intercultural skills and recommended behaviours: The psychological perspective for training program. In O. Shenkar (ed.), *Global Perspectives of Human Resource Management*, pp. 112–13. Prentice-Hall.

CHAPTER 12

Alghamdi, Saleh Y. (2023). A review of blood delivery for sustainable supply chain management (BSCM). *Sustainability*, *15*(3), 2757. https://doi.org/10.3390/su15032757

Bimpikis, K., & Markakis, M. G. (2016). *Inventory pooling under heavy-tailed demand. Management Science*, *62*(6), 1800–13.

Christopher, M. & Towill, D.R. (2000). Supply chain migration from lean and functional to agile and customised. *Supply Chain Management: An International Journal*, *5*(4), 206–13.

Ciravegna, L., & Michailova, S. (2022). Why the world economy needs, but will not get, more globalization in the post-Covid-19 decade. *Journal of International Business Studies*, *53*(1), 172–86.

Dutta, P., Choi, T. M., Somani, S., & Butala, R. (2020). Blockchain technology in supply chain operations: Applications, challenges and research opportunities. *Transportation Research Part E: Logistics and Transportation Review*, *142*, 102067.

Gligor, D. M., & Holcomb, M. (2014). The road to supply chain agility: An RBV perspective on the role of logistics capabilities. *The International Journal of Logistics Management*, *25*(1), 160–79.

Grossman, G. M., Helpman, E., & Lhuillier, H. (2023). Supply chain resilience: Should policy promote international diversification or reshoring? *Journal of Political Economy*, *131*(12), 3462–96.

Hastig, G. M., & Sodhi, M. S. (2020). Blockchain for supply chain traceability: Business requirements and critical success factors. *Production and Operations Management, 29*(4), 935–54.

Holmström, J., Holweg, M., Lawson, B., Pil, F. K., & Wagner, S. M. (2019). The digitalization of operations and supply chain management: Theoretical and methodological implications. *Journal of Operations Management, 65*(8): 728–34.

Imamkulieva, E., & Kondakova, K. (2022). International cargo transportation through the Suez Canal and alternative routes (by the example of China-EU). *SHS Web of Conferences, 134*, 00135. https://doi.org/10.1051/shsconf/202213400135

Ivanov, D., Dolgui, A., Das, A., & Sokolov, B. (2019). Digital supply chain twins: Managing the ripple effect, resilience, and disruption risks by data-driven optimization, simulation, and visibility. In D. Ivanov, A. Dolgui, & B.

Kauppi, K. (2013). Extending the use of institutional theory in operations and supply chain management research: Review and research suggestions. *International Journal of Operations & Production Management, 33*(10), 1318–45.

Ketokivi, M., & Mahoney, J. T. (2020). Transaction cost economics as a theory of supply chain efficiency. *Production and Operations Management, 29*(4), 1011–31.

Klöckner, M., Schmidt, C. G., & Wagner, S. M. (2022). When blockchain creates shareholder value: Empirical evidence from international firm announcements. *Production and Operations Management, 31*(1), 46–64.

Lee, J. M., & Wong, E. Y-c. (2021). *Suez canal blockage: An analysis of legal impact, risks and liabilities to the global supply chain*. MATEC Web Conf. 339: 01019. https://doi.org/10.1051/matecconf/202133901019

Maskell, B. (2001). The age of agile manufacturing. *Supply Chain Management: An International Journal, 6*(1): 5–11.

Oh, C. H., & Oetzel, J. (2022). Multinational enterprises and natural disasters: Challenges and opportunities for IB research. *Journal of International Business Studies, 53*(2), 231–54.

Oliveira-Dias, D., Maqueira-Marín, J. M., & Moyano-Fuentes, J. (2022). The link between information and digital technologies of industry 4.0 and agile supply chain: Mapping current research and establishing new research avenues. *Computers & Industrial Engineering, 167*, 108000.

Prater, E., Biehl, M., & Smith, M. A. (2001). International supply chain agility: Tradeoffs between flexibility and uncertainty. *International Journal of Operations & Production Management, 21*(5/6), 823–39.

Seuring, S., & Müller, M. (2008). From a literature review to a conceptual framework for sustainable supply chain management. *Journal of Cleaner Production, 16*(15), 1699–1710.

Sokolov (eds), *Handbook of Ripple Effects in the Supply Chain*, 309–32. Springer.

Tallman, S. (2011). Offshoring, outsourcing, and strategy in the global firm. *AIB Insights, 11*(1), 3.

Tay, M. Y., Abd Rahman, A., Aziz, Y. A., & Sidek, S. (2015). A review on drivers and barriers towards sustainable supply chain practices. *International Journal of Social Science and Humanity, 5*(10), 892.

Tiwari, S., Sharma, P., Choi, T. M., & Lim, A. (2023). Blockchain and third-party logistics for global supply chain operations: Stakeholders' perspective and decision roadmap. *Transportation Research Part E: Logistics and Transportation Review*, *170*, 103012.

Van Hoek, R. I., Harrison, A., & Christopher, M. (2001). Measuring agile capabilities in the supply chain. *International Journal of Operations & Production Management*, *21*(1/2), 126–47.

Weixel, N. (2022) Infant formula shortage worse. *The Hill*, 11 May.

Williamson, L. M., & Devine, D. V. (2013). Challenges in the management of the blood supply. *The Lancet*, *381*(9880), 1866–75. https://doi.org/10.1016/S0140-6736(13)60631-5

Zhan, J. X. (2021). GVC transformation and a new investment landscape in the 2020s: Driving forces, directions, and a forward-looking research and policy agenda. *Journal of International Business Policy*, *4*(2), 206–20.

CHAPTER 13

Alexopoulos, A., Becerra, Y., Boehm, O., Bravos, G., & Chatzigiannakis, V. et al. (2022). Big data analytics in the manufacturing sector: Guidelines and lessons learned through the Centro Ricerche FIAT (CRF) Case. In E. Curry, S. Auer, A. J. Berre, A. Metzger, & M. S. Perez et al. (eds), *Technologies and Applications for Big Data Value*. Springer.

Al-Lozi, E., Alfityani, A., Alsmandi, A. A., Al-Hazimeh, A. M., & Al-Gasawneh, J. A. (2022) The role of big data in financial sector: A review paper. *International Journal of Data Network Science*, *6*(4), 1–12.

Alpaydin, E. (2020). *Introduction to Machine Learning*. MIT Press.

Bell, R. G., Filatotchev, I., & Rasheed, A. A. (2012). The liability of foreignness in capital markets: Sources and remedies. *Journal of International Business Studies*, *43*(2): 107–22.

Berrar, D. (2018). Cross-validation. In S. Ranganathan, M. Gribskov, K. Nakai, C. Schönbach & M. Cannataro (eds), *Encyclopedia of Bioinformatics and Computational Biology* (542–5). Elsevier.

Bhattacharyya, S., Jha, S., Tharakunnel, K., & Westland J.C. (2011). Data mining for credit card fraud: A comparative study. *Decision Support Systems*, *50*, 602–13.

Brynjolfsson, E., & Mcafee, A. (2014). *The Second Machine Age: Work, Progress, and Prosperity in a Time of Brilliant Technologies*. Norton.

Choudhury, P., Starr, E., & Agarwal, R. (2020). Machine learning and human capital complementarities: Experimental evidence on bias mitigation. *Strategic Management Journal*, *41*(8), 1381–1411.

Cowgill, B. (2019). Bias and productivity in humans and algorithms: Theory and evidence from résumé screening. Columbia University, Upjohn Institute working paper, 19–309.

Dash, S., Shakyawar, S. K., Sharma M., & Kaushik, S. (2019). Big data in healthcare: Management, analysis and future prospects. *Journal of Big Data*, *54*(6), 1–25.

Erevelles, S., Fukawa, N., & Swayne, L. (2016). Big Data consumer analytics and the transformation of marketing. *Journal of Business Research*, *69*(2), 897–904.

Frey, C. B., & Osborne, M. A. (2017). The future of employment: How susceptible are jobs to computerization? *Technological Forecasting and Social Change*, *114*(1), 254–80.

Giri, C., & Chen, Y. (2022). Deep learning for demand forecasting in the fashion and apparel retail industry. *Forecasting*, *4*(2), 565–81.

Goodfellow, I., Bengio, Y., & Courville, A. (2016). *Deep Learning*. MIT Press.

Heath C., & Tversky A. (1991). Preference and belief: Ambiguity and competence in choice under uncertainty. *Journal of Risk and Uncertainty*, *4*(1), 5–28.

Ivanov, S., Kuyumdzhiev, M., & Webster, C. (2020) Automation fears: Drivers and solutions. *Technology in Society*, *63*, 101431. https://doi.org/10.1016/j.techsoc.2020.101431

James, G., Witten, D., Hastie, T., & Tibshirani, R. (2013) *An Introduction to Statistical Learning: With applications in R*. Uncorrected edn. Springer.

Klayman, J. (1995). Varieties of confirmation bias. In J. Busemeyer, R. Hastie, & D. L. Medin (eds), *Decision Making from a Cognitive Perspective*, pp. 365–418. Academic Press.

LeCun, Y., Bengio, Y., & Hinton, G. (2015). Deep learning. *Nature*, *521*, 436–44.

Litjens, G., Kooi, T., Bejnordi, B. E., Setio, A. A. A., Ciompi, F., et al. (2017). A survey on deep learning in medical image analysis. *Medical Image Analysis*, *42*, 60–88.

Maitland, E., & Sammartino, A. (2015). Decision making and uncertainty: The role of heuristics and experience in assessing a politically hazardous environment. *Strategic Management Journal*, *36*(10), 1554–78.

Mäkelä, K., Andersson, U., & Seppala, T. (2012). Interpersonal similarity and knowledge sharing within multinational organizations. *International Business Review*, *21*(3), 439–51.

Mittelstadt, B. D., Allo, P., Taddeo, M., Wachter, S., & Floridi, L. (2016). The ethics of algorithms: Mapping the debate. *Big Data & Society*, *3*(2), 1–68.

Nebus, J. & Celo, S. (2020). Cognitive biases in the perceptions of country distance. *Journal of International Management*, *26*(3). https://doi.org/10.1016/j.intman.2020.100774

Niittymies, A. (2020). Heuristic decision-making in firm internationalization: The influence of context-specific experience. *International Business Review*, *29*(6). https://doi.org/10.1016/j.ibusrev.2020.101752

Noble, W. S. (2006). What is a support vector machine? *Nature Biotechnology*, *24*(12), 1565–7.

Paksoy, T., Kochan, C. G., & Ali, S. S. (2020). *Logistics 4.0: Digital Transformation of Supply Chain Management*. CRC Press.

Raisch, S., & Krakowski, S. (2021). Artificial intelligence and management: The automation–augmentation paradox. *Academy of Management Review*, *46*(1), 192–210.

Ripley, B. D. (1996). *Pattern Recognition and Neural Networks*. Cambridge University Press.

Rugman, A. M., & Verbeke, A. (2004). A perspective on regional and global strategies of multinational companies. *Journal of International Business Studies*, *35*, 3–18.

Russell, S., & Norvig, P. (2016). *Artificial Intelligence: A Modern Approach*. Pearson Education.

Samuelson, W., & Zeckhauser, R. (1988). Status quo bias in decision making. *Journal of Risk and Uncertainty*, *1*(1), 7–59.

Schmidhuber, J. (2015). Deep learning in neural networks: An overview. *Neural Networks*, *61*, 85–117.

Scrucca, L., Fop, M., Murphy, T. B., & Raftery, A. E. (2016). mclust 5: Clustering, classification and density estimation using Gaussian finite mixture models. *R Journal*, *8*(1), 289–317.

Seetharaman, A., Niranjan, I., Tandon, V., & Saravan, A.S. (2016). Impact of big data on the retail industry. *Corporate Ownership & Control*, *14*(1), 506–18.

Simon, H. A. (1956). Rational choice and the structure of the environment. *Psychological Review*, *63*(2), 129–38.

Sirignano, J., & Cont, R. (2019). Universal features of price formation in financial markets: *Perspectives from deep learning*, *19*(9), 1449–59.

Srivastava, N., Hinton, G., Krizhevsky, A., Sutskever, I., & Salakhutdinov, R. (2014). Journal of Machine Learning Research: *JMLR*, *15*(1), 1929.

Suthaharan, S. (2016a). Supervised learning models. In *Machine Learning Models and Algorithms for Big Data Classification: Thinking with Examples for Effective Learning*, pp. 145–81. Springer.

Suthaharan, S. (2016b). Support vector machine. In *Machine Learning Models and Algorithms for Big Data Classification: Thinking with Examples for Effective Learning*, pp. 207–35. Springer.

Tversky, A., & Kahneman, D. (1974). Judgment under uncertainty: Heuristics and biases. *Science*, *185*(4157), 1124–31.

Vidgen, R., Shaw, S., & Grant, D. B. (2017). Management challenges in creating value from business analytics. *European Journal of Operational Research*, *261*(2), 626–39.

Vlahogianni, E. I., Karlaftis, M. G., & Golias, J. C. (2014). Short-term traffic forecasting: Where we are and where we're going. *Transport Research Part C: Emerging Technologies*, *43*(1), 3–19.

CHAPTER 14

Ambrose, J. (2019, 13 June). World's biggest sovereign wealth fund to ditch fossil fuels. *The Guardian*. www.theguardian.com/business/2019/jun/12/worlds-biggest-sovereign-wealth-fund-to-ditch-fossil-fuels

Andrade, G. (2019). Medical ethics and the trolley problem. *Journal of Medical Ethics and History of Medicine*, *17*(12), 3.

Bansal, P., & Song, H.-C. (2017). Similar but not the same: Differentiating corporate sustainability from corporate responsibility. *Academy of Management Annals*, *11*(1), 105–49.

Berry, H., Kaul, A., & Lee, N. (2021). Follow the smoke: The pollution haven effect on global sourcing. *Strategic Management Journal*, *42*(13), 2420–50.

Broccardo, E., Hart, O., & Zingales, L. (2022). Exit versus voice. *Journal of Political Economy*, *130*(12), 3101–45.

DesJardine, M., Marti, E., & Durand, R. (2020). Why activist hedge funds target socially responsible firms: The reaction costs of signaling corporate social responsibility. *Academy of Management Journal*, *64*(3), 851–72.

Donaldson, T., & Preston, L. E. (1995). The stakeholder theory of the corporation: Concepts, evidence, and implications. *Academy of Management Review*, *20*(1), 65–91.

DW (2020). Brazil's Odebrecht changes name to Novonor. DW. www.dw.com/en/brazils-scandal-hit-odebrecht-changes-name-to-novonor/a-55994035

European Commission (2011) Communication from the Commission to the European Parliament, the Council, the European Economic and Social Committee and the Committee of the Regions: A Renewed EU Strategy 2011–14 for Corporate Social Responsibility. Document 52011DC0681. https://eur-lex.europa.eu/legal-content/EN/TXT/?uri=CELEX:52011DC0681

Freeman, R.E. (1984). *Strategic Management: A Stakeholder Approach*. Pitman Publishing.

Friedman, M. (1970, September 13). The social responsibility of business is to increase its profits. *New York Times Magazine*. www.nytimes.com/1970/09/13/archives/a-friedman-doctrine-the-social-responsibility-of-business-is-to.html

Gillan, S. L., Koch, A., & Starks, L. T. (2021). Firms and social responsibility: A review of ESG and CSR research in corporate finance. *Journal of Corporate Finance*, *66*, 101889.

Gillani, A., Kutaula, S., & Budhwar, P. S. (2023). Heading home? Reshoring and sustainability connectedness from a home-country consumer perspective. *British Journal of Management*, *34*(3), 1117–37.

Grappi, S., Romani, S., & Bagozzi, R. P. (2020). Consumer reshoring sentiment and animosity: Expanding our understanding of market responses to reshoring. *Management International Review*, *60*(1), 69–95.

Jones, T.M. (1995). Instrumental stakeholder theory: A synthesis of ethics and economics. *Academy of Management Review*, *20*, 404–37.

Marquis, C., Toffel, M. W., & Zhou, Y. (2016). Scrutiny, norms, and selective disclosure: A global study of greenwashing. *Organization Science*, *27*(2), 483–504.

McWilliams, A., & Siegel, D. (2001). Corporate social responsibility: A theory of the firm perspective. *Academy of Management Review*, *26*(1), 117–27.

O'Gorman, P. A., & Dwyer, J. G. (2018). Using machine learning to parameterize moist convection: Potential for modeling of climate, climate change, and extreme events. *Journal of Advances in Modeling Earth Systems*, *10*, 2548–63. https://doi.org/10.1029/2018MS001351

Oh, C. H., & Oetzel, J. (2023). Natural disasters and multinational enterprises: In denial and unprepared, or ready to respond? *AIB Insights*, *23*(3). https://doi.org/10.46697/001c.77303

Parmar, B. L., Freeman, R. E., Harrison, J. S., Wicks, A. C., Purnell, L., & de Colle, S. (2010). Stakeholder theory: The state of the art. *Academy of Management Annals*, *4*(1), 403–45.

Quinn, B. (2012, 2 October). Ikea apologises over removal of women from Saudi Arabia catalogue. *The Guardian*. www.theguardian.com/world/2012/oct/02/ikea-apologises-removing-women-saudi-arabia-catalogue

Reuters (2019). Brazil's Odebrecht files for bankruptcy protection after years of graft probes. www.reuters.com/article/us-odebrecht-bankruptcy-idUSKCN1TI2QM

Riedl, A., & Smeets, P. (2017). Why do investors hold socially responsible mutual funds? *The Journal of Finance*, *72*(6), 2505–50.

Seele, P., & Gatti, L. (2017). Greenwashing revisited: In search of a typology and accusation-based definition incorporating legitimacy strategies. *Business Strategy and the Environment*, *26*(2), 239–52.

Transparency International (2024). What is corruption? Transparency International. www.transparency.org/en/what-is-corruption

United Nations. (n.d.). The 17 Goals. United Nations. https://sdgs.un.org/goals

United Nations Development Programme (UNDP). (2024). UNDP and the Private Sector. United Nations. www.undp.org/partners/private-sector

United Nations Human Rights Office of the High Commissioner (OHCHR) (n.d.). What are human rights? United Nations. www.ohchr.org/en/what-are-human-rights

Walsh, J. P. (2005). Taking stock of stakeholder management. *Academy of Management Review*, *30*(2), 426–38.

Whoriskey, P., & Siegel, R. (2019, June 5). Cocoa's child laborers. *The Washington Post*. www.washingtonpost.com/graphics/2019/business/hershey-nestle-mars-chocolate-child-labor-west-africa

World Economic Forum. (2021). *What is stakeholder capitalism? Its history and relevance*. World Economic Forum. www.weforum.org/agenda/2021/01/klaus-schwab-on-what-is-stakeholder-capitalism-history-relevance

INDEX

NOTE: page numbers in *italic* type refer to figures.